THE CHAPTER

The Chapter

A SEGMENTED HISTORY
FROM ANTIQUITY TO THE
TWENTY-FIRST CENTURY

NICHOLAS DAMES

PRINCETON UNIVERSITY PRESS

PRINCETON & OXFORD

Published by Princeton University Press
41 William Street, Princeton, New Jersey 08540
99 Banbury Road, Oxford OX2 6JX

press.princeton.edu

All Rights Reserved
ISBN: 978-0-691-13519-9
ISBN (e-book): 978-0-691-25363-3

British Library Cataloging-in-Publication Data is available

Editorial: Anne Savarese and James Collier
Production Editorial: Jenny Wolkowicki
Cover design: Katie Osborne
Production: Erin Suydam
Publicity: Alyssa Sanford and Charlotte Coyne
Copyeditor: Maia Vaswani

This book has been composed in Arno Pro

Printed on acid-free paper. ∞

Printed in the United States of America

10 9 8 7 6 5 4 3 2 1

For Kathleen
who also remembered the *Magicicada septendecim*

CONTENTS

ILLUSTRATIONS

Figures

Tables

ABBREVIATIONS

AA   *Albert Angelo,* by B. S. Johnson

BEC   *Chrétien de Troyes in Prose: The Burgundian "Erec" and "Cligés,"* by Chrétien de Troyes

C   *Cléo de 5 à 7,* by Agnès Varda

D   *Discourses,* by Epictetus

DC   *David Copperfield,* by Charles Dickens

DOM   *Dom Casmurro,* by Joaquim Maria Machado de Assis

EJ   *Esau and Jacob,* by Joaquim Maria Machado de Assis

EST   event segmentation theory

EW   *Excellent Women,* by Barbara Pym

GS   *A Visit from the Goon Squad,* by Jennifer Egan

IN   *The Interesting Narrative of the Life of Olaudah Equiano,* by Olaudah Equiano

M   *Middlemarch,* by George Eliot

MA   *Le morte d'Arthur,* by Sir Thomas Malory

PM   *The Posthumous Memoirs of Brás Cubas,* by Joaquim Maria Machado de Assis

QB   *Quincas Borba,* by Joaquim Maria Machado de Assis

R   *Reservoir 13,* by Jon McGregor

T   *Trawl,* by B. S. Johnson

TS   *Tristram Shandy,* by Laurence Sterne

U   *The Unfortunates,* by B. S. Johnson

WD   *Wives and Daughters,* by Elizabeth Gaskell

WM   *Wilhelm Meister's Apprenticeship,* by Johann Wolfgang Goethe

WP   *War and Peace,* by Leo Tolstoy

PART I

Envisioning the Chapter

Are there sections? Consider transitions.

—BRIAN ENO AND PETER SCHMIDT,
"OBLIQUE STRATEGIES" CARD (1975)

The history of the chapter (*caput, κεφάλαιον*) has yet to be written . . . it would take an entire book.

—HERMANN MUTSCHMANN, "INHALTSANGABE UND
KAPITELÜBERSCHRIFT IM ANTIKEN BUCH" (1911)

On Segmented Time

THERE IS NO LIMIT to the ways we can imagine the divisions of time. The swell and crash of a wave; the disappearance and return of an axial rotation, an orbit's centripetal curve; the ripening and rotting of a fruit; arboreal concentric rings, radiating outward in alternating shades; the crossing of an invisible meridian; the transit of an eclipse into and out of totality; sedimentary layers of rock, striated by subtle gradations of color; a pattern of stitches, knit and purl together creating a rhythm of textures; the opening and closing of a shutter, darkness falling to isolate one moment from the next; the cresting and descent of pitch as a sound dopplers past; separate celluloid frames merging into continuity as they pass by at the rate of so many per second; manifold and crease, pulse and echo, call and response, downbeat and upbeat, systole and diastole, ones and zeroes; even, if we prefer, the unmarked flow, the continuous stream of duration impossible to cut or mark. And among them, the chapter: that artifact of the book, giving us an image of time as a series of ordered linear segments. Intelligible units, these chapters, each one tagged or numbered and neatly sequential. Puzzling ones as well, somehow speaking to us of both the feeling of being in a unit and of transitioning to the next—the enclosed space and the wall promising an obverse side, the organ and the membrane attaching it to another.

This is a book about ruptures. But traversable ones: gaps one crosses, fissures within continuities, the marks within an individual life. William James: "The conjunctive relation that has given most trouble to philosophy is *the co-conscious transition*, so to call it, by which one experience passes into another when both belong to the same self."[1] Even nonphilosophers have reason to be troubled by this mystery, and can use a figurative hook by which to grasp it. A gifted analyst remarked to me once, by way of encouragement and explanation at one such rupture: "You're starting a new chapter." For a bookish type, the remark was instantly clarifying. It gave me the hook I needed at a particular juncture: the sense of being propelled forward, the sense of being lodged within a linearity that had just passed over a gap, the sense as well of being narrated. Above all it gave me the sensation, in Donald Winnicott's terms, of being "held" in a time, my pieces gathered together by the new time I was entering.[2] While it did all this, the remark also kindled a search. I was a novel reader, I had some pretense at being practiced at it, I'd devoted years to making it into an occupation. Yet this instant novelization of my life—that was how it felt; I'd eagerly accepted the time signature of a novel—was something whose effects I couldn't as yet explain to myself. I clearly knew how to think in chapters. I'd been doing it my entire reading life; it had created an orientation to time that I would struggle to erase even had I become conscious of it, which until then I hadn't been; it was in some sense what I'd been thinking all along, without knowing it. The little release of the chapter break, the tidiness of its sequencing, the quiet space of resonance it opens, all these were rhythms to which I had learned to respond without effort and without much thought; chapters were occasionally pleasures to encounter, but more often a cognitive and even haptic habit, a discipline, a training. Its bearing on me was precisely its way of helping me find my bearings. A temporal GPS, a way of finding your location: here, in this chapter, this is where I am. (Like the chapter- and book-ending line of Henry James's *The Ambassadors*, a plangent but also reassuring deictic demonstrative: "Then there we are!")[3] But I had no idea why chapters existed—a historical question—nor what exactly they did to our sense of time, a theoretical question. So this book came slowly into being.

I finished this book in the midst what felt like a series of breaks in collective life. They were far from common, even if they could well have been predicted. Again, a series of adjustments seemed necessary, as if everyone were engaged in adapting to some kind of weather condition, trapped as we were in a transitional historical moment—in fact, in several overlapping transitional historical moments. There were of course literal weather conditions: planetary time seemed to have decisively shifted. Some others (say, a presidential term) were discrete, however infinite they felt. Others (a pandemic, outbursts of collective outrage over the immiserations of racial subjugation, a widespread coming to terms with the ruinations of capitalism's latest phase) were more amorphous, as it was unclear whether they served as a boundary—as the gap between temporal units, the transition to something new—or as the unit themselves, something into which we were sealed, no threshold visible. The

Jamesian question of "where we are" beckoned again, if differently. Everywhere the language of chapters was invoked as a way of answering it. That language was often abused, tendentious, or merely glib. It has featured, for instance, in the rhetoric of American presidential speeches stretching back for well over a century, in order to declare any number of national perils, however prematurely, concluded.[4] And in the years of this book's development it returned continually. Take two recent presidents, one who spoke of "a new chapter of international cooperation," the other "a new chapter of American Greatness."[5] The juxtaposition is politically significant for its similarity as well as for its difference. Both are assertions of change within continuity, progress as repetition, the rupture as merely a resumption. If the metaphor can be so tamed by the banalities of power, the experience of temporal fissure the chapter break evokes can also ramify unpredictably. A new chapter might be more of the same, but intensified: long-prepared causes exploding into effects, long-delayed reckonings awaiting. Or new, untold horrors awaiting. So it seemed to me at the most recent turn of the decade: the logic of a linear segment coming to an end, of sequential advance and of the caesuras of transition, possessed a newly heightened communal-historical force, even if instead of feeling "held" by these collective chapters, more often recently I felt trapped, stuck, or strangled by them, without feeling as if their conclusion would offer comfort.[6] We can be lacerated by shifts in time just as well as relieved by them.

Between those two orientation points, an experience of personal and then collective transition, both articulated by the same metaphor, this book took shape. What became apparent was how deeply embedded, how durable, the metaphor of the chapter was. As the American idiom "chapter book" still tells us, mature literacy, a familiarity with how to use a book, is defined by the expectation of the chapter break. We "start a new chapter" in our lives with dread or excitement; we "close that chapter of my life" with regret or relief. It is an old metaphor, its bookishness signaling its longevity. But its antiquity—both in cultural-historical terms and in our individual lives as readers, taking us back to some of our earliest experiences with books—allows it to modulate between the personal and the collective. It is almost always both: the life lived as a historical narrative, historical change lived as an individual itinerary. Thomas De Quincey, writing in 1853: "About the close of my sixth year, suddenly the first chapter of my life came to a violent termination; that chapter which, even within the gates of recovered paradise, might merit a remembrance."[7] Vilém Flusser, in 1991: "On the one hand, the history of the human species is one of the final chapters in natural history. On the other hand, natural history is a late chapter of human history."[8] We live stretched between many different clocks, many different temporal rhythms: the abstraction of an hour, the inevitability of diurnal repetition, our different biological rhythms and phases, the measures provided by a historical or cultural or economic phase. The chapter is not just one of those clocks; it has become a metalanguage for the interrelationship, the intricate polyrhythm, of those various clocks in their simultaneous operation. If it still works for us this way, for how much longer? I have attempted here to trace the history of this temporal construction, this bookish way of parsing time, and to consider its phenomenological nuances. It did not escape me that I was perhaps standing near the conclusion of its long history, the end of the chapter of the chapter. In a culture, and on a planet, where our temporal frames seem as unlocked or mismatched as ever before, and where the influence of the book on our mappings of time could be waning, it may be that this study is written as almost an elegy. But if I was foretelling a transition, taking the attitude of anticipatory poignancy, it did not escape me either that I had learned that habit from chapters.

This book can then be thought of as a study of the long, slow coming into being of the conditions of the chapter metaphor and its persistent grip on how we speak and think of change, transition, boundaries in time. It starts, however, with some naïve and nonfigurative questions: Why do books have chapters, and when did they start to have them? How has the chapter, and the idea of the chapter, changed over the two millennia of the practice of writing and reading in them? What kinds or durations of experiences do chapters encapsulate? What I aim to detect are some patterns in the history that help give shape to what otherwise might seem too hopelessly shapeless, irregular, and nebulous to be anything like the phenomena literary scholars usually study. Such a purpose, however, necessitates a few opening explanations, a provisional map to the peculiarly organized terrain that follows and the compromises I've adopted in charting it.

Norms and Exceptions. That there are broad, enduring logics to the chapter, affinities across different genres, languages, and historical occasions, is one of this book's contentions. Necessarily therefore it is in search of representative, model examples, those that seem to best (or, most quickly) encapsulate normative practices in the long history of chaptering. This is not a history of resistances to the chapter or flagrant refusals of its protocols. Much of my attention has been devoted to the *usual* chapter and its almost unthinking repetitions of technique, as well as the subtleties of that technique. And yet, often the exception has proven too important to ignore: the "bad" or flawed version of chaptering, the deliberate adjustment to a habitual gesture, the idiosyncratic stamp put on an old template. Some of those eccentricities, in the eddies of stylistic history, have spawned their own microlineages. Which is to say that the tension between the norm and the exception runs throughout this book's choice of examples, in a way that is not finally resolvable; their relationship is unstable. But that tension even goes to the heart of my arguments about the chapter's form itself. The chapter metaphor might seem to indicate— particularly given its presence in the lexicon of the powerful, in the rhetoric of governments—not just the presence of a norm but the influence of normativity. Yet the chapter, as the following pages will demonstrate, is far stranger than that, far more porous and recalcitrant than the regulatory goals to which it is sometimes put. This is an irony that my book pursues throughout. The chapter is indeed one of the primary exemplars of linear time, still a significant way of expressing the dread and hope associated with that mode of futurity. Yet it is also a means for prying linear time apart, making it conspicuous and peculiar, balking or taming its relentlessness. A chapter is a way of paving a linear path and of marking gaps or tears in that path; it is the progress and the impasse both, the space of hesitation between them, the hiccup or delay as well as the leap across or thrust forward. It is a norm, and a way of imagining an escape from or interruption to that norm.

Counting and Reading. Chapters have an intimate relationship with numbers. It can even sometimes seem as if numbering is all they exist to do. George Gissing's 1891 *New Grub Street*, providing a tableau of writer's block: "At the head of the paper was inscribed 'Chapter III.,' but that was all. And now the sky was dusking over; darkness would soon fall."[9] More cynically consoling, Elizabeth Taylor's 1947 *A View of the Harbour*: "The best part of writing a book is when you write the title at the top of the page and your name underneath and then 'Chapter One!' When that's done the best part's over."[10] A chapter numerates a text, even in the absence of literal numbers. And so it is not an accident that one intellectual mode this book adopts is that of counting. Word counts, in particular, will matter here, as one way of measuring size; size will matter as one way of measuring stylistic change over time. None of these quantitative elements are particularly sophisticated or have required feats of computational power. I have wanted to stay close to the rudimentary arithmetic of chaptering itself: Chapter One, Chapter the Second, the chapter-as-next-in-a-series. I have not refused the aid of counting, nor some of the analytic styles (the graph, the grid, the chart) that accompany it. That said, this is not a study that operates solely, or even largely, at the level of the quantitative. Its interest is finally phenomenological: how a chapter organizes both diegetic and readerly time. Counting is one way to capture elements of chaptering style that can operate below the threshold of consciousness, and of recognizing patterns and deviations from them, but it is always accompanied by reading, the procedure of investigating a select few instances in granular detail. At a moment when the relationship between quantitative and hermeneutical impulses is fraught and sometimes polemical, my method here—eclectic, rudimentary, and even happenstance as it might be—is an experiment in companionship between these modes.

Archives and Itineraries. The scope of this book is necessarily broad in time and geography, and necessarily highly partial in its examples. There are countless forms of textual segmentation in the world: cantos, stanzas, paragraphs, dramatic acts, Qur'anic surahs, Vedic mantras, Attic strophes. Few, if any, however, have become so mundanely widespread, so adaptable to different geographical and generic climates, so pervasively figural; one does not speak of "paragraphs of my life," nor of a "new canto" in the history of a nation. Some part of this ubiquity is the effect of the chapter's multicultural and multilinguistic spread; whether *capitolo, chapitre, capítulo, kapituła,* or *Kapitel, глава* or *bab* or *kabanata* or *κεφάλαιο,* it is evidently unmoored from any particular linguistic or national tradition. It is an enormously diverse terrain, and what this book offers is one itinerary through it, weaving its way across a number of locations and times, starting with a 2,200-year-old Italian legal tablet and leading to, among many others, scriptoria and schoolrooms in third-century Caesarea, sixth-century Vivarium, and thirteenth-century Saint Albans; a courtly coterie in Burgundy and a London printer's workshop in the fifteenth century; a host of eighteenth- and nineteenth-century locations from Britain to Germany, Russia, Brazil; and finally to the Paris of the early 1960s captured on film and the United States, sometime around now, captured in a slide presentation. That itinerary is admittedly limited by the linguistic and interpretive tools with which I am familiar, and its stopping places have been significantly determined by something like an individual readerly education and taste. There are enormous gaps here, of culture, region, and historical time. My examples are drawn from Western languages and locales only, already just a portion of the chapter's wild global proliferation, and this is also literary scholar's book, oriented toward the highly self-conscious presence of chapters in novels. A version of this book written by a theologian, or philosopher of science, or historian, might imagine a different trajectory; the alternative paths that could have been taken are limitless, in language, geography, and genre. But the route this book sketches is not just a matter of disciplinary training or eccentric preference. Certain inarguably pivotal examples loom large, among them the Bible itself, in its long history toward becoming one major paradigm for a chaptered text. At other moments I have chosen examples because archival evidence permits us to glimpse chapters in the process of formation—where, as in my instances in chapters 3 and 4, we can directly compare texts chaptered by editors, scribes, or printers to the older, undivided texts to which they applied breaks, or to different attempts at chaptering the same texts, these before-and-after comparisons revealing the poetics of the chapter at particular moments. Chapters are everywhere, but they are not everywhere so visibly *worked*, and one principle of my approach has been to try to locate moments where the thinking behind chaptering might be most visible. Whether my landmarks were chosen for their cross-cultural influence or the fact that they bear useful traces of their construction, the goal has been to extract from these stopping places a list of stylistic and tonal traits of the chapter that have endured over long stretches of time and found their way into very different historical occasions. Each of my own chapters is focused, not just by a particular set of texts embedded in its cultural-technological specificity, but by an identifiable chaptering style that is there generated and that would last beyond its initial moment. Neither this list of styles, however, nor the examples out of which it has been derived are in any way exhaustive. It is meant instead to suggest that, however infinite the possibilities of chapter division might be, the repertoire of its uses is much less than infinite. A set of tropes around the chapter tend to recur across its long history: a rhetoric of hands and fingers (grasping, reaching, pointing); a set of architectural images (thresholds, doors, staircases, steps); a frequent recourse to daily biorhythms (resting, sleeping). The chapter is a set of familiar styles and justifications: broad, and flexible, and far from doctrinaire, but recognizable. Recognizable not just as a way of writing but as a way of conceiving of a life in time.

What follows is in three parts: The first is a theoretical portion, laying out synchronically some of the conceptual terrain around the chapter; the second a history of the editorial chapter, which studies moments in which legal texts, philosophies, Scripture, and prose romances from antiquity to the early days of print are segmented, sometimes in multiple ways, by scribes, compilers, or printers after their initial composition, creating durable habits of division that would remain influential for later writers composing in chapters from the outset. The third is a final portion on the novelistic chapter, where I argue for the novel form's unique ability to use the chapter—the numbered or titled section, the blank space of its caesuras—as a way to articulate how the experience of time is the experience of time's segmentations. So while this book's second part generates a set of nouns to identify techniques, or topoi, that never quite disappear (the threshold, the syncopation, the cut, the fade), the third, or novelistic, portion turns to the adjectival (the postural, the tacit, the diurnal, the antique-diminutive) to describe some of the styles in which those early techniques were used and transformed at particular moments in the novel's history. One motto for the book's final section might be: how the novel is like other kinds of books, and what it takes from, and does to, that likeness.

Nothing in this story, however, is irreversible or entirely forgotten; older kinds of labor arrangements or stylistic emphases have a habit of returning. As such, the chapters of this book are in a tense relation to some of the basic presumptions of chapters per se, particularly their linearity. This is a story, but with eddies, loops, persistent motifs. In its broadest sense, however, the trajectory of these three parts is from the chapter's use as an editorial technique performed on texts not originally written for or with the chapter to its use as a compositional unit—inevitably if not always deliberately, willingly if not always happily. So it goes with my own arrangement of this book. You must, after all, write about chapters in chapters. Writing this book forced me to contend with how I'd learned to write literary-critical chapters, through no precepts or explicit instructions, just by a vague slow osmosis absorbed from countless examples; in this I very much doubt I'm alone. And as the novelists Gissing and Taylor both knew, with that pause before the new—and particularly first—chapter, comes the pleasure and anxiety of trying out something that is also too invitingly open, and too seemingly blank, to instruct you in how to use it. If the white space after a chapter's last words can sometimes feel like falling through open sky, a pen or cursor hovering as if in zero gravity, one might as well try to savor it as exhilaration before the terror returns. Here, then, is the first leap in a book about crossing gaps.

1

In Which an Object
Is Proposed for Analysis

WHAT IS A CHAPTER that we might study it? The very object itself is difficult
to conceptualize. Countless are the world's narrative forms, we know; how
much more beyond counting the segments known to us as chapters that so
often organize, interrupt, and in various ways mark them: chapters in histories,
textbooks, memoirs, children's stories, sacred writings, guides, theories, mani-
festos, pornographies, realist novels, and yes, academic monographs.[1] They
pullulate; they spawn. Yet they are almost never an object of notice as such.

An opening comparison, then: two pages from almost five hundred years
apart. The first comes from the second volume of an unexceptional manuscript
Bible of the late thirteenth century produced in Bologna and held at the British
Library (Add MS 18720); the second is from the middle volume of Charlotte
Lennox's 1752 novel *The Female Quixote* (figure 1.1). They share neither physical
material, size, mode of production, genre, conventions of authorship, nor
many operating assumptions of page design, although neither was particularly
unusual for its time and genre. The word "chapter" is not present in any form
in the Italian Bible, and its chapter openings—here, Luke 13 and 14—are not
titled. Instead a colored initial begins each chapter, as well as Roman numerals
indicating the chapter number, rubricated in alternating red and blue and inserted in the line space remaining at the end of the previous chapter. These numbers correspond to no table-of-contents-style list (or "capitula list") elsewhere
in the volume; they exist alone. A running head, spreading across the volume's
facing pages, announces the name of the book only, while slender borders on
the left of each column trail off into thin winding scrolls.[2] The British novel,
on the other hand, has a thirty-two-word chapter heading and a "drop cap" for
the chapter's first letter, the weight of segmentation falling on the heading

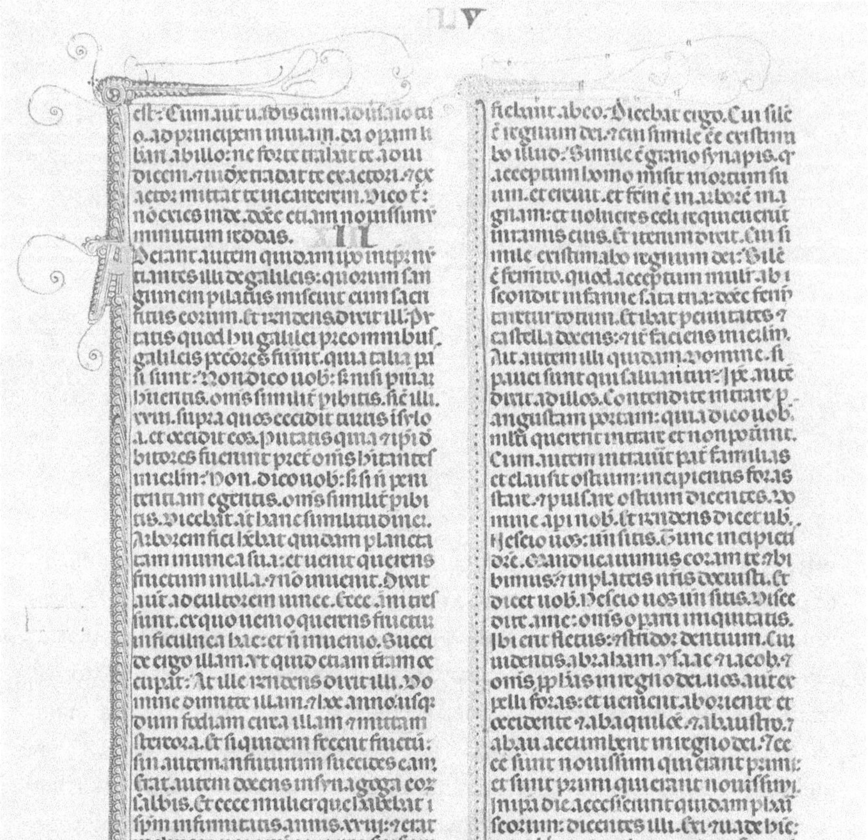

FIGURE 1.1 Two varieties of the chapter: *left*, chapter openings of Luke 13 and 14 in British Library Add MS 18720/2, fol. 438v; *right*, the opening of book 5, chapter 5, of Charlotte Lennox's *The Female Quixote: or, The Adventures of Arabella*, volume 2 (London, 1752), page 32.

Left courtesy of the British Library; *right* courtesy of the Rare Book and Manuscript Library, Columbia University.

CHAP. V.

*In which will be found one of the former
Miſtakes purſued, and another cleared
up, to the great Satisfaction of Two
Perſons; among whom, the Reader, we
expect, will make a Third.*

*A*RABELLA no ſooner ſaw Sir *Charles*
advancing towards her, when, ſenſible of
the Conſequence of being alone with a Per-
ſon whom ſhe did not doubt, would make uſe
of that Advantage, to talk to her of Love, ſhe
endeavoured to avoid him, but in vain; for Sir
Charles, gueſſing her Intentions, walked haſtily
up to her; and, taking hold of her Hand,

You muſt not go away, Lady *Bella*, ſaid he:
I have ſomething to ſay to you.

Arabella, extremely diſcompoſed at this Be-
haviour, ſtruggled to free her Hand from her
Uncle; and, giving him a Look, on which Diſ-
dain and Fear were viſibly painted,

Unhand me, Sir, ſaid ſhe, and force me not
to forget the Reſpect I owe you, as my Uncle,
by treating you with a Severity ſuch uncommon Inſolence demands.

Sir *Charles*, letting go her Hand in a great
Surprize, at the Word Inſolent, which ſhe had
uſed, aſked her, If ſhe knew to whom ſhe was
ſpeaking?

Queſtionleſs, I am ſpeaking to my Uncle,
replied ſhe; and 'tis with great Regret I ſee
myſelf obliged to make uſe of Expreſſions no
way

FIGURE 1.1 (*continued*)

more heavily than the initial words of the unit; the word "chapter" is present but abbreviated, as if too informal to bother with the full label one already knows; and a moderate amount of white space, equivalent to one line of text, separates title from chapter proper. Lennox's chapter number competes with other location devices at the page's head—both a page and a book number—and therefore is nested within one finding scheme while overlapping with another. Both the chapter number and title are recapitulated in a list of "Contents" at the start of the first volume. The chapter breaks of both Bible and novel hail a reader, but they do so with a wide tonal difference: the tacit expectation of the Biblical chapter number, that it will be used as a finding aid or citational marker, contrasts with the occasion Lennox seizes to playfully address the reader directly—this despite the fact that her novel has a more elaborate finding apparatus, its table of contents. Finally, Lennox's chapter is self-evidently understood to have authorial sanction; the division here is intrinsic to the text. Could a differently chaptered version of *The Female Quixote* possibly exist? Quite the opposite with the thirteenth-century biblical page: its chaptering is, as of the likely date of the manuscript, a fairly new scheme of division developed in the first decades of the thirteenth century, inserted into a text that had been divided quite differently over the preceding eight hundred years. One would seem to be essential and unalterable, the other provisional.

Are these chapters at all the same? What do two such things share other than a name, which might seem just a flag of convenience? What, to extend our thought experiment further, of other frequent variations—the "chapter" that is not even announced as such, marked only by a number, if that? Can these instances be said to belong to a category that could become an object of analysis?

Further confusions abound: what, in each instance, looking for a "chapter," are we supposed to see? For the literary theorist Gérard Genette (perhaps encouraged by the fact that *chapitre* or *chapter* derives from a diminutive of *caput* in Latin, or "little head"), chapters are essentially their titles, or *headings*—the labels or "intertitles" that, like the other "paratexts" Genette studies, such as prefaces, epigraphs, or dedications, exist in a space auxiliary to the text itself.[3] In the case of the biblical chapter here, these are minimal; in Lennox's novel, lavish. In both cases these are largely conventional for their time. Yet what of the unit of text so marked off, the stretch more commonly referred to as a "chapter," which is far less conventionally—perhaps even somewhat casually, or idiosyncratically—measured? In not being quite sure whether a chapter is a unit of a text or a way of marking off that unit, a label or

the textual contents so labeled, we are accordingly uncertain how much freedom it permits. In either case a suspicion lingers that only half the story is
being told. The writer of a chapter feels constraint, no doubt; the very fact of
writing in a chapter is less chosen than expected, and the appearance it will
take, its length, the extent to which it will be set off by blank space on the page,
how or if it will be titled, tends to be far more conventional to a time and a
genre than freely manipulated, and in any case not often completely within
authorial power. Yet a massive freedom exists in between. What a chapter is
meant to do—how it must begin and end—is nowhere codified. Is such a
composite thing any kind of "form"?

A "form," stretching back to the term's uses in Kant, is an identifiable feature
that negotiates between limitation and invention; it realizes itself by adhering
to, if not a rule, at least a pattern or external constraint, and yet it cannot seem
entirely rote or predetermined.[4] The chapter violates that balance. It seems at
once infinitely various and wholly routine, both too weak to be any constraint
and so ubiquitous that it can be nothing but a passively acquired constraint. As
a result, the chapter has almost never been accepted in the range of elements
that constitute a literary form.[5] But it will not do to be too nice about what we
allow into that category, if only because of what it prevents us from seeing—
here, the durable consistency and manifold variations of the chapter's segmenting work. In this I am following the call of literary critics Jonathan Kramnick and Anahid Nersessian for a pragmatist understanding of form, one that
resists any totalizing definition in favor of a flexible usage that is largely osten-
sive: to use the term "form" is to point to something, and by doing so isolate
it among a host of overlapping and competing phenomena.[6] (As we will see,
this approach is appropriate for the chapter, which is itself a kind of pointing.)
To designate a "form" is not necessarily to posit something objective about
what one points to, but instead, in the philosopher Rodolphe Gasché's phrase,
to name "a subjective condition concerning the representability" of that object
or category of objects; to call the chapter a "form" is above all to make it visible.[7] This is no small thing. There are many reasons not to see chapters: their
dull, even remedial ordinariness, their omnipresence across so many kinds of
prose documents, and also, across the millennia of their existence, what can
look like their deep unlikeness from one another.

Those obvious dissimilarities, and the chapter's oddly composite status
between text and paratext, have tended to restrict the historical and generic
scope of the few studies of the chapter that do exist, which by and large concentrate on the logics of chapter form in specific genres or even particular

writers, usually those locations where chapters are within authorial control.[8] In the foremost instances, the sophisticated and broadly synthetic work of Georges Mathieu and Ego Dionne, the result is something closer to taxonomy than history. This book proposes a more drastic kind of abstraction and a longer genealogy: to move across the difference between the authorial chapter and the kind produced by editors, scribes, and scholars at other points in the lifecycle of the text, and to move therefore across almost two millennia of textual production. It means thinking of the thirteenth-century medieval Bible, not to mention much older material, and the novelistic chapter, even many newer such examples, together. It means often adopting an uncomfortable or embarrassing literalism: if the unit was at any point called a chapter, it is a chapter, however it looks and however it was made.

I want then to propose a highly abstract object of analysis, and as a result a fairly new one, and so I began with a comparison meant to suggest a level of abstraction sufficient to gather together two such disparate instances. Where that abstraction will take us is primarily toward the question of time. The difference between medieval Bible and satirical eighteenth-century novel is of course vast, and the idea that the chapter develops slowly with every shift in genre and technology of publication will be fundamental to this study. Equally fundamental, however, is that the object of analysis is bound together and given its cultural weight by one quality every instance shares: the chapter is a form of textual segmentation that articulates time. That function is not, as we will see, one of its original purposes. It is to some extent an accident occasioned by its migration from informational to narrative genres in late antiquity. But even in its earliest instances it is present, and as the chapter spreads into an inevitability of almost any codex, it is what gives chaptering a cultural purchase not afforded other kinds of segmentation. To the extent that this mess of individual objects belongs to a class, it does so because each chapter participates in the project of imagining a temporal experience, one that is organized into flexible yet regular units, punctuated by breaks, and loosely, at times very loosely, tied in a developing sequence. It is this kind of temporal experience that gives the metaphor of the chapter—the "chapter of my life," the desire to "start a new chapter"—its power. The claim my following pages will press is that this innocuous, ubiquitous device, not just a format but not quite a genre, has a purchase on one of the grander claims of written narrative: to be capable of representing, and even structuring, what it feels like to have an experience in time. Chapters locate a reader. They fit us into a scheme that is at the same time chronological and topical; they "commensurate" our lived time, to use Nan Da's term, to textual time.[9] As such this book is a study of the gradual diffusion, long preexisting the novel but flourishing in it, of something that can be called *chapter time*.

The distinction I am making here is between what might seem like the chapter's most obvious function—its ability, particularly when indexed to a table of contents or other tabular representation, to produce a synchronic map of a text—and how chapters segment, interrupt, and articulate a diachronic or linear process through a text. By emphasizing diachrony, I am alluding to a historical argument that this book will make: the chapter, more swiftly than has been understood, outgrew its initial function of mapping or outlining and became a caesura or temporal measurement, an implicit evaluation of what is possible in the time given us by a chapter. I am also making here an argument as to essential function. Insofar as the chapter has meaning—a meaning that can become a metaphor—it is because it speaks of a sort of time analogous to, but crucially different than, the other time units we live in: hours, days, months, years; eras, periods, epochs, phases. In fact, the charged tension that seems to inhibit us from calling the chapter a "form," the tension between something that seems so abstractly conventional and yet so free to be filled in so many distinct and personalized ways, is exactly the tension of any unit of time. That is the "form" of this particular form: it marks time. And it marks time in ways that absorb and compete with other ways of marking time, at different historical moments stretching or compressing in a constantly elastic relationship to other, often more rigid, temporal concepts.

Ten Premises

From this initial comparison, I want to move to some hazarded generalizations: a list of ten premises about the chapter, an abbreviated overview of aspects of chaptering that later parts of this book will illuminate more fully. These are general observations, closer to sociological norms than ironclad distinctions. Quite often they present features that cry out, at particular moments and for particular writers, to be resisted. Yet they are surprisingly durable across a long historical stretch, and together they define a practice that, however different in material appearance or authorial intent, remains recognizably similar.

1. *The chapter is stylistically distinct; it is not fully explicable by analogy to units in other media or to psychological models. It is only loosely like a*

*musical phrase, a dramatic scene, or what cognitive scientists call "event
perception," however tempting the analogy becomes. It is its own practice,
peculiar and peculiarly useful.*

"A new chapter in a novel is something like a new scene in a play," begins
chapter 11 of Charlotte Brontë's *Jane Eyre*.[10] Sketching out chapter plans in his
notebooks, Henry James had frequent recourse to similar language. On *The
Spoils of Poynton* (1896): "I seem to see the thing in three chapters, like 3 little
acts"; on *What Maisie Knew* (1897): "Each little chapter is, thereby, a moment,
a stage." Ruminating in late 1914 over the project that would be *The Sense of the
Past*, James considered the means by which he "ended my chapter, or dropped
my curtain."[11] The comparison between chapter and scene is recurrently ap-
pealing, just as other such comparisons tend to offer themselves as suitable
explanations of how chapters operate. In *Jane Eyre*, the comparison seems motivated by embarrassment: so much has happened in the preceding chapter
break, so much more than ordinarily occurs in that space—a complete change
of life, from years spent at Lowood School to a new life among strangers—that
the typically more modest interval of a chapter break seems scarcely capable
of accommodating it. Too much has changed, as if in that space stagehands
were busily arranging a new set.

Chapters exist, then, in a matrix of different temporal units, comprising the
vocabularies of other aesthetic media, such as the "scene," as well as a more
diffuse vocabulary of time measurement. The ingredients of daily time, from
social to physiological or circadian rhythms, like a day, an hour, a visit, an
event; the human political units of reigns and revolutions, wars and careers,
and the periods in which an ideology dominates; the abstractions of small and
large time, from minutes to geological eras: the chapter is not only porous to
all these, potentially, but often explained with reference to them, depending
on the particular speed and scope of the individual text. Similarly, the chapter
exists in a matrix of different marks of punctuation.[12] It is often grouped with
the page, the paragraph, and even the separation between words as a protocol
for parsing text into distinct entities.[13] Yet by existing within *both* matrices, the
chapter remains stubbornly, if partially, independent of either, and maintains
its difference. It can absorb other units while not being reducible to them.

The occasional comparisons of chapters to other temporal segmentations
are just that—comparisons, catachreses. The chapter is tied to the materiality
of text, yet can float free of it; it can help shape more notional units of narrative, such as the "episode," without remaining beholden to them either. A

chapter can be "scenic"—limited to one continuous scene or action—or pure summary; more usually it is a combination of both, only obliquely related to either, making it difficult to parse through one particular narrative speed.[14] The chapter's relation to other kinds of temporal or narrative measurement is constituted by fleeting and changeable kinds of mimicry, making it, necessarily and paradoxically, ever more itself. More prosaically: it can encompass, at times, something like an episode, an era, a scene; and it can take on other documentary forms, such as the testimony, the affidavit, the letter; but it absorbs these within its own rules and tends to violate, or reshape, their boundaries. To echo Laurence Sterne's novel *Tristram Shandy* (1759), the chapter will observe other kinds of time measurement, like the pendulum, while rejecting "the jurisdiction of all other pendulums whatever."[15]

If the chapter is not reducible to some other unit, either specifically aesthetic or more generally cultural, a suspicion remains, familiar in our moment, that it might be explicable with reference to properties of the human brain: that the chapter satisfies, or can be derived from, ways in which time is cognitively processed. A large body of work within cognitive science has been devoted, for the last four decades, to the question of how stretches of time are segmented in ways that either make them amenable to coding as memory, or simply reviewable as coherent experiences. Such experiments have focused on the ordinary perception of events as well as the special case of reading. The basic claim of this work seems important for any theory of the chapter: boundary making is a ceaseless activity of the brain in its encounter with time, and is essential for any recall or experiential coherence. As one of the earliest such studies insisted, "ongoing behavior is perceived in units."[16] The initial and still-popular term "chunking" described exactly that aspect of perception: the spontaneous, automatic division of temporal experience. Later work in what is now known as event segmentation theory (or EST) has described some of the specific mechanisms by which the data of continuous temporality are parsed, and from the standpoint of a literary theorist, the workings of event segmentation are surprisingly Aristotelian. EST argues for a ceaseless cognitive labor of marking time into basic plot units characterized by actions and the intentions of the actor; that is to say, we scan for completed actions, where "action" is defined as a goal-driven human act.[17] Our default cognitive template for the shape of a narrative unit, which becomes the basic unit of our temporal experience, is according to logic of EST the inception and completion of a human intention, however fleeting. Simply put, the history of the chapter is inconsistent with this theory. Human intention is not the inevitable, or even a particularly frequent, grammar of chapter boundaries.[18] Or perhaps EST has a merely negative relation to the chapter: if, as is the contemporary consensus of research in the field, our episodic memory—that is, our narrative memory—is organized by the activities of event segmentation, we would have some help in understanding how difficult it can be to remember the events of any one particular novelistic or scriptural chapter.

The chapter, in other words, does not fit with current accounts of cognition the way a tool fits with an intended use. As a tool, its original purpose was never perfectly aligned with the task of chunking temporal sequence into memorable units, and it has outlived that tool-purpose in any case. As an artifact, it is best thought of as addressing virtual states of affairs—as an experiment in imagining different kinds of temporality than those spontaneously or habitually produced by our cognitive acts of segmentation.[19] Theories of other modes of dividing time can be at best suggestive in any account of the chapter, and at worst will be misleading. We will need to respect its strange, stubborn autonomy.

2. *It is so ubiquitous as to be almost invisible: the essence of conventionality.*

It is hard to *see* chapters, such is their banal inevitability. The chapter possesses the trick of vanishing while in the act of serving its various purposes. In 1919, writing in the *Nouvelle revue française*, Marcel Proust famously insisted that the most beautiful moment in Gustave Flaubert's *Sentimental Education* was not a phrase but a *blanc*, or white space: a terrific, yawning fermata, one "sans l'ombre de transition," without, so to speak, the hint of a transition.[20] It is the hiatus, Proust explains, that directly ensues from a scene set during Louis Napoleon's 1851 coup, in which the protagonist Frédéric Moreau watches the killing of his radical friend Dussardier by Sénécal, a former militant republican turned policeman for the new regime. After this sudden and virtuosic blanc, Frédéric is in 1867; sixteen aimless years elapse in the intervening silence. It is, Proust argues, a masterful change of tempo, one that liberates the regularity of novelistic time by treating it in the spirit of music. And yet this blanc is not entirely blank. What Proust neglects to mention, whether out of forgetfulness or disdain for such editorial and typesetting detail, is that the hiatus he is praising here is a chapter break.[21] However masterful and unprecedented its handling of time, it is also to some extent procedurally typical—a blanc like countless others in the history of the novel, dully routine in visual terms, simply the transition between the fifth and sixth chapters of the novel's third part, marked in the early editions published by Michel Lévy Frères not just by the

Roman numeral that prefaces the new chapter but by a change of page between the two units, an arrangement most subsequent editions followed. It
was an arrangement already present in the novel's manuscript, where across
six different rewritings Flaubert indicated this transition with a horizontal line
and a carefully, even dramatically, indited "VI." The blanc has more than a
shadow to indicate it; it has conventional marks. Flaubert was writing a chapter break. It is easy to see, but also, apparently, easy to forget, or too common
to be worth mentioning.

This is the chapter's usual fate, to be considered dully expedient but embarrassingly common, the musty old furniture of the book. We cannot entirely forget
chapters because we do not ever really have to learn about them. The conventionality of the chapter places it in the middle of a spectrum of form: too ordinary to
be easily apparent as a particular aesthetic method or choice, too necessary to
eliminate in the name of an antiformal freedom that claims to speak on behalf
of pure "life." That intermediate position is a place, we might say, where form's
deliberate artifice and life's unruly vibrancy mix most intimately. The chapter has
one foot in both restriction and freedom, diluting the force of both: a not very
severe restriction, a somewhat circumscribed freedom.

Put another way, the chapter, like any pervasive conventionality, feels natural. It is old-fashioned, but that old-fashioned aura nonetheless does not need
to rise to the level of a conscious reference to its history. To write a chapter is
to be aware of working within the preferences or norms of a genre, to think of
its vaguely usual length, to be conscious of the reader's need to pause. In fact,
that weak but persistent inevitability, that which we often mean when we speak
of the conventional, is one of its determining characteristics, and something
that any account of the chapter will have to bear in mind. Recovering what
chapters do, and a history of their changing shapes and uses, should not tip
into a psychoanalytic account that imagines readers as excessively, even if unconsciously, aware of their presence.[22] An essential element in how chapters
have developed is toward a functional innocuousness, an insistence, in fact, on
their own vagueness, flexibility, and resistance to rising to any flagrant notice.
As a result chapters escape the structure/ornament distinction; in their long,
slow history, they become ever more tacit and recessive, ever farther from their
initial structural purpose as an indexical device, and as a result ever more indispensable, something that cannot be removed without damage to the whole.

Put in a more dismissive vein, we might say that a chapter is usually, in fact
possibly always, "just" a chapter. Its claims on our attention are marginal. This
is not the whole story, but neither is it something to be ignored. In an attempt

to keep the chapter's ubiquity and innocuousness from sliding into something more vivid and unusual, my instances of chapters in what follows will more often come from a range of ordinary, typical, customary examples than from those that seem to call for our attention through intense self-consciousness or experimentation. My bias is toward the example that just barely calls out for notice, that takes part in the chapter's usual near-invisibility. Although even these examples will have intriguing lessons for us, beyond providing the ground against which more experimental instances could be understood.

3. *As a result, the chapter has no explicit canons of construction, no theory of its own.*

Like any paratext, as Genette defined the term, the chapter is "constrained."[23] It is a place where norms are obeyed more often than flouted, a space of repetition rather than innovation. But the fact of obedience does not mean that there are explicit rules being obeyed. Obscure norms do the work of regulating the chapter's shape rather than anything like a set of hard prescriptions. There is not even a canon of illustrious examples to be followed, parodied, or rejected—so diffident is the chapter's demand to be noticed. A few landmarks of metacommentary rise to the surface across the centuries, clustered in particular places and times: the "chapter on chapters" in *Tristram Shandy*, the chapter titled "Of Divisions in Authors" in Henry Fielding's 1742 *Joseph Andrews*, the "Table of Instructions" to Julio Cortázar's 1963 *Hopscotch*. But these do not function as models so much as places to explore metaphors or possible alternate uses for chaptering, and they are not widely emulated. The chapter has no foundational or primary instance, no explicit tradition, no set of guidelines; it is in this sense that Ugo Dionne, speaking of the novelistic chapter, calls it *"informalisable,"* resistant to any grammar.[24]

Such resistance gives the chapter its durability. Its shape is never so hard as to become brittle. This suggests that the chapter is most itself when least self-conscious, most habitual or automatic, when its elastic norms are most taken for granted and not pressed into the mold of a specific metaphor or function. No small part of that elasticity is that the chapter allows for a considerable confusion as to the question of agency. If a chapter is a shaped object, who shapes it?[25] The question is never easily settled, even in the cases where it becomes most apparent. "The division of the novel into parts, parts into chapters, chapters into paragraphs—the book's *articulation*—I want to be utterly clear," Milan Kundera insists in the interview with Christian Salmon collected as "Dialogue on the Art of Composition." But such clarity is a somewhat diffuse responsibility: "I also want each of the chapters to be a small, self-contained entity. This is why I insist that my publishers make the numbers prominent and set the chapters off sharply from each other. (Gallimard's solution is best: each chapter starts on a fresh page.) Let me return to the comparison between novel and music. A part is a movement. The chapters are measures. These measures may be short or long or quite variable in length."[26] Without quite acknowledging the dilemma, Kundera nonetheless points it out: the chapter, even at its most consciously shaped, is at least in part a collaboration, an effect of typography as well as of composition, a paratext as well as a form. As a result the ensuing musical metaphor expresses nothing so much as the wistfulness of the novelist in regard to another medium; composers, after all, do not thank their publishers for setting off the measures with sufficient distinctness.

In its will-to-metaphor, its implicit admission of the limits here of an author's agency, and its veering from a statement of intent ("I want . . . I insist") to something that takes the form of a definition ("chapters are measures"), Kundera's explanation is a model of how the conventions of the chapter are muddled, if productively so. Like any convention, it exists whether or not anyone wants to participate in it, but one is free—as Kundera does here—to invest in the convention, even imagine a way to transform or rationalize it. But this is not the same thing as obeying a rule. Nor is it even something like constructing a theory. It is closer to finding a way, a compromise with one's will, to live with a norm.

> 4. *And yet for all its unformalized conventionality, the chapter is also, perhaps inevitably, metafictional; it cannot help but attempt to explain itself.*

To say that the division of a narrative must in some way become a comment on that division is true in multiple senses. It is of course most notable in the category of statements that dot eighteenth-century fiction in which a narrator refers to the chapter itself, as in this characteristic chapter ending from Fielding's *Amelia* (1751): "That we may give the Reader Leisure to consider well the foregoing Sentiment, we will here put an End to this Chapter."[27] Those closing tags need not be so explicit, as the following selection of chapter-ending clauses from Eliza Haywood's *The History of Miss Betsy Thoughtless*, published the same year, demonstrates:

the reader shall presently be made sensible.

the reader will presently be informed of.

how she was amused will presently be shewn.

as will hereafter appear in the progress of this story.

will in due time and place appear.

Although such comments cluster at chapter endings, they can appear anywhere as useful cross-referencing. Haywood, for instance, has recourse to this phrase: "as related in the sixth chapter of this volume."[28] These are obvious examples, culled from two novels published within months of each other, but by no means peculiar, and they reveal that the very presence of a break in the action tends to occasion a shift in which the break becomes the subject of the discourse. Genette has called these "advance notices and recalls"; Monica Fludernik refers to them as "metadiscursive."[29] It might be more fruitful still to turn to the branch of linguistics known as pragmatics, where such a reference is understood as a deixis—technically a "discourse deixis," a gesture that locates an utterance within a surrounding discourse, lifting figure from ground. Such deictic moments tend to blur temporal and spatial registers: "presently" and "hereafter" can merge with demonstratives such as "this" or "that," "later" can also be "below."[30] Like any deixis, these moments refer to anchoring points in both space and time, pointing from the relative viewpoint of the now toward some larger temporal scheme: like proprioception, but for time.

All chapter titles, in this sense, are essentially deictic, and therefore metafictional, no matter their individual styles. The shift from a seventeenth-century heading—"How Simplicissimus Was Changed from a Wild Beast into a Christian" (Simplicius wird aus einer Bestia zu einem Christenmenschen)—to an early twentieth-century one like "Initial Inquiry" (Erste Untersuchung) is stylistically large but functionally minor.[31] Both point outside of the story world to a reader, situating the "now" of narrative within some broader and usually sequential context. (Grimmelshausen's title tells us we will be left with a Christian protagonist in what follows; Kafka's promises at least a second interrogation, and possibly several.) In fictional prose where the presence of an implied author is for whatever reason illicit, the chapter heading nonetheless refers to a world occupied by that author. "Who speaks the chapter heading?" is an unavoidable question. In more openly metafictional novels, that question can become explicit, and chapter heading can cross over into narrative (figure 1.2). In others, devices such as epigraphs signal an exterior world commenting on the world of the narrative.[32] Yet even that most discreet of

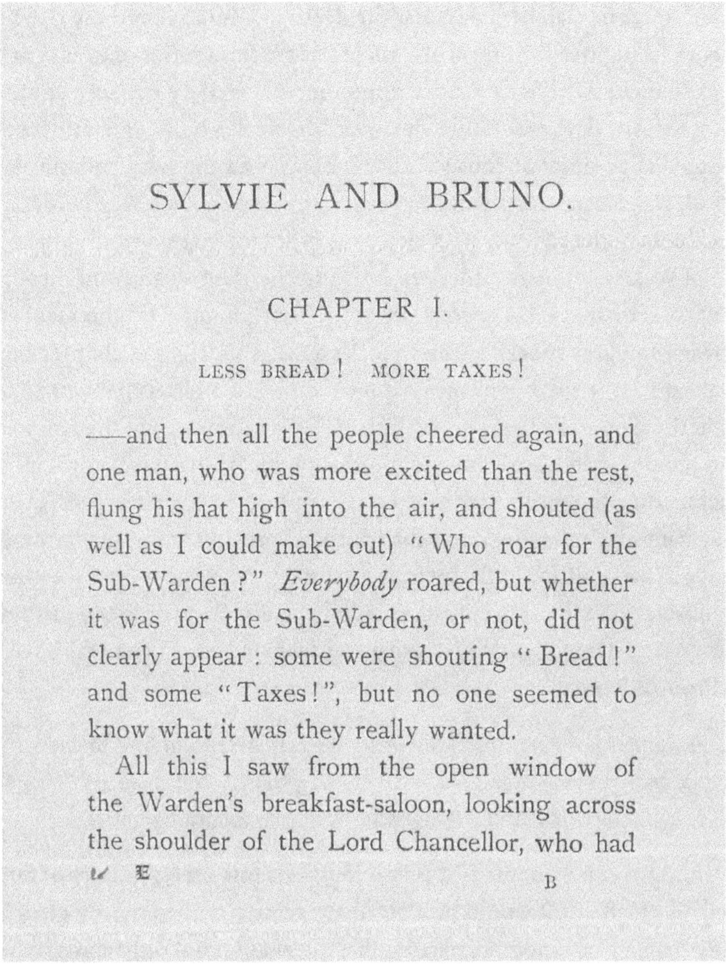

SYLVIE AND BRUNO.

CHAPTER I.

LESS BREAD! MORE TAXES!

——and then all the people cheered again, and one man, who was more excited than the rest, flung his hat high into the air, and shouted (as well as I could make out) "Who roar for the Sub-Warden?" *Everybody* roared, but whether it was for the Sub-Warden, or not, did not clearly appear : some were shouting " Bread!" and some "Taxes!", but no one seemed to know what it was they really wanted.

All this I saw from the open window of the Warden's breakfast-saloon, looking across the shoulder of the Lord Chancellor, who had

FIGURE 1.2 The cross-contamination of chapter head and narrative: Lewis Carroll's *Sylvie and Bruno* (London: Macmillan, 1889), page 1. Courtesy of the Rare Book and Manuscript Library, Columbia University.

chapter headings, a simple number, points to an outside order and sequence as well as an attitude—mocking or reluctant—toward that order.

Of course, the metafictional dimension of the chapter can be handled with varying degrees of willfulness and explicitness. Take one eventful chapter from Elizabeth Gaskell's 1854 *North and South*, "Home at Last," in which Margaret Hale's mother dies shortly after the clandestine arrival from abroad of her brother Frederick, a naval mutineer who had been living in a Spanish refuge.

It is a chapter of major transitions: the death of a mother and the dangerous presence of fugitive brother will initiate a more fluid series of events in Margaret's Manchester life as a more unpredictable anxiety replaces another. It ends at the first daybreak of the vigil over Mrs. Hale's body, and with it several "chapters" align simultaneously: "The night was wearing away, and the day was at hand, when, without a word of preparation, Margaret's voice broke upon the stillness of the room, with a clearness of sound that startled even herself: 'Let not your heart be troubled,' it said; and she went steadily on through all that chapter of unspeakable consolation."[33] That "chapter" is John 14, of which we hear Margaret speaking the first verse. As that Gospel chapter begins, "Home at Last" ends, novelistic chapter yielding to biblical chapter in a deftly metafictional gesture that yokes Margaret's recitation within the story world to our temporary release from it in the chapter break. In a novel not at all given to metafiction, the suturing of novel and Scripture through the word "chapter" is unusually sly. It demonstrates the continual pressure upon the framing of a chapter to account for itself, by finding some way to link a hiatus within the fictional world to the exigency of a readerly pause. To go one step further: we can even detect, in the history of the novel, fashions or recurrent styles of such synchronization.

5. *A chapter is a particular kind of segment. It is resistant to wholeness, autonomy, being excerpted; it prefers irregularity and elasticity. Its orientation is linear or syntagmatic rather than paradigmatic.*

A thought experiment: Is it possible to imagine an anthology of famous novelistic chapters? It would be a peculiar exercise, and no more or less compelling than an anthology of paragraphs; the chapter not only tends to be too embedded in the context of a plot to be excerptible but is not often shaped with enough attention to internal coherence to be memorable on its own. Harry Levin, in 1958, on "The Whiteness of the Whale," chapter 42 of *Moby-Dick*: "one of the farthest-ranging chapters in our literature."[34] Who else speaks of chapters in this way? A chapter is an *articulation* of a text, in the sense of the links in a chain, the bones of one's hand, or the interwoven steps of an escalator.[35] Alone, it is shorn of its function and therefore much of its effect.

Those metaphors—chain, skeleton, escalator—are also, however, slightly misleading. The chapter does always exhibit some minimal difference, despite its place within a larger working scheme, and is never quite identical to others, either in length or procedure. It has an uneasy relationship to isometry or any nested, hierarchical, regular structure. It has rhythm rather than architecture.

One way to understand this resistance to higher-order formalization is by a second thought experiment, along the lines of a quiz: How many chapters are in *Gulliver's Travels, I promessi sposi, Uncle Tom's Cabin, Der Mann ohne Eigenschaften, Invisible Man*? Any correct answer would be definitionally trivial. Chapters imply numeration but not usually numerology; there is no widely acknowledged numerological tradition proper to the chapter or the chaptered book, unlike the twelve or twenty-four "books" of epic, the three or five acts of drama, or Dante's hundred cantos divided into three canticles.[36] Those texts that adopt a chaptered numerology are deliberately eccentric, such as the unlucky thirteen chapters of Horace McCoy's 1935 noir allegory *They Shoot Horses, Don't They?*; the twelve chapters of Malcolm Lowry's 1947 *Under the Volcano*, with that number's Kabbalistic, mythological, and calendrical significances; or the thirteen books of Lemony Snicket's *A Series of Unfortunate Events* (1999–2006), each with thirteen chapters.[37] Where it is not eccentric, such numerology is deliberately countercultural: there is the example of the early sixteenth-century *Book of a Hundred Chapters*, authored by the anonymous Revolutionary of the Upper Rhine during the Peasant's Revolt, although, as if to illustrate the oddity of such totalizing numerical schemes, the book in fact includes only eighty-nine chapters.[38]

The tension the chapter occupies is that between complete autonomization and distinctness—"even the assing girouette of a postfuturo Gertrudo Steino protetopublic dont demand a new style per chapter," Ezra Pound exhaustedly warned James Joyce in 1919, having just struggled through a draft of the "Sirens" chapter of *Ulysses*—and complete totalization, or absorption into any schema that would enforce regularity.[39] It intersects with a more regular material rhythm (the page) and with different kinds of narrative rhythms (the day, the episode), cutting aslant each of them and resisting being wholly incorporated into their order.[40] In this sense, the chapter attunes us to a sense of time as multiple, overlapping, irregular. "Intervals of time," Ricoeur noted, "do not simply fit into one another according to their numerical quantities, days into years, years into centuries."[41] Nor do the slippery cadences of the chapter fit easily into larger, graduated orders. There are different ways of understanding this unevenness, different value judgments and aesthetic terms that could be applied: organic versus mechanical, self-aware rather than externally imposed, embodied rather than abstract and automatic. It is not necessary to choose; and in fact, at various historical moments, chapters may generate their impetus from any one of these vocabularies.[42] What is most important is to recognize the stubborn way in which the chapter, as a segment, defies subordination to some master scheme and evades any excessive consistency.

Which is to say that an understanding of the chapter cannot be oriented upward, toward the paradigmatic or the schematic, but forward, to a syntagmatic or linear series. The inescapable relation of chapters to ordinal numbers ("Chapter the Second") suggests how crucial linearity is to its function. This might suggest that the chapter enforces what Elizabeth Freeman has called "chrononormativity" and José Muñoz "straight time," a way of suturing the collective to the personal by enforcing a rhythm of linear, forward-directed sequence, lockstep "progressive" movement, the denial of alternative timelines or the curlicues of other-directed temporalities.[43] But its linearity is not a regular, Newtonian time; it comprises nonuniform leaps or transitions, interrupted flows, voids and blancs, that fissure linearity into an often eccentric modularity. We might now call this time "digital": discontinuous, segmentary, discrete.[44] Both comfort and foreboding can arise from its directionality, its irresistible pull to one more unit, one more chapter, promising escape and dread in equal measure. What order exists for the chapter inheres in the idea of *next, more to come, and yet.*

> 6. *As a segment, its work is primarily interruptive; it is a caesura, an aeration. Interruption is one of its primary communicative modes—it is a way of talking to a reader. To the reader it says: rest is now permitted. What we are meant to do with that rest, depends.*

For all the attention paid to "closure," we prize the experience that refuses to be firmly end-stopped: the concert-goers humming a tune while heading for the exits, the students who keep discussing after the class is done, the children still possessed by the fantasy game they've been forced to finish. In such cases "closure" is the incorrect term, even if each experience depends on the halt it elides for its force. We would do better to speak of a pleasure in *lingering*. These are not always protests against endings per se; they are more likely to seize the opportunity of an ending in order to allow it to diffuse into the outside air, to permit it to gently haunt us, to let it pass into our preoccupation. Such a pleasure needs the boundary of an ending, and needs that boundary to be a little porous. It desires a respite. Here again the American idiom "chapter book" is suggestive; such a book requires not only the stamina to read for long stretches but the maturity to want to resume it after a pause, which means acquiring a taste for interruption.

This is not reading, exactly, nor is it quite *not* reading. It poses the question of how we are to understand the role of interruption, usually ignored by literary historians and theorists because of the continuing power of immersion in the value systems that surround reading.[45] The interruption/immersion binary is, however, a false one. Cognitive approaches to literary form have been best at understanding this self-evident, if persistently ignored, fact: attentiveness requires its opposite.[46] The chapter break solicits immersion in ongoing narrative because it permits release. But it does something else as well: it encourages a diffuse resonance, allowing long narrative all the pleasures other aesthetic media possess, like the pianist's fingers lifting while a chord still echoes. It is what Jean-Luc Nancy calls "sonorous time": a not-yet-sense-making willingness to let an experience spread, extend, pass away.[47] That "lingering" of narrative spilling over into the everyday is produced by the pause.

Unlike so much else in the history of the chapter, the function of interruption has long been understood and frequently restated. Sterne in *Tristram Shandy*: "Chapters relieve the mind. . . . [T]hey assist—or impose upon the imagination."[48] Thomas Mann, as Serenus Zeitblom, in *Doctor Faustus* (1947): "It is only out of consideration for the reader, who is always keeping an eye out for places to pause, for caesuras and new beginnings, that I have divided into several chapters what in my own conscientious authorial opinion can really lay no claim to such segmentation."[49] Playful or sententious, the sentiment is nonetheless commonplace, and remains so.[50] The chapter is, to adopt the language of contemporary media, an interface: a space that connects media and user, where a direction is given (here, pause your reading) but where different possible behaviors (put the book down for a minute, put it down for the day, ignore and continue) are possible in response.[51] The direction is merely to rest, pause, suspend in some manner.

But not—it must be repeated—end. The chapter break is not a unit of closure but of hiatus. It is not a division *of* so much as a division *within*, a caesura within an ongoing experience, an internal bracketing.[52] We might think of the chapter in this sense as the enjambment of narrative prose. Prose, as so many of its theorists insist, is defined by its lack of enjambment, its continuous, blocklike quality; the chapter break is among the oldest techniques to provide prose what it otherwise resists, the space of a breath.[53] That space can have particular aesthetic qualities. It can vary in frequency across a text, in predictability or regularity, and in its relation to the narrative it articulates. It can also have particular cultural qualities. The "one chapter a day" habit of biblical reading in Protestant societies can and did often lead to an idea of any narrative reading being meted out similarly; in certain regimes of labor and leisure, this might mean the association of the chapter break with a longer pause, that for sleep, the end of day. The matching of chapter break with nightfall will then in turn have a feedback effect upon the shaping of the novel, as chapter 7 of this book will explore. But these particularities, however numerous, all stem from a structural condition of the chapter's interruptive work: the chapter break synchronizes, however temporarily, a reader's time with story time. Pause matches pause. Like a conductor's baton, the break signals a rhythmic coordination of worlds.[54]

7. *It is both material and immaterial; tied to the book, it nonetheless has no physical, three-dimensional referent.*

Many kinds of textual division are based in distinctions between discrete objects or material practices, even if those distinctions have become merely figural. Dramatic "acts" are normally marked by a pause or curtain fall. The division of long texts—epic poetry most notably—into "books" refers to the separate *bibloi* of papyrus scrolls, even if the size of scrolls may not have been directly responsible for the length of these divisions.[55] Then there are the tablets, or *tuppu*, of Babylonian cuneiform, such as those that compose what is left of the epic of Gilgamesh, which would be numbered and listed in a colophon tablet. These *tuppu* are now often called "chapters" as well as tablets, in an attempt to naturalize them for Western audiences.[56] One can then begin to imagine that all textual divisions have some physical referent, a constraint borrowed from some previous technology that time has rendered invisible to us.

It is a persuasive idea and often justified. Yet as Bonnie Mak has argued, even a textual unit like the *page*, which seemingly is defined by its tactile qualities, may be at least partially independent of its usual objecthood.[57] So it is, even more emphatically, with the chapter—like the page, older than the codex with which it is so often associated. Its physicality is ghostly, inaccessible. It is not amenable to the hand: one cannot ordinarily hold, grasp, or clasp a chapter. It is not even susceptible to the eye, given how rarely a chapter is visible in one glance. The result is the extreme difficulty in imagining its materiality at all. Even its relationship to the page is historically contingent; the fashion for starting a chapter at the top of a new page is a relatively modern one, and for much of its history any coalescence of page and chapter would have been accidental. A common kind of chapter heading, beginning with the playfully locative "in which," alludes to a container or position while committing itself to no fixed spatial concept—"in" may simply mean "during the next period of reading." While tied to the book as part of its "bibliographic code"—its format—it is also a "linguistic code," a form, not wholly identifiable with the particular typographical norms that articulate it and the material container in which it exists.[58] As a result it can float free of the book—both films on DVD and podcasts alike can have "chapters"—while providing, in these newer media, a whiff of bookishness.

The chapter is what the sociologist Erving Goffman called an "episoding convention," a frame that marks out a particular temporality, and such a frame, Goffman reminds us, is "neither part of the content of activity proper nor part of the world outside the activity but rather both inside and outside," a paradox that is both familiar and hard to grasp conceptually.[59] No one material element completely defines the chapter, not its heading or label, not the (minuscule or lavish) white space that surrounds it, not even the stretch of text between those spaces. It is all of those things, text and paratext both, in a gestalt that perceives the segment and its apparatus against the ground of the text as a whole. The materiality of the chapter is no more or less palpable than the materiality of time itself.

8. *Its long history is that of a shift from utility to aesthetic form, or from indexicality to significance—but it never quite sheds its relation to utility, which remains available for use in either sincere or parodic modes.*

The chapter is an intersection—at times a collision, at others a negotiation—between two kinds of reading: one that is continuous and immersive, and one that is informational and consultative. The halt a chapter break permits and even encourages is a place where the "tabularity" of reference intrudes directly into the text, far more directly than a page number, which remains literally marginal; it inserts the discontinuous directly into the flowing.[60] Originally a method for citation and nonlinear access, the chapter evokes partial reading, excerpting, and scanning, even in texts (like narrative fiction) that do not otherwise invite such a use. It is a reminder that our books are not just narratives but also, however slightly or vestigially, reference books. A chapter heading and a chapter number are both memories of an indexical function, even when they have been shorn of any accompanying apparatus like a table of contents. Yet that function has been largely replaced by a wider repertoire of uses that we can call formal, among them being: composing a rhythmic alternation of immersion and aeration; providing occasion for metafictional comment; sculpting a temporality that modulates between story time and readerly time.[61]

The key point here is that one of those two forces existed before the other, so that the collision in reading modes evoked by the chapter points to a past that has been (largely) superseded and can be (occasionally) recovered. The chapter begins its life, even before the full development of the codex, as a technology produced by scribes and editors for discontinuous access; only gradually will it become a "form" of its own, produced by writers as part of the compositional process and not afterwards by various others in the communications circuit. That is the story this book will tell, and it is why this book must in fact take the form of a story—of a history, not a taxonomy or map. The lesson could be put as follows: The chapter's history is ancient, preceding the norms of continuous, solitary reading. It means that a turn to the indexical or citational function of chapters will present itself usually as self-consciously antique. In the case of the novel, it means that the chapter serves as a reminder of the novel's historical lateness; the apparatus of chaptering is older than the form that is being segmented. "The novel," Peter Stallybrass put it with polemical force, "has only been a brilliantly perverse interlude in the long history of discontinuous reading."[62]

A further consequence is that the original citational function of chaptering is vestigial and largely irrelevant. It is of course peculiar that we now use page numbers to cite texts rather than chapter numbers, given that chapters are not as susceptible to change, via new editions, translations, or formats, in the way pagination must be.[63] We simply use chapters differently than their originally intended function; we have adaptively reimagined them, taking a tool and applying it to new materials and tasks. Some of those new tasks, such as the "sample chapter" beloved by literary agents, publishers, job and prize committees, are still purely functional rather than aesthetic. The chapter has not shed every practical use. Yet the original "infrastructural context" of format often persists, as Jonathan Sterne argues, as a "style" long after the initial purposes of a format have vanished.[64] The memory of that original use of the chapter—citation or discontinuous access—lingers as part of the chapter's significance, and is available for homage, parody, and even, perhaps, resumption.

9. *Its history, for writers and readers both, is deep, demotic, passed by anecdote, rediscovered anew in each moment. A recurrent amnesia turns the chapter's history into a series of long silences and strange repetitions.*

The chapter's history operates at a scale broader than literary history tends to adopt. It cannot be situated in any one recognizable "period," and moves through such periods often without any long-term or consequential

AN OBJECT IS PROPOSED FOR ANALYSIS   33

alterations. Like any story told at a broader scale, it will have long silences, dips into routine and sudden rises of some new development; it will fall into abeyance somewhere and then erupt somewhere else; the chains of causality are not always evident. It will involve recurrence and persistence as much as progression.[65] It will look strikingly stable at the broadest scale, while seeming unpredictable, and amenable to human creativity, at the smaller scale. It isn't located in any one period, while being a model, demotic and widespread, for time's periodization. In fact, the chapter is a practice of segmentation already far more self-conscious than the segments into which the historical gaze habitually falls.[66]

It is therefore a history marked by amnesiac recurrence, as a cento of citations might suggest. The earliest is from the *De re rustica* of Columella, a first-century CE compendium of agricultural lore, in regard to the list of chapter headings that prefaces the text:

> Since it generally happens that the recollection of the things which we have learned fails us and must be renewed rather often from written notes, I have added below a list [*argumenta*] of the contents of all my books in order that, whenever necessity arises, it may be easily possible to discover what is to be found in each of them.[67]

A century later, Aulus Gellius prefaces his *Noctes Atticae* with a similar disclaimer:

> Summaries of the material [*capita rerum*] to be found in each book of my Commentaries I have here placed together, in order that it may at once be clear what is to be sought and found in each book.[68]

Discontinuous, consultative reading is the rationale here, identified with the summary work of the heading rather than the divisions of the units themselves, although the latter is implied by the former. This is still the stated rationale in the sixth century, when the Ostrogothic textual scholar Cassiodorus clarifies, in his *Institutiones divinarum et saecularium litterarum*, why the Bibles produced by his scriptorium include chapter headings at the start of each individual book:

> To make the text of the Octateuch available to us in a summarized version, I thought that the chapter-headings [*titulos*] should be set down at the beginning of each book, chapter-headings that had been written by our ancestors in the course of the text. The reader might thus be usefully guided and made

profitably attentive, for he will easily find everything he is looking for, seeing it briefly marked out for him.

Similarly, on the Solomonic, or wisdom, books, Cassiodorus remarks:

> With the Lord's aid I have taken care to mark the chapter-headings [*capit-
> ula*] on these books so that in such indispensable reading, as I have often
> said, the inexperienced beginner may not be left in confusion.[69]

Jump ahead again, this time five hundred years, to the middle of the twelfth
century, and one can find this, from the prologue to Peter Lombard's *Four
Books of Sentences*, one of the first medieval compilations of patristic
wisdom:

> Again, so that what is sought might appear more easily, we have begun by
> providing the titles [*titulos*] by which the chapters [*capitula*] of the indi-
> vidual books are distinguished.[70]

Something has changed here—the terminology of heading versus unit has
been settled, "title" and "chapter" differentiated; but the rationale is recognizably the same. Yet another four hundred years elapse, and the 1560 preface to
the Geneva Bible will argue that its elaborately subdivided presentation, including chapter headings and prose summaries or "arguments"—along, now,
with verse numeration—are necessary "that by all meanes the reader might
be holpen."[71] This recurrent historical amnesia, which discovers in the chapter
a potentially needless encrustation that must be described in terms of a consultative reader's convenience, then migrates into the novel, where the argument
is recognizably the same despite a tonal difference. There is, famously, Henry
Fielding in *Joseph Andrews*:

> Secondly, What are the Contents prefixed to every Chapter but so many
> Inscriptions over the Gates of Inns (to continue the same Metaphor), in-
> forming the Reader what Entertainment he is to expect, which if he likes
> not, he may travel on to the next: for, in Biography, as we are not tied down
> to an exact Concatenation equally with other Historians, so a Chapter or
> two (for Instance, this I am now writing) may be often pass'd over without
> any Injury to the Whole.[72]

Less famously, and now delivered into the voices of characters, from *The
History of Charlotte Summers* (1750), often attributed to Sarah Fielding,
in which a Miss Arabella Dimple, lying half naked in bed, calls to her

maid to fetch "the first Volume of the Parish Girl I was reading in the Afternoon":

> —Pray, Ma'am, where shall I begin, did your Ladyship fold down where you left off?—No, Fool, I did not; the Book is divided into Chapters on Purpose to prevent that ugly Custom of thumbing and spoiling the Leaves; and, now I think on't, the Author bid me remember, that I left off at the End of—I think it was the 6th Chapter. Turn now to the 7th Chapter, and let me hear how it begins—[73]

Discontinuous reading has gradually been redefined as the interruption of a sequence rather than nonlinear access, but the essentials are recognizable, despite local differences of tone or terminology, across 1,700 years: the chapter is a solicitation of the reader's convenience. Each instance here treats the chapter as an innovation, then proceeds to rationalize it along similar lines, with little consciousness of the long rhetorical tradition of that rationalizing. Only Fielding notes, unusually, that chapters "have the Sanction of great Antiquity."[74]

We can then speak of a continual rediscovery of a fact that never disappears long enough to seem to need rediscovering. The tendency extends to scholars as well, who have sometimes insisted, with pardonable pride, that it is in their own chosen period in which chapters arise. The feeling of novelty associated with its continually recurrent defenses has perhaps misled them.[75] It is as if the memory of the chapter's justifications resides somehow in the form itself, which bears its marks despite, or without, the intentions of its users. As a result amnesia is accompanied by a tenacious implicit memory: no resource, technique, or rationale associated with the chapter is ever wholly forgotten, and each is always available for reuse.

10. *Long as the chapter's history is, the novel is where the creative potential of that history culminates, the place of its flourishing. But the chapter's role in the novel is troubled, ironic, part of the novel's inevitable tension with discontinuity.*

Perhaps the most significant moment in the chapter's history is its insertion into narrative genres. The chaptering of narrative, rather than texts intended for informational or consultative use where the chapter is originally developed, assigns to the chapter a new purpose: segmenting time. It begins the process by which the weight of the chapter falls ever more decisively on the unit of text, and the amount of time the narrative (and the reading experience)

within it occupies, rather than the label or heading. Many notable early examples of chaptered narrative—from some early chaptered Bibles to the chaptered prose narratives published by William Caxton—omit descriptive headings entirely, demonstrating the gradual etiolation of the chapter's indexical
function. It is a history that will be recapitulated by the novel itself, in which
the garrulous headings common to early realist fiction give way to tactfully
restrained headings or simple numeration. Tables of contents pegged to chapter headings begin to vanish in novels, and where they remain, they are more
ornamental than functional, telling us nothing that we can know without having already read the novel, and possibly not much even then; they are a
hollowed-out index, often perfectly useless.

The shift in the chapter's purpose inaugurated by its application to narrative
texts, from index to rhythmic rest, may have initially been accidental, but quickly
becomes in the novel a series of deliberate effects, often to the point of self-
parody. In the novel, *chaptering becomes itself a narrative technique*. That is, it becomes a "form." Format becomes form when intentionally adapted for some
artistic purpose.[76] While not entirely relinquishing its status as a paratext with a
defined range of possible *functions*, it develops into a tool with a wider range of
possible *meanings*; meanings that are, however, not entirely divorced from those
initial functions. The meanings the novel accrues around the chapter cluster
around the subject of time. This is a reinvention of the chapter—or, perhaps, the
discovery and display of something latent in it from the beginning.

In general, the *functions* of the chapter in the novel do not easily relate to
the purposes for which it was originally *designed*, or at least as that design was
recurrently described.[77] But that design, in the form of a paratext's ability to
permit discontinuous access, cross-reference, and tabulation, lingers, even if
ironically, playfully, or begrudgingly. And so the chapter's place in the novel,
while entirely conventional, is never wholly comfortable and at times acutely
irritating. It is from the beginning a slight embarrassment, announced by co-
medic or otherwise self-conscious headings, modulating gradually into the
even deeper and more tacit embarrassment signaled by the absence of headings entirely. The chapter's conventionality must be resisted, denied, partially
dispensed with. Its segmentation—governed by outdated norms—does not,
so we are often told, reflect the continuous texture of lived consciousness. It
is purely linear, so incapable of complexity. John Berger in G. (1972): "The relations which I perceive between things—and these often include casual and
historical relations—tend to form in my mind a complex synchronic pattern.
I see fields where others see chapters."[78] It openly solicits the reader, to allow

a pause or provide helpful labels, when such solicitations seem insulting to the dignity of the genre. It breaks up what should be continuous, interrupts what should be immersive. If the chapter is an almost inevitable element of the novel, to the point of becoming virtually synonymous with it, a hard kernel of discomfort remains in this otherwise durable relationship.

Chapter Time (the Example of Pym)

If the novel is the place where chapters finally flourish as formal possibilities, it should already be evident that they do so, by and large, quietly. It will take an adjustment of the ear to surface their rhythms. So I conclude these abstract ruminations on chapters by turning to a single, highly innocuous, if no less finely shaped, example: the ninth chapter of Barbara Pym's 1952 *Excellent Women*. This sample chapter comes from a moment and a genre in which the chapter is thoroughly conventional and naturalized, no longer the subject of ironic commentary as in *The Female Quixote*, although Pym's subject is another, more recessive kind of female quixotry. It is an unexceptional chapter in the middle of its novel, without the burdens of originating or concluding. Far more so than in Lennox or the manuscript Bible, it is typographically modest: only "Chapter Nine" sits at the top of its first page, without the heading or corresponding table of contents that British fiction had been in the process of abandoning for almost two centuries. At a little over three thousand words, it is also unassuming in length, calling attention to itself for neither excessive amplitude nor noticeable condensation.

It does not advertise itself as unique or outside its moment's norms. But it is no less a puzzle for all that, however ordinary the puzzle. The question it asks: Why is this chapter—not a single event, scarcely a series of events—a unit of time? What if anything distinguishes it, marks out its boundaries, frames its action? So weak is its framing, in fact, untitled and summarized by neither character nor narration in any obvious way, that we might suspect nothing distinguishes it at all aside from its very ordinariness, a "chapter effect" akin to a "reality effect." But still the fact of its being so distinguished, at least typographically, as "Chapter Nine," calls for an answer, and the answer might be a different route to some useful generalizations about how chapters, that technique of discontinuity, are engineered within continuous narrative.

Pym's chapter opens on a March morning, a Wednesday during Lent in postwar London. Mildred Lathbury, the novel's protagonist spinster and mordantly observational narrator, has the day before—narrated in the previous chapter—had her annual lunch with William Caldicote, the brother of a close friend, a confirmed bachelor who greets any hint of Mildred's erotic or sentimental life with alarm; in mutely rebellious response, she drinks a bit too much wine, and impulsively purchases a bouquet of mimosas. Upon returning to her flat, she meets the smoothly ingratiating Rocky Napier, husband of her new upstairs neighbor, Helena. Unlike William, Rocky enthuses over the mimosas and impulsively invites Mildred to tea, an invitation she accepts, stopping only to let Rocky put the flowers in water in the Napiers' apartment. That evening, overhearing Rocky and the returned Helena laughing upstairs, Mildred realizes she has left the mimosas in their flat, and has for compensation "only a disturbed feeling that was quite unlike me" (EW, 75).[79]

As Chapter Nine's morning begins, Rocky, in his dressing gown, returns the mimosas; too embarrassed to encounter him in this way, Mildred reaches out her hand for them without looking at him, noting that they had faded in the interval. She heads to work—at an organization for "impoverished gentlewomen"—where a coworker reminds her of their plans to attend a lunchtime church service. A hurried and dispiriting cafeteria lunch precedes the service. The service itself is dominated by a long, uncomfortably febrile sermon on the Last Judgment, which Mildred passes over in summary. Upon departing the church, Mildred encounters Everard Bone, the dryly enigmatic anthropologist and friend of Helena Napier's for whom Mildred has a puzzled curiosity; Everard remarks that he had been moved to laughter by the sermon, and after a short exchange, issues an unenthusiastic invitation to see his upcoming talk at the Learned Society. After work, Mildred visits her friends Father Julian Malory, with whom Mildred shares a perennially baffled nearcourtship, and his sister Winifred, only to find them helping to arrange the rooms of the vicarage's new lodger, the clergyman's widow Allegra Gray, a rather younger and "faster" specimen than her status would normally indicate. Mildred is brusquely pressed into the service of helping hang curtains; she notes signs of rapidly acquired intimacy between Julian and Allegra, and leaves abruptly, almost impolitely. As she leaves, Sister Blatt, a member of Julian's congregation and a brusquely observant commentator on parish affairs, comments on Mildred's evident gloom. Back home, Mildred gathers some underclothes to wash, making in the chapter's last sentence its closest approach to metafiction: "Just the kind of underclothes a person like me might wear, I thought dejectedly, so there is no need to describe them" (EW, 85).

Something a bit more than a dozen hours, over the course of an unremarkable, if stubbornly dispiriting, Lenten and leaden weekday: this is what paraphrase reveals. What seems at first to give it shape is its mood, signaled by the fading of the mimosas during the previous chapter interval. In any adequate summary of a Pym chapter, adjectives loom large; here the quality of wilting, and its attendant disappointment, lingers for the rest of the day. At first this is something like the mystery of how one day can be so unlike another, the Tuesday of the eighth chapter ("suddenly it was almost spring" [*EW*, 66]) switching during the night, and the white space of the chapter break, into a familiarly gray Wednesday. The unaccountability of mood gives the chapter a theme of balked cognition: What made the day this way? None of the proffered possibilities (among them: having missed the short freshness of the mimosas; regret at the previous day's costly and ill-nourishing indulgences; a confusion at the oscillation between the previous day's two differently impossible erotic objects, William and Rocky, as well as their combined mismatch with the ambient longing for which they were insufficient occasions; a shame at solitude accentuated by close, unchosen proximity to so many other couplings, potential or actual; the weather) entirely satisfies. So the chapter—identical with a mood—is constituted by a frustrated relation to event. Whatever happens, and it is not quite nothing while not amounting to much of something, does not seem in an apposite relation to what Mildred feels. Which is a challenge to paraphrase, even in Mildred's narratorial recollection; to retell is not the same thing as to explain, even as retelling seems the only plausible route to explanation.[80]

Along with mood's decoupling from causality is its paradoxical temporal vagueness. How long a mood lasts is both unknowable and yet intimately, rhythmically familiar; it *could* be interminable—a bad mood always threatens to become a lifelong condition, or to seem like the truth of that condition— but experience tells us that, like every other mood that has preceded it, it has a natural duration, if one that seems untethered to any regularly recurring punctuation. It will simply lapse at some future point.[81] The frustration arising from that vagueness requires other, more reliable temporal frames for reassurance. Leaving the vicarage, Mildred thinks: "Today was obviously not a good day, that was it" (*EW*, 84). The diurnal frame, in fact, gives the chapter some of its shape; it is an account of most of Mildred's waking hours in one day's scope, structured by daily social rhythms: waking for work, lunch, tea, washing. But other references to days cut across that mundane dailiness. The Judgment Day sermon that disconcerts Mildred invokes a perspective of ultimate, terminal, emblematic days, and if Mildred's coworker grouses at the subject—"'That talk about the *Dies Irae*,' she said, 'that's Roman Catholic, you know. It ought

not to be allowed here'" (*EW*, 73)—the suspicion that this particular Wednesday is a day of ruth rather than wrath, typical and typological rather than an
accident, is harder for Mildred to erase. At times, if with habitual deprecation,
Mildred arrives at something like a cosmic or revelatory sense of the moment
in which she is enveloped. Looking around the cafeteria, she remarks on the
"hopeless kind of feeling" it inspires:

> "One wouldn't believe there could be so many people," I said, "and one
> must love them all." These are our neighbors, I thought, looking round at
> the clerks and students and typists and elderly eccentrics bent over their
> dishes and newspapers.
>   "Hurry up, dear," said Mrs. Bonner briskly, "it's twenty past already."
> (*EW*, 78)

This slightly Vergilian vision of a multitude of souls is, like so much else in
Excellent Women, only hesitantly epiphanic, but it hinges on a vision of unarticulated, endless time; the remark is prefaced by Mildred's memory, appropriate for a clergyman's daughter, of two lines from Isaac Watts's "Our God, Our
Help in Ages Past": "Time like an ever-rolling stream / Bears all its sons away."
Another, more circumscribed temporal frame—that of social time, the
clock—interrupts and relieves the gesture. It points to a time that is potentially
interminable, as well as a moral demand that would be limitless, in precisely
the way the *Dies Irae* will shortly do during the post-lunch church service. The
collision between these two "days" occasions much of the chapter's perplexity:
Is this a passing day or something pivotal, permanent?

Alongside this dilemma sits another temporal crux in this chapter, that between linearity and repetition. Harried by the moving tray belt during her path
through the cafeteria line, Mildred's indecision results in "a tray full of things
I would never have chosen had I had time to think about it, and without a
saucer for my coffee." When Mrs. Bonner explains correct procedure, Mildred
makes one of her characteristic self-implicating jokes, of the kind that, by inviting both laughter and agreement, ends up disappointed at receiving one at the
expense of the other: "I think one ought to be allowed a trial run-through first,
a sort of dress rehearsal" (*EW*, 77). Linearity: if only one knew what was coming. This day will be for Mildred a record of small unpleasant surprises, toward
which she feels in a position of keen, unprepared susceptibility. Yet it is also,
in its way, entirely expected, a line she has already been through; the chapter
ends with her undergarment washing, of which she observes: "It was depress-
ing the way the same old things turned up every week" (*EW*, 85). Repetition:

one always tends to know what is coming. The play between unsettling, hurried novelty and complete dreary familiarity may help define the trap of Mildred's mood, but it throws a reader back to the implicit question of this untitled unit: what kind of time is this chapter that it is a chapter at all?

Attending to the chapter's beginning and ending provides some possible answers: it is the curve of a mood (from its onset with the wilted mimosas to a purgative climax in the minor masochism of choosing to wash undergarments); it is an abstract or natural unit of time (the day, or diurnal path, from shortly after first light to "dusk," the chapter's final time indication); it is a record of social or human time, bracketed by an initial awkward interaction and the day's final withdrawal from conversation. Other time units—the brief period of a cut flower's freshness, the week's washing, the gloom of early spring, the Lenten season, the gradual yet sudden onset of permanent spinsterhood—uneasily coincide as well. To which one might add the question of the rhetorical occasion of the chapter itself rather than just its purely diegetic dimensions. If a chapter is a unit for its reader, the modest scope of this particular one suggests a similarly modest expectation, perhaps even on the part of the narrator herself, of what a reader can endure of Mildred before a break is necessary. How much is too much is a constant concern of *Excellent Women*; the previous chapter had in fact contrasted Mildred's unaccustomed indulgence in good cakes and Nuits St. Georges, the prelude to the ninth chapter's surfeited regrets, with what awaits her at home, "a small wedge of sandwich cake" inside a tin (*EW*, 75). Small things, it might be, are here the most anyone is expected to easily digest.

Beginnings and endings offer one approach, if several different answers. A different analysis would look for a core, a kernel, something transformational in the chapter inside its various kinds of temporal bracketing.[82] Such a supposed kernel might point beyond the chapter—set off reverberations that will alter the plot in subsequent chapters—or could remain intrinsic to it, organizing in one moment or gesture the contour of the chapter's actions, serving as its key, its culmination, its meaning. Mildred's day offers no easily detectable candidates. Its stubborn ordinariness tends to level her actions into a series of identically futile, or balked, gestures. But a claim could be made for one particular trajectory. We have her rather sudden epiphany at the cafeteria ("one must love them all"), occasioned by the lines from Watts's hymn, which transform the long cafeteria line into a vision of the afterlife, "like something in a nightmare," with its "file of people . . . fenced off from the main part of the room by a brass rail" (*EW*, 77). It is accentuated uneasily by the sermon on Judgment

Day that immediately follows lunch, although Mildred does not comment on the reverberation. Following the sermon, primed by the moral injunction her lunchtime epiphany evoked, her meeting with Everard Bone—for whom she has had a curious distaste—seems to demand action, some triumph of intention over inclination. So she asks him about his Learned Society paper, to be presented with Helena. His response is offhand, without particular warmth, although it does result in his suggestion that Helena get Mildred an invitation. The result for Mildred is the mildest form of moral elation:

> I felt that I had made a slight advance, that an infinitesimal amount of virtue had gone out of me, and although I did not really like him I did not feel so actively hostile to him as I had before. But how was it possible to compare him with Rocky? All the same, I told myself sternly, it would not do to go thinking about Rocky like this. Yesterday, with the unexpected spring weather and the wine at luncheon there had perhaps been some excuse; today there was none. The grey March day, the hurried unappetising meal and the alarming sermon made it more suitable that I should think of the stream of unattractive humanity in the cafeteria, the Judgment Day, even Everard Bone. (*EW*, 80)

If this is the result of the Christian injunction to "love them all"—to ask an academic about his work—so be it. As an extrinsic kernel it functions, if weakly; it reminds her of the previous day's false elation, and lays the ground for the following chapter, in which Mildred attends the lecture. It is her first independent, affirmative gesture toward Everard, if a characteristically self-effacing one; it presages the eventual progress of their acquaintance, even beyond the novel itself, if we want to believe the evidence of *Jane and Prudence* (1953) and *Less than Angels* (1955), in each of which we hear secondhand accounts of their marriage and Mildred's fate to be the "useful wife" of an anthropologist, who types his manuscripts and "got on well with the missionaries they were meeting now that they were in Africa again."[83]

As an intrinsic kernel, however, it explains the chapter differently: as a fleeting response to the incitation of Mildred's cafeteria vision, one to which she is unequal in the rest of the chapter. It is one thing to express interest in Everard's anthropology, quite another to pretend to enjoy the company of Allegra Gray, to laugh at her cheaply amusing wit and to accede to her having supplanted Mildred in the social life of the vicarage and, perhaps, in Julian's affections. It is an impulse without a lasting effect, quashed by the day's conspiracy to demoralize Mildred. This reading would explain the chapter as the victory of contingencies—mood, chance, quotidian reality—over moral intention, whereas the "extrinsic" reading would read the chapter as the glimmer of future events seen through the scrim of the day's preoccupations. Neither reading, however, identifies anything like the "kernel" of narrative theory. The impulse to treat Everard with ordinary solicitude, as a moral resolution, fails to catch fire; as spark to her developing entanglement with him, it is damp enough that it might as well not have happened at all. Helena had already promised to take her to the talk; her attendance is anticipated anyway. If anything, *Excellent Women* presents Mildred's intentions and actions as superfluous to the history of her social relations, as if she is passively beset by a series of unchosen circumstances (who is lodging in the flat upstairs, who has moved into the parish) rather than afflicted by the results of her choices.

Which is to say that this chapter is not reducible to an event, an action, or an intention, however small or frustrated. Yet its being marked *as* a chapter nonetheless promises some significance, some shape to the experience that is not quite equivalent to the actions narrated within it. It has both an independent shape—the persistence of Mildred's mood, the failure of her impulse to universal love to displace that mood, the limits of the individual day—while also being a minor node in the advancing chain of actions that will propel all its participants, Rocky, Everard, Allegra, and even Mildred, to some more consequential resolutions. It is dependent on what surrounds it but remains, however partially or weakly, separate; and it offers an uneasy, stymied relation to action, just as any analysis of it is in an uneasy relation to paraphrase.

If this all sounds as if the ninth chapter of *Excellent Women* is in some way structurally allegorical of Mildred's character, that is a happy accident. My intention here is different: to use it as an allegory of chaptering itself. Much of how this particular chapter operates, from its slightly displaced relation to action or event to its foregrounding of temporal parameters like the day, is crucial to the long history of the chapter as a form, particularly as a novelistic form, as my own following chapters will outline. In this sense, a certain sleight of hand was operative in my choice of Pym; as a traditionalist in narrative techniques, she is clearly aware, likely even more than she knew, of how a novel chapter usually feels, what it can usually do, how long it can usually last, what it is usually in tension with. She then employs those potentialities and limitations to sculpt a time that allegorizes, and grounds, Mildred's plight: small-scale, repetitive yet capable of minor surprise, bounded and distinct while also being porous to its surround. This goal necessarily involves Pym in a close engagement with a long, uncodified, felt-more-than-known generic habit. And as we will see, the particular generic habit of chaptering, the chapter's inevitable place in the novel, is tied to a series of pre-novelistic developments.

In a broader sense still, Pym's chapter helps demonstrate that chapters are a primary means by which time is sculpted within a novel. A chapter is a novel's usual rhythm or cadence, in the sense that Jean-Luc Nancy gives to rhythm: the "time of time," the portioning of a linear succession into a beat, a rise and fall, a repeated incitation and resolution, that by segmenting time makes it palpable.[84] It is a time that is neither wholly public or conventional—not strictly bound to the clock, to any particular collective regularity—nor purely internal or psychological; it is ironic, aslant of those two possibilities, a temporal third dimension. Mildred closes the ninth chapter at the end of day, as if adhering to a social norm, dismissing the reader as the last of her lingering visitors. Yet the ninth chapter is also a record of a mood's rise and fall, something that is only partially dependent on the public time of the day's labors. Extrinsic and intrinsic metrics meet, and by meeting transform into something distinct from either.[85]

The novel, in E. M. Forster's famously gnomic claim, always has a clock.[86] The chapter is its familiarly strange non-Newtonian clock, relative and elastic rather than precise, abstract, and independent. It evokes the funny duality of the future perfect, in which the unit of time is imagined both from present-tense inhabitation and from an outside retrospect. "Today was obviously not a good day," Mildred thinks, the jolt of the present "today" and past tense "was" encapsulating the chapter's odd relativity; it is not just that it will be a bounded segment of time in retrospect, but it *already* feels like it. And this peculiar time synchronizes the diegetic world with the world of the reader. A chapter break, that invitation to halt, that aeration of the continuity of reading, puts us in rhythm with the imaginary world that observes that same break. The chapter break blurs, or sutures, inside and outside.

If all this is true of a novel, it is because novels are in this respect an accentuated version of any chaptered book, rendering self-conscious and often allegorical the chapter's place in the history of text. Books are containers of time, and chapters give that time its most visible, and yet flexible, expression.[87] Chapters, in this sense, are where novels are at their most bookish and their most time-engaged. To grapple with their shape and intent, even in the case of something as faintly etched as the ninth chapter of *Excellent Women*, one must take a long detour back into the history of textual division, beyond the birth of the codex. Such a history will have lessons for the most commonplace and the most outlandish handlings of chapters alike.

PART II

Two Millennia of Capitulation, from Heading to Unit

The information is carried by the cut, the splice.

—ALEXANDER KLUGE, IN A 1989 INTERVIEW
WITH GARY INDIANA

2

On the Shape of the Classical Heading (the Threshold)

TABULA BEMBINA—AUGUSTINE— ARRIAN'S EPICTETUS

A FORUM in the region of Urbino in the late second century BCE: if not an origin for the chapter, a moment and location where the commonplace appears in an unfamiliar ancient guise, where we can learn some lessons from the contrast. There, and for an indeterminate time afterward, a large bronze tablet stood, measuring more than two meters wide. On it were inscribed legal statutes dating to the Gracchan land reforms of 133–121 BCE, in particular a *lex repetundarum*, or "recovery law," which established a special court, comprising a jury of equestrians without senatorial connections, to determine compensation for extortionate senatorial confiscation of money or property; a public, technical matter, by no means literary. For historians of Roman law, the tablet memorializes a fleeting era of judicial and agricultural reform.[1] But a different kind of gaze would see in that tablet and in that site the trace of a much quieter history: one of the earliest extant examples of a chaptered text.[2]

It is a curious witness to the early story of chaptering. Broken into fragments, the tablet came into the possession of the Duke of Urbino, from whom the fragments were passed in the early sixteenth century to Cardinal Pietro Bembo; the surviving pieces are now distributed between the Museo Nazionale in Naples and the Kunsthistorisches Museum in Vienna. But it is after Bembo that the fragments received their name: the *tabula Bembina*. The tablet's size and official function seem far from the scroll or codex, where the chapter seems native. It is monumental rather than intimate, designed for public display rather than for individual consultation. It is also peculiar in technical respects: the engraver wrote in lines of almost four hundred letters rather than the more commonly narrow columns of public text, and it was sloppily transcribed, with several lines devoted to recopying previous sections in order to correct errors.[3] Yet already one can see a form that the technology of the book would slowly absorb over the next several centuries and that would endure long after the tablet had been shattered and deposited in Bembo's library. That element is the chapter heading, which appears in the *tabula Bembina* in a nascent but still recognizable shape. Whatever its haste or amateurism otherwise, the chapter headings at least are signaled with particular care. Each section is prefaced by a chapter heading, or rubric, and each heading is set off on either side by a *vacat*, or small space the size of a few characters.[4] The attention devoted here to the subdivision of the text by labels is unusual for the era; it seems not to have been repeated in an inscribed Roman legal text until the Flavian period, roughly two hundred years later.[5] Yet even in this early and in some ways defective text—scholars suggest that the tablet was too poorly produced to actually be displayed, and that the text on its reverse side, featuring a later and unrelated agrarian law, would have ended up as its actual purpose— the chapter headings seem strikingly modern.[6]

Some examples include:

"de nomine deferundo iudicibusque legundeis" (concerning prosecution
    and the choosing of juries)
"de reo apsoluendo" (concerning the acquittal of the defendant)
"de reo condemnando" (concerning the condemnation of the defendant)
"de leitibus aestumandis" (concerning the assessment of damages)
"de praevaricatione" (concerning collusion)[7]

As with chapter headings in later formats and genres, these serve two purposes: they are graphic features (designed to segment the text, to provide a place for a gaze to land), and also summaries (of the passage they preface). That is, they perform both a visual and analytic function. The combination of the two functions forces a certain tension in terms of their length; concision is clearly one goal here—a shorter heading is more visually arresting amid the tablet's long lines of text—but some moderate amplitude, amounting to several words, has occasionally to be supplied in order to allow for a summary that is not too terse or elliptical. More remarkably still, their syntax—in its Latin form, a noun phrase introduced by the ablative *de*—persisted for centuries, in a variety of languages, as the default, familiar form that signaled the particular textual division of the chapter. Concerning, in which; *peri*; *en el que*;

où; enthält, in dem; in cui: the formulae are legion.[8] Each in some vague but functional way points to a space, both the literal space of the text that follows and the virtual space, or time, of its reading.

The *tabula Bembina*'s chapter headings here are not yet numbered, a slightly later development in Roman legal practice.[9] They are not yet quite citable in that way, not yet exactly indexical. The visual design of the tablet's text, while clearly intending to present a kind of segmentation, is at odds with itself; its long lines mitigate against the later practice of starting a chapter on a new line, reducing the possibilities of how visible the text's articulation could be. It is possible to say that the tablet was designed for a symbolic purpose—to declare the statutes they inscribe fully public, fully operative—rather than for actual consultation or reference. But we should be skeptical of the idea that, because it does not conform to later norms, it was not meant to be read at all. The clear attempt by the engraver to make the law's segments immediately apparent is a decisive first step toward the abstractions that facilitate not only reading but also memorability: a division into, and well-marked labeling of, segments.

The tablet's headings are also studiously neutral; they don't offer much in the way of rhetorical embroidery. Two significant later modes—the explanatory and the interrogatory—are absent. One can compare their terse modesty with the more garrulous headings of later writers, at least those whose headings are fairly certain to have been written by the text's author. In the imperial grammarian and polymath Aulus Gellius's miscellany *Noctes Atticae* (*Attic Nights*), from the second century CE, the headings are stylistically varied and flexible, less parasitic on the text and more of a separate text itself. Gellius can at times adhere to the tact of the legal heading, mirroring his subject's parsimony with a traditional brevity:

On the ancient frugality; and on early sumptuary laws

Yet he can also mix rhetorical occasions, and even provide some evaluative terms:

Who Papirius Praetextus was; the reason for that surname; and the whole of the entertaining story about that same Papirius

On some extraordinary marvels found among barbarian peoples; and on awful and deadly spells; and also on the sudden change of women into men

How Publius Nigidius with great cleverness showed that words are not arbitrary, but natural.[10]

These are much more than summaries; they are lures, promises, almost advertisements, oriented to the adjectival and evaluative as much as to names and things. The heading can by Gellius's time do more than segment or inform, it can solicit, beckon, play, argue, suggest questions, provoke interest.[11]

There is a wide stylistic gap between the *tabula Bembina* and Gellius. The three hundred years between the Republican legal tablet and the urbane sophistication of Gellius's compendium clearly saw a widening in the tonal register a chapter heading could employ. That can perhaps be ascribed simply to the question of authorship; Gellius, like his forerunner Pliny the Elder, composed his own headings, with flourishes that are recognizably his own, while it is impossible to establish the origin of the tablet's terser headings. Yet as much as they stake out the extent of the classical chapter's spectrum, from stark utility to sophisticated play, they belong to the same regime of chaptering, one in which the heading is of paramount importance. It is there—with the insertion of a label, the "heading" proper—that the chapter begins.

Starting with the Heading

What the *tabula Bembina* suggests is that chaptering does not begin as the special property of any kind of book, neither the scroll nor the codex. It might possibly have migrated into the book from the specific "topography" of legal inscriptions and texts.[12] And indeed in Gellius's time at least, references to chapters (*capita*) tend to refer to legal statutes; when Gellius uses the term he refers either to his own chapters or to citations, at times even numbered references, from legal authorities.[13] Yet some interpretive modesty is necessary here. The earliest uses of chapters belong to informational or reference texts, a broader category in which legal texts play a prominent but not exclusive role. Technical manuals, florilegia, treatises on religious or philosophical edification, compilations: this is the initial habitat of the chapter, one that would remain remarkably consistent well past the Christianization of the Empire.[14]

The earliest extant texts supplied with authorial headings—Pliny the Elder's, Gellius's, Columella's, and the *Compositiones* of Scribonius Largus, a first-century CE compilation of medical prescriptions—are all miscellanies, more informational than literary, designed, or so it seems, to be consulted rather than read sequentially. At the very least, these texts make no claims to the necessity of being consumed as a whole. Their form is both too large to be easily recalled in any detail and too fragmented, presented as a series of relatively isolated—if perhaps loosely organized—topics, anecdotes, divagations.

Chapter headings, and the tables in which they were most commonly assembled as a list, provided a map for the navigation of these cumbersome, multivolume collections. At this early stage the chapter heading does not interrupt a linear path through the text so much as indicate where a brief, individual itinerary across it might begin. One can think of these headings as a cultural response to what seemed like an explosion of information itself, the provision of quick summaries for an audience forcibly aware of the inability of any one person to read, or recall, the totality of current knowledge.[15]

To adopt the terminology of the early chapter's defenses, we need to speak not of a reader but of a "seeker." In his preface Gellius explains that headings ease both "searching" and "finding" (or, *quaerere* and *invenire*), a pairing that echoes earlier extant defenses of chaptering, including those of Columella and Largus.[16] The relation between these two acts may not be so simple, but neither term, it can be said, is exactly "reading" in our sense.[17] For "seeking," we might now say "discontinuous access." Yet the term "seeker" carries with it not simply a description of a particular mode of nonsequential access but also an intellectual framework or attitude: a practical intention, to locate the answer to a question or doubt, that is also a reductive desire for the pith, the nugget, the detail. The text is not an experience, is it a storage place from which information is extracted; the condensed summary is not only possible, but desirable. Too much tarrying with immersiveness risks turning "seeking" into something like excessive finding, or information overload.

Authors who produced their own chapter headings were keenly aware of this dynamic, even if they might have prodded it gently and explored the ways in which "seeking" might bleed into more diffuse forms of inquiry. But it is important to note that at no time, even in the early phase of its existence, was the chapter purely an authorial prerogative. It was instead an exercise of reading that authors might occasionally preempt but did not wholly control. To be provided a map was of course helpful, but one kind of intellectual mastery—never that far from ordinary reading—involved producing the map oneself. This involved two different tasks that could be carried out either in isolation or together: marking the text to indicate its constituent parts or significant divisions, and labeling those parts with summaries.

This was a genre of knowledge work so long-lasting that I will only gesture to it here, although it plays a role in many of the instances and trends I will discuss later; indeed, for a long while, the subsequent chaptering of texts by editors and readers will be a more significant actor in our story than authorial headings. There is, for instance, the marginal letter "K," found in various manuscripts from the first century onwards; Isidore of Seville's seventh-century *Etymologiae* explains it as referring to a "caput" or "head," although it has been suggested that a Greek derivation, possibly from the equivalent term *kephalaia* ("headings," "chapters"), may be the actual origin.[18] It seems to have indicated the shift to a new "head," or significant division, in the text, as applied by a reader—as both a notation and an analysis. For students practicing oratory, the presence of the "K" indicated both a place for stress and something like a fermata, a place to pause before launching into a new *periodus* or semantic unit; while oriented toward recitation, it was also the mark of a higher-order comprehension of the text, one that had identified its seams and leaps, that had observed its structure. In the far less articulated texts of antiquity, the "K" mark was a trace of an individual's articulation, the beginning of a reader's mastery. Of course, such marks had a way of parasitically attaching themselves to the host text, as they were often passed down by copyists to subsequent readers, ossifying into a part of the text itself. A first-century manuscript containing part of Cicero's *In Verrem* (Against Verres), the so-called Giessen fragment, contains "K" marks that seem to have been provided by the initial scribe, either thought out in the process of writing, or copied from an earlier exemplar; if we take the latter surmise, they might even be derived from Cicero himself.[19]

The "K" is just one intriguing element in a whole repertoire of methods by which readers or scribes could take on the editorial function—which was a critical function, needing considerable attunement to the text in question—of chaptering. Pliny, Gellius, Columella, and Largus are exceptions; most chaptered texts from antiquity, even other miscellanies, were likely provided with divisions and headings as part of a later manuscript tradition, as in Valerius Maximus's first-century *Factorum et dictum memorabilium libri IX* (Nine books of memorable doings and sayings) or Lucius Annaeus Florus's early second-century historical *Epitome*. Dividing and heading are, of course, different aspects of the same general work of capitulation, and each could be applied without the other. For texts segmented from the start, like Valerius's anecdotes, the heading was the key element; for texts presented in more continuous fashion, such as Cicero's speeches, division was the key work. Chaptering, or capitulation—the work of dividing, as a way of analyzing, extant texts—encompassed both, and both could last as legacies, however unwelcome, of the text they articulated. The rarity of authorially derived classical headings, in fact, lent to the classical heading its poor reputation in later centuries as inauthentic encrustation upon a text that was once pure and unmediated.

Capitulation, then, was comprehension by way of division. It is related to the "seeking" that explanations like Gellius's described, but not identical to it. What it sought was more global—almost an outline—although in so doing, it provided the possibility for a more targeted seeking, for potentially turning any work into a reference work. The division imagined by ancient capitulations needs some further explanation, however, because it involved a conceptual knot, an uneasy compromise between two different ways of imagining the work of the "head." We could, given some testimony, imagine capitulation as the identification of textual wholes, or sense-making units coherent in and of themselves. Pompeius, a fifth-century North African grammarian who produced a starkly clear, remedial commentary on Aelius Donatus's fourth-century *Ars grammatica*, defined a "period" as follows: "A period is a complete utterance, a complete heading [*caput*]; the parts of that heading are called clauses or phrases [*cola et commata*]."[20] The caput is here is a unit identified on the basis of its inner coherence. Any actual heading would be a material distillation or encapsulation of that conceptual unit. There can be subdivision within a caput—the phrase-length units of *cola* and *commata*—but still a recognizable wholeness. But this is not the only version of capitulation. We can imagine the work of capitulation as far less oriented toward identifying unity, unmoored from the "period," and much closer to something like the mark on the page itself: an incitation, a trace, a break in the service of memory. If Pompeius's definition emphasizes the *gathering* function of the caput, we could also think of the caput as *pointing*—and thereby intervening, tearing, splitting.

In this second sense the chapter mark is not the summary of a unit but the trace of an interaction, left for later consultation—a wave, hailing a future reading. It is less rhythmical (attuned to the rise and fall of a "period") than it is irregularly punctual, and what it records may not refer to some larger unity.[21] Memory is the key element here. The first-century CE rhetorician Quintilian's *Institutio oratoria* (Institutes of oratory) recommended memorizing speeches in "piecemeal" fashion (*per partes*) and advised a balance between too many such divisions, which are a burden to memory, and too few, which are less useful as a mnemonic aid. Where this process of readerly tact resulted in something literally tactile was in the mark on the text itself: "If certain portions prove especially difficult to remember, it will be found advantageous to indicate them by certain marks [*notas*], the remembrance of which will refresh and stimulate the memory."[22] It is not, of course, necessarily the act of capitulation that Quintilian refers to here, although it could be; and in any case, the impulse is identical—to preserve a record of an individual itinerary through the text. There is clearly an inescapable relationship between the mark and the unit in capitulation, where the difference appears less as a negation of the opposite pole and more as a matter of relative stress, but the distinction matters nonetheless because it orients a reader differently in relation to the division: Is the chapter mark an incitation, a place of momentary acute importance, or the threshold to a unitary experience?

One way to describe the difference is between the idea of the heading as an introduction and the heading as itself an instrument of forceful distillation. Commentators often bring a language of impress to bear on discussions of chapter division. The following, from the prologue to Gregory of Nyssa's fourth-century *Peri kataskeuēs anthropou* (On the making of man), is in this respect typical: "For clearness' sake I think it well to set forth to you the discourse by chapters [*epi kephalaiōn*], that you may be able briefly to know the force of the several arguments [*epicheirēmatōn*] of the whole work."[23] Chapters—the work's kephalaia—are identical here to what we would normally call headings, and as such are a way to register the force of "arguments," or *epicheirēmata*. They are different manifestations of the same intellectual content; the argument is more notional, something the text hopes to bring into being, whereas the chapter is a brief material inscription, a rapid or condensed translation, of the conceptual argument. Each is potentially translatable to the other. Nothing in the language here indicates units as such, or relies on a notion of a natural unit like the "period." If the chapter as a "gathering" exists somewhat parasitically on a host text, indicating its natural divisions, the chapter as "pointing" seems to envisage a substitutability, the possible replacement of the text itself by its headings—as if one could read a table of headings alone and still reach a sufficient comprehension of the text.

Would this have been possible? Here we need to retreat from more abstract considerations to the material facts of how a chapter was usually placed in ancient texts, particularly in the miscellanies or compilations where they tended to be found. The most common modern format—a table of contents providing chapter headings indexed to particular page numbers, with those headings repeated at the start of each chapter as an intertitle—is not how ancient chapters would have commonly appeared. Gellius's *Attic Nights* is in this respect exemplary. His chapter headings would not, in their initial format, have served as intertitles; they were instead gathered together in one list that preceded the body of the text itself, and were themselves preceded by an explanatory preface. The term Gellius gives to this list is *capita rerum*, "main things," "summaries," or "headings." Before foliation and pagination, it is almost easier to imagine reading this list of headings sequentially, to discern what topics the work covers, than it is to imagine using it to locate particular topics. Gellius's description, however, toggles between those two modes, his notion of *invenire*, or "finding," a sequential perusal, matched by the more focused, nonsequential scanning of *quaerere*, or "seeking." And of course those two can bleed into each other. As Joseph Howley puts it, "one might see a *caput* in the listing, have one's interest somehow piqued, and then consult that essay."[24]

In this respect Gellius was following the important precedent of Pliny's *Historia naturalis* (*Natural History*). The first book of the *History* is made up entirely of a list of headings, prefaced by a dedicatory letter to the emperor Titus, which explains the list's purpose:

> As it was my duty in the public interest to have consideration for the claims upon your time, I appended to this letter a table of contents of the several books, and have taken very careful precautions to prevent your having to read them. You by these means will secure for others that they will not need to read right through them either, but only look [*quaerat*] for the particular point that each of them wants, and will know where to find [*inveniat*] it.[25]

"Table of contents" here is the translator's approximation of Pliny's more periphrastic description of his list; some scholars, such as Aude Doody, prefer to call the list Pliny's *summarium*.[26] Even more explicitly than Gellius, Pliny invokes here the idea of the list largely replacing the text itself, in an ironic gesture of encyclopedic self-canceling.[27] Whereas Gellius's notion of "finding" holds out the possibility of a general curiosity, Pliny collapses "finding" and "seeking" into a single act of consultation that can dispense with the body of the text. Yet the logic of the *Natural History* itself, where items follow each other with a loosely associative order, invites a sequential reading that the list or *summarium* seems, however ironically, to deny.[28] This confusion leaves the status of Pliny's *summarium* as a problem for future editors, and in fact it ends up being deployed, across the subsequent history of the text, in multiple formats: some later editions of the *Natural History* divide the list and distribute its items before the book to which they each refer; some—including, strikingly, early print editions—maintain its place in the first book, in a nod to the original arrangement; some do both. Some used the headings as running titles to facilitate discontinuous access; in so doing, they often tweaked or replaced the original headings. Eventually the list's items were numbered, although this involved complexities, including splitting what seem like single items in the list.[29] Fifteenth-century editions thus begin to turn the list into an "index" in the modern sense, tying its items to intertitles, softening its possible availability for being sequentially read itself. These are decisions that were forced upon editors and copyists early in the tradition; it would be cumbersome, of course, to imagine consulting a book list, particularly as a separate scroll, in a text running to thirty-seven books, and that technological dilemma was solved in various ways.[30] What is at stake here is the indexical function of the list and how it is to be used.

Pliny's example suggests that the chapter had no stable location or appearance in its initial guises, and that there is no clear evolutionary process in which the unmarked list of the *Natural History*'s first book yields to the numbered heading inserted into the text's breaks as an "intertitle." The *tabula Bembina*, at least, tells us that the chapter heading as an intertitle was already being used within legal texts and inscriptions. Rather than a teleology moving from simple to complex, from ancillary to ever more embedded, we have a wide repertoire of practices and possibilities that overlap, collaborate, and conflict, all of them serving as ways of imagining texts as composite objects. A default idea that technology determines patterns of use often seems to stand in the way of envisioning the full complexity of ancient thinking in this respect; it has been hard, for instance, to imagine readers using the scroll in the same discontinuous ways as the codex. Isidore of Seville's definition of the codex seems to stress the scroll's essential unity: "A codex is composed of many books; a book [*liber*] is of one scroll [*voluminis*]."[31] It seems more possible to imagine the scroll as an unmarked whole, the smallest monad of ancient literary culture, and any further subdivision of a text initially produced for the scroll as an inauthentic later addition. So it is that in 1787 the classicist Johann Matthias Gesner claimed that ancient writers did not divide their texts into units smaller than the "book," or scroll, which division was merely forced upon them by the technical limitations of the average scroll size, and which they sought to hide in elegant ways—just as, Gesner added, the different sections of a Corinthian column are meant to join seamlessly.[32]

Such an approach does not only miss the shifting material practices of capitulation, it overlooks the conceptual dilemmas that these practices negotiated. The basal unit of the chapter, if not necessarily its "original" form, is the heading—the label. Yet that label, from the first, performed multiple tasks, and also created multiple ancillary forms. It satisfied an existing desire, which the earliest defenses called *quaerere*, or "finding": the task of the finding aid. Yet it could also stimulate new curiosities, which Gellius seems to indicate by his uses of *invenire*. In this sense the heading both supinely awaited the reader's use and actively hailed the reader's passing gaze. It could both inform and advertise. The heading necessarily summarized, although it could do so in sly, or extended, or perfunctory fashions; on the whole, however, what would have been most apparent is its intense reductiveness.[33] Yet it did more than summarize: it divided, or cut—either implicitly, when it was confined to a prefatory list, or explicitly, when it was used as an intertitle. The two actions coexisted, but with a certain conceptual tension between the idea of the heading as gathering into a sensible whole or as tearing a whole into parts—imagining, that is, two different tactile approaches, one that grasped and one that pointed.[34] The act of providing headings immediately suggested different possible uses, and different imaginaries, which are masked by the overall similarity of the explanations offered for their existence.

Augustine's Finger

If the heading is then an identifiable object, wherever it is found, in a prefatory list or as an intertitle, what it creates is a hybrid object that is more abstract than material, one that would paradoxically come to bear the name by which the heading was first known: the chapter. Several centuries elapse before the host of terms around the chapter settle somewhat into a recognizable pattern in which the terms for the unit ("chapter") and its label ("heading," "title") are clearly divided. From the late Republic well into post-imperial Europe, the terminology of the chapter is muddled and provisional, reflecting the conceptual cruxes that the heading inevitably introduced. This makes most appearances of the ancient vocabulary of capitulation difficult to parse.

Take, for instance, an early text of Cicero's, the treatise *De inventione* (On invention): "The lawmakers are accustomed to make exceptions. Then it will be in point to read laws that include exceptions and in particular to see if there is any exception in any chapter [*capite*] of the law in question or in laws by the same law-maker, in order that it may be better established that he would have made an exception if he had thought one ought to be made."[35] It is a touchstone reference in the history of the chapter, because an insoluble dilemma appears for the translator: does Cicero here mean by caput/*capite* a material aspect of the text, a unit marked out as a formal property, or something closer to a notional idea of the "main" thrust of an argument, its "head" or "chief" aspects? Given the context here—the reading of legal texts—the translator has decided on "chapter," suggesting a formal division, but the matter is far from simple, as elsewhere in the text uses of caput are rendered here as "topic" or "head," indicating a more abstract use.[36] A persuasive argument has it that what Cicero here refers to is a segment of a text beginning with a slightly offset line, something like a modern paragraph, which may have been called a "head" in the same way that a protruding end of any common tool is often called its "head."[37] But the very fact that the term can be unmoored from this possibly specific, technical usage elsewhere in the same text indicates that it is always modulating between materiality and abstraction. A caput can refer to a unit marked on the page or marked only in the mind; there is an equation, but a nonidentity, between a "head" and a "topic" or "main thing."[38]

Further confusions abound, because caput was not the exclusive term in play.[39] Columella's term for his list of headings was *argumenta*, meaning something like "outline"—a usage that veered closer to abstraction than to material mark, even if its referent was the list itself. Pliny, for his part, had no specific term for his list of headings. His rough coeval Sextus Julius Frontinus provided a general summary in the first book of his *Strategemata*, a collection of illustrative examples of military craft, as well as a list of headings at the start of each book; here too no specific bibliographic term is employed, as Frontinus referred to the items of each list as *species*—that is, "types" or "classes"—of strategy, even if their syntactical form and general function operate like Gellius's *capita rerum*.[40] More importantly, as we get farther from the initial chaptered Latin compilations, other terms proliferate in what seems like an effort to specify a difference between the heading itself and the unit to which it refers. Plotinus's *Enneads*, in the late third-century edition prepared by his student Porphyry, contains a table of contents in Porphyry's prefatory "life"—a combined biography and bibliography—of his master, a table that essentially creates the composite fact of the *Enneads* itself.[41] The *Life of Plotinus* concludes, however, by describing another more elaborate apparatus to the *Enneads*, now lost:

> In this way, then, I have arranged the treatises, of which there were fifty-four, in six Enneads, and I have attached discourses to some of the works, haphazardly produced on account of friends who urged me to write about such matters as they themselves desired to have clarified for them. Furthermore, I have composed chapter-heads [*kephalaia*] for all of them, except On Beauty, because they were missing in my copies, and in this I follow the chronological order in which the treatises were distributed. But in this

matter, not only have the heads [*kephalaia*] been affixed to each book but summaries [*epicheirēmata*] also, which are numbered in sequence with the chapter-heads.[42]

This is difficult to picture with any confidence. It is possible that each separate heading, or *kephalaion*—the Greek analogue to caput—was accompanied with a slightly longer summary or synopsis. It is also possible that by kephalaia here Porphyry is referring to the act of division, or the furnishing of units, for which the *epicheirēmata* serve as the kind of useful summary we have otherwise known as an early table of contents.[43] But some attempt to articulate different elements of capitulation is going on here, either between heading and unit or between different kinds of headings, although those different elements are nonetheless both meant to help a reader navigate a difficult, sprawling text.

By the end of the fifth century the term *titulos* was common, employed by Priscian to describe the labels of his subdivided *Institutiones grammaticae* (Grammatical foundations); in the sixth century Cassiodorus, in his *Institutions of Divine and Secular Learning,* explains his mode of handling the Books of Chronicles with the same term: "Since I have not discovered ancient chapter-headings [*titulos*] like the chapter-headings existing for the preceding books, I have, as I thought best, added them in an orderly fashion to each passage so that by any kind of service in letters the quality of my devotion might be recognized."[44] The term is an old one, employed previously for titles of entire works, here used to denote what Gellius had called his *capita rerum*—headings, organized into a list—but the semantic difference is crucial: *titulos* is more specific and technical, no longer referring to the act of summary or abstraction that was always part of the sense of caput, its ability to mean "main things." It has become separated from the unit to which it refers, more purely indexical.

Yet if in the long run *titulos* would have a victory of sorts—we still commonly speak of chapter "titles"—in a slightly shorter time frame, derivations of caput would persist, maintaining a tension between the unit (or the act of division) and the heading (or the act of summarizing). The figure who seems to have devoted much thought to both sides of the chapter's double task of segmenting and labeling was Jerome, whose late fourth-century commentaries on the Hebrew prophets show consistent attention to questions of how texts are articulated in these two distinct yet complementary ways. His use of the word *capitulum*, a diminutive of caput, tends to indicate a particular *passage*—even a passage not necessarily marked out on the page as such. In a much-discussed aside in his commentary on Isaiah, Jerome alludes to a line present in Alexandrian copies of the text but missing from the Septuagint as well as his Hebrew sources: "In the beginning of this passage [*hujus capituli*] in the Alexandrian exemplar is added . . ."[45] The explanation of this extra line requires Jerome to gesture to a particular moment, section, or passage, what we might call with some greater technical precision a *pericopē*—and the word he employs to do so is a variant of capitulum. This does not mean that he is inattentive to whatever actual divisions or labels existed in the texts before him. But it does mean that he recognizes a tension between the divisions he has inherited and the divisions he feels to be natural, or necessary for a given task.[46] Elsewhere, in the preface to his Isaiah commentary, he complains of the commentary of Apollinaris of Laodicea, whose too-abstract overview reads like only "a list of chapters [*indices capitulorum*]."[47] Capitulum modulates between those two uses, the airy abstractions of headings and the greater precision of indicating a unit. In its latter use, indicating a capitulum means something close to perceiving a new beginning—a slight turn in the text's attention to something new. It is a notation, meant to preserve *notabilia*.[48]

These several usages, drawn from over half a millennium's slow shifts in the semantic cloud around the "chapter," demonstrate curiously persistent qualities. They are attached to prose, particularly informational, or nonliterary, prose. Prose is the chapter's native habitat. Yet they seem independent of any given book format; the chapter seems to move easily across those seismic material changes of ancient literary culture. The caput and its cousins migrate from tablet to scroll to codex without much alteration in the way they are articulated, defended, discussed. This suggests that, however much capitulation was a material practice—however tied to particular marks, page arrangements, lexical formulae, all of which changed more slowly than the book formats they inhabited—from the start it had a tendency toward the intangible. Prose itself, perhaps, already less embodied than verse, helped generate the second-order conceptualization of the heading, an act of summary that further dematerialized the text. Consider the continual oscillation between four possible referents that the "chapter" demonstrated:

1. The individual *heading* itself, wherever it may be placed
2. The *list* of headings as a collection, placed usually but not exclusively at the start of the text, often in a separate "book," and in its totality expressing a condensation of the text available to different kinds of searching

3. The *unit of text* marked by the heading, either by an intertitle, white space, hanging indentation, or any other method
4. An individual *passage*, not necessarily marked at all

These are referents of mounting abstraction. They indicate how resistant the chapter was, already in its ancient guises, to becoming identified with a physical object like the Babylonian *tuppu* (chapter-tablet) or Greek *tomos* (book), both of them units associated with the limits of a container or surface. It seems instead that a chapter was a mental construct, formed by a specific gesture: the conjoined gesture of labeling and segmenting, identifying by isolating. To call a chapter a gesture is to suggest the way it starts with a physical intervention or manipulation and yet lifts off into the notional. The act of pointing is the ideal analogue: a conventional, familiar, concrete act of the hand that invokes, or summons, a segment out of what had been something whole.

Necessarily, up to this point, my examples have themselves been somewhat abstract, derived as they are from the metacommentary of authors or editors upon their own work's divisions. What is harder to come by is an account of a reader facing a text, enacting exactly this gesture—in other words, capitulation in action. One such instance lurks in plain sight, in the climactic moment of Augustine's *Confessions*. Hearing the "take it and read" of children chanting in the adjoining garden while in the midst of a spiritual crisis, Augustine famously turns to a book:

> I checked the flood of tears and stood up. I interpreted it solely as a divine command to me to open the book and read the first chapter [*caput*] I might find [*invenissem*] .... I seized it [*arripui*], opened it [*aperui*] and in silence read the first passage [*capitulum*] on which my eyes lit. ... I neither wished nor needed to read further. ... Then I inserted my finger or some other mark in the book and closed it. With a face now at peace I told everything to Alypius.[49]

I leave out Augustine's quotation from the text itself, known to us as Romans 13:13–14, in order to concentrate on one aspect of the combined physical and mental action involved: the isolation of the life-changing caput/capitulum. First, it is important to note that caput/capitulum here can be rendered in two ways: as marked "chapter" and also as a "passage," unmarked except by the reader's gaze. To offer both equivalents in the passage is a wily compromise with the term's trickiness in the period. That said, it is unlikely that the codex Augustine consulted here had isolated the phrase from Romans as its own formal caput.[50] The act Augustine performs is therefore not *recognizing* a chapter but instead *performing his own capitulation*—spontaneously segmenting the text, in an act that is initially purely visual but will then need the intervention of his finger to mark and save it. It is an act even more habitual and embedded in habits of reading than the *sortes Virgilianae* that structures the scene. It is the same kind of "seeking" as Gellius's *invenire*, one that may not initially know what it wants, but knows that something is there to be found, precisely by isolating a part of the text by pointing to it. There is a halo effect produced by the combined act of eye and finger: out of an unmarked stream, a unit emerges.

All the elements of capitulation are present here, except for the actual scribal indication of the chapter.[51] First, there is a break: *arripui*, the almost violent act of seizing the book itself, a lexical echo of how Augustine's emotional upheaval, just before hearing the children's song, "tore" (*abripuit*) him from attending to Alypius; but also *aperui*, the opening of the book itself, a more crisp act of rupture—a breaking in two—than the gradual unrolling of a scroll.[52] The break, the tear, the discontinuity, are all focused, at the pivotal moment, on the separation of one passage from another. Then there is the mark. For this the gesture of Augustine's finger suffices, touching the page to retain the caput in question and to keep its boundaries intact. This involves a transfer from the eye to the hand, moving from the visual to the tactile: something has been perceived as distinct, and then there is an insertion (*interiecto aut digito*) to materialize that distinctness. It is the common process of capitulation, a widespread and often humble sort of intellectual labor that extended from antiquity to centuries following—segmenting and labeling a long text— but rendered here as both even more ordinary and far more consequential.

If Augustine can elsewhere in the *Confessions* speak of the caput with metaphorical offhandedness—referring, for instance, to "chief kinds of wickedness [*capita iniquitatis*]"—he is nonetheless continually preoccupied with what it means to divide into parts, and how reading is both a spontaneous generation of segments and an encounter with preexisting units.[53] Augustine did not, it seems, divide his works himself. That was left, as was usual in late antiquity, to the later efforts of students, editors, and redactors, such as the sixth-century Neapolitan scholar Eugippius, whom Cassiodorus later testified had excerpted portions of Augustine's collected works and organized them into "a collection of 338 chapters."[54] Eugippius seems to have, at the very least, supplied the headings to the *Literal Commentary on Genesis* and perhaps the chapter divisions to the *City of God*.[55] Yet hints survive of how Augustine himself thought about the practical work of segmenting large texts. There is, most famously, his "letter to Firmus," first published in 1939 by Cyril Lambot. The letter was meant to accompany the twenty-two books (*libros*) of the *City of God*, presumably in some unbound state, because it proceeds to advise on different possible arrangements for its binding into separate codices: if in two volumes, then ten books followed by twelve; if in more than two, Augustine advises five volumes, of which the first volume should contain five books, followed by four volumes of four books each.[56] Augustine here imagines two different higher-order schema for his work, each with its own different taxonomical justification, creating different sense units that respect, if in divergent ways, the contents of the separate *libros*; he has conjured alternate possibilities for nested structures of meaning, each resting on the integrity of the individual "book."

It is the letter's final line, however, that is most tantalizing: "The summary [*breviculus*] attached will give you an idea of how much is in these twenty-two books."[57] What might this breviculus have looked like? Lambot argues that it cannot have been a list of headings, but rather some collection of summaries that could be attached in the margins of the text at relevant moments, and others concur, using the logic that as the text had not been divided into chapter units as yet, it could not have been "headings" per se.[58] Yet the list of headings, unindexed to particular divisions, was as we have seen well within the repertoire of ancient textual arrangements; and at any rate, attempting to keep the distinction between "heading" and "summary" airtight will not hold. Whatever this breviculus might have been, it was at the least a consultative aid, intended to be used in both "seeking" and "finding" modes, allowing Firmus to locate moments of preexisting interest as well as to gain a quick survey of the work's full extent in order to elicit some new, possibly transformative, interest.[59] The way in, the path of access to the book and to the heart, is through the small unit: the breviculus, the caput, the capitulum. Where that unit is not already marked or summarized, it can be summoned into being by the reader's own gestures.

The chapter, then, whatever term it went by, was both a tool for and an *ethos* of reading, a meditation on the possible significances of partial, nonlinear, or segmented textual consumption.[60] Rooted in a culture of consultation, in legal texts, practical guides, and even more learned, information-rich compilations that were accumulating already by the late Republic, the chapter nonetheless expanded to take in other genres, particularly as chaptering became increasingly something done *to* texts rather than coinciding with their initial publication. Capitulation mediated between the careful annotation of philosophy and the production of much more common, public, and even ephemeral texts.[61] It also spanned formats: deriving perhaps from legal inscriptions, and initially inhabiting the scroll, it survived intact into the new technological ecosystem of the codex, where it would thrive—just as it would thrive in the new generic ecosystems of texts that were not compilations, miscellanies, or treatises. The codex did not create chapters, but chapters were ideally suited to flourish in a literary culture dominated by it.[62] Capitulation may have in fact been one of the first steps, initially awkward and associated with only certain kinds of texts, in which the continuity of the literary prose scroll was disrupted for good.[63]

The capitulum that Augustine marks with his finger is in one sense the culmination of this early history, and not simply because it demonstrates the ability of the chaptering impulse to unmoor itself from the mechanics of actual marked headings and divisions and therefore to become conceptual rather than material. It is because in the moment of isolating and marking his pivotal "passage," Augustine has dramatized the emergent meaning of the chapter. The caput or capitulum—like kephalaia, *titlos, argumentum, breviculus*—is what we would now call an "interface": the place where reader and text touch, either by the text reaching out to hail a reader's possible curiosity, need, or haste (the already-chaptered text), or by the reader's reaching in to segment it themselves (the act of capitulation, whether deliberate or spontaneous). The finger in the book, marking what the eyes had found, offers a bridge, a route of access preserved for later memory, a point of contact. Augustine imagined the chapter as a traversable threshold. This is where the "heading" leads us.

Arrian's Preconceptions

Few of these chapter-thresholds are as provocative, and self-conscious, as those of Epictetus's *Discourses*, because the mechanics of headings as they existed in the second century CE—the distinction between seeking and finding; the question as to how experience could be, and why it perhaps should be, segmented; the act of abstraction involved in any heading—are, as we will see, already deeply embedded in Stoic thought. To provide headings for passages of Epictetus's teaching is necessarily to engage in a form of his thinking; capitulation is here yet another aspect of practical philosophy. In this case, the philosophy was enacted by Arrian of Nicomedia, a disciple of Epictetus and later high-ranking public figure under the emperor Hadrian. Arrian likely produced the *Discourses* sometime after 130 CE, arranged them into what may have been as many as eight books—of which four survive—and provided ninety-five extant headings. We do not know how these headings were arranged in original versions of the text, whether as a list, as intertitles, or both, although the roughly contemporary practices of Pliny and Gellius would suggest the first possibility. A prefatory letter by Arrian does not mention the headings or account for how they were deployed, but does explain the work's content as *hypomnemata*, or "memoranda," of Epictetus's teaching, less an act of writing than of direct transcription of Epictetus's conversation. Most modern commentators are skeptical about the performative modesty of Arrian's letter.[64] His headings are, at least, clearly more than transcriptions of Epictetus's speech, and would be the most obviously "written" elements of the work— thus, perhaps, Arrian's silence about them.

Perhaps unsurprisingly, the headings are almost uniformly critiqued as a botched job—clumsy, misleading, shallow. Robert Dobbin, one of the *Discourses*'s most recent editors, notes the most flagrant offenders and even, in one instance, supplies a replacement.[65] For Dobbin, some of the headings seem simply to have misunderstood the contents of their respective passages; for others who have studied them, even where the headings are not simply incorrect, they are often too partial, ignoring the twists of their respective chapters in favor of some single, often inessential, element.[66] They are certainly, by the standards of many classical headings, highly varied: terse in some places, unexpectedly prolix in others, syntactically heterogeneous. We may owe this stylistic diversity to the deliberate informality of the units they index. The *diatribai*, or discourses, are records of particular interactions Epictetus had with various unnamed interlocutors, be they students or skeptical bystanders.[67] They can veer from stark urgency to digressive, playful irony, and they can be indirect as to their intended targets. Epictetus's unsettling tonal shifts are their most consistent element. At the very least they are not formally pedagogical; Pierre Hadot imagined them as records of the discussions that followed the technical part of Epictetus's teaching.[68] With such tricky material, the headings necessarily take some risk of being inapposite.

Arrian often hews to the familiar "about" (*peri*) clauses of the classical heading, as if to promise a straightforwardly terminological, or taxonomical, approach. These are the most traditional of his headings:

"On steadfastness" (1.29)
"On friendship" (2.22)
"On freedom" (4.1)

Just as often, however, he changes his rhetorical and syntactical strategy. One species of interrogatory heading suggests an elenchic situation:

"What does philosophy promise?" (1.15)
"What is the law of life?" (1.26)
"What is the point of departure of philosophy?" (2.11)

Others seem to more narrowly recommend specific kinds of conduct:

"How may everything be done in a way that is pleasing to the gods?" (1.13)
"How ought we to bear our illnesses?" (3.10)

Some apostrophize an individual or collective interlocutor, situating an addressee who is also a target:

"To those who have set their hearts on advancement in Rome" (1.10)
"To the inspector of the free cities, who was an Epicurean" (3.7)

While others, starting with the propositional *hoti*, offer an axiom that seems to promise a proof to come in the subsequent dialogue:

"That logic is indispensable" (1.17)
"That confidence does not conflict with caution" (2.1)
"That we should not allow news to disturb us" (3.18)

There are also hybrid modes ("That we should not be angry with others; and what things are small, and what are great, among human beings?" [1.28]), as well as three chapter headings that are essentially a shrug: "*Sporadēn tina,*" or "Miscellaneous" (3.6, 3.11, 3.14).[69]

The stylistic variety would seem to be an attempt to match the unpredictable nature of the *diatribai* themselves. Yet the match often seems imperfect nonetheless. At times they seem to overspecify the following passage's more capacious boundaries: "Against the Academics" (1.5) identifies one particular target, although the following discourse offers a much more general critique of the human tendency to resist rational persuasion. This sly specification provides a comfortable and possibly ironic exculpation—surely if we are not an Academic, this fault cannot be ours. At others the heading is more directly misleading, playing with what it would mean to instantiate a general term: "On calmness of mind" (2.2) centers in fact on its opposite, and is addressed to someone, about to go to court, who is presumably consumed by the desire to retain their possessions; the example of *ataraxia* here is largely provided through its obverse, a perpetual helpless anxiety. Some of the interrogatory titles find clear answers in their accompanying passages; in others, like "What does philosophy promise?" (1.15), any answer is withheld. Finally, there are strange misdirections, often seeming like simple errors: "To those who have set themselves on advancement in Rome" is actually addressed to Epictetus's students, to whom he speaks *about* those mentioned in title, recommending their ceaseless activity if not their specific goal. The "head" of each dialogue often has a riddle-like, or simply confusing, relation to what ensues.

Here is where we need to understand Arrian's chaptering practice not as a series of blunders but as an attempt to model Stoic epistemology, meaning ultimately an attempt to enact Stoic time. The root conceptual problem of Arrian's headings, which as it happens is also their rationale and their opportunity for ingenuity, is that they exist in a temporal process: they do not merely label, they preface—they *come before*—and they also *suspend*. They are the data that we bring to an experience before it begins, forcing a brief but crucial hesitation, a threshold pause. In the context of Epictetus's Stoicism, this is not particularly surprising. His *diatribai* imagine themselves as both descriptions and enactments of a process of mental training; their goal is not to provide information so much as incite a gradual change in our cognitive relation to the world. Thus the appropriateness of athletic endeavor as one of Epictetus's privileged metaphors; philosophical engagement is the softening of mental tissues in order to stiffen them correctly, an act that is an inevitably repetitive, routinely reapplied, gradual, teleological unfolding.[70] The *diatribai* consistently ask us to imagine beginnings and endings, in between which the individual exists, moving slowly. "In each action that you undertake, consider what comes before and what follows after, and only then proceed to the action itself" (*D*, 171). Time has direction and momentum: "And say while you are training yourself day after day, as you are here, not that you're acting as a philosopher (for you must concede that it would be pretentious to lay claim to that title), but that you're a slave on the way to emancipation" (*D*, 229). We are not composite entities so much as temporal ones, changing through accretion and loss.[71]

In this way the seriality of reading itself—particularly the reader's continually percussive reimmersion in Epictetus's brief and pointed lessons, with their ability to leave even a willing participant wrongfooted—is a useful metaphor for the Stoic training process.[72] But Epictetus's technical vocabulary is more precise than this general comparison might indicate, and in fact provides a specific model for the initial hesitation-with-a-label that Arrian's headings enact. In Epictetus's conception, each of our perceptions, or the bundle of perceptions that compose an experience, are prefaced by what he calls a *prolēpsis*, which can be rendered as "presupposition," "anticipation," or "preconception."[73] This is a term not unique to Epictetus, although he gives it an unusually wide range of application, extending it to our encounter with natural objects of any kind.[74] A *prolēpsis* is the set of concepts, formed from earlier experience, that define for us the general force and meaning of the things we perceive. Although produced spontaneously, by induction, from perceptions, they can still be developed or rationalized, and they embody general truths that are communally held. They can be thought of as a naturally indexical knowledge: useful, like the chapter heading, for organizing and tagging experience into categories. They express our general sense of what items fit within general concepts, and so they guide our expectations, circumscribing our range of possible responses.

The problem for this theory is that not every label or preconception fits well with the particular instance it tags. This is the dynamic that Epictetus is at pains to explain in the chapter titled "On preconceptions" (1.22), which begins as follows:

> Preconceptions are common to all people, and one preconception doesn't contradict another. For who among us doesn't assume that the good is beneficial and desirable, and that we should seek to pursue it in every circumstance? And who among us doesn't assume that what is just is honourable and appropriate? When does contradiction arise, then? It comes about when we apply our preconceptions to particular cases, as when one person says, "He acted well, he's a brave man," while another says, "No, he's out of his mind." (*D*, 48)

The problem is not that preconceptions can be in themselves mistaken; it is that they can be, in the same way as Arrian's headings, misleading or inapposite, a mismatch with the experience they preface.[75] They can fail at the indexical task they are meant to perform. As such, Epictetus recommends a constant temporal back-and-forth, comparing the preconception with the given perception, thereby becoming self-critical enough about the spontaneity of our preconceptions that they become what he calls "systematically examined preconceptions" (*D*, 94–95). The term used here—*diērthrōmenais*, or to "divide by joints," to "articulate"—underlines one of the key dynamics of this process.[76] The preconception and the perception must be kept separate in order to be accurately compared. Similarly, the boundaries of the perception itself must be set, segmented into a coherent unit capable of being judged in relation to a preconception. To distinguish, or to separate, is fundamental. Alongside careful discrimination is hesitation, a momentary, cautious delay. "But first of all, don't allow yourself to be dazed by the rapidity of the impact, but say, 'Wait a while for me, my impression, let me see what you are, and what you're an impression of; let me test you out'" (D, 116).

This is the famous Stoic present: an act of the attention, temporarily slowing and thickening time, that hovers on the threshold of a new experience in order to set the incipient experience off from others, to gauge its parameters, and to adopt a critical relation to the label that spontaneously prefaces it.[77] If this general account also seems like a way of describing the seriality of reading a segmented text, Epictetus's own language tends to confirm that suspicion. The language of textual arrangement is palpable in his description of how preconceptions can be correctly applied: "But it is impossible for us to adapt these preconceptions to the corresponding realities unless we have subjected them to systematic examination, to determine which reality should be ranged under [hypotakteon] which preconception" (D, 110). Hypotaxis, subordination, the relation of general to particular: this is at once the structure of Epictetus's epistemology and the structure of Arrian's arrangement of the Discourses. The act of subjoining headings is also the act of "determining which reality should be ranged under which preconception," or which label is appropriate to which experience. That labels are tricky, Epictetus is quick to warn. They are handles, but, in a formula the Discourses repeats, "use is one thing, and understanding is another" (D, 15, 102). To understand means to compare the label to the unit of experience, a process that begins with that initial act of hesitation.

Hesitation makes preconceptions conscious. "Bring out your preconceptions," Epictetus exhorts; "perfect your preconceptions" (D, 53, 242). This making-conscious is something Arrian's headings mimic. They are reflections upon their own indexicality; different versions—some disarmingly direct, some oddly oblique, others frustratingly imprecise—of how generalities and specific cases can match and mismatch. His seemingly infelicitous headings provoke testing and reflection: Can I trust this label on the threshold of this experience? To say as much, of course, risks seeming as if my goal is to rescue Arrian's reputation by turning even his flaws into canny virtues. But some self-consciousness about headings and divisions, in the context of arranging Epictetus's diatribai, would have been inevitable; one consistent theme of the master's teachings was the difficulty of matching a prefatory label to an experience, and the urgency of doing so well. To this incitement the student responded, using, with curiously mixed results, the repertoire of heading styles that existed in his time, while also slightly expanding them. The result is a constant, embedded theorization of the chapter heading itself, however inadvertent.[78]

In many of the *diatribai*, Epictetus displays a critical relation to the culture of information out of which the chapter heading arises. Titles in particular seem to earn his suspicion. With a monitory tone addressed to his presumably literate audience, he ridicules those who would prefer to consult texts rather than change their behavior: "That is just as if, in the sphere of assent, when we're presented with impressions, some of them convincing and others not, we should refuse to distinguish between them and want to read a treatise *On Understanding* instead" (*D*, 240). Yet we cannot do without indexical tags. One sort of informational reading, lightly curious and indiscriminately wide-ranging, is to be supplanted with another, vital and pressing, that is also in need of titles:

> But if we read treatises *On Motivation* not merely to know what is said there about motivation, but so as to be able to direct our motives rightly; or a treatise *On Desire and Aversion* so that we may never fail in our desires or fall into what we want to avoid; or a treatise *On Appropriate Action* so that we keep in mind our social relationships and never act irrationally or in a way that conflicts with them—if we approached our reading in that spirit, we wouldn't be vexed at being hindered with regard to our reading, but would be satisfied to accomplish the actions that are in accord with them. (*D*, 241)

This, in a chapter bearing the title "To those who have set their hearts on living at peace." A label is a guide and a lure, necessary in a world with an excess of information, but potentially delusory nonetheless, because a merely categorical knowledge is sterile without a systematic comparison between categories and their contents. One way to encapsulate Epictetus's argument here is that the heading, like the preconception, gains from the richer and more detailed experience of the unit itself—it becomes "systematically examined." Or we might say that the heading's job is to vanish at the threshold of the experience.

Epictetus's skepticism about information culture necessarily produced a critical attitude toward the textual apparatus of that culture, to titles and the scanning reading they invite, to the *peri*-constructions that were the mark of that culture's learning and thereby also a mark of the limits of that learning.

This is something Arrian seems to have both understood and undercut. By supplying headings to the *Discourses* he drew Epictetus into that culture; by doing so in ways that are inconsistent and unexpected, so that the shrewd cannot be separated from the inattentive, he tests a reader's ways of inhabiting that culture. In the process, the uneasy collaboration of Epictetus's transcribed teachings and Arrian's way of dividing and labeling them produced a multifaceted theory of the heading as a space of hesitation, the place where the categorical and the temporal meet in tense, if temporary, negotiation.

In the process, the *Discourses* develops ways of thinking about segmented experience, and segmented texts, that will have enduring effects. Even Epictetus's figurative illustrations will linger. At one point he offers this analogy for the process of arriving at understanding through texts:

> People behave like a traveller who, when returning to his homeland, passes through a place where there is a very fine inn, and because he finds it pleasant, remains there. Man, you've forgotten your purpose, you weren't travelling to this place, but passing through it. "But it's a lovely inn." And how many other lovely inns are there that are just as nice, and how many meadows too! But only as places on the way. (*D*, 135)

Reading as traveling, the inn as the temporary space along the way—it is one of the primary symbolic resonances that, down at least to the birth of the realist novel, will be invoked by the pause of the chapter.[79] We will see it elaborated in centuries to come: the bills of fare, the length of the stay, the quality of the refreshment. From the start it bears a degree of strain. The theory of the chapter as threshold, and its attendant vocabulary and image repertoire, arises here out of a fortuitous collision between the dependency on and suspicion toward informational texts of the Stoic philosopher, and the unusual ways in which his later editor reinserted his words into the textual matrix from which the philosopher had tried to keep his distance. But as chapter deviser, Arrian was nonetheless reasonably tactful, and he operated with a text that seems to already know very well that it was fated to be so arranged. When three centuries later many unnamed figures took turns repeatedly chaptering texts that were less suited to segmentation and labeling, and the chapter attached itself to the textual culture of early Christianity, the theory and practice of the chapter would take on more peculiar characteristics.

3

Concerning the Division of the Gospels (the Abstract Syncopation)

EUSEBIUS—ALEXANDRINUS—
THE PARIS BIBLE

IT LOOKS like a deliberate experiment, so elegantly designed that it might have been carried out in a controlled environment. Take a text—better yet, a series of related texts—of considerable historical importance, written initially without any of the subdivisions and headings with which the compendia of antiquity were often equipped. Ideally these would be narratives, but narratives that stuttered under the weight of the teaching, or information, that they were also intended to convey—hybrid narratives without any preexisting model for their internal articulations. Now observe these texts as they pass through centuries of circulation, translation, and changes of book format, not to mention immense changes to the institutional settings and cultural situations in which they were read. Under the pressure of these shifts, and without any traditional guide to their segmentation, they develop a history of different kinds of internal divisions and labels, a history that would mutate unpredictably and usually without any explicit justification. As a result, this history of segmentation would look like a geological record, or core sample, of atmospheric changes. There would be periods of rapid change, and others that seemed more settled, almost permanent; but even in the long calm of agreement there would be stirrings of disquiet, because without any authorial sanction to any one scheme of subdivision, it would always be possible to imagine a better way to do it.

Atmospheric changes to what, exactly? There would be two possible answers. These core samples would have much to tell us about how those particular texts were understood differently at different moments, in ways that were
not fully captured by the exegeses produced to explain them. Yet it might also
be true that tracing the changes to the way a set of texts were segmented differently over a long period of time would give us a record of how textual division
itself was conceived at different times—indeed, a record of thinking, implicit
and unrecognized, of what it means to read narrative in units at all. The history
of the narrative texts of Christian Scripture, the Gospels and Acts, is exactly this
phenomenon: a natural experiment in the history of the chapter. It is there that
the evolving finding technique of the chapter had its first significant intersection with prose narrative. This collision fundamentally, if gradually, shifted the
meaning of chaptering, from a means of organizing *information* to a new sense
in which it organized *time*. Temporal measurements enter the world of the
chapter, and competing imaginaries around how we understand time and its
relation to human action become inevitable questions every time the Gospels
are resegmented. This is where the significance of the various Gospel chapter
systems becomes a question of literary form.

Biblical chaptering is not a common object of attention for literary historians, theologians, or lay readers of Scripture. The long-lasting convention of
their current arrangement, which dates from the thirteenth century, has gradually rendered their history and peculiar shapes invisible. Their supplementa-
tion in the sixteenth century with Robert Estienne's division into numbered
verses has consigned them even further into the territory of the purely functional, the thing you use to cite a passage.[1] "Chapter and verse": it is a conventionally banal term for the act of excerpting, quoting, memorizing, a neutral
grid laid on top of the text and no more significant than that. The history of
how the biblical chapter arrived at that state of banality, however, is fraught
and illuminating. It reveals significant changes to ideas about segmentation,
changes that—given the cultural centrality of these texts—had real importance for other narrative genres. With each shift in the way the Gospels were
chaptered, a tacit statement was made about the uses to which chapters could
be put, the shape they could take, and the phenomenology of a reader encoun-
tering them. These were responses to various cultural pressures, but they
ended up exerting their own outward pressure.

Biblical paleographers and codicologists of course have long wrestled with
the vexed history of chaptering, but either as a means to date manuscripts and
establish lines of transmission or with an eye to doctrinal or liturgical

questions.[2] While I will lean on the work of these scholars, I have different questions to ask here, questions that are literary in orientation: How does the history of the chaptered Gospel reveal to us shifts in how the articulation of time itself, particularly in relation to human agency, is apprehended? How did the different solutions to this question spread out to other cultural spheres, through the specific techniques of chaptering developed to render those solutions visible? This more literary survey of the Gospel's textual history will mean alighting at different times and places, from the fourth to the thirteenth century, sometimes with known individuals, sometimes only with specific versions of the texts—even, sometimes, a single surviving manuscript witness. It will have to leap over geographical and historical chasms. But it allows us to perform something that the chapters of classical culture did not: the comparative reading of the same text across different regimes of segmentation. We can see the same scenes or passages distributed in contrasting ways, with new and sometimes unexpected fissures; familiar moments, sutured unfamiliarly. In the process we can discover some almost accidental innovations to the shapes of narrative division, developments that give us a new kind of syncopated narrative time, alien rhythms stuttering the flow of human intention.

Caesarea and the Synoptic Impetus

Christian texts, and Christian intellectual needs, torqued classical habits of textual segmentation in distinctive ways. Most methods of intellectual labor, of course, were still broadly continuous between classical antiquity and early Christianity; as late as the sixth century, as in the Calabrian monastery of Vivarium where Cassiodorus oversaw a tremendous labor of textual reproduction and emendation, the *titulos*—the word that, as we have seen, modulated between "title" and "summary" of a demarcated unit—was still a major tool of scholarly knowledge production, along with other kinds of *notae* or marginal glosses.[3] Beneath the surface continuity, however, were momentous changes. The first is that the "book" had become, inescapably, a codex. Although the indexical work of chaptering preexisted the codex, certainly the codex offered it a more amenable environment. The extent to which the desire of Christian readers for such reference tools was a significant, or perhaps even the primary, driver of technological change from scroll to codex is still a live subject among scholars of the period.[4] Whatever the influence of Christian communities in driving this change, however, and whatever their reasons for preferring the codex, it seems clear that two of the advantages of the new format were its comprehensiveness and the ease with which it could incorporate finding aids, from chapters to pagination—a codex could contain multiple texts and permitted their quick cross-referencing.[5]

The codex therefore fostered new creativity in the development of finding aids and textual arrangement because of how it encouraged *comparative* modes of reading. Comparison was required by the unique textual dilemma of Christian textual culture: the possession of four texts—each amounting to roughly the length of an average scroll, and therefore necessitating a codex to collect together—that told the same story in sometimes subtly, and occasionally widely, divergent ways. To enable quick cross-referencing of the similar elements of the respective Gospels, it was necessary to divide them into the constituent elements that could be so compared, and then devise a method for marking these divisions in such a way that similar passages could be indicated and swiftly located. This work, the earliest native segmentation of the Gospels, can be traced back to the early fourth century and the library at Caesarea, the research center or workshop led by Eusebius, bishop of Caesarea and pioneering Church historian, whose intellectual signature was the application to key Christian texts of finding apparatuses and summaries.[6] Eusebius's solution to the technical dilemma of Gospel comparison would initiate an enormous mutation to the norms of classical capitulation. It was a step, inadvertent but decisive, toward the chapter's millennium-long shift away from a finding device to something more purely rhythmic, more a part of narrative experience, more attuned to the experience of time.

Not all of the work at Caesarea was radical in form. Eusebius's foundational *Ecclesiastical History* includes chapters usually judged as authorial that are not widely dissimilar, in either syntactical form or textual arrangement, from Arrian's heads for Epictetus: noun phrases opened by *peri* that announce a subject or particular moment, or the historical *hōs* ("how") that opens a causal account, placed in a table at the start of each book but not, in the earliest manuscripts, serving as intertitles.[7] This is a habit shared not only with the classical compendium but also with the Greek historians of preceding centuries.[8] It is also the heading style associated with the so-called Euthalian material, a surviving composite textual apparatus of chapter divisions and headings for Acts and the Epistles that is persistently if not conclusively associated with Caesarea.[9] The intellectual problem posed by the Gospels, however, was not amenable to this familiar approach. Because they were narratives—and narratives that were not always sequentially identical to one another—they necessitated a unit of segmentation that was not primarily oriented around topics or short propositional summaries, and they demanded a new method by which to organize these notations in a comparative manner.

The solution was to be known as the Eusebian canons, a strikingly elegant and durable method by which parallel passages in the Gospels could be identified. As Eusebius explained it in the "letter to Carpianus" that prefaced many Greek Gospel manuscripts, each Gospel was divided into numbered passages, along with a canon number, from I to X, that referenced its place in an accompanying table. Those ten canon numbers each indicated a particular category of similarity: I standing for passages to be found in all four Gospels, II standing for passages shared by the synoptic gospels Matthew, Mark, and Luke only, III standing for passages present only in Matthew, Luke, and John, and so on to VII–X, which stood for passages found only in a single Gospel. The explanation is remarkable for its effort at terminological precision:

> Hence, if you were to open any one of the four Gospels, and wish to light upon any chapter [*kephalaio*] whatever, to know who else has said similar things and to find the relevant passages [*pericopēs*] in each, in which they treated of the same things, then find the number [*arithmon*] marked against the passage which you have before you, look for it in the canon [*kanoni*] which the note in red has suggested, and you will immediately learn from the headings at the start of the canon how many and which have said similar things.[10]

Here a "chapter," or kephalaion, is distinguished from, and yet seems to contain, a "passage," or pericopē—the latter by implication smaller, which indicates, tantalizingly, that Eusebius may have already known of, or produced, Gospel texts segmented into marked "chapters," although the more general sense of kephalaia used by Augustine may be the referent here. But the pericopēs of which Eusebius speaks here need two separate marks, a "number" and a "canon," the first segmenting the text in a linear fashion, the second indicating its place in a nonlinear table where the various pericopē numbers are sorted into categories and available for quick comparison across different Gospels. There is no known precedent for this act of bibliographic creativity.[11] Perhaps there could not be, so unique was the opportunity, or dilemma, presented by the Gospels. But the solution is codex dependent, and indicates significant thinking about the technology of the codex and how it could permit new kinds of textual articulation.

The canon table itself and its diagrammatic arrangement of information is the most visible legacy of Caesarean ingenuity, but for a history of the chapter

the interest of the Eusebian canons is the pericopē. The term is significant in
its distinction from "kephalaion," which refers to "heading" and therefore exists in the complicated ecosystem of the classical tradition of capitulation.
"Pericopē," on the other hand, is etymologically related not to the heading but
to the act of division—to *cut*, to detach. The necessary prelude to the complicated comparison work of the canons is to divide the Gospels, and the
Eusebian pericopē is a foundational act of interpretive segmentation. It is not,
admittedly, wholly original to Eusebius himself. The letter to Carpianus refers
to an Alexandrian scholar, Ammonius, as the inspiration for the subdivision,
although the Ammonian pericopē is arranged differently; the Ammonian
"fourfold Gospel," as Eusebius calls it, left Matthew intact while placing corresponding sections (*pericopas paratheis*) of the other three Gospels alongside their precedents in Matthew. The Eusebian canons no longer need to
privilege any one Gospel, as they allow any Gospel to serve as a reference
point for any other. But that is not the burden of Eusebius's critique in the
letter. Ammonius's text, as Eusebius complains, disrupted the continuity of
three of the four Gospels, preventing a "consecutive reading" of any of them
aside from Matthew.[12] The Eusebian system is intended instead to restore this
linear reading experience while maintaining the divisions, which were likely
borrowed from Ammonius. This is already a strikingly new concern: to balance the continuity of a narrative thread with the segmentation needed for
cross-referencing. Eusebius, that is, no longer treats the Gospels as a collective
reference work, but as *a temporal narrative process intersecting with nontemporal
reference points*. The four timelines of the Gospels run differently, and those
differences inspire the need for an atemporal grid, but the separate timelines
need nonetheless to be respected.

The result, however, looks nothing like the chapters of antiquity, and it is
here that Eusebius departed from previous segmenting norms most violently.
His units can be widely divergent in size, but their most distinctive quality is
compression: they are quite often shorter than anything that could be distinguished as an episode, action, or even continuous discursive segment. Seen
through the lens of the Eusebian canons, the Gospels have been pulverized.
Matthew, for instance, was divided into 355 units; even Mark, the shortest by
word count, is divided into 233 such segments. Insofar as they are for comparison purposes, they need to respect the law of the smallest coherent shared
segment. What they seek to identify, therefore, are textual monads: the bits of
Gospel narrative that cannot be subdivided any further, because in their intact
state they were passed between Gospels (or, in the case of the final four

canons, exist nowhere else).[13] That can sometimes be reasonably large, but is equally often the size of a sentence or phrase, and at any rate does normally not adhere to any narrative logic. Take, for instance, the Mission Discourse as it is found in Matthew, not simply a single scene but a single speech act. Later systems of division tend to situate this, with unusual uniformity, as a single unit; it is, in our current system, Matthew 10, but it is divided into twenty-two Eusebian units. Not that the scale of the cutting is consistent; the entirety of the Feeding of the Four Thousand, in what is for us Matthew 15:29–39, is a single Eusebian pericopē.

As the earliest form of division in Christian Scripture, the Eusebian system tore apart the norms of classical segmentation and rearranged its values to new ends. By treating the Gospels as both a mutually collaborative reference work and yet also as four distinct narrative experiences, it accentuated the tension between the linear and nonlinear models of reading. These are not yet, of course, chapters. Nor are they kephalaia, the word that Eusebius uses with mysterious application in the letter to Carpianus. But they are a sign of ferment, an innovation that reveals not only the creativity of the environment in Caesarea but also the particular problem that called forth those energies: the need to bring intellectual tools not designed for continuous narrative to bear upon a textual corpus that was narrative in its essence. The Gospels are not narratives in any mundane or accidental sense; the insertion of the divine into a human and therefore temporal world is their subject, and therefore narrative itself, as Eusebius surely recognized, demands to be treated carefully. The canons implicitly recognize this fact. Yet the specific problem they solve does not yet require a particular understanding of narrative segmentation per se, but rather how to stage the encounter of narrative with nonnarrative or indexical reading modes. Thus the canons remain, emblematically and literally, marginal to the text.

Eusebius's thinking may not have stopped there, and may have taken on the subject of the internal rhythms of Gospel narrative. There is some circumstantial evidence that the ingenuity of Eusebius's efforts was not exhausted by the system of canons, and may have extended to what we might recognize as the first kephalaia proper of the Christian tradition. The hint lurks in Eusebius's use of the word "kephalaia" in the letter to Carpianus. What may he have been referring to? It is open to us to assume that he used the word in its vaguest, purely conceptual sense, as a "passage" that a reader happens to alight upon, as opposed to the more specific sense of pericopē as a textual unit shared by one or more Gospels, a unit of transmission. Nor does he use the term "kephalaia" to refer to his headings for the *Ecclesiastical History*, so there is some sense in believing that Eusebius's use of the term floated, as would have been common in the fourth century still, between the specifically marked and the merely notional. Yet there remains a second plausible reading of that sentence from the letter: that he is referring to a textual unit larger than the pericopē that his system marks out—something that either sits alongside, or encompasses, the unit of the "passage." What might incline us to this reading is the evidence of the Codex Vaticanus, one of the earliest extant Greek pandects, or complete, one-volume Bibles, and one that bears a plausible connection to Caesarea, and displays a new shift in the New Testament's unit segmentation.

Vaticanus dates from the mid-fourth century, and although there is no firm evidence for its place of production, debates on each tend to oscillate between Alexandrian and Caesarean provenance.[14] Vaticanus, unlike its slightly near-contemporary Codex Sinaiticus, lacks the Eusebian apparatus. What it possesses in the Gospels instead is among the earliest systems of Christian capitulation, if not the earliest.[15] These are purely unit divisions, without any accompanying heading, and although the units are on the whole larger than a Eusebian/Ammonian pericopē, they are still numerous; Vaticanus's text of Matthew, for instance, contains 170 such marked segments. Like the Eusebian canons, they are indicated by marginal notations—Greek letters serving as numeration, again in red ink—but also with a short horizontal line, or *paragraphos*, placed above the first whole line of the unit, and occasionally with a letter protruding into the left margin, something like the "head" of Ciceronian manuscripts.[16] The marginal numeration is not in the same hand as the two scribes identified for the text itself, although it was likely not added significantly later.[17]

What purpose could these early units have served? A return to the Mission Discourse of Matthew 10 will help provide a feel for their breadth.[18] Here is one single Vaticanus unit, encompassing what in the Eusebian apparatus were four complete units and parts of a fifth:

[V 65] When you are persecuted in one place, flee to another. Truly I tell you, you will not finish going through the towns of Israel before the Son of Man comes. The student is not above the teacher, nor a servant above his master. It is enough for students to be like their teachers, and servants like their masters. If the head of the house has been called Beelzebul, how much more the members of his household! So do not be afraid of them, for there is nothing concealed that will not be disclosed, or hidden that will not be made known. What I tell you in the dark, speak in the daylight; what is whispered in your ear, proclaim from the roofs. Do not be afraid of those who kill the body but cannot kill the soul. Rather, be afraid of the One who can destroy both soul and body in hell. Are not two sparrows sold for a penny? Yet not one of them will fall to the ground outside your Father's care. And even the very hairs of your head are all numbered. So don't be afraid; you are worth more than many sparrows. (Mt 10:23–31)

Yet this unit is still a small portion only of the Mission Discourse as a whole, which Vaticanus divides into nine segments—fewer than the twenty-two Eusebian units into which it is divided, but still several for what narrates a single recognizable episode and speech act. The reasoning behind this segmentation practice is difficult to discern, particularly without headings to provide us with any guide. Yet in one respect we can operate through negative proof: the Vaticanus segmentations do not line up across the Gospels, so they cannot have been developed to solve the synoptic problem.[19] They might have operated as lectionary units—intended for some liturgical purpose—although they seem far too small in extent for such use.[20] They might have functioned as a citational apparatus, although aside from their reproduction in two later extant codices, they have no lasting presence as such; but such a guess would at least explain the careful numbering as well as the lack of headings.[21] If they are an attempt to capture narrative rhythm, or some rhythm of reading, their method is obscure. Perhaps they are simply a minor fermata for a reader, a place for the eye, or voice, to pause.

What Vaticanus does signify is some effort, contemporaneous to Eusebius if not necessarily produced by him or the Caesarean library, to provide a segmentation for the Gospel narratives that has a purpose other than cross-referencing. Its proto-chapters might have been inspired by the Eusebian canons—the presence of marginal numeration might have led to the notion of a system of segmentation that, unmoored from a comparative table and slightly expanded in size, could serve other purposes, as an example of exaptation in the evolution of the chapter. They might look instead like an experimental dead end, an attempt to imagine a new apparatus for the text that was never satisfactory enough to take hold, yet pointed the way to a further development. Regardless, once the search for the smallest possible shared unit— the presupposition of the canons, the premise upon which the synoptic problem was and still is conducted—was discarded, a new imagination for how to distribute breaks into Gospel narrative could take rise. The next step, it is just possible, might have been Eusebius's as well.

Codex Alexandrinus's Incitations

The first fully evolved capitulation of the Gospels, segments that are in form and function recognizably "chapters" to a modern eye, belongs to the youngest of the three great uncial Greek biblical codices, Codex Alexandrinus. The codex dates from the late fourth or early fifth century, and its provenance is uncertain; while Caesarea has been suggested, Constantinople, Ephesus, and the traditional ascription to Alexandria remain more popular.[22] It contains the Eusebian canon numbers, and in that respect has some relationship to the Caesarean tradition. Its chapters, however, are entirely its own. Referred to as either the Old Greek Divisions, the *kephalaia majora* (as compared to the *kephalaia minora*, the Eusebian divisions), or the "Byzantine" divisions after the subsequent textual tradition where they were used, these are not later additions to the codex but thoroughly integrated aspects of it. Each Gospel has a prefatory list of numbered headings, or *titloi*, something very like a table of contents. Those headings are tied to the text by being repeated in the upper margin, as a kind of running head, although many of these were destroyed by the binding of the codex upon its arrival in England in the seventeenth century, when its pages were cut to a standard size. In Luke and John, the kephalaia numbers are repeated in the margin at the start of each, accompanied by a cross; in Matthew and Mark, a marginal mark something like a "7"—a *koronis*—indicates the start of a kephalaion, without the accompanying numbers.[23]

Compared with the capitulations of Vaticanus, not to mention the *capita* of classical antiquity, these kephalaia involve specialized elements that nonetheless are fused into a single complex mechanism. The divisions involve both unit demarcation and headings rather than one or the other, and numeration linking the two—and these are now clearly understood as interdependent functions, each relying on the others for its proper operation. The headings in list form permit both "finding" (discontinuous access) and "seeking" (a perusal in search of something of interest), while the running heads tie any sequential reading experience back to the latticework of the headings; their numeration allows for citational use. These are textual divisions that are at once narrative sense units, a summary list providing an overview for a novice or curious reader, a technique for discontinuous access as in a reference work for a

practiced reader, and citational units for use in secondary scholarship or liturgical directions, all fused into a whole.[24] In this sense the kephalaia are more
comprehensive than most, if not all, of the systems that followed. If Alexandrinus was not a product of the Caesarean workshop, it bears the marks of the
thinking that emerged there: a sophisticated approach to the question of how
continuous narrative could be articulated into segments for multiple overlapping uses.[25] A plausible hypothesis is that what the synoptic dilemma
initiated—the question of how narrative could be rendered as units—led to
the development of the kephalaia, a supple and variously useful tool that, by
coordinating all the techniques of segmentation that preexisted it, signified
something new.

It is the novelty of the kephalaia, if anything, that gives off a Eusebian scent,
because the question of why they were produced has no clearly satisfactory
answers, at least not of the usual kind. They are certainly related to the Eusebian canons, perhaps even partially derived from them; almost three-quarters
of the kephalaia begin at the same location as a Eusebian pericopē.[26] The titloi
of similar passages in different Gospels are often identical, suggesting some
use in locating synoptic parallels. Yet the competing presence of the Eusebian
canons in the text indicates that the kephalaia are doing something different,
something supplementary. That other function, in the views of some scholars,
can only be to serve as lectionary units in a yearly cycle. Alexandrinus's Mark,
for instance, has forty-eight kephalaia, intimating a relation to the number of
sabbaths in the Jewish lunar year minus the high holidays.[27] This surmise involves some selective attention, as the number of kephalaia in each Gospel and
the length of the kephalaia themselves vary widely enough to make apportion-
ing the divisions to a yearly cycle an exercise in ingenuity. These explanations
are part of a general effort to discern a technical and extratextual problem to
which the Alexandrinus divisions were the solution. What if, instead, the problem to which the kephalaia responded was not extratextual but intrinsic: the
problem of how a narrative text could be at once atomized into units while also
being understood as necessarily and inescapably sequential and continuous?

This is where a more strictly literary consideration, an account of the intrinsic shape of the kephalaia and how they implicitly understand the narratives
they measure, becomes necessary. If this intrinsic viewpoint has rarely been
taken, it is in part because what the kephalaia do is so peculiar at times—so
stubbornly odd, not naturalized by centuries of familiarity—that they come
to a modern reader as flawed reflections of what might have been a more coherent, rational procession of segments. But the logic they possess deserves

considerable attention. They are spare, most not taking more than single line of text in the list where they are collected, as in the table of forty-eight headings that prefaces Mark (figure 3.1). What is remarkable is how these clauses intersect with the narrative material they organize.

A sampling from the titloi to Mark reveals a narrative poetics:

[A 1] "Concerning the possessed man [peri tou diamonizomenou]"
[A 2] "Concerning Peter's mother-in-law [peri tēs pentheras Petrou]"
[A 4] "Concerning the leper [peri tou leprou]"
[A 5] "Concerning the paralyzed man [peri tou paralytikou]"
[A 15] "Concerning John and Herod [peri Iōannou kai Herōdou]"
[A 19] "Concerning the Phoenician woman [peri tēs Phoinikissēs]"
[A 23] "Concerning the blind man [peri tou typhlou]"
[A 26] "Concerning the epileptic man [peri tou selēniazomenou]"
[A 29] "Concerning the inquisitive Pharisees [peri tōn eperōtēsanton Pharisaiōn]"
[A 31] "Concerning Bartimaeus [peri Baltimaiou]"
[A 38] "Concerning the Sadducees [peri tōn Saddoukaiōn]"
[A 39] "Concerning the scribes [peri tōn grammataiōn]"
[A 44] "Concerning the woman who anointed the Lord with myrrh [peri tēs alipsasēs ton Kyrion myrō]"
[A 47] "Peter's denial [arnēsis Petrou]"[28]

As these indicate, the majority of the titloi to Mark function as a record of *others*—of the entrance into the narrative of peripheral figures, whose intersection with the protagonist is limited in extent, often to the single kephalaion whose title they furnish. It is something like a list of encounters. They are of course often miracle-encounters, but not exclusively so: they can be hostile encounters, questioning ones, moments of solicitude or doubt or even error. As for the protagonist of this text, he is almost entirely missing from the list, referred to by *nomina sacra* five times only: once by name (A 25: "Concerning Jesus's transfiguration") and four times by title, as "the Lord." Actions that Jesus carries out are syntactically emptied of their actor, as in A 17, "Concerning walking on the sea." Where the titloi do not simply indicate a minor figure, when they refer instead to a parable, their form does not differ from the miracles, to such an extent that that the literal and figurative become hard to distinguish: A 21, "Concerning the seven loaves," is directly followed by A 22, "Concerning the Pharisees's leaven." The titloi blur an action—a miraculous multiplication performed before a crowd—with the figurative speech act that

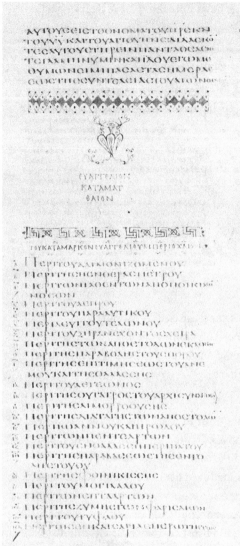

FIGURE 3.1 The list of *titloi* prefacing the Gospel of Mark in Codex Alexandrinus. British Library Royal 1 D. VIII, fol. 5v. Courtesy of the British Library.

follows it, by removing the actor from the formulation. To the extent that the titloi have named actors, they are largely the cast of incidentals, who exist to be acted upon by a force greater than they know. Jesus, however, is the absent center around which these segmentations revolve with a tacit silence. The protagonist has been detached from the logic of the units of his own story.[29] Seen from the vantage point of the titloi, Mark has been almost de-protagonized, and looks more like a series of quasi-autonomous interactions.

The collapsing of speech acts into actions—the way the titloi make a discursive topic merge with a literal enactment—indicates something crucial: these are clearly *segmentations of a narrative*, not an arrangement of concepts.[30] There are occasional exceptions, as in A 34, "Concerning the forgiveness of evil," but these are crowded out by an attention to the accumulation of persons and events. This might explain why Alexandrinus's John has only eighteen kephalaia, despite being significantly longer than Mark; John is simply too dedicated to *talk*, particularly talk of an abstract nature, to be pegged to persons or events in quite this way. Alexandrinus's titloi are in this sense the opposite of the informational headings of Gellius or Arrian, whose headings strive toward conceptual abstraction to aid a consultative reader. Alexandrinus locates a reader instead in a procession of personal encounters and acts, not a list of theological or even more broadly homiletic topoi. As such the combined machinery of the kephalaia offers something in addition to any potential synoptic, citational, or liturgical use: it presents an implicit theory of narrative measurement. This is the shockingly innovative aspect of the work of the kephalaia—what, in a history of capitulation, is unprecedented.

The titloi are, however, only one aspect of Alexandrinus's theory; they cannot fully encapsulate the feel of the kephalaia themselves, their amplitude and rhythm. In comparison to the Eusebian pericopē and the Vaticanus section, a kephalaion tends to be longer, more capacious. The Mission Discourse in Matthew is, for instance, a single unit in Alexandrinus; although this is the broader end of their spectrum, the Alexandrinus units do usually linger with actions to a greater extent than their predecessors, indeed far greater than the Eusebian canons. There is admittedly a high degree of variability involved. The aforementioned "Concerning the forgiveness of evil" encompasses only two contemporary verses, Mark 11:25–26. But while the units are shaped by actions of some kind, those actions—and even most longer discourses—are allowed a continuity that the Eusebian pericopē interrupted. This too indicates a dilution of the precision that a consultative reading might require, in favor of a rhythm that seems adapted instead to a linear mode of access. It is closer, that is, to a rhythm of reading for the story.

These units have further surprises still. Take, for instance, their orientation around secondary actors, as signaled by the titloi. It is part of Alexandrinus's procedure that the first kephalaion does not begin at the start of each Gospel, which it treats as an incipit or prologue, but with some initial decisive action. In Mark, the first unit begins with a speech act: "Just then a man in their synagogue who was possessed by an impure spirit cried out, 'What do you want with us, Jesus of Nazareth? Have you come to destroy us? I know who you are—the Holy One of God!'" (Mk 1:23). The cry opens the kephalaion here, as the possessed man accosts Jesus, inciting an immediate healing when Jesus responds to the spirit, "Come out of him!" It is not entirely coincidental, perhaps, that this initial unit is a pair of performative speech acts: a recognition and an exorcism. Just as the titloi collapse speech acts into actions, the units themselves understand speech as at the very least the instigation of action, if not indeed equivalent to action. They are known less by their abstract content and more by the events they enact. Parables are more usually gathered into long kephalaia than separated out; A 9, unlike the Eusebian design, collects the parables of the sower, lamp, and seeds, as if what matters in this scheme of division is the continuous action of speaking, not the particular concepts that are spoken about. And so, repeatedly, the kephalaia begin with speech—most often, in fact, the sudden hailing of one person (usually Jesus) by another that incites an event.

Such a starting point does not, however, necessarily imply that the unit has to confine itself to that action. A 1 in Mark, somewhat anomalously, does; the demon is cast out, onlookers are amazed, and news of the incident spreads, at which point the unit concludes. Even if it is brief, this kephalaion is shapely, discrete, comprehensible: a challenge, an immediate response, a ripple of consequence. This is, however, an unusual procedure for Alexandrinus. The later casting out of an impure spirit is traced over by Alexandrinus in its more typically peculiar manner. The Gospel narration gives it a setting, and sutures it to earlier action: Peter, James, and John have accompanied Jesus to witness the Transfiguration, and immediately upon their return to the other disciples, they are met by a crowd, out of which a man emerges to declare that he has brought his son: "He foams at the mouth, gnashes his teeth and becomes rigid. I asked your disciples to drive out the spirit, but they could not" (Mk 9:17). This scene of casting out is more richly personalized than the earlier one: as the boy convulses, Jesus asks the father for the affliction's history, and notes the doubt in the father's plea for help; the father responds with the uncanny "I do believe, help me overcome my unbelief." Such a paradox threatens to linger—unanswered, it presents a brief tear in the scene—but the advancing crowd prompts Jesus to cast out the spirit, which creates such physical violence upon its exit that the boy is taken for dead, until Jesus takes him by his hand. A brief exchange follows with the bemused disciples, who ask why they could not have cast it out themselves; Jesus responds that "this kind can only come out by prayer" (Mk 9:29).

This event is the subject of A 26, "Concerning the epileptic man." Yet this kephalaion's boundaries are at some odds with the scene's narrative contours. It begins not with the scene setting at 9:14–16—the transition from the Transfiguration to the approach to the crowd, which even includes the question Jesus asks, to which the boy's father responds—but with the father's request at 9:17. Here again, an urgent, dialogic speech incites the kephalaion. What we might normally understand as necessary scenic preparation or "pre-proceeding" tends to be excised from the formal unit in Alexandrinus, which moves straight into the proceeding proper.[31] If as a result the previous unit, on the Transfiguration, has a somewhat ragged, chaotic end, this is consistent with the emphasis these units place on an immediate instigation of action. Yet A 26 does not conclude with the action's ending, either its immediate consequences in the boy's revival or the subsequent bewildered questioning by the disciples. It continues as the disciples leave Galilee, during which Jesus predicts the death of the Son of Man, to 9:33, when they arrive at Capernaum. A 27 begins at Mark 9:33, again with an inquiry: Jesus asking the disciples what they had been arguing about on the road. Neither the change of location nor the separate incident of Jesus's puzzling prophecy brings the unit to its close. Only a new speech incitement—a question demanding an answer—can initiate a new unit.

The logic here is difficult to parse. Such a division severs the scene from its physical and emotional setting: the descent from the mountaintop vision of the transfigured Jesus to a dissatisfied and needy crowd, a sobering reimmersion in everyday distress and tepid faith that might be the immediate spur for Jesus's frustrated rebuke to an "unbelieving generation." Yet if it foregoes this particular setting, it oddly enough appends a setting that does not seem integral to it: the departure from the incident, the roadside prophecy, the subsequent squabbling of competitive disciples. The segment flares into life instantly, with a cry erupting from the crowd, and then drags on past its dramatic conclusion, slowly burning out. If we look to prior divisions as a source for this scheme, we come up empty. The Eusebian system divides the scene in several units, but one of them extends from the father's anguished request to the boy's recovery, the curve of a coherent and isolated action. Vaticanus configures the scene in an intriguing apposition, as half of one lengthy unit that starts with the Transfiguration and ends with the boy's rise. There is no precedent for Alexandrinus's articulation of this moment. Any presumed attention on the part of the Alexandrinus scribes to particular lexical formulae in Mark is also not quite explanatory; although forty-three out of the forty-eight Mark kephalaia begin with *kai* ("and," "and yet," "and then," or simply "also"), usually followed by a verb with an aorist tense form, this is such a common grammatical construction in Mark that it is scarcely avoidable; it has been rightly called a "weak signal."[32] This syntactical cue may have been a necessary condition for the Alexandrinus scribes when they sought a place to begin a new unit, but given its sheer copiousness in Mark it was scarcely a sufficient one.

Nor is the strange rhythm of the Transfiguration/epileptic-healing episode unique within the codex, even within its version of Mark. When Mark's scene setting directly explains some aspect of the ensuing action, it is as likely as not to be disconnected from the action proper by a new kephalaion: A 5, the scene of the paralytic man's healing, begins with the man's arrival at Mark 2:3, omitting the preceding account of the large Capernaum crowd that pressed up to the door of the house where Jesus was staying—a necessary prelude to the detail that the man is lowered to Jesus on a mat through the roof. There is the further example of A 45, which encompasses the preparations for the Last Supper but stops before it begins, while A 46—titled, somewhat elliptically, "Concerning the prophecy of the surrender"—begins with Jesus's dramatic assertion that "one of you will betray me," and then extends over the rest of the meal, the waiting in Gethsemane, the arrest, and the trial before the Sanhedrin, ending only before the scene of Peter's denial. Most remarkably, the very long A 47, "Peter's denial," starts with that scene of challenge and then encompasses the rest of the Passion narrative, about which the title is silent. The kephalaia seem to start almost in medias res, but then ramble, even fizzle, accumulating addenda until they bump into another moment of impetus.

The unity of an action is simply irrelevant here. The stress falls audibly on the beginning of a kephalaion and then lapses away in a vaguely dactylic fashion. It is, after all, to the sparking moment or incitement that the titloi allude, as in the heading to A 47, which simply omits Jesus's condemnation, torture, and death. To understand such a method requires us to find a new bearing, something not oriented toward closure or significant wholeness. One particularly curious example, Alexandrinus's solution to a knotty moment in the synoptics, will help surface this strange temporal rhythm. Here the scribes developing the codex's capitulation would have been faced with an unusual dilemma within Gospel narration: one action interrupted by another before being completed. None of the synoptics narrate the scene by disentangling its elements; in each, the text adheres to the linearity in which Jesus's intent to perform one miracle is suspended, if only temporarily, by a request to perform another. Two separate events are thereby entwined, in a manner that the stubbornly sequential nature of Gospel narration, its one-thing-and-then-another texture, tends to avoid, making this braided scene a challenge for any capitulation.

In all three of the synoptic versions of this scene, Alexandrinus divides it into two kephalaia. In Mark, the first such unit, "Concerning the synagogue-leader's daughter," is a kind familiar enough in this codex: the sudden entrance into the narrative of a new figure. As is Alexandrinus's fashion, the Gospel's scene setting—the crossing of the Sea of Galilee by boat, the arrival of a crowd, out of which Jairus emerges—in excised in favor of the immediate spark of speech (A 12): "Then one of the synagogue leaders, named Jairus, came, and when he saw Jesus, he fell at his feet. He pleaded earnestly with him, 'My little daughter is dying. Please come and put your hands on her so that she will be healed and live.' So Jesus went with him. A large crowd followed and pressed around him" (Mk 5:22–24). The action cannot continue, because a second incitement follows. Alexandrinus adheres to its normal procedure and starts a new kephalaion—"Concerning the bleeding woman"—at exactly this point:

[A 13] And a woman was there who had been subject to bleeding for twelve years. She had suffered a great deal under the care of many doctors and had spent all she had, yet instead of getting better she grew worse. When she heard about Jesus, she came up behind him in the crowd and touched his cloak, because she thought, "If I just touch his clothes, I will be healed." Immediately her bleeding stopped and she felt in her body that she was freed from her suffering. At once Jesus realized that power had gone out from him. He turned around in the crowd and asked, "Who touched my clothes?" "You see the people crowding against you," his disciples answered, "and yet you can ask, 'Who touched me?'" But Jesus kept looking around to see who had done it. Then the woman, knowing what had happened to her, came and fell at his feet and, trembling with fear, told him the whole truth. He said to her, "Daughter, your faith has healed you. Go in peace and be freed from your suffering." (Mk 5:25–34)

Here the episode of the bleeding woman concludes and the scene returns to the continuing action of A 12. There is a new eruption of speech, the attempted dissuasion of "some people," who announce the death of Jairus's daughter. Alexandrinus, however, does not begin a new kephalaion as one might expect, refusing to isolate the incident of bleeding woman. A 13, the unit of the bleeding woman, simply continues long past her departure, and in fact past the healing of the daughter to the return to Nazareth:

> While Jesus was still speaking, some people came from the house of Jairus, the synagogue leader. "Your daughter is dead," they said. "Why bother the teacher anymore?" Overhearing what they said, Jesus told him, "Don't be afraid; just believe." He did not let anyone follow him except Peter, James and John the brother of James. When they came to the home of the synagogue leader, Jesus saw a commotion, with people crying and wailing loudly. He went in and said to them, "Why all this commotion and wailing? The child is not dead but asleep." But they laughed at him. After he put them all out, he took the child's father and mother and the disciples who were with him, and went in where the child was. He took her by the hand and said to her, "*Talitha koum!*" (which means "Little girl, I say to you, get up!"). Immediately the girl stood up and began to walk around (she was twelve years old). At this they were completely astonished. He gave strict orders not to let anyone know about this, and told them to give her something to eat. Jesus left there and went to his hometown, accompanied by his disciples. When the Sabbath came, he began to teach in the synagogue, and many who heard him were amazed. "Where did this man get these things?" they asked. "What's this wisdom that has been given him? What are these remarkable miracles he is performing? Isn't this the carpenter? Isn't this Mary's son and the brother of James, Joseph, Judas and Simon? Aren't his sisters here with us?" And they took offense at him. Jesus said to them, "A prophet is not without honor except in his own town, among his relatives and in his own home." He could not do any miracles there, except lay his hands on a few sick people and heal them. He was amazed at their lack of faith. (Mk 5:35–6:6)

At this point, with Jesus's mission instruction to the apostles, a new unit begins.

Alexandrinus is here distinctive, even eccentric. Both the Eusebian system and Vaticanus treat this moment as one combined unit, restoring to it the scene setting at Mark 5:21, and concluding just before Jesus's departure, with his instruction to give food to the healed daughter. Both previous systems, that is, understand this narration as a frame story (Jairus's daughter) surrounding an inset digression (the bleeding woman), and follow the curve of the initial action to its completion. So too with later systems. Codex Amiatinus, the eighth-century Northumbrian pandect that is the earliest complete exemplar of Jerome's Vulgate, segments it into a capitulum of the same extent, entitled "He hurries to raise from the dead the daughter of Jairus, he heals the woman with the flow of blood, and then goes onward to raise the girl" (Vadens mortuam suscitare filiam Iairi, mulierem a profluvio sanguinis sanans, suscitat protinus et puellam).[33] These are strongly proairetic arrangements: they understand request, performance, and completion as linked in a monad we might call an "event." The performance is complicated here by a particular delay, but still brought to closure. One might understand this composite event thematically, as an implicit pairing of two forms of strong faith, one forthright and the other furtive and abashed; in terms of narrative mechanics, it has been suggested that Mark inserted the story of the bleeding woman in order to demonstrate that the interval between the father's request and the news of the girl's death covered a significant period of time.[34] Whatever one believes about Mark's interest in providing an illusion of duration, this reading understands the bleeding woman as necessarily secondary, serving some explanatory purpose in relation to the frame story, because a larger conceptual grid of proairesis—incitement, performance, resolution—encompasses it. The resolution of the action, in these various systems, matters; they give us a world where intent, performance, and completion are indissolubly linked.

Alexandrinus invites us to think differently. Its narrative understanding is concentrated on the *catalyst*: the inciting figure, the arrival of a new spur to action, a newly complicating element, an addition of some kind, usually in the form of an outside figure. If, as has been claimed, a miracle starts a new kephalaion, the arrangement of these segments suggests that the key element is the provocation offered by a figure entering the narration rather than the miracle itself, which is often severed from its scenic placement and whose successful conclusion may not even merit the emphasis of a chapter ending.[35] Efforts to understand these units as rounded wholes, with thematic through lines, are ingenious but strained. There is of course always a way to read one of Alexandrinus's ragged units as a cleverly masked totality—hermeneutic practices invested in coherence tend to be highly resourceful—but the units themselves, with their pronounced orientation to how they begin and relative neglect of how actions conclude, seem indifferent to well-wrought concords between beginnings and ends. As episodic brackets, to use Goffman's terminology, they demonstrate the tendency of the opening bracket to be a stronger signal.[36] Put simply: the kephalaia are not unities but instead *incitations*: editorial markings for the moment when a new element enters the text. They are signals to a reader's memory, insertions or bookmarks that denote the collision of an ongoing stream and the descent of a new catalyst. These are not shapely segments but *notabilia*, orientation points, mnemonic hooks. They record the dropping of the stone into the water but are vague as to the extent to which the ensuing ripples need to be traced—instead, they tend to wait for a new stone.

A record of moments in which the even continuity of events is punctuated by an entrance, a hailing of some kind: is this a reflection, however unwitting, of Christian time, even if a strangely inverted one in which the entrances are those of often nameless individuals in need of healing, and the continuity belongs to Jesus, the being whose time it is that is ruptured? Such a guess will seem far-fetched only to the extent that chaptering seems too innocuous, too workmanlike or technical, to merit any attention. At the very least, by decisively moving away from a method that prioritized episodic wholeness, Alexandrinus's kephalaia might come closer to matching some of the ironies of Christian soteriology. Of course, one further irony is that even in doing so, those who developed Alexandrinus's system might not have possessed an intent that matched the result of their performance. In grappling with the local peculiarities of Gospel narration, and attempting to divide the text into units that might be useful for readers of both the consultative and continuous varieties, these unknown scribes may have found themselves sidestepping proairesis almost by accident, and in the process opening up possibilities for understanding narrative segmentation—as a series of orientation points and incitations rather than unities of action—that were not initially obvious. That may have been Alexandrinus's own incitation.

The Langton–Saint Albans Abstractions

Different places, different times, different divisions: the Eusebian canons have had a long life, and Alexandrinus had its own more limited Byzantine influence, but the history of biblical segmentation within the Christian world is for centuries a welter of competing methods. The most authoritative history of the capitulary list of the Latin Vulgate, published in 1914 by the Benedictine scholar Donatien de Bruyne, counts eighteen different list traditions for Mark alone, which divide the text into as few as thirteen and as many as ninety-six different units.[37] With the increasing importance of citation in the labor performed with and on Scripture, the proliferation of local systems was fated to end in some consensus; and so it did, in the first decades of the thirteenth century, when the chapters still in modern use were first developed.[38] The place of their invention and the identity of their inventor—if they had only one—are not settled matters. That debate has significance as far as how we understand why these chapters were fashioned the way they were. The chapters Bibles currently possess are compromise formations, but the exact nature of that compromise is opaque, and if we knew more about the exact situation in which that compromise was first achieved we would have a better sense of the form it took. Unlike the cases of Vaticanus or Alexandrinus, then, we can weigh details of milieu and even personality, institutional histories and individual predilections. But just as with those early codices, the new system also bears all the traces of its peculiarity on its surface, however used readers have grown to them, and an approach to them as literary forms as well as historical artifacts is necessary to understand their subsequent influence.

So I begin with time and place; those frames will, as it happens, have a role to play in the texture of the chaptering system that would quickly become standard. It is Paris in the first two decades of the thirteenth century that is usually cited as the birthplace of the modern biblical chapter. At the very least, Paris is where that system was widely disseminated and where it made its claim to universality. What seems to have spurred the new system's growth to dominance was the formation of a distinctively medieval conurbation, the university. The young and gradually incorporating university in Paris inherited capitulation as an intellectual exercise from previous centers like Caesarea and Vivarium, but the needs that chapters were asked to satisfy were different, and were likely dictated by the classroom milieu and the particular population it served. As the center of western European education for at least a century already, Paris attracted a cosmopolitan body of students and masters whose cultural and political allegiances lay for the most part well outside the Île-de-France.[39] They found themselves in an environment where the *lectura* (the oral commentary upon a set text) and the *reportatio* (the written transmission of the master's oral teaching) were the preeminent techniques of instruction.[40] A master could be expected to make frequent textual references at a speed and density that necessitated the student's rapid consultation of a shared text. It was a milieu where the accurate and searchable citation was paramount.[41] Particularly in the matter of Scripture, this state of affairs created a conflict: between an international population who were familiar with different versions of the text that contained varying reference systems and a pedagogical situa-tion that increasingly necessitated standardization.[42] At least by the 1190s this was a dilemma acknowledged by the institution's authorities.[43]

Unlike the situation in Eusebius's Caesarea, the eventual solution was to some extent extramural. The stationers of Paris, through the *pecia* system by which authorized portions of scriptural texts were loaned to copyists for pro-duction in installments, began to confect a type of pandect Bible that, if not directly bearing the imprimatur of the university, filled its need for a relatively affordable and standardized school text.[44] The transmission from university authorities would have been informal and indirect, and the copies themselves were not uniform in every respect, nor were they for the exclusive use of the classroom; this was an initiative of collective private enterprise rather than an institutional product of either school or Church, and as such bore the marks of its somewhat haphazard development.[45] But the "Paris Bible," as it came to be known, had characteristics nonetheless that distinguished it from the produc-tions of the twelfth century and earlier and that indicate a fit for the exigencies of the Parisian academy. As objects, these Bibles were pedestrian, streamlined, shorn of most of the paratextual accumulations of previous centuries. Gone were capitula lists, the Latin offspring of elements like Alexandrinus's list of titloi; gone were the Eusebian canons.[46] In some ways this made the text *less* searchable, at least for certain uses, such as synoptic comparisons. In its rela-tively plain two-column format, however, one element stood out: chapter numeration. The example provided in figure 1.1a is typical: red and blue Roman numerals, inserted into the line space left at the end of the previous chapter, along with colored initial letters, are easily visible marks set within a page design that is otherwise uncluttered by marginal notations. Given the usual size of letterforms in these texts and the length of the newly devised chapters they include, most pages will have at least one such mark. The eye is oriented, that is, to chapter breaks—to the suture points between units. No other articulation of the text, save the beginnings of individual biblical books, is allowed to compete with this primary reading frame. In its own way, the Paris Bible was, starkly and programmatically, a chapter book.

Why foreground chapter breaks and their numbers in this way? The interest was not philological; the new chapter system that the Paris Bible contained did not spur a revision to the Vulgate text.[47] What seems to have been the interest was the creation of a text that was easier to navigate than previous versions by virtue of a single and easily visible method of division and numera-tion. Shorn of accompanying headings, its numbered units appeared as neutral marks for citational purposes and for easy location within longer texts—as well as a neutral grid for interpretive work, as the units were not already equipped with guiding rubrics. The chapter was a tool, but also, possibly, a puzzle, a relation to the whole that could be worked out in different ways. The retrieval system of the new chapters was in this way flexible, adaptable for university use as well as for the extramural uses, like the preaching of mendicant orders, in which highly trained literacy was enacted in public. They facilitated browsing or other kinds of consultative reference but presumed nothing about the uses to which such a reading might be put. Seen from the perspective of Alexandrinus's intriguingly sophisticated and integrated modes of segmentation, the Paris Bible seems like a simplification. It would be better to say that it was a *rationalization*, something like the invention of the metric system. It put into place a deliberately flexible and clearly arbitrary system of reference and division that was intended, in its nontendentious simplicity, to become the common apparatus. In this sense it succeeded wildly. Its page design and manner of indicating chapters survived the remediation into print—when captured by Gutenberg, it would become something like a scriptural standard—and its chaptering system exists still.[48]

What was newest about this Bible, its chapters, was the very thing it foregrounded by erasing other kinds of segmentation. If the Paris Bible was a collective enterprise, however, the chapter system it highlighted likely had a more specific, possibly even individual origin. Here two possibilities emerge, each pointing to a slightly different rationale for the shape of these chapters, and each picking up on something that these intriguingly flexible units could be said to do. The most widespread such account is the one that is most personalized: that this chapter system was the work of Stephen Langton, the English lecturer on theology who, until his elevation to cardinal in 1206 and eventual election as archbishop of Canterbury, had been a major figure in Paris as part of the circle around Peter the Chanter. Langton is an intriguing figure to single out from the Paris masters; a prolific commentator who would go on to play a significant and complex role in the English struggle between baronial, papal, and royal power during the years that surrounded the signing of Magna Carta, he was both a speculative theologian and a capable public figure, an academic, that is, with a serious interest in institutional and even more narrowly pedagogical questions.[49] And as the account has it, before his removal from Paris, in the early years of the century, he joined theory and practice by developing a more satisfactory chaptering system for use in the classroom.[50]

Capitulations, however, do not usually have a signature. In the case of Langton, the attribution rests largely on circumstance—his having the right profile, at the right time and place, to have tried his hand at solving the logjam of competing biblical reference systems—and on scattered and tenuous references. There are some lists of rubrics or chapter *incipits* that cite Langton, dating from shortly after his death in Paris.[51] The first explicit attribution of the entire chapter system to Langton is an early fourteenth-century reference, from the English annalist Nicholas Trevet, who noted in his entry for 1228: "Stephen, archbishop of Canterbury died. He commented upon the whole Bible and divided it into the chapters [*capitula*] which we moderns use."[52] This is somewhat slender, dating as it does from a century after Langton's death; but it does connect the work of Langton's commentaries to his supposed capitulation. Those commentaries, as several scholars have noted, were not indifferent to the question of textual division. Notoriously, Langton cited Jerome on the need to divide the text "by *portions,* that is by chapters [*per membra* id est per capitula], which are necessary for finding what you want and for remembering. Here you have authority for chapter division."[53] If we take this combination of circumstantial evidence and a slightly later tradition of attribution as dispositive, we have the following narrative: a creative and practical-minded English churchman, steeped in the chaotic environment of a cosmopolitan academy, takes on the chaptering of the Bible in order to provide a universal system of reference appropriate for classroom use and citational use more broadly. The inciting milieu is academic; the purpose is pedagogical. A neutral reference structure is the goal.

Although well enshrined, the Langton story has its skeptics, who offer a different narrative. One alternative hinges on the discovery by Paul Saenger of a late twelfth-century Bible, produced at the royal abbey of Saint Albans in Hertfordshire around 1180, that contains modern chapter numeration.[54] Saenger's comparative study of several other codices from the same period, many of them also produced at Saint Albans, suggested that the modern chapter system developed earlier than previously supposed by some two decades, and in a wholly different locale: an English monastic setting, not a Parisian scholastic one. It also suggested an alternative rationale. Saenger's chief instance, held at Corpus Christi College, Cambridge, contains an expertly calligraphed Hebrew alphabet, the only such example in a twelfth-century Latin Bible, suggesting that a Jewish scribe may have been employed at the abbey.[55] Further details of numeration, style, and page design from Saint Albans Bibles indicate familiarity with Jewish practice. Saint Albans seems to have had rabbinical contacts of a kind unusual for the time; the local schoolmaster Alexander Neckham was a noted Hebraist, and the abbey was a center for the period's interactions between Jewish and Christian scholars. If Jewish learning was available to the Saint Albans community, and the modern chapter system was gradually developed there, the reason for the latter may be tied to the former. As Saenger argues, this is indeed the case, because the modern chapter divisions of the Pentateuch bear a close resemblance to the Palestinian *sedarim*, the system of divisions developed from the third century BCE that shaped a triennial reading cycle of the Torah.[56] The Saint Albans scholars, that is, might have derived from Jewish practice a general shape or length of biblical division, adhering closely to it in the shared scriptural tradition and then adapting it to the specifically Christian texts of the New Testament, for a similar reason: to organize a ritualized cycle of scriptural *lectura continua*.[57] Such a theory would explain a key difference the new chapters offered to previous Vulgate versions: their length and relative homogeneity. In this version of the story, the inciting milieu behind the modern biblical chapters is monastic, and the purpose is liturgical. The goal is not reference or citation, but communal reading tied to a ritualized calendar.

These distinct historical narratives have competing kinds of allure. The first appeals to individual creativity spurred by an academic environment; it asks us to imagine the pressures of a scholarly milieu spilling out, thanks to a personal innovation, into a far-reaching impact. Like many such individualized accounts, it might also have a sectarian interest, particularly to a later Protestant and British historiography eager to claim Langton as its own.[58] The second narrative appeals to an ideal of cross-cultural contact and ferment, a more gradualist and communal account of reuse and adaptation. These narratives center on different reading imaginaries: one scholastic and consultative, the other monastic and performative. If we call the system, for the sake of compromise, the Langton–Saint Albans model, it is clear that it owes its eventual triumph to the first of these functions, thanks to the energy of the Parisian stationers and the spread of their Bibles. But the system's original intent may have been otherwise. The question of intent will help shape a study of the Langton–Saint Albans chapters' *design*; however, it cannot fully account for their *effect*, because their ultimate fate was to shape a reading environment far from either Paris or Hertfordshire, the classroom or the chapel: private continuous reading of narrative texts.

One other way to consider intent is to reverse engineer these chapters from an abstract consideration of their shape. The first obvious fact is their unmooring from headings. In the history of capitulation this prioritizing of the unit over the heading is peculiar and eventually decisive. Dispensing with the norms of the capitula list, the Paris Bible broke with a tradition in which the chapter had a *topical* basis that could be summarized. Those topoi could be treated in playful or ironized ways, as in the *Attic Nights* or the *Discourses*; they could become attuned primarily to narrative sequence, as in Alexandrinus's Gospel titloi, by highlighting incidental figures or particular speech acts; regardless, they were broadly conceptual and summarizable, and in fact came presummarized. The Bibles that spread from Saint Albans or Paris no longer offered chapters that were this capable of being encapsulated. One possible result is to drain the chapter of any pretense toward topical organization; chapters would then figure merely as reference marks, as indifferent and regular as milestones. The other possibility is that they produce a hermeneutic puzzle: What makes this chapter a chapter? Langton was no stranger to this kind of contextual reading. One of his classroom lectures, discussing Matthew 18:15 ("If your brother or sister sins, go and point out their fault, just between the two of you"), takes up the question of whether it is a universal injunction, and answers by asserting that "this chapter is inserted between a chapter on scandal and a chapter on forgiving injuries; and as the chapters on either side [*extrema*] are addressed to all, this is also."[59] Langton is here using some earlier system of "chapters"—all the sections he addresses here fall into Matthew 18— but he is nonetheless considering placement as a clue to an overall tendency or purpose. A chapter without a heading might invite such an interpretive maneuver, by its very silence inviting a reader's reconstruction of its overall topos. It was not an uncommon move; the Dominican Hugh of Saint Cher, master of theology in Paris two decades after Langton's departure, often returns in his *Postilla* or Bible commentary to summaries of a chapter's contents and coherent effect—using, of course, the modern chapters.[60] Yet a chapter shorn of the heading might also present an even more peculiar neutrality—a tacit distance from its own material, like the respectful detachment of the yardstick from the fabric being measured.

The other significant aspect of the Langton–Saint Albans chapters, both less immediately apparent and yet more crucial still, is their size. They differ from the tradition in two drastic ways: they are far longer, and their length is far more homogenous. Table 3.1 shows chapter frequencies from some major codices and widespread chaptering systems and reveals a stark truth: from Caesarea to thirteenth-century western Europe, biblical chapters grew in size and declined in number. A certain looseness in regard to textual material

TABLE 3.1 Sample chapter frequencies in the Gospels, 3rd–13th centuries

	Matthew	Mark	Luke	John
Eusebian/Ammonian units (3rd–4th century)	355	236	342	232
Codex Vaticanus (Codex B) numbered units (mid-4th century)	170	62	152	80
Codex Alexandrinus (Codex A) *kephalaia majora* (late 4th–early 5th century)	68	48	83	18
Codex Amiatinus (Vulgate A) *capitula* (ca. 700)	88	46	94	45
Book of Durrow (ca. 650–700) and Book of Kells *capitula* (ca. 800)[1]	76	46	79	36
Langton–St. Albans or "modern" chapters (ca. 1180–1230)	28	16	24	21

Sources: de Bruyne, *Summaries, Divisions, and Rubrics*, 421; Scrivener, *Criticism of the New Testament*, 68.
Note: 1 Both codices are examples of a widespread capitulary system, categorized by the siglum I in de Bruyne. For a fuller description of this category, which spans from the 7th to the 10th centuries in diffusion, see Houghton ("Chapter Divisions," 340–43).

develops—more and more material can be packed into a textual unit—while a counterbalancing regularity of the unit size emerges. If a spatial metaphor is necessary, we might think of these chapters as undergoing something like *containerization*: the size of the package is no longer tailored to its contents with as much individual sensitivity, but the container has become much larger and much more capable of holding anything, in fact many different things. The increased uniformity of the modern chapters has been acknowledged ever since modern scholarship settled on Langton as their creator; Paulin Martin noted it at the end of the nineteenth century as one of the system's defining features.[61] This fact accords with either Langton's Parisian origination or the Saint Albans hypothesis. Uniform size, or equal spacing, could speak to an almost quantitative objectivity that a system devised for citational purposes alone would strive to attain, but it might just as easily be ascribed to an outside constant that dictates its uniformity, like the vaguely appropriate duration of a public recitation, suggesting the monastic rationale. The chapters' increased size, however, is rather more mysterious. A longer unit, or so it would seem, is actually less suitable for citational use. The modern chapters would in fact be quickly equipped with the so-called Dominican subdivisions indicated by the marginal letters A–D or A–G, devised by Hugh of Saint Cher to facilitate more precise forms of discontinuous access, to be followed centuries later by verse numeration.[62] Greater length might permit liturgical or recitational uses, but the gradual shift to the modern chapter—a continual, if in its details erratic, process of steady expansion in size—suggests that a thirteenth-century liturgical use alone was not the driver of the change. The chapter form was already inexorably swelling, and the possible impulse of the Saint Albans scribes toward imitating Jewish lectionary practice would only have clinched a much longer and more diffuse trend.

The idea that compels the expansion of the chapter—the element that is more and more palpable as it grows larger—is abstraction, particularly abstraction from the narrative motors of intent, action, and result. The chapter breaks of earlier systems, which often hinge on the onset of action or, as in the case of Alexandrinus, the incitement of speech, were now buried within longer units; and the new transition points seemed more weakly derived from the text, incited in more oblique ways and slightly out of step with the main narrative or theological interest. If this was a rhythm, it was oddly syncopated, and slower, more spacious, as if beats were being withheld. If it offered topoi of any kind, it would often be difficult to say what they were. No rubrics existed to help, and their disappearance might have seemed intentional, as if the new units were incapable of being encapsulated. To borrow a metaphor that Laurence Sterne would much later explore: it is as if one were forced to walk up a staircase that included two sets of steps placed at irregular intervals to each other, alternating between them with each stride.

We can better understand this new experience of abstraction by returning to the interweaving of the stories of Jairus and the bleeding woman. The Langton–Saint Albans chapters produce a solution that is completely unlike any previous model: they resolve the question of how chapters can handle embedded narrative by simply absorbing both frame and inset stories into a larger and peculiarly heterogeneous unit. It is a vivid, capsule version of the general tendency of these units to shift away, by enlarging, from the level at which the incitations of action and intent can drive narrative division. Alexandrinus divided this combined narrative into two; other systems (the Eusebian units, Vaticanus, the Alcuinic system of Codex Amiatinus) combined it into one moment. What all three share is the sense of a distinct gap that opens at either Mark 5:21 or 5:22, where the crowd that gathers by the lake awaiting Jesus opens to allow Jairus to speak his request. The rhythmic beat of this moment in Mark is so strong that, of fifteen different systems studied by de Bruyne, eleven place a division at 5:21, a strong majority of opinion and practice rare in the history of Mark's text.[63] Here, however, the thirteenth-century system looks elsewhere. It adjoins to the Jairus-and-*haimorrousē* narrative the previous visit to the country of the Gerasenes, and the casting of the impure spirits of the Gerasene demoniac into a herd of swine; Mark 5, as it happens, will become a container for three miracle stories, one of which happens to occur within an interval of another. They are unlike in kind: an exorcism, a raising from the dead, a healing of an affliction. The onset of each is situationally distinct: the spirits inside the demoniac react in fear to Jesus's appearance and ask to be spared; Jairus falls to Jesus's feet and beseeches him for help; the bleeding woman attempts to covertly secure the aid she is too afraid to ask for directly. Nor are these three actions part of a continuous or linked episode. They occur in different locations, the first in Gerasa and the next two back on other side of the Sea of Galilee—at Capernaum, if the version of the interwoven stories in Matthew is to be taken as authoritative. An uneventful journey by boat separates the two, a journey that, at 5:21, is the "strong beat" identified by so many previous systems, the crossing that signals a decisive change of scene. Indeed, it could be said that the Gerasene exorcism, and the perilous travel in a storm there that starts at 4:35, is itself an inset episode within an ongoing performance of miracles in Capernaum. What the Langton–Saint Albans divisions give us is a segment that is something closer to an loose anthology rather than any thematic or narrative unity.

What does motivate, at least at a lexical level, this particular chaptering? The first place to look would be the opening formulae of Mark 5 and 6 in English and the Vulgate of this system's initial use:

"They went across the lake to the region of the Gerasenes [Et venerunt trans fretum maris in regionem Gerasenorum]" (Mk 5:1)
"Jesus left there and went to his hometown, accompanied by his disciples [Et egressus inde, abiit in patriam suam: et sequebantur illum discipuli sui]" (Mk 6:1)

These are both departures, decisive changes of location. It is possible to say that one form of abstraction the thirteenth-century chapters take is spatial, or geographical, with particular attention to short tags that establish a named or otherwise precise space. The journey to the Gerasenes actually begins on 4:35—in which Jesus commands the waves to be calmed, another strong beat in the list of older divisional systems—but the exact name of their destination is not present until 5:1. The Langton–Saint Albans system, it could be said, seems to prefer the naming of location as a signal rather than the starting of the action that leads to that location. This is the chapter division as map.

Yet there is another element operating here, one that is not quite visible from within Mark 5. The journey to the Gerasenes that starts at 4:35 occurs, Mark tells us, "that day [*in illa die* in the Vulgate; *in ekeinē tē hēmera* in the original] when evening came." The demonstrative pronoun here is intriguing. Its deixis indicates that the series of parables told in Mark 4, which starts "Again Jesus began to teach by the lake," happens on the same day as the departure for Gerasa—that Mark 4, in other words, is the record of a single day's action. As for Mark 6, it begins with a Sabbath scene: the teaching in the synagogue, which leaves the Nazarene congregation unimpressed. What if the three healings in Mark 5 are collected not for any particular thematic, conceptual, or narrative unity but because they are bracketed by identifiable *days*? If, that is, the person or persons who developed the new system looked for that particular unity as one guide to an appropriate unit, and when those were found—as in Mark 4 and 6—whatever fell between them could be gathered into a chapter that was more of a miscellany, a blurred collection of events between two distinct diurnal shapes? As we might say: I know what I did last Tuesday, and I can tell you what I did on Saturday, but between that, a few different things come to mind. The day is a familiar mnemonic frame, while for those details that have slipped out of that frame there is a looser mode of recollection, which might take the form of a string of similar actions. Between two distinct days, three miracles.

If this seems hard to credit, it is likely because such an organizational principle manages to insult two competing, and seemingly primary, criteria for narrative segmentation: the topical and the scenic. The day is not a concept in a strong sense, not necessarily linked to any of the topoi—transgression, forgiveness, consummation—that even Alexandrinus's highly concrete titloi addressed on occasion. With the exception of its use in a prophetic sense (Mk 13:32: "about that day or hour, no one knows, not even the angels in heaven, nor the Son, but only the Father"), the day is conceptually inert or empty, merely an aspect, or so it seems, of narrative background, a realist notation amid the "conciseness" of Gospel narration, in which events are generally of a much shorter duration than one day.[64] Similarly, it is not exactly a narrative unit, neither a "scene" nor an event, although it can encapsulate several of either. In narrative terms it is an exceptionally weak boundary. If previous chaptering systems treated the Gospels as a series of actions or scenic moments, the diurnal unit acts differently.[65] It hovers above, or around, any framing that takes human intent or performance as primary. Nor does Gospel narration usually insist on the diurnal frame in any overt way; it doesn't shout "how much occurred on this one day, how extraordinary it was!" Where a day is mentioned, it is done through the subtle deixis that is the Gospel writers' usual method. To pay attention to such syntactic niceties, and such a barely visible frame, seems like a curiously inconsequent reading, both narrowly attentive and yet disengaged.

The Langton–Saint Albans chapters are, of course, trickier, or more eclectic, than this example might indicate. As a compromise between size and sense, they are more opportunistic than formally consistent, and they do often coincide with earlier divisions. Of the eighty-nine modern chapters in the Gospels, thirty-nine of them start in the same place as a kephalaion in Alexandrinus, including a surprising half of the modern chapters in Matthew. There are several thematic or scenic unities among these chapters. As mentioned before, the Mission Discourse, largely in line with Alexandrinus, is a single chapter, Matthew 10. Matthew 3 is an elegantly shaped small unit, starting with a character portrait of John the Baptist and a pseudo-iterative quotation of his denunciation of the Pharisees and Sadducees that ends with a prophecy of his successor, and moving to the scene proper of the chapter, the baptism of Jesus. Luke 2 is something like an even further condensed novella of youth, combining the stories of Jesus's birth, presentation in the Temple, and lingering in the Temple at the age of twelve into an epoch of life—material that in Alexandrinus is divided among four *kepahalaia*. Yet these unities, which are themselves of different kinds—a speech act, a pivotal scene and its background, a quasi-montage of several years—are comparatively rare. What tends to motivate chapter transitions in the Langton–Saint Albans version is some attention to time or place, and particularly a discourse around the frame of the day.

Often this framing is explicit from a chapter's initial phrase, which situates the chapter's event as transpiring on a particular day set within a sequence of days, and thereby tacitly insisting upon a human calendar that the events of that day will presumably mark and possibly transcend:

That same day Jesus went out of the house and sat by the lake (Mt 13:1)

A few days later, when Jesus again entered Capernaum, the people heard that he had come home (Mk 2:1)

Now the Passover and the Festival of Unleavened Bread were only two days away (Mk 14:1)

Very early in the morning, the chief priests, with the elders, the teachers of the law and the whole Sanhedrin, made their plans (Mk 15:1)

One day Jesus was praying in a certain place (Lk 11:1)

One day as Jesus was teaching the people in the temple courts and proclaiming the good news (Lk 20:1)

On the third day a wedding took place at Cana in Galilee (Jn 2:1)

It should be noted that this tendency is not limited to events characterized by the particular day named, as with a Sabbath day or Passover; it is equally likely to occur in relation to blander, unmarked days, where the invocation of the diurnal frame is inessential—*chronos*, one might say, rather than *kairos*. Location is the other major frame, and the phrasing of the opening statement can at times combine departure and arrival into one act of threshold crossing that produces a temporal echo out of the sound made by a geographical name:

Jesus then left that place and went into the region of Judea and across the Jordan (Mk 10:1)

As they approached Jerusalem and came to Bethphage and Bethany at the Mount of Olives (Mk 11:1)

When Jesus had finished saying all this to the people who were listening, he entered Capernaum (Lk 7:1)

Jesus entered Jericho and was passing through (Lk 19:1)

but Jesus went to the Mount of Olives (Jn 8:1)

The last of these notoriously places the chapter break in the middle of a sentence; while an embarrassment that has often been refused or critiqued, it is simply an extreme version of the modern system's technique.[66] It places a strong beat at the moment that the narrative departs from the Pharisees and shifts back to Jesus, a threshold moment in John's shuttling between Jesus and those discussing him that is both spatial and temporal. When both diurnal and spatial frames coincide, the resulting signal is too strong for the Langton–Saint Albans chapters to resist:

One day as Jesus was standing by the Lake of Gennesaret, the people were crowding around him and listening to the word of God (Lk 5:1)

The syntax here is particularly appropriate for an opening to one of the modern chapters in the way it depicts an ongoing situation about to be pierced by the specificity of an action. Yet whereas other systems could often prefer the immediate onset of action in speech, this tends when possible to look for a time-and-place bracketing. Where that is not indicated by the invocation of a particular day or named location, the Langton chapters gravitate toward the different modes of temporal deixis preferred by each Gospel writer, such as Matthew's "at that time" (either *en ekeinē tē hōra* or *en ekeinō tō kairō*) or John's terser "after this" (*meta tauta*).

The insistence upon temporal-locative framings could not, given the texture of Gospel narrative, be the system's exclusive method. Speech, particularly that of Jesus, opens many chapters, often unavoidably so, as in the long monologues of John. It even occurs at places where presumably capitulation might have easily been carried out differently. The opening of Mark 9 is particularly famous for its eccentricity: here the chapter begins with the final words of Jesus from the previous chapter's discourse ("Truly I tell you, some who are standing here will not taste death before they see that the kingdom of God has come with power"), turning then to a seemingly far more appropriate chapter opening, that of the Transfiguration episode's beginning: "After six days Jesus took Peter, James and John with him and led them up a high mountain, where they were all alone" (Mk 9:2). As if in a strange switch of practices, both Vaticanus and Alexandrinus begin their units at 9:2, preferring to go with scene setting rather than speech, while the modern chapters elect, even when it would not necessarily be called for by the narrative rhythm, to start with speech rather than scene setting.[67] One interpretive move to justify this odd modern chaptering would be to see the Transfiguration as fulfilling the prophecy with which the chapter begins, explaining the unit's peculiarity as a canny linkage of word and fulfillment that the Greek pandects, more conservative here, do not attempt.[68] It can also be thought of as a formally daring gesture, a way of detaching word and scene in the mode of what film editors call an "L cut," where audio from a previous shot persists into the next shot. Yet, given the modern system's usual preferences, this departure can seem more like an accident than a proto-modern experiment, a peculiar oversight in the midst of a complicated and necessarily imperfect task. Regardless, Mark 9 is an excellent example of the widely divergent—and possibly inadvertent—effects possible with capitulation, even when two different divisional systems are placed only one sentence apart.

There are many oddities in the Langton–Saint Albans model, as well as many familiarities. Yet the question finally is of its overall effect: the shift in narrative perception afforded by its newly capacious size and its consequent partial disengagement from action. As a system it had and has a peculiar, if accidental, gestalt: impersonal abstraction. These chapters are syntheses, attempts to bring discrete actions under the umbrella of a category—a time, a place—that is outside or beyond personal agency. They seem to *situate* actions more than they are incited by them; they tend to stand a bit apart from action, regarding it as it from an external perspective. Geographical thinking, ephemeral or diurnal thinking: these are conceptual frames that, by placing events into categories independent of the intent or will of those events' participants, invent a new perspective, that of the distant, retrospective whole. As in: the things that happened that day; the things that happened in that place. It is a standpoint that is slightly aloof, almost a structural irony, invoking as it does the view from above, the realm of the Author, the Narrator, the Arranger.

Thanks in large part to the influence and industry of the Parisian stationers, the Langton–Saint Albans chapters were adopted, and naturalized as the inevitable inhabitant of Christian Bibles, with remarkable speed. So thorough was their triumph that by the late fifteenth century they had even been introduced into Hebrew Bibles, closing the circle of influence that may have begun with rabbinical contact in Hertfordshire in the late twelfth century.[69] If the Franciscan Nicholas of Lyre inveighed in the early fourteenth century against chapters and associated finding aids—"they have chopped up the text into so many small parts, and brought forth so many concordant passages to suit their own purpose, that to some degree they confuse both the mind and memory of the reader and distract it from understanding the literal meaning of the text"—his lament was too belated to matter.[70] Yet the work of Langton or the Saint Albans scribes had a double fate, more complex than the longevity, up until the current day, of their presence within Bibles. It is of course remarkable enough that as citational or liturgical units they continue to serve the purpose for which they were designed, eight centuries on. Yet their durability within Bibles as a *system* has obscured their importance as a *style*—as a practice of muted abstraction that, diffused beyond Scripture and into other narrative genres, has lasted just as long.

4

How Fifteenth-Century Remediators Did Their Work (the Cut, the Fade)

THE BURGUNDIAN CHRÉTIEN DE TROYES—CAXTON'S MALORY

UP TO THE LATE medieval period, one thing above all is true of the chapter: if it could occasion technical critiques, or judgments according to varying criteria of utility, it did not then inspire anything like an aesthetic appreciation. The possible felicities of the chapter, the way a particular break might awaken an innocuous moment into some kind of surprised life, is not yet a thought attached to the editorial labor of capitulation. Not so with William Caxton's 1485 printing of Thomas Malory's *Morte d'Arthur*, however, which despite a legacy of critique attached to its arrangement may be one of the earliest examples of chaptering to have occasioned a connoisseur's delight. Even if the *Morte*'s chapters can resemble biblical methods of narrative division, they offer a subtly altered visual grammar and a distinctively abrupt rhythmic patterning—the sheen of having been polished by a printer's eye and the pleasing jar of having been arranged by a composer's ear. The *Morte* does not simply represent a technological leap into the chapter's machine age; it reveals how the capitulator's editorial task became an arranger's art through an occasionally brazen, and just as often subtle, use of the "cut."

Caxton's edition of the *Morte* contains 507 chapters, and their styles of opening and closing are many. But one particular silence can ground us in the new landscape of the aestheticized chapter break. In the middle of book 6, Launcelot remains trapped, if willingly, by his pursuit of Arthur's wife

Guinevere; it is a dilemma whose various solutions he refuses to entertain, preferring instead to simply keep moving on. As the tenth chapter of the book proceeds he comes to a bridge, one of the countless threshold points that he can never stop himself from traversing. He is there challenged by a "foul churl" for crossing the bridge without a license; having slain the churl for his presumption, he enters a village whose inhabitants upbraid him for having killed the porter of their castle. To this Launcelot pays little heed, and rides on still:

> Sur Launcelot let them say what they would, and straight he went into the castle; and when he came into the castle he alit, and tied his horse to a ring on the wall, and there he saw a fair green court, and thither he dressed him, for there him thought was a fair place to fight in. So he looked about, and saw much people in doors and windows that said, "Fair knight, thou art unhappy."[1]

Here the chapter ends, with that resonant cry of the castle's prisoners reaching Launcelot in an entrance court. It is a pause in a threshold space, as if literalizing the ancient chapter's self-understanding. Chapter 11 begins immediately after this, with the words "thou art unhappy" still hovering in the air: two giants arrive, Launcelot slays them both, and then frees sixty women who have been imprisoned there for seven years. Then he learns that he is in Tintagel Castle, the place of Arthur's conception. With an impenetrable remark—"I understand to whom this castle belongeth"—Launcelot departs, and the chapter continues with a new series of events (*MA*, 1:214).

This particular journey of Launcelot's occupies multiple chapters in book 6, but the break between chapters 10 and 11 is perhaps its signal stylistic event. In George Saintsbury's 1912 *History of English Prose Rhythm* it comes in for special praise as the "best of all" of several examples of Malory's rhythmic sense, his deft joining work by which dialogue and narrative sequence are braided, his "breaking and knitting again of the cadence-thread."[2] Too long as the passage is to quote sufficiently, Saintsbury laments, he nonetheless cannot resist quoting "thou art unhappy" as a brilliantly satisfying chapter ending, a rhythmic pause worth savoring. The dark warning, with its enigmatic lack of specificity as if addressing some larger mischance in his destiny, points to the specific bad luck facing him in the two giants, while resonating beyond that immediate danger. At the height of an action, a note is struck that resounds in the chapter interval while slowly receding into harmonic background once action resumes. Saintsbury's sense of its felicity is far less antique than many of his other judgments; it is easy to see what he admires. Unlike the bridge that takes Launcelot directionally across and forward, the chapter break here is a halt to look in some other direction, a fall into another temporality.[3]

Yet the trouble is that this is not exactly, or even primarily, Malory's effect at all. Not that Saintsbury could fully know it; it was not until 1934 that a version of Malory's text predating Caxton's printed edition was discovered in the library of Winchester College. In the so-called Winchester manuscript there is no chapter break here, as it did not possess any chapters; Caxton had, after all, boasted in the preface to his edition that the chapter divisions were his, and in assigning them to Malory, Saintsbury was ignoring Caxton's claim in favor of assuming an authorial control taken for granted in his era. The Winchester manuscript employs a large rubricated initial letter to mark the break, however, which Caxton likely used as his guide.[4] Yet Caxton has altered the sentence as well; in the manuscript it reads: "Fayre knyghte, thou art unhappy to com here!"[5] Caxton had, evidently, taken an effect in Malory and heightened it—by truncating the sentence to achieve a more oracular effect, and by replacing the manuscript's rubricated capital with the new white space of his book's page design. The felicity is actually a collaboration, where Caxton has been responsible for the effect's modernization: the rendering of a deliberate discontinuity in Malory's prose into an artful segmentation, a resonant silence, in the printed volume's visual patterning. The break amplifies the prose. What Saintsbury identified as an aesthetic effect of Malory's syntactical rhythm is in large part the result of Caxton's remediation.

"Thou art unhappy" is a useful example in a special and a general sense. It is a vivid instance of a new aesthetic of narrative chaptering that is particularly common within fifteenth-century remediations of Arthurian legends: a habit of momentary suspension in the middle of a continuous action. The interstitial space between chapters becomes a potential marker of stilled time— sometimes eerie, sometimes plangent, sometimes tense—and, as such, a way of rendering the intensity of presentness, its onset and falling away. This segmentation may look like some of the odder effects of biblical chaptering but is far more intent on exploring the chapter break as a dynamic marking, an elongated resonance held long enough to alert a reader to its suspension. Long enough, possibly, to produce a momentary discomfort, but as Saintsbury shows us, certain forms of discomfort can be relished. Yet this chapter ending is also an example of a general fact about chaptering in the fifteenth century: its peculiarly collaborative nature. Capitulation is no longer understood simply as an invasive procedure but instead as an act of translation, rendering a prior text by prying open its preexisting, if only incipient, transitions and accentuating those effects with a new medium's technical possibilities. It is a practice of tactful emphasis, the discerning application of an editorial hand to both cut and connect. And it centers in the second half of the fifteenth century, primarily in two locations and with two new media: in London, where Caxton gave Malory's *Morte* the articulation of print, and in Burgundy, where anonymous redactors rendered Chrétien de Troyes's legends into a modernized French prose.

Prose and the Atomic Present

For the most part, fifteenth-century remediators advertise their chaptering, but they tend to omit or amend the usual justifications. Caxton addresses the matter in his preface shortly before detailing the number of chapters in each book: "And for to understand briefly the content of this volume, I have divided it into twenty-one books, and every book chaptered as hereafter shall by God's grace follow" (*MA*, 1:6). The syntax here is ambiguous; it is not entirely clear whether the "brief understanding" Caxton references is that of the reader of the preface wanting to know how his book works, or the reader of the table of contents seeking a quick summary of the narrative. Philippe de Vigneulles, the draper and chronicler from Metz who produced an early sixteenth-century prose version of parts of the twelfth-century poetic cycle of Lorraine called the *Geste des Loherains*, simply nods to his having remade the older poem "in chaptered prose," as if chapters were a common consequence of prosification and needed no special justification aside from that pertaining to prose in general.[6] The anonymous fifteenth-century figures known as "prosateurs" of the Burgundian court under Philip the Good, who rewrote older epic verse in modernized prose *remaniements*, or remediations, saw no need to mention capitulation at all. The brief prefaces to their reworking of Chrétien de Troyes's *Cligès* and *Érec et Énide* both use the term "transpose" (*transmuer*) to describe their work.[7] Chaptering goes unmentioned, again as if it is simply an inevitable component of prose itself. Prose, that is, is understood as a practice of discontinuity.

The absence of citational or informational justifications for chaptering in these instances suggests that it is no longer primarily understood through the familiar duality of *quaerere/invenire*, or seeking/finding. When thirteenth-century compilers refer to capitulation, they still rely on those terms. Stephen of Bourbon's *Tractatus de diversis materiis praedicabilibus*, a handbook for preachers, is in this way firmly traditional: "We have divided the material of this book by titles [*titulos*], titles by chapters [*capitula*], and each chapter is in turn divided into seven parts [*partes*] indicated by the first seven letters of the alphabet, a, b, c, d, e, f, g, so that the reader can more quickly find that which they are searching for."[8] Vincent of Beauvais's enormous mid-thirteenth-century encyclopedia *Speculum maius* avoids the traditional vocabulary while making the same claim: "So that each of the parts of this work will appear more easily to the reader, I wanted to divide the whole work into books and chapters [ipsum totumopus per libros, & per capitula distinguere volui]."[9] Both the *Tractatus* and the *Speculum maius* are reference works rather than narrative works, but the fifteenth-century segmentation of Arthurian tales has been understood similarly, as a division into units that refer to particular virtues or vices, or that offer condensed and labeled episodes useful for consultative readers interested in particular moral dilemmas, as if the goal was to retrofit poetic narrative for informational uses.[10] Yet those rationales are not found in any of the places where editors or translators explain their work, and it seems as if seeking and finding have begun to vanish from both the explicit lexicon of capitulators and perhaps even their operational understanding of their task. That understanding is instead increasingly bound to prose—that is, to linear temporality and its rhythms.

These fifteenth-century texts understand prose and chapters as inseparable, because they are both modes of temporal expression. Chapters now *divide* more profoundly than they *index*; indeed the shift from *distinguere*, a function of intellectual abstraction, to "divide," a function of temporal rhythm, is subtle but crucial. It means the divisions produced will no longer be considered primarily as information design but as the articulation of a temporal process— often, indeed, as *interruptions* of that process. They will mark moments rather than topics. It is a new signifying practice for capitulation, even if it can appear indistinguishable from earlier versions; the erosion of the usual language of justification, and its replacement by terser and even somewhat confusing gestures ("to understand briefly the content of this volume"), can be taken as evidence of the tremors underneath what looks like surface stability. Prose is understood as linear, but jointed; not continuous, but rather stitched together out of pieces.[11] It is the chapter where the seams show. Chaptered prose is a synthesis of time's seeming flow with its capacity to be quantified and experienced as discrete units.

What is visible in fifteenth-century prose remediations is something like the *de-informationalizing* of the chapter, and its new use as a technique of the pause. Throughout these texts we can see an emphasis on blanks: the chapter hinge, the white space between units, the interstice. Something, that is, begins to happen *between* chapters, and the emphasis of the editor or prosateur is not so much to outline complete episodic units to the extent possible, but to locate moments where a rupture—a splintering of continuity—can, by stopping narrative time and prying it open, allow that minute but not quite impalpable segment of time to blossom in the blank space. Which is to say that what chaptering increasingly does in these texts is insert a feeling of presentness. There is a weight to these interstices that is lacking from even the most peculiarly interruptive Gospel chapters; they seem to be identifying an infinitesimal unit of time, so small that it can be taken to be nothing, and yet insisting on holding it in a way that it, too, can seem to possess duration or quality. "Thou art unhappy": the space between the words' sound and the onset of the threat of which they warn is empty, a void. For Caxton the page designer, it is a space of definite dimensions, a line or two of white on either side of a chapter numeral. That emptiness has a temporal intensity, however, that forces our attention to the span, however brief, of a moment's passing.

The notion of the duration of the present was, as it happens, a continuing dilemma during the centuries prior to the reworkings of Arthurian narrative that are my instances here. The classic formulation of the problem was Augustine's argument in book 11 of the *Confessions* that the present cannot be said to have any duration, and it is an argument that turns on the infinite divisibility of temporal units. Can the present have extension, be called "long," be given any quality at all? That would depend on finding a proper unit of measurement for it, against which it could be compared. When we turn to the conventional units of time, we find that they contain too much to be called properly "present": the present century, the present year, the present month, the present day, all comprise times past and times future. We cannot localize the present to them. This is true, naturally, of even smaller times:

> One hour is itself constituted of fugitive moments. Whatever part of it has flown away is past. What remains to it is future. If we can think of some bit of time which cannot be divided into even the smallest instantaneous moments, that alone is what we can call "present." And this time flies so quickly from future into past that it is an interval with no duration. If it has duration, it is divisible into past and future. But the present occupies no space [praesens autem nullum habit spatium].[12]

The present is therefore essentially unrepresentable—a blank without extension, incapable of being captured by any particular unit as there can be no base unit to confine it. A paradox then emerges. The present cannot be said to have any duration, yet it is the only time that can be said to properly have existence; duration belongs to registers of time—the past and the future—that have no existence. Much of the rest of book 11 turns on how this extensionless present is a negative image of God's eternity, a connection we could make if we could manage somehow to hold the present still long enough to give its absence of duration some durative quality.[13] Modes of attention then become Augustine's concern. It will in fact emerge that if time can be said to have any existence, it is as a property of mind extending itself between past and present through acts of focus. How the mind "extends" through focus is, as Paul Ricoeur judged it, Augustine's "supreme enigma," if a necessary one in order to resolve the crisis created by the impossibility of measuring the present.[14]

But a later and more demotic theory sidestepped the paradox of the Augustinian present by assigning to it a unit of measurement of the sort that Augustine denied could possibly define any sort of presentness. Augustine had written of "the smallest instantaneous moments" (*minutissimas momentorum*), and it is here that a broadly medieval conception of the present took shape. It is best captured in Bede's *The Reckoning of Time* (*De temporum ratione*), his attempt in 725 to standardize a calendrical system both for purposes of historical chronology and to enable the accurate calculation of the date of Easter. This involves Bede in assessments of temporal units along the full range of current usage, from ages or epochs (*saecula, aetates*) to moments—largely because, as Bede insists, "times [*tempora*] take their name from 'measure' [*temperamentum*]," whether according to conventional or natural categories.[15] These categories have a reality independent of the mind that Augustine's thorough skepticism had leveled.

For the purposes of Bede's calendrical computations, the day is the root unit. But it is divisible, Bede explains, into conventional units: twelve or twenty-four hours, four *puncti*, ten *minuta*, fifteen *partes*, and forty *momenta*. This has its confusions, depending upon whether the hour so divided is considered in its artificial or sundial sense (the day divided into twelve equal segments of sunlight, which would each expand in northern regions in the summer) or its equinoctial sense (one twenty-fourth of the day, where in the summer daylight would simply cover more hours). Each *momentum* would, judged by the latter as seems to be Bede's preference, cover ninety of our seconds. This cannot be the *minutissimas momentorum* of which Augustine speaks, however, and Bede does not stop there. "The smallest time of all," he explains, and one which cannot be divided by any reckoning, they call by the Greek word "atom," that is, "indivisible" or "that which cannot be cut." Because of its tiny size, it is more readily apparent to grammarians than to computists, for when they divide a verse into words, words into feet, feet into syllables, and syllables into quantities [*tempora*], and give double quantity to the long [foot] and single to the short, they are pleased to call this an *atomus*, as they had nothing more beyond this which they could divide.[16]

This is that bit of time which cannot be divided, whose existence Augustine had denied; rather than a dimensionless void it has some minimal and definite shape. If there is a present, it is here that it exists, in the "atom."

What does this atomic present feel like? In the process of acknowledging that ordinary language has adopted various usages for this unit, including the technically incorrect *momentum*, Bede illustrates its contours with a lovely image:

> The Apostle uses the term for this kind of time in a better sense, to suggest the swiftness of the Resurrection, stating, *We shall all rise, but we shall not all be changed, in a moment, in the twinkling of an eye, at the last trumpet.* This deserves our attention, because although computists make a strict distinction [between these terms], many writers indiscriminately call that tiniest interval of time in which the lids of our eyes move when a blow is launched [against them], and *which* cannot *be divided or distributed*, either a *momentum*, a *punctus*, or an atom.[17]

That "tiniest interval of time in which the lids of our eyes move when a blow is launched" is Bede's present: a twinkling of an eye, a coup d'oeil. Call it the interval between the eye's will to close, if we can speak of "will" here, and its closing. The present lives in the minimal space between perception and response. The atom is in this sense a gap or void, but unlike Augustine's dimensionless point, it possesses the smallest quantum of duration.

The disagreement between Augustine and Bede here predates the work of fifteenth-century remediators by a considerable historical distance, and cannot have influenced them in any direct way.[18] But there is a consequence to the debate that centers on how exactly these competing notions of the present are linked to linguistic or even textual formats. Augustine's interest in how attention could produce a simulacrum of temporal extension in the mind, a synthesis of passing moments into something like a present with a dimensionality, turned on the oral performance of verse. His pivotal example is the recitation of a psalm, in which however much time its repetition takes, the ability of the mind to hold the poem entire prior to and even during any such performance mimics the simultaneity of past, present, and future in God's eternity. The infinitely divisible and therefore nonexistent "present" of recitation, each syllable passing away to the next, can be felt to stretch (*distendere*) between memory and anticipation in order embrace a broader continuum; it is a palpable duration of the mind's own construction, one that is both premised on meter yet thereby able to transcend meter's divisibility. The reciter, put another way, sutures linguistic gaps—between lines, words, syllables—into a "stretched" whole.[19] "The same is true of a longer action in which perhaps that psalm is a part," Augustine remarks, with his characteristically allegorical reading of all temporal units; it is "also valid of the entire life of an individual person." Or, more simply: "my life is a distention" (ecce distentio est vita mea).[20]

Bede similarly uses verse as an example, but with a characteristically different emphasis. That grammarians call a short syllable an *atomus*, he explains, is a model for the temporal meaning of the term. As in time, so in language: the minimal unit exists.[21] What stands out in Bede is the absence of that transcendence, or at least moderation, of linearity that marks Augustine's description of the psalm reciter stretched in two ways between past and present. The atomic present seems premised instead on a punctuated continuity and directionality. Indeed, that continuity may be the best way to access the present: in the one-thing-and-then-another procession of language, we can attend to the minute elements of which that continuity is composed.[22]

If atomic time is best appreciated in conditions of continuity—if it is in an unmarked stream, oddly enough, that its constituent units stand out—then the continuous reading of prose will help access the atomic present better than the recitation of memorized verse. Indeed, it is in later medieval prose writers that an emphasis on the atomic present emerges most clearly, often in the context of meditations upon their own chosen medium. As Eleanor Johnson has argued, perhaps the clearest such example is *The Cloud of Unknowing*, the late fourteenth-century English devotional manual that connects its own prose to the atomic present of Bede. The *Cloud* author outlines a practice of minimal units, particularly monosyllabic prayer, which in its indivisibility most closely approaches the eternity of divine time. This would seem to be an Augustinian emphasis, but the *Cloud* author understands these moments of monadic presentness as emerging not out of an attentive synthesis of past, present, and future, some mental or inner duration, but instead out of pure continuity. God shows that time is precious, the book's argument runs, because he forbids simultaneity: "God, that is gever of tyme, geveth neuer two tymes togeder, bot ichone after other"—that is, in succession.[23] Seriality, not the transcendence of seriality, is our access to the divine. What does immersion in seriality give us access to? Again the answer is the atomic present, described in terms that would have been familiar to Bede. Contemplative prayer, the author insists, is the shortest work that can be imagined because it takes the time of an "atho-mus," the unit that "is the leest partie of tyme . . . so litil that, for the littilnes of it, it is undepartable and neighhonde incomprehensible"; indivisible and almost incomprehensible as it may be, this atomic present can nonetheless be described as the time of a single impulse of the will.[24] The sudden, even anguished utterance of a monosyllable, such as "help," "God," and "love," is the linguistic equivalent of such minimal time, and therefore much of the purpose of the *Cloud* is to recommend such utterances as the best form of prayer, an emphasis that has its effects on the *Cloud*'s own prose.[25] Indeed, prose itself comes to seem like an environment designed to foster such minimal units; it is a linearity that is visibly, because irregularly, punctuated. Human nature, the *Cloud* author insists, is "acordyng to o tyme only"—we live one impulse at a time, serially.[26] God has provided us with temporal seriality in order for those acts of will to be salient to us; salient in their indivisibility, salient in their irrecoverableness. They are, in multiple senses, precious.

The *Cloud* ties together several strands in its theory of time: presentness as tied to an atomic, indivisible duration; the necessary relation of that duration to a single act of our will; the salience of these acts in a punctuated continuity, which is best reflected by prose, with its seeming fluidity pried open by the minute gaps between words—as so often in the *Cloud*, between monosyllabic words. But the *Cloud* is not simply in prose; it is, of course, in chaptered prose, "disyngwid in seuenty chapitres & five," as the prologue has it, brief chapters often scarcely longer than a couple hundred words.[27] A table of chapter headings prefaces the work, although the headings are not repeated as intertitles, an arrangement that will later be taken up in Caxton's *Morte*. The table's headings are only elliptically topical, and they instead make frequent reference to the time they evoke, a time both of the chapter and of the prayer work they describe:

> The secound chapitre A schort stering to meeknes & to the werk of this book.

> The feerthe chapitre Of the schortnes of this werk, & how it may not be comen to by the corioustee of witte, ne by ymaginacion.

The six chapitre A schort conceyte of the werk of this book, tretid by questyon.[28]

The modifier "short" blurs the chapters' brief duration with the unity and instantaneity of a mind's movement toward God; both are brief, pointed, and set within an ongoing flow. Here with particular vividness we see the torque of the chapter away from an aid to consultation—the *Cloud*'s headings are more incantatory than informational—and toward a temporal self-consciousness: the chapter not only takes (brief) time, the "werk" of reading, but mimics the atomic time of the "werk" of contemplation and prayer. To the extent possible, the chapter is a frame for the elusive, minute, monadic present.

This highly abbreviated intellectual history is meant to suggest the ways in which prose, temporal divisibility, human will, and textual segmentation become tangled together in any consideration of how presentness could be felt or evoked. The relation between these elements can shift, and at times reverse course; Augustine's durationless void will remain relevant. But the lure of the atomic present gained in force from Bede's time to the fifteenth century, and the role of prose—and the almost inevitable accompaniment of prose, the chapter—in gaining access to this elusive now-time grew in prominence. Certainly the capitulators and prosateurs of the very late medieval period understood their work as accessing the places in the host text where the present could be evoked. They were not simply modernizing Arthurian legend, they were often giving it the immediacy of the *atom*. One of their chosen methods to do so, in an ironic echo of Augustinian time, was a new poetics of white space that ruptured narrative seriality with gaps or voids.

Burgundian Interruptions

That poetics had awkward, even maladroit beginnings, arising out of experiments performed on older texts. The most vivid such example is the group of anonymous writers who, at the Burgundian court of Philip the Good in the 1450s, produced prose versions of centuries-old romances and chansons de geste, including those of Chrétien de Troyes. They left little record of the principles or guidelines animating their work; if they comprised a studio or literary "laboratory," their purposes have to be inferred from the surviving results.[29] The work was simultaneously a quasi-translation and a quasi-remediation. These prose versions departed freely from the sense units of

Chrétien's octosyllabic couplets and significantly abridged his prolonged dialogues and interior monologues; narrative paths were streamlined, interactions truncated, and even, occasionally, new elements inserted, while his playful and complex prologues were simply cut. The *mises en prose* were not attempting to be faithful renderings so much as modernizations—a form of "intralingual translation," in Roman Jakobson's term—that attempted to make the originals readable in a new cultural context.[30] The liberties taken by these adaptations suggest the need to present the old epic stories in a fashion that reflected updated sensibilities and updated formats. These were courtly productions, often dedicated to their royal patron, and as such they can read as having an appropriative function, as if their task is to make the old chivalric tales Burgundian property reflecting Burgundian values. The prosateurs were functionaries of sorts, and the labor they performed was a curious mixture of the authorial and the editorial, in several respects without equivalent, if somewhat akin to the work of a screenwriter adapting a classic novel. They translated, rewrote, abridged, and chaptered.

For all the complications of this labor, the results have never quite been treated as successes. It is even a question whether they were popular in their own time, as they exist in only a few copies, in some cases having just a single exemplar.[31] For centuries they were entirely neglected. The first appearances in print of the prose *Erec et Enide* and *Cligès* were as appendices to the editions of Chrétien's verse produced by Wendelin Förster in the late nineteenth century, and only with Georges Doutrepont's magisterial 1939 *Les mises en prose des Épopées et des Romans chevaleresques du XIVe au XVIe siècle* did the efforts of Burgundian prosateurs become a subject of scholarly interest in their own right. The manuscripts are inelegant enough to sometimes be considered as merely rough drafts.[32] As for the governing aesthetic, contemporary scholars are at best politely dismissive; the prose *Cligès*, in one mordantly expressed opinion, is only "a solid exercise in subtlety reduction."[33] Certainly the adjustments of the prosateurs are intended to clarify where Chrétien is ambiguous, render exact what Chrétien has left suggestive, summarize where Chrétien has been expansive.[34] They are, consciously it seems, simplifications.

Not so with their chaptering, however, which achieves effects, even if inadvertent, that went beyond ideological or linguistic ambiguity reduction, and that justifies a glance at these otherwise workmanlike productions. The introduction of regular caesuras into Chrétien's largely undivided verse perhaps inevitably produced complications; to aerate is not necessarily to clarify, and more creative resonances were often the result.[35] At first glance, however, the

Burgundian capitulations look to neatly fit the general effort to scour away whatever opacities the original text possessed. In the case of both the prose *Erec* and *Cligès*, chaptering appeared in the reverse mode to what it would look like in Caxton: the insertion of headings as intertitles, and an absence of any table of contents. The headings were inserted in red ink in the manuscripts, occasionally in the same hand as the main text, and likely, as would have been usual with "rubrication," as a final touch.[36] With almost total uniformity, they display a syntax used by Eusebius and Bede, common to narrative history: phrases introduced by "how" (*comment*) and usually centered on verbs in the past definite, such as "How the king kissed Enide."[37] So expected is this pattern that Philippe de Vigneulles even referred to his titles by the term "coment," instructing a future reviser to insert an omitted chapter title as follows: "take this 'how' here and put it in the following book."[38] The "hows" serve not so much an indexical function as an exemplary one: they further abridge an al-ready streamlined remediation. Nor are their placements entirely discon-nected from the rhythms of Chrétien's verse. Subtle transitional markers in the source text such as "when" (*quand*), or the "but" or "meanwhile" (*meis, antre-deus*) of a scene shift, frequently motivate a new chapter in the prose versions.[39] The prosateur of *Cligès* often explicitly turned to the original for justification, as in chapter-opening formulae like "The story recounts then [Dist l'istoire doncques] . . ." and "In this part, the story tells [En ceste present partie dist l'istoire] . . ." (*BEC*, 91, 107).[40] Both the prose *Cligès* and *Erec* reserve *histoire*, or "story," for Chrétien's original, and are more apt to insert a mention of what the *histoire* "tells" at a chapter break, which functions therefore as a frame break as well, an occasion to nod dutifully to the authority of the source.[41] Certainly the prosateurs did not describe their work as violations or reinven-tions of the verse originals, and the chapter break is often a place to issue reas-surances to the contrary.

Yet these acts of obeisance to the verse original also express an anxiety about chaptering: how exactly is the segmenting of Chrétien's continuous verse to be justified? Is it as the periodic insertion of a time external to the story, a calling of the attention to the manner of its telling, a subtle alienation effect? Is it a dampening of narrative tension, an aeration that comes as a rhyth-mic relief, or can it be an emphasis of its own? The *histoire* provides no strong pattern for how the prosateur cuts its fabric. To remind readers of the original is, at least in part, to remind them that the *histoire*'s continuity has been frac-tured. With understandable indecision, the prosateurs tended to justify their chaptering by having it both ways. Often enough, chapter breaks tie themselves to the original explicitly, as if in embarrassment at their presumption. Yet just as often the break works directly and flagrantly against the tendency of the original, refusing the deft seamlessness of Chrétien's narrative procedure and insisting, even at the cost of an almost violent emphasis, on a more heavily accented, atomized temporality. Chrétien's narrative, in Erich Auerbach's admiring account, "flows," its "progress is steady": "Its parts are connected without any gaps . . . there are no strictly organized periods; the advance from one part of the story to the next is loose and follows no set plan. . . . But this does not harm the narrative continuity; on the contrary, the loose connections make for a very natural narrative style," he adds appreciatively.[42] This is the dexterity with which Chrétien naturalizes and subtilizes what could often be the mechanical kinds of epic enchaînement in the older chansons de geste. It is exactly what the prose remediations disrupt, and that disruption is at once their most clumsy technique and their most daring maneuver.

Take the prose *Cligès*, dated March 1454 [1455] in its *explicit*, divided into seventy-five chapters of widely varying length, with some headings simply missing and spaces for illustrations empty as if unfinished or even abandoned.[43] The original's interior monologues, with Chrétien's fondness for exploring the fluctuating ambivalences and rationalizations of eros, are truncated, sometimes drastically, while details of tournaments and siege warfare are expanded.[44] More to the point, the prosateur has a marked tendency to signal disjunction where the *histoire* preferred seamless transition and interlacing. *Cligès* itself is a two-generation story, narrating a father's and son's loves and combats, in which the son's story involves uncanny echoes and intensifications of the father's: where the father Alixandre finds his love and proves his mettle at Arthur's court, the son Cligès will find his love in his uncle's betrothed, will head to Arthur's court to escape the complications of that sentiment, and will need to depend on his love Fenice's constancy to an extremity (faking her own death and surviving torture) that his father's wife Soredamours had not needed. Yet the prosateur insists on these as two distinct narratives. At the end of his chapter 28, Alixandre on his deathbed having just exhorted the young Cligès to serve King Arthur for a time, the prosateur adds: "And thus ended the life of Alixandre, Cligès's father, about whom we have made a brief account, and now we shall begin the second account as follows" (*BEC*, 102).

The break between the two atomizes a transitional moment that Chrétien's narrative had ominously linked. What in the *histoire* is an overlapping series of anticipatory plans, hints of future discord, rearward gazes to the dying father's past in England, and oracular pronouncements about future combats becomes in the prose version a swift disjuncture, turning on the prose's insistent "and now." The father is dead; now is the son's time. By contrast, Chrétien is everywhere devoted to interweaving. It is his chosen motif; Alixandre's beloved and eventual wife Soredamours makes him a chemise of gold thread, into which is woven a strand of her hair, of a gold brighter than that of the metal. Combat scenes are refracted through multiple viewpoints, from the participants to various anxious onlookers; dialogues, such as that between Cligès and Fenice when they mull their dilemma and devise the plan to stage her death, spread over multiple days. Chrétien's interest, we might say, is in perpetuation: what lasts or lingers, the dual directionality of phases and times in which the now moment, as in Augustine, recedes into a durationless point the more it is packed with the stuff of retrospect and anticipation. The prose version is instead focused on serializing these layered moments into small monads. In practice this means that the chapter break disrupts, as if with intentional violence, some of Chrétien's more carefully prepared effects of temporal transposition. When Fenice is wed against her will to the emperor Alix, she and her nurse Thessala, with Cligès's consent and participation, plan to drug Alix with a magic potion that will send him every night into a deluded sleep where he will dream of having possessed Fenice while no such thing has occurred. On their wedding night the plan works seamlessly, yet Chrétien's narration of Alix's false consummation explodes into multiple temporalities:

De neant est an si grant painne
Car par voir cuide et si s'an prise
Qu'il ait la forteresce prise.
Einsi le cuide, einsi le croit,
Et de neant lasse et recroit.

A une foiz vos ai tot dit,
C'onques n'en ot autre delit.
Ensi l'estovra demener
Toz orz mes, s'il l'en puet mener,
Mes ainz qu'a salveté la teigne,
Criem que granz anconbriers li veigne,
Car quant il s'an retornera,
Li dus pas ne sejornera
Cui el fu premerains donee.

Great were his effort and his pain,
and all for nothing and in vain,
For he believed he held the fort,
had captured it from his consort,
Was spent, and needed some repose.
Thus he believed; thus he'll suppose.
I've told you once for all, he'll savor
no other joy, so his behavior
must be forever and a day,
if he can take the maid away.
Before she's safely home, I sense
he faces great impediments.
The emperor came from his bridal;
the Saxon duke had not been idle
to whom she had been given first.[45]

This "une foiz" is also "tot"—one time is somehow all time, encapsulating a life story. The past collapses into a lie, as all the effort Alix had taken to prize Fenice from her previous suitor the Duke of Saxony is undone by the potion's trick; meanwhile the future looms, as the duke himself reappears, preparing his army simultaneously with Alix's deluded wedding night, two temporal tracks aligned by the *retornera/sejornera* couplet. Alix is undone by past and future both. Tenses flit from the preterit to the future while outlining a continuity between them; the poet gathers a wide temporal continuum and knits it together. In this concatenation of ramifying consequences, the present moment of the dream itself dissolves into nothing: "With nothing to embrace and kiss, / he talked to nothing, nothing held, / hugged nothing, nothingness beheld."[46]

The prosateur, however, unties these interlacings, and instead slices through the midst of narrative episodes, leaving characters momentarily frozen in attitudes of unselfconscious intensity before their fates are revealed. A chapter here is a record of a short-term, individual position, with minimal reference to prior events or future consequences.[47] In dialogues, a character's speech concludes a chapter before a response can be given; in combat, a blow can end a chapter before it is returned. The lead-in to Alix and Fenice's wedding night is parceled into small segments: one chapter for the preparation of the potion by Thessala, one for the serving of the potion to Alix by Cligès, one for the nighttime dream, one for the relating of the news of the wedding to the duke, and one for the duke's preparations for battle and the joining of combat. Instead of the transition to the duke's preparations occurring within a single couplet, the fall of a chapter break descends as if to segregate Alix from his antagonist, halting the action in the moment of his happy awakening: "We shall now suspend [*se taira*] for a time our account of the relations between Fenice and Alix and proceed to speak of the duke of Saxony" (*BEC*, 113). It is a shift without any of Chrétien's dark irony, and as a result more of a leap, a rending apart of time. The "suspension" of the chapter break traps Alix in his delusion, and prolongs his perspectival ignorance, its blissful segregation from past mistakes and future costs. Earlier in the prose *Cligès*, when Arthur lays siege to Windsor Castle to punish a traitorous count, the initial chapter of that episode ends by modulating into the present tense, catching the count's forces in a doomed act of defiance that the chapter break oddly prolongs into a tableau: "they issue from the castle mounted on good horses and each equipped with shield and lance alone and, because they want to show King Arthur that they do not fear his intelligence, force, or great host

of knights, they leap and pirouette on the gravel as if wishing to amuse themselves" (BEC, 92). That dance is the prosateur's grim invention; Chrétien had
them only taking a ceremonial walk before Arthur's troops to show themselves unafraid. It is a structure that has a constant allure for the prosateur:
sharply bounded moments of the present so disconnected from the dual directionality of time and its usual affects—regret, foreboding—that one hovers between admiration and pity for the people caught there. With the brief
time of the chapter break to consider the dancers, might even our sense of
their foolishness soften into something like an appetite for the narrowed temporal horizon, the vivid and almost durationless "now," that allows them their
defiant posturing?

The prose Erec, meanwhile, persistently linked to the Cligès revision and
likely also a product of the 1450s, approaches its similar task in a different
spirit.[48] Where the Burgundian Cligès used capitulation to disentangle Chrétien's complexly interwoven narrative, the Erec prosateur was confronted with
a much more streamlined story: Erec's bringing Enide to Arthur's court to
prove her beauty and to wed her with properly royal sanction, followed by the
series of tests he puts her through after she reluctantly informs him of his
knights' complaints that he has sacrificed arms for uxorious leisure. The story's
episodes are in Chrétien accumulative rather than multifocal, a mounting tension that explores marriage as itself a dilemma for the chivalric ethic. Perhaps
for this very reason Chrétien felt the need to explicitly note one of the story's
major divisions, when Arthur kisses Enide, completing the ritual of the white
stag and marking her as the court's most beautiful woman shortly before her
marriage to Erec:

Li rois, par itele avanture,	By this adventure, watched by all,
randi l'usage et la droiture	Arthur fulfilled the ritual;
qu'a sa cort devoit li blans cers:	now the old custom could prevail.
ici fenist li premiers vers.	Here ends the first part of this tale.[49]

A capitulator, presumably, looks for places in the host text where a chapter
break could be inserted naturally. Here is one such moment, and it is almost
ostentatiously refused. It occurs instead in the middle of the chapter titled
"How the king kissed Enide," and the prose formulation simply moves on,
indeed fairly jumps: "Here our tale will leave off speaking of Enide's gracious
demeanor for a little while and will now turn to say that Erec had five pack-
horses loaded with gold, silver, and great riches and sent them to his father-in-
law and to his mother-in-law of Lalut" (BEC, 40).

It is a curiously willful chaptering. Eliminating Chrétien's "here ends the first part" turns Arthur's formal acknowledgment of Enide from the culmination of a long episode to just another event in a flattened series; the prose version's leveling seems to deliberately counteract the gradually escalating process of the verse. It silences Chrétien's ordinal sequencing, his sense that one item necessarily presumes its next from the standpoint of a teleology, a complete set whose meaning inheres in its end. The prosateur seems to prefer a *cardinalization* of the story's events—not so much first and second as one thing after another, a bumpy and paratactic seriality rather than Chrétien's causally oriented hypotaxis. If the poet has an eye on counting the number of items in a total set, the prose writer prefers the immediacy of transition, passing from one thing to the next.[50] Headings themselves occasionally articulate pure sequence, as in those to chapters 21 ("How Erec killed five brigand knights, one after the other"), 27 ("How Erec and Guivret jousted together, and afterwards fought with their swords"), and 31 ("How Erec killed two giants, one after the other, in a wood") (*BEC*, 47, 55, 60). The paradigm here is not the working out of fate but the arrival of a new present—then, next, and after that—whose content is never wholly predictable, while the timing of its interruptions is eccentric, even glitchy. A thoroughly linear time, after all, has its surprises as much as its repetitions.

The prose *Cligès* and *Erec* are similar experiments in chaptering, each applying the lancet of the chapter break to Chrétien's verse, that nonetheless result in different textures. Where the former inserts gaps to dilate time, the latter's styptic and jagged breaks confine time to a linear, leveled series of small moments. One temptation, given the brief Burgundian court taste for such productions, is to assess these atomized styles as some kind of ideological effect catering to the relatively new, and centralized, dynastic ruling coterie for whom they were written. Perhaps such an audience, freshly arrived at what would be its historical apex, would not love the momentum and suspense of Chrétien's gradually unfolding ironies, and would prefer modes of intense now-time; perhaps the prose versions usefully softened Chrétien's imagination of consequence, retribution, and disaster. But there remains the likelihood that the Burgundian prosateurs fashioned these new temporalities by accident, by a clumsy or hurried application of prose chapters to a verse fabric that resisted easy cuts. The Burgundian *mise en prose* was in any case a fairly ephemeral genre. But the nature of the experiment persisted. What its example preserves for us is the chaotic playfulness of writers exploiting, as if with a new tool not yet fully naturalized, the possibilities of inserting pauses into narrative.

The Capitulum in the Press: Caxton

Burgundy, as it happens, leads us back to Caxton. In the same years that the prosateurs were transposing Chrétien, Caxton had settled in Bruges as a merchant with significant connections, and was becoming a prominent figure in the Burgundian hierarchy. In the 1450s he had access to ducal libraries, and was even empowered to purchase books and manuscripts for the duchy; in 1463 he achieved the position of governor of the English Nation at Bruges, an ambassadorial role that would be expanded by Edward IV the following year.[51] We cannot know which, if any, of the Burgundian prose *remaniements* he read, although his immersion in the court where the taste for segmented prose adaptations had become so prevalent suggests some acquaintance with them, at least. But when Caxton began his career as a printer in the 1470s, first in Bruges and then by 1476 in Westminster, the texts he published were often in prose, and frequently already chaptered into discrete segments, either because they were miscellanies or because chaptered narrative was the literary fashion. However it came, Caxton seems to have had an education in styles of division, and would later apply it.

Caxton's editorial prologues were often ambiguous as to his responsibility for chaptering, and tended to echo, if more swiftly and elliptically, conventional defenses of the indexical uses of chapters. A 1481 production, *Godeffroy of Boloyne*, introduces its table succinctly: "Henne for to knowe the content of this book, ye shal playnly see by the table folowynge / wherof every chapytre treateth al alonge."[52] In *The Mirrour of the World*, published the same year, Caxton simply advises that the text "conteyneth in alle lxxvii chapitres and xxvii figures, without whiche it may not lightly be vnderstande." Here he admits that the chapters are not his own, the *Mirrour* having been "engrossed and in alle poyntes ordeyned by chapitres and figures in ffrenshe" sixteen years before he translated and published it.[53] Yet as early as 1480, in his printing of the *Chronicles of England*, there is a hint that capitulation—either the composition of headings, or their arrangement in a table—is his special contribution: "that euery man may see and shortly fynde suche mater as it shall plese hym to see or rede I haue ordeyned a table of the maters shortly compiled & chapitred as here shall folowe."[54] By the time of the 1485 *Morte*, with its prefatory boast that "I have divided it into twenty-one books, and every book chaptered," capitulation is not just one of the services performed by the printer, it is something like the value added by the act of printing itself and a signature intellectual style. What is quickly emerging in Caxton's practice in the early

1480s is an understanding that print, translation or adaptation, and capitulation exist in a tightly bound nexus. Narrative prose in print requires the aerated punctuation of chapters, which are the quasi-compositional acts of the printer/editor; segmentation in multiple senses—casting off a manuscript into a certain number of pages, locating places in the manuscript for the insertion of chapter heads—is their métier.[55]

Yet Caxton's chapters do not perfectly resemble the chapters of later fictional prose. In appearance they are minimal and discreet. Contrary to his usual practice, his *Morte* does not repeat the headings in his table as intertitles. Chapter breaks are signaled only by a relatively unobtrusive indication: the typographical mark known as a pilcrow or paraph, and the word "capitulum" followed by a roman numeral or the number spelled out in Latin—this combination usually, if not always, centered.[56] White space, often of one line on either side although sometimes less, accented these signals; Caxton did not employ a larger display type to highlight this brief interruption any further, although a woodcut initial, of around three lines' height, started the text of the chapter proper (figure 4.1). Nor did his chapters automatically start a new page; such lavishness with white space would take centuries to emerge. But when a chapter break occurs near a page division, these breaks do tend to accumulate more white space around them, and in one place Caxton shortened his normally thirty-eight-line page to twenty-two lines as a result.[57] The amount of white space was therefore variable, susceptible to the vagaries of the casting-off process in which he would have calculated, taking into consideration the size of his page and his chosen type, how much of Malory's manuscript would fit on a printed page.[58] Visually, at least, Caxton's chapter breaks are regular but not rigid, easily visible but not ostentatious, with the modesty of a stippling or graining effect. In their diminution of the summary function of the heading, which has been restricted to the initial table, there seems to be an intent here to avoid halting the continuity of reading while nonetheless opening up a space in that continuity and offering a rhythm of rests. Which is to say that the indexical function of these chapters has started to recede, and what predominates instead is the feeling of aeration.

Caxton's *Morte* is an excellent occasion to imagine how chaptering worked in the early decades of print. The current assumption is that Caxton must have possessed at least two manuscripts of the *Morte* in his workshop: the Winchester manuscript, which bears indications of having been in Caxton's possession but has no casting-off marks or chapter indications, and a hypothetical second that would have been used as the setting copy.[59] Caxton would presumably have had to make two markings in the setting copy: casting-off marks to indicate where page divisions would fall, and chapter and book divisions to indicate where the white space and "capitulum" numbers should be inserted. The two divisions would have had a mutual impact: Caxton's casting-off estimates would have had to assume a page of thirty-five rather than thirty-eight lines to leave room for the space of chapter divisions.[60] The restrictions of operating only a single press meant this work needed to be done before printing began. Translating the result to the printed page was not without snags; occasionally, certain chapter-break indications seem to have been overlooked by whoever handled the casting-off, and the result was the half-dozen times in the finished edition where chapter breaks are missing and the numeration has to jump one number, along with other occasions where the break is crowded into the end of a line of text rather than given any space of its own. These internal segmentations of the manuscript, into both pages and chapters, preceded the composition of the chapter headings of the opening table, which seems to have been carried out in a spirit that was anything but comprehensive; the headings often are simply borrowed from a chapter's first lines, or refer to the first of a chapter's actions.[61]

This was tricky enough mechanical and arithmetical work, a continual process of balancing the different articulations of the chapter and page. But it was result of the even trickier work of capitulation itself, where Caxton had to identify places in Malory's text to segment. Here we know less, although we can infer at least some of the various considerations he juggled as he marked chapter divisions in his setting copy. These would have included external factors—considerations for the visual aspects of either the manuscripts involved or the final printed product—and internal factors, deriving from how Caxton preferred to handle the texture of Malory's narrative. The most mechanical of the external considerations seems to have been his following the 111 large capitals that exist in the Winchester manuscript, its major divisional indications. Of these, Caxton employed 108 as chapter or book divisions, and 19 of his 21 book divisions coincide with one of these capitals.[62] It seems as if this would have been his most inflexible rule, but it was hardly exhaustive; there remain almost 400 chapters not accounted for in this way. It has been suggested that Caxton also aligned his chapters with a double-slash punctuation mark that is employed in Winchester, although these are frequent enough that some further criteria must have been in play.[63] One hypothesis is that Caxton attempted to divide the text into chapters of roughly equivalent size between the divisions he inherited, although his chapters come in varying

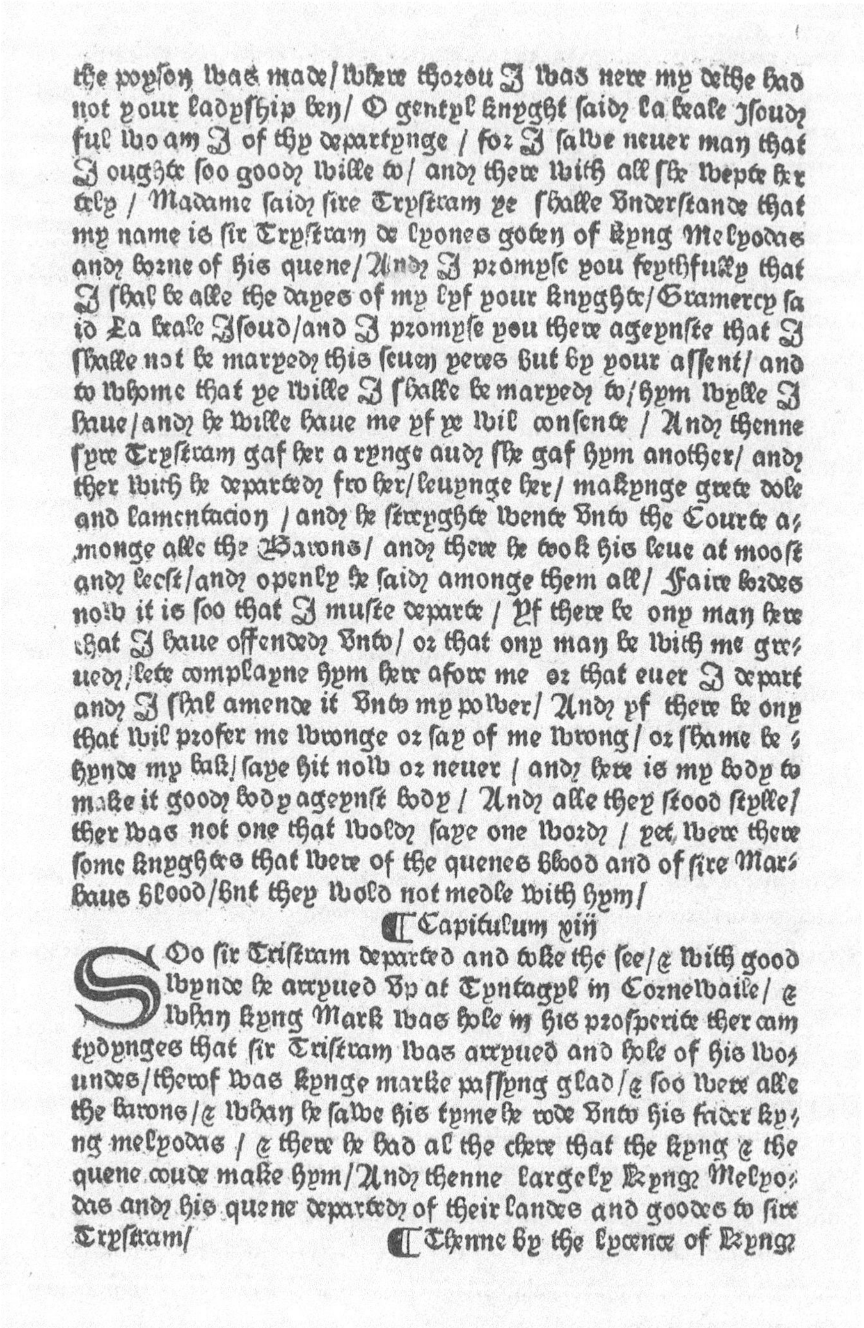

the poyson was made/ where thorou I was nere my dethe had
not your ladyship ben/ O gentyl knyght said la beale Isoud
ful who am I of thy departynge / for I sawe neuer man that
I oughte soo good wille to/ and ther with all she wepte ter
tly / Madame said sire Trystram ye shalle vnderstande that
my name is sir Trystram de Lyones goten of kyng Melyodas
and borne of his quene/ And I promyse you feythfully that
I shal be alle the dayes of my lyf your knyghte/ Gramercy sa
id La beale Isoud/ and I promyse you there ageynste that I
shalle not be maryed this seuen yeres but by your assent/ and
to whome that ye wille I shalle be maryed to/ hym wylle I
haue/ and he wille haue me yf ye wil consente / And thenne
sire Trystram gaf her a rynge and she gaf hym another/ and
ther with he departed fro her/ leuynge her/ makynge grete dole
and lamentacion / and he strayghte wente vnto the Courte a
monge alle the Barons/ and there he took his leue at moost
and leest/ and openly he said amonge them all/ Faire lordes
now it is soo that I muste departe / yf there be ony man here
that I haue offended vnto/ or that ony man be with me gre
ued/ lete complayne hym here afore me or that euer I departe
and I shal amende it vnto my power/ And yf there be ony
that wil profer me wronge or say of me wrong/ or shame be
hynde my back/ saye hit now or neuer / and here is my body to
make it good body ageynst body / And alle they stood stylle/
ther was not one that wold saye one word/ yet were there
some knyghtes that were of the quenes blood and of sire Mar
haus blood/ but they wold not medle with hym/

¶ Capitulum viij

Soo sir Trystram departed and took the see/ & with good
wynde he arryued Vp at Tyntagyl in Cornewaile/ &
whan kyng Mark was hole in his prosperite ther cam
tydynges that sir Trystram was arryued and hole of his wo
undes/ therof was kynge marke passyng glad/ & soo were alle
the barons/ & whan he sawe his tyme he rode Vnto his fader ky
ng melyodas / & there he had al the chere that the kyng & the
quene coude make hym/ And thenne largely kynge Melyo
das and his quene departed of their landes and goodes to sire
Trystram/   ¶ Thenne by the lycence of kyng

FIGURE 4.1 Some varieties of Caxton's chaptering aerations in his edition of the *Morte*, from the copy at the Morgan Library: *left*, the compressed opening of book 8, chapter 13, fol. 147v; *right*, the more common spacing, from book 17, chapter 19, fol. 367v. The Morgan Library and Museum. PML 17560. Purchased in 1911.

¶ Capitulum xix.

So departed he from thens / and commaunded the bre ‧
theren to god / and soo he rode fyue dayes tyl that he
came to the maymed kynge / And euer folowed Percyual the
fyue dayes as kynge where he had ben / and soo one told hym /
how the aduentures of Logrys were enchyeued / So on a daye
it bifelle that they cam oute of a grete foreste / and there they
mette at trauers with sir Bors the whiche rode alone / hit is
none nede to telle yf they were glad / & hem he salewed / & they
yelded hym honour and good aduenture / and eueryche told
other / Thenne said Bors hit is more than a yere and an half
that I ne lay ten tymes where men dwelled / but in wylde fo
restes and in montayns / But god was euer my comforte /
Thenne rode they a grete whyle tyl that they came to the castel
of Carbonek / And whan they were entryd withyn the Castel
kynge Pelles knewe hem / thenne there was grete Joye / For
they wyst wel by theire compnye that they had fulfylled the
quest of the Sancgreal / Thenne Elyazar kynge Pelles sone
broughte to fore hem the broken suerd wherwith Joseph was
stryken thurgh the thygh / Thenne Bors sette his hand therto /
yf that he myght haue souded hit agepne but it wold not be /
Thenne he took it to Percyual but he had no more power ther
to than he / Now haue ye hit agepne sayd Percyuall to Gala‧
had / for and it be euer enchyeued by ony worldy man / ye must
doo hit / and thenne he took the pyeces and sette hem to gydere
and they semed that they had neuer ben broken / and as wel
as hit had ben fyrst forged / And whanne they withyn aspyed
that the aduenture of the suerd was enchyeued / thenne they gaf
the suerd to Bors / for hit myght not be betterset / for he was a
good knyghte and a worthy man / and a lytel afore euen the
suerd arose grete and meruepllous / and was ful of grete he
te that many men felle for drede / And anone alyght a voys
amonge them and sayd they that ought not to syttе at the ta
ble of Jhesu Cryst / aryse / for now shalle veray knyghtеs ben
fedd / Soo they wente thens all sauf kynge Pelles and E ‧
lyazar his sone / the whiche were holy men and a mayde which
was his nece / and soo these thre felawes and they thre were

lengths, at times widely so.[64] A second hypothesis is that he sought a rhythm of visual interruption in which most of the printed pages, and certainly most pairs of facing pages, were aerated at least once by a chapter break to avoid the monotony of an uninterrupted text block. As Takako Kato has determined, fully 61 percent of the book's pages include a chapter division, and an additional 15 percent include white space of some kind.[65] Only eleven pairs of facing pages fail to include a chapter division's aeration or some other white space within the text block. Attention seems, that is, to have been paid to the relationship between the page and the chapter, and chapter lengths seem to have been tailored to make sure the graphic element of the chapter break appeared with regularity. The regularity worked in the other direction as well, against excess: only four pages in the book include multiple chapter breaks.

These observations suggest that Caxton was thinking of pages when chaptering, and that therefore during the act of capitulation he must have had in mind simultaneously a rough casting-off estimate, to keep the general balance between pages and chapter breaks intact. Perhaps rather than two separate acts of segmentation, pages and chapters, he performed both at once, in an intricate double act of patterning, the stricter regularity of the printed page oscillating with a slightly more flexible scanning for places to interrupt Malory's narrative—one that located them, when it could, in the manuscript's directions, but that nonetheless had to invent other occasions for itself at fairly regular intervals. Those last inventions would be what we might call the internal factors driving capitulation. Some of these seem to be a set of verbal formulae Malory used to manage narrative attention—"now turn we to," "now leave we," and the like—as well as the shifts of plot strand that these locutions signaled.[66] Amid all of these complex and interrelated considerations, involving the look of the printed page as well as the sense its text made, any possible higher-order conceptual organization of Malory's text vanishes. The chapters address themselves to sequences of action rather than becoming individual moral or philosophical exempla.[67] The first five chapter headings of book 6 are typical:

1   How Sir Launcelot and Sir Lionel departed from the court for to seek adventures, and how Sir Lionel left him sleeping and was taken
2   How Sir Ector followed for to seek Sir Launcelot, and how he was taken by Sir Turquin
3   How four queens found Launcelot sleeping, and how by enchantement he was taken and led into a castle

4   How Sir Launcelot was delivered by the mean of a damosel
5   How a knight found Sir Launcelot lying in his leman's bed, and how
    Sir Launcelot fought with the knight (*MA*, 1:194–201)

The actions itemized here lack any higher-order labeling or assessment, even any adjectival color. Instead, the headings concentrate on lexical echoes that establish a chain of repeated actions.[68] It is a circuit of pursuit and capture, free wandering and sudden seizure, drawing ten characters, four of them named, into its orbit. The headings do not conceptualize, even in the playful or partial manner of late antiquity; they abbreviate or dilute. What results is a table that is ill adapted to its putatively indexical function. Caxton's concentration was oriented toward the shape of his units, not their labeling; it is evidence that his guiding principle was narrative progression and rhythm.

Not that, for some time now, it has been the fashion to see any consistent principle at all in Caxton's arrangement. Following the discovery of the Winchester manuscript, the *Morte* underwent what has been called a "Malorization," in which the text was imagined by scholars as in need of rescue from the "obtrusive," or merely "solid and foursquare," craft labor of Caxton's workshop, which like some badly trained renovator fell too in love with a pet technique and thereby botched a more elegantly designed original.[69] There is a veiled class distaste operating here—the plodding tradesman Caxton as having cut up the rakishly aristocratic Malory's tapestry—as well as what Jerome McGann has called "the nostalgic attachment which textual criticism has always had for original authorial documents."[70] The nostalgia in this case takes the form of an embedded preference for the elegance of prechaptered continuity, one that echoes the older humanist idealization of unmarked, unsegmented editions of the classics rather than the clutter of medieval glosses. Yet this preference, which governed studies and editions of the *Morte* for most of the twentieth century, overlooks both Caxton's general aims and the specific means by which he tried to achieve them. His goal was precisely to unify the *Morte*—gathering Malory's separate tales into a work centered on Arthur and his court, a "book," the key term that is dotted throughout his preface, that would signify a wholeness Malory's collection lacked. The unity effect depended paradoxically on a periodic recurrence of rests, which by irregularly cutting into Malory's narrative paths gave a rhythmic signature to the whole. Caxton seems to have imagined that the articulation of his unity into books and chapters actually *sutured* Malory's diffuse episodes rather than dispersed them further. The chapter in Caxton's book is not a presentation of discrete episodes or exempla. It is much closer to a rhythmic unit that offers breathing space while simultaneously binding episodes together; its goal is as much linkage as fissuring.

Caxton's considerations when chaptering were therefore many, and they ranged from those that seem far from Malory's text, such as breaking up the text block with white space, to those that are intimate with it, such as the identification of transitional formulae. But the result, however accidental or contingent, essentially invented for prose narrative a form: the brief *subepisodic chapter*—a unit of time too short to encapsulate a complex series of related actions brought to a conclusion, but long enough to gather one or more particular actions understood as a segment of a much longer set; a unit that has no pretension to wholeness, but that can isolate units within a larger whole and present them in their momentary isolation, their ironic or splendid illusion of distinctness that holds for only the briefest of moments. Caxton splinters Malory into slivers—507 of them—and the syncopated relation these units have to the rhythm of the host text is similar to that of the Burgundian prosateurs, whom he may have read. But print has had its effect on these units. They are more regular; and they seem to accentuate, play with, stretch, and even exist for the blank caesuras that follow them.

The regularity can best be understood at an abstract, quantitative distance, which will also help establish Caxton's relation to later prose fiction. Chapter size mattered to Caxton, it seems, at least in part because of the frequency of the chapter's visual interruption in the standard but arbitrary measure of the thirty-eight-line printed page, and its size was modulated in accordance with that need. An even more abstract measure, one that may or may not have figured in his thinking, is word count. His work results in a roughly 700-word unit— 669 words, to be exact, is the average length of the *Morte*'s printed chapters.[71] Given that Caxton's normal printed page holds a bit more than 400 words, we can call this the either the 700-word form or the page-and-a-half form, the interval shaped by the capacity of his printed pages and therefore deliberately compressed below the threshold of a narrative episode. The overall average is reasonably well maintained in each separate book, with the primary exceptions being the heavily rewritten book 5, the much longer book 10, and the final four books, which begin to press upward slightly (figure 4.2).[72] The form admits of some variability; the standard deviation of these chapters, taken as a whole, is 208 words, allowing for moderate distention when events in the narrative demand it. Average variability, as the figure demonstrates, moves in tandem with length, as longer chapters necessitate shorter ones to follow in order

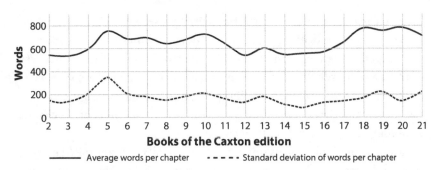

FIGURE 4.2 Chapter word counts in Caxton's 1485 *Morte*.

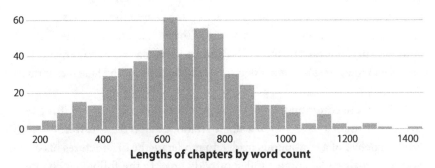

FIGURE 4.3 Distribution of chapter lengths in Caxton's 1485 *Morte*.

to maintain the overall balance of length Caxton attempted to keep. The short-est chapter, in fact, directly follows its second-longest: chapter 4.24, at 157 words, presents a brief conversation that simply concludes the action of 4.23, which comes to 1,344 words. Altogether this two-chapter episode—the story of a vexed ménage between Lady Ettard, Sir Gawain, and Sir Pelleas—averages out to well within the general length norm of Caxton's edition, as the histo-gram in figure 4.3 reveals. However Caxton calculated the norm, he attempted to self-correct as soon as he could when he was forced, for whatever reason, to transgress it. This distribution of average lengths is part of the generic signa-ture of Caxton's chapters. A prose form of roughly 500 to 800 words: what can be told in that limit? The answer in the *Morte* is portions only of ongoing ac-tions, usually not discrete episodes.

The subepisodic length of these chapters means that a stress falls on the break between chapters, on concluding and commencing sentences, to link these subepisodes into longer chains. Fully 205 of Caxton's chapter breaks interrupt an ongoing narrative, offering a brief pause only, rather than shifting a scene, a plot strand, or introducing any larger temporal gap. These momentary suspensions even in one case span the slightly harder division between books 9 and 10. Whether by accident or design, the fact of these suspended chapter breaks, which follow the Burgundian precedent, is an important aspect of Caxton's procedure. At the very least he does not think of the chapter as needing anything stronger than a small aperture in an unfolding action to occasion its onset or conclusion. In fact those small apertures might even be taken as the most felicitous occasions for the adapter's skill. They allow Caxton to present the *Morte* as comprising semi-discrete moments in a single process, rather than entirely different narratives, and they allow him to give texture to, and even dramatize, the implicit permission the chapter break gives a reader to pause or suspend a continuous reading. These dramatizations are slightly and crucially different from the Burgundian *remaniements*, softer, subtler. They seem to express an art of lingering—the aesthetic of the fade rather than the cut.

In the more common uses of the chapter break, such as the shifting between plot strands or scenes in a single strand, Caxton demonstrates a concern, on behalf of a continuous reader, to moderate the disjunctures his own division creates. Closing formulae provide links to the following chapter, throwing a bridge over the gap. Some of these gaps are reminiscent of Burgundian divisions: suspensions occurring at the height of action, introducing a momentarily frozen present. So 1.23 ends with Arthur supine and Pellinor's sword raised as if about to cut off his head, a momentary halt of the kind favored by the prosateurs; 1.24 begins with "Therwithal came Merlin and said, 'Knight, hold thy hand, for and thou slay that knight thou puttest this realm in the greatest damage that ever was realm" (*MA*, 1:54). The Winchester manuscript has a double slash where Caxton places his break, likely one cause of its placement, although Caxton trims the opening "and" of Malory's sentence, as if preferring the white space's tact to Malory's parataxis.[73] Often these gaps are located with a particular ingenuity, aslant of the familiarly vivid tableaux of one combatant caught at the moment before triumph. One of Caxton's favorite techniques is to close a chapter with the announcement of a dialogue to follow, and then to open the next with the promised speech, rather than placing his break in the midst of a dramatic action. The result, like the hush produced by the conductor's raised baton, accentuates the rhetorical occasion, and gives the interchapter silence a forward-tending movement, as if to refuse the possibility that the reader's pause would be anything but momentary; it tends to

bury significant action within chapters rather than use those actions to motivate conclusions.[74] Unlike the combat pause among Arthur, Pellinor, and Merlin, these effects do not derive from any indication in the Winchester manuscript; here Caxton often pries apart the space between Malory's sentences,
or even within a sentence, to create his aeration. So 14.9 ends midsentence,
with Sir Percival having just realized the danger he was in of losing his virgin-
ity: "And then he was adread and cried aloud" (*MA*, 2:289). His cry to Jesus,
and self-chastening puncturing of his thigh with his own sword, follow after
the break.

If we can surmise what Caxton might have learned from Burgundian capitulation, then, it is a set of topoi in which interruption of actions might
occur: between apparent victory and its swift reversal, between illusion and
disenchantment, between anticipatory entry and the unforeseeable effects of
having crossed a threshold. When in book 17 Launcelot comes to the door of
the Sangrail chamber, Caxton locates a chapter pause at the moment when he
"set his hand thereto to have opened it" (*MA*, 2:355)—a chapter, it should be
added, in which he says his final farewell to his son Galahad. The much earlier
scene of Galahad's conception, in which Elaine uses her art to enchant Launcelot into the belief he is lying with Guinevere, is marked by a break signaled by
a different kind of aperture:

> and so they lay together until undurn on the morn; and all the windows
> and holes of that chamber were stopped that no manere of day might be
> seen. And then Sir Launcelot remembered him, and he arose up and went
> to the window.

Caxton's white space intervenes, and then:

> And anon as he had unshut the window the enchantment was gone; then
> he knew himself that he had done amiss. (*MA*, 2:192)

The Winchester manuscript provides no indication of a pause in either location; these are examples of Caxton's own artfulness, however reminiscent they
are of Burgundian style. But Caxton's editorial technique gives a delicately
muted quality, a peculiar gentleness, to these interstitial moments. He is attentive to tactile contact: the hand on the door, the opening of the window, ordinary kinesis caught at the moment of its becoming extraordinary. It is as if the
white space is expressing an embodied tenderness, a desire to linger with
Launcelot's touch before it produces its transformations. Malory has provided
the occasion, but Caxton the capitulator demonstrates a heightened sensitivity

to these swiftly passing gestures, and gives them a space to breathe. It is as close as chaptering comes to sheer play.

It is in segmentations like these that we see a different tonality in Caxton from the *mises en prose*, one that amounts to an aesthetic of its own, however similar the initial technique might be. Instead of the break as a sharp cut—ironic possibly, distinct always—Caxton has a fondness for a stillness that seems to diffuse or slowly dissolve; he prefers the fade to the sudden silence. In keeping with his emphasis on linkages across the chapter break, his endings often employ sentences in Malory that, when set off by a caesura, expand in the vacuum and linger there, casting a foreboding shadow on what is to come. Much of this is accomplished by locating chapter transitions with significant character speech, and even editing Malory lightly in order to carve these lines in an even deeper relief. Between 5.7 and 5.8 Caxton has worked to give the resonance of white space to one of Launcelot's arguments about chivalry; however slight an intervention, it is a trace of the capitulator's art. The Winchester manuscript has Arthur weeping at the news of Launcelot's near death in an ambush set by the Emperor Lucius, and reminding him that it is folly not to flee when so severely outnumbered. Launcelot disagrees, responding that "the shame would ever have been ours," to which Sir Clegis and Sir Bors assent. Caxton locates his chapter break, as is his frequent practice, with the "Now leve we" of the following sentence and the familiar double slash of the Winchester manuscript that precedes it.[75] As far as location, Malory is here his guide. Yet he cuts the extraneous agreement of the two knights and rewords Launcelot's argument, so that his chapter ends with a firmer, more categorical, and more darkly ironic assertion: "'Nay,' said Launcelot and the other, 'for once shamed may never be recovered'" (*MA*, 1:180). Given amplitude by its position at the end of the chapter, the statement detaches itself from the immediate situation under discussion and floats uneasily over Launcelot's broader story; will the aphorist of shame remember this when he later begins to flirt with his own, very different kinds of shame?

If the impress of Caxton's chaptering is in general toward the subepisodic—the 700-word chapter cannot usually fully encompass one of Malory's episodes in anything like its full reach—the endings seem often bent slightly to become, as with Launcelot's words on shame, *extra*-episodic: utterances that reach outside of their immediate occasion to encompass a broader time scheme. Eliminating response of any kind to these utterances is in many cases how Caxton accomplishes this peculiar resonance. When in 10.8 Sir Dynadan chides King Mark—"And because ye are no men of worship, ye hate all men of worship, for never was bred in your country such a knight as is Sir Tristram"—Caxton breaks off the chapter there, cutting King Mark's silent, abashed response (*MA*, 2:18). The words achieve a motto-like generality by the break's slight detachment from a specific scenic context. These cuts achieve a more expansive effect than is found in the Winchester manuscript. Caxton is not disambiguating or clarifying his source text; he is instead aerating it, where the aerations will allow particular sentences within scenes to rise above the occasion of their saying and to become plural in their possible meanings. Rather than the clean cut, he is after what we might call today the slow dissolve, something that might even force a momentary pensiveness to arise from the chapter's caesura.[76]

The most telling such effects occur when Caxton has enunciations of the narrator to work with rather than those of characters. Here he will occasionally pluck some of Malory's sentences, unmarked in the Winchester manuscript with any divisional indication, and simply by their placement give them a temporal reach that is only incipient in Malory. When Tristram agrees to believe his rival Sir Palomides's false assurance that he had not realized whom he was attacking, Isoud looks on, unbelieving: "Thenne La Beale Isoud held down her head and said no more at that time" (*MA*, 2:164). As Launcelot and Guinevere's liaison begins to have directly catastrophic effects on the Round Table, Sir Bors passionately defends her to an assembled group, with only partial success: "Then some said to Sir Bors, 'We may well believe your words.' And so some of them were well pleased, and some were not so" (*MA*, 2:382). These are Caxton's signature chapter endings, close kin to "thou art unhappy," but as they are unmarked in the Winchester manuscript we can take them as even more profoundly his own work. They are the narrative articulations of an editor whose preferred modulations are toward lingering, fading, distant resonance, the feel of situations that have only temporarily and incompletely concluded. They are descriptions of tact: Isoud's silence, the withheld dissent of the knights. It is a tact mirrored in Caxton's own placement of his narrative rests, the soft touch of an editor whose delineations are also unobtrusive, fluid linkages.

Tact may take us back to Launcelot with his hand at the window and at the door, to the ways in which these chapter breaks, set in the midst of ongoing episodes, express the attempt to *grasp* something: a change in the situation; a modulation, whether merely a seam or as much as a tear, in an experience that is nonetheless possessed of a discernible continuity; a sudden check to the will that elicits a flinch. (As Bede had it, the "tiniest interval of time in which the lids of our eyes move when a blow is launched.") Necessarily the pause of that grasping reintroduces duration into the "now" moment that the Burgundian prosateurs had preferred to render as frozen or discrete. So much is packed in these interstices: tense interplays between dread and denial, hope for the new and the resignation to what was already feared, shock and dulled confirmation. As a result they are a good fit for the elegiac tone of Malory's epic, whose attention is always facing two ways at once, to former glory and its future disappearance. They will also become part of the familiar apparatus of the novel, a genre even more tied to duration, where opening temporary blank spaces in unfolding experience will have a recurrent attraction.

PART III

Dividing Time in, and beyond, the Novel

Their progress, meanwhile, was not of the straightest; it was an advance, without haste, through innumerable natural pauses and soft concussions.

—HENRY JAMES, *THE WINGS OF THE DOVE* (1902)

It was after two in the morning before I got to bed. I remember how the doings of my day appeared again before me, rich with inexplicable life. I fell asleep with a strange sense of sadness and promise meeting and holding hands.

—MURIEL SPARK, *LOITERING WITH INTENT* (1981),
END OF CHAPTER 2

5

Attitudes of the Early
Novel Chapter
(the Postural, the Elongated)

LOCKE—STERNE—EQUIANO—GOETHE

THERE MAY BE, as Tristram Shandy puts it, "no end, an'please your rever-
ences, in trying experiments upon chapters."[1] But it is in the slightly more than
two centuries of the European novel's early development that such experimentalism seems wildest, at its most unregulated and also most uncertain, since
for much of this period no standard stylistics of the novelistic chapter existed
by which to measure any deviation. The absorption of the chapter by prose
fiction was slow and partial; it remained, well into the eighteenth century,
optional rather than obligatory, and as such kept the aura not just of a choice
but of a mild curiosity. Any list of significant fictions, prior to *Tristram Shandy*
at least, will include both chaptered and unchaptered examples, and the distinction will not fall into any easy before-and-after narrative. Among chaptered
fictions one could mention *Lazarillo de Tormes* (anon., 1554), *Los siete libros
de la Diana* (Jorge de Montmayor, 1559), *Guzmán de Alfarache* (Mateo
Alemán, 1599), *Historia de la vida del Buscón* (Francisco de Quevedo, 1626),
Der abenteuerliche Simplicissimus Teutsch (Hans Jakob Christoffel von Grimmelshausen, 1669), and *Candide* (Voltaire, 1759), not to mention the inescapable examples of *La vie de Gargantua et de Pantagruel* (1532–64), *Don Quixote*
(1605, 1615), and *Gil Blas* (1715). Speaking for the other side might be the
notably unchaptered *Countess of Pembroke's Arcadia* (Philip Sidney, 1590),
Artamène ou le Grand Cyrus (Georges and/or Madeleine de Scudéry, 1649–53),
La Princesse de Clèves (Madame de Lafayette, 1678), *Oroonoko* (Aphra Behn,

1688), *Les aventures de Télémanque, fils d'Ulysse* (François Fénelon, 1699), *The New Atalantis* (Delarivier Manley, 1709), *Love in Excess* (Eliza Haywood, 1719), *Robinson Crusoe* (Daniel Defoe, 1719), *Memoirs of a Woman of Pleasure* (John Cleland, 1749). At the same time, the enormous importance of epistolary fiction meant that segmentation could exist without any chaptering at all. If the chapter need not be there, then, it need not be any one thing in particular. So experimentalism arose in one sense at least: that of unconstrained possibility, without the guardrails of a normative practice.

The proliferation of possibility; along with it, the proliferation of discussion: the novelistic chapter of the eighteenth century is volubly self-conscious. Figurations and explanations abound. In Henry Fielding's *Joseph Andrews*, as we have already seen, there is famously the comparison of the chapter break to "an inn or resting-place, where he [the reader] may stop and take a glass, or any other refreshment, as it pleases him. Nay, our fine readers will, perhaps, be scarce able to travel farther than through one of them in a day." Meanwhile, an unchaptered text is a voyage by ship rather than by land, offering us "the opening of wilds or seas, which tires the eye and fatigues the spirit when entered upon."[2] Fielding's comparisons are cited in the anonymous *History of Charlotte Summers*, which offers in addition a more purely literary comparison: a chapter is like a scene in a play, for which, "to step into the next Room, next House, Street, or even a Town, a short Interval serves without any great notice being taken, that an Alderman's Wife, who perhaps weighs about half a ton, has mov'd with greater Velocity than either Light or Sound."[3] A chapter is very like many things, as long as those things have the qualities of stuttered motion, time experienced as space and space understood as an effect of time.

Both the period's memorably peculiar and varied chapter types and its farrago of similitudes and justifications are experimental in a second and perhaps more pertinent sense: they are tests whose purpose is to determine what the substance under experimentation really is and does. After all—and it is both the most obvious and most obscure truth of the novelistic chapter—once fictional narrative embraces an indexical technique associated with informational texts, that technique loses much of its original function without as yet having acquired a new one. The chapter's directional or guiding task remains as an increasingly empty gesture. In a culture of the book where, in Henri-Jean Martin's formulation, white space triumphs over black type after the seventeenth century, and where paratexts become less precise and less informative, the fate of the chapter seems therefore to lie in some new conceptual function.[4] The chapter no longer offers assistance to the actively seeking reader, in Gellius's terms, but sculpts experience for a reader who, as Christina Lupton has argued, has begun to embrace, even if masochistically, a passive role.[5] This is a reader who no longer plots their own route with a GPS, but who instead is being conveyed down a linear path with a mixture of curiosity and apprehension, needing cajoling and encouragement, wanting occasional rest and release, a reader above all undergoing something that they do not wholly control.

These new temporal functions, of course, remain entangled with the old signposting, and various possible accommodations made between them mark the novelistic chapter for much of its early development. Novels retain traces of a more purely informational design; lengthy tables of contents and elaborately summative titles persist throughout many seventeenth- and eighteenth-century examples, although their assistance to first readers rather than rereaders would be minimal at best; they would be signposts for those who already know where the road goes.[6] The maintenance of indexical technique within long narratives produced odd tensions. Francis Coventry, writing in 1751 on contemporary fiction, complains of Tobias Smollett's overly informative chapter titles, and praises Lesage and Fielding for their reticence: "what admirable Titles," he writes of Fielding, "has he invented for his Chapters to keep him [the reader] the longer in the Dark!"[7] Coventry applied his theory: one typical title from his *History of Pompey the Little: or, the Adventures of a Lapdog*, exemplifies his anti-informational bias: "Containing what the Reader will know, if he reads it."[8] The ideal here seems to be *talk, don't reveal*—the "show, don't tell" of the mid-eighteenth century. Along with this uncomfortable resistance to techniques originally aimed at discontinuous readers is a tendency to disarray, instances in which the strain between the indexical and the continuous occasions peculiar mistakes. The various 1605 editions of *Don Quixote* are riddled with errors that cluster around its divisions: they include no chapter 43, and instead skip blithely from 42 to 44; the title to chapter 36 announces events that occur in the previous chapter; the break between chapters 5 and 6 occurs, in an inadvertent echo of the Langton–Saint Albans placement of the start of John 8, in the middle of a sentence; there are misnumberings, and indecisiveness between Arabic and Roman numeration, among other inconsistencies. One theory holds that Cervantes's chaptering of his text begins only midway through the writing of *Quixote*'s part 1, meaning that his retroactive divisions resulted from sloppiness, which would later be taken for metafictional wit. Confusions between hastily inserted divisions and the nature of an early modern typesetter's task may have had even more to do with these slips.[9] But the larger lesson is that chaptering in the early European novel existed within a complex middle ground, somehow both conventional and inessential, functional yet inert. When done, it did not always need to be done systematically, or thoughtfully, or seriously. Insouciance and inattention are as important here as experimentation—indeed, part of it.

What follows does not pretend to be a full catalogue of the ingenious syntheses and carelessly mangled solutions to the hosting of an indexical device within fictional narrative. There are many ways to tell the story of the chapter's early presence in the novel. This chapter will in fact take two non-novelistic detours, into Enlightenment theories of biblical editing and slave narrative, to outline the vague boundaries within which novelists employed the chapter. My emphasis here will take an unexpected trajectory. It is not that novelists slowly rationalized the chapter's presence in fiction, assigning to it common clock functions or emphasizing its topical, indexical properties. Instead, the chapter appears as a barely stable compound of different tasks, a compound repeatedly reconfigured when, as happens most signally toward the end of the eighteenth century, changes occur to the ways in which the divisions of individual experience are conceived. The path, that is, gets twistier, not straighter; the logic of chapters more, not less, opaque. Think, for instance, of the novella *Lazarillo de Tormes*, a paradigm for the picaresque narrative mode, whose seven chapters, or *tratados*, each narrate Lázaro's servitude under a different master: a blind man, a priest, an impoverished "gentleman" or *escudero*, a friar, a pardoner, an artist, and then finally, after time with a constable, marriage and an end to subordination.[10] Time, and text, is divided by one simple rule: who now controls me? The question of domination never quite goes away in the early history of the novelistic chapter, but the transparency of *Lazarillo de Tormes*'s segmenting method is an aberration. The later novelistic chapter will almost never look so clean, will rarely answer so lucidly the question, Why am I done this way? The chapter as an elegantly intelligible sense unit is a fantasy often held but, in the history of the novel, constantly and with frequent resourcefulness, rejected.

Rationalizing the Biblical Chapter

The pressures around sense-making segmentation in the novel were identical to those that had long operated in Scripture, but it is in biblical commentary and editing that such pressures were most exposed, and most unresolved.[11] In the case of the Enlightenment Bible we can see a particular failure to experiment with segmentation, produced by a fantasy of an unmarked, unsegmented reading that could not, finally, manifest itself. I mean here specifically the belated and finally futile resistance in Protestant Britain to the Langton–Saint Albans biblical chaptering system. Starting in the seventeenth century and extending until the dawn of the nineteenth, British scholars and editors attempted to rethink the model of biblical capitulation they had inherited. The extant chapters were critiqued and frequently denounced, their particularities often described and widely labeled as defects. It was a moment destined to eventually recede; the Langton–Saint Albans system would survive it essentially unaltered. But it was, for some time, a moment in which the operations of chapters were newly available for reconsideration. The impetus for this rethinking of the chapter was initially a newly popular textual historicism, spurred by the arrival of manuscripts from the East into centers of western European learning. Codex Alexandrinus arrived in England in 1628, a gift from Cyril Lucar, Patriarch of Constantinople, to the court of Charles I; many scholars hailed it as the oldest and purest scriptural text.[12] When fire broke out in Ashburnham House in 1731, where it was then held, the famed scholar and editor Richard Bentley chose it for a last-minute rescue. Witnesses observed the sixty-nine-year-old Keeper of the King's Libraries emerging in his nightgown and wig carrying a few select treasures, including the sole manuscript of *Beowulf*, and with Alexandrinus tucked under one arm.[13] But the lessons of historicism inevitably tended to produce new theories of textual division that were not necessarily tethered to historical example—in particular, a series of attempts to rationalize the erratic nature of now historically distant paradigms of segmentation.

Historicism initially had the effect of denaturalizing choices made centuries ago. However well known the story of Langton's creation was—and it had become widely if not universally accepted, often mentioned by English scholars and essayists with some element of national pride—the sanction of long use had protected the chaptering system in place from any critique.[14] As biblical textual criticism developed, however, this creation began to seem more recent and more contingent; what had been long understood as a reader's aid shifted into an obstacle. Even by the mid-seventeenth century, only a few decades after Alexandrinus's arrival, Langton's reputation was in decline. The critique of the natural philosopher Robert Boyle is exemplary for its moment: while acknowledging the "seeming Immethodicalnesse of the New Testament," he laid much of the blame upon "the inconvenient Distinction of Chapters and Verses now in use":

> which though it be a very great help to the Memory, and be some other wayes serviceable; yet being of no Greater Antiquity than its Contriver, *Stephanus*; and being (though now of General use) but of Private Authority, and by him drawn up in haste; it will be perhaps no slander to that Industrious Promoter of Heavenly Learning, to say, he hath sometimes Severe'd Matters that should have been left United, and United others which more conveniently he might have Sever'd, and that his Lucky Attempt ought not to lay restraint upon other Learned Men, from making use of the same Liberty he took in altering the former Partitions (for of them I speak, not of the Punctuation) of the New Testament; in altering his alterations, to the best Advantage of the Sense of Method.[15]

Boyle's reference to "the former Partitions" gives him the historical perspective necessary for an otherwise audacious proposal: redivide Scripture. If it has been done once, it can be done again, and better. The accusation is as yet general—simply that divisions are present when not needed and absent when needed—but comprehensive, and rooted in a sense of the system's contingency. The critique could run toward restoration rather than reinvention: as early as 1587, the Huguenot philologist and theologian Isaac Casaubon had expressed a wish, in his notes to Henri Estienne's edition of the Greek New Testament, that more ancient divisions of the text might be revived.[16] This scholarly preference for restoration rather than reinvention was at times contradictory, as it could imagine at once a purer, original text unmarked by clumsy divisions and also an original set of divisions that, by virtue of their antiquity, were preferable to any later confection. The Spinozistic textual criticism of Richard Simon, the French scholar whose influence in late seventeenth-century England was considerable, negotiated exactly this dual nostalgia: while well aware of ancient capitulary traditions, including that of Alexandrinus, Simon also asserted that the oldest exemplars of the New Testament had been elegantly unmarked, marred neither by chapters, verses, nor even spaces between words.[17]

Yet an appreciation for the long and complex history of biblical capitulation was not, in and of itself, sufficient to motivate the burgeoning distaste for the modern biblical chapter, even with the usual scholarly preference for the older over the newer. Nor was a thorough acquaintance with the modern system's occasionally puzzling decisions. The root question here, which cannot be entirely explained by the new presence of texts like Alexandrinus, is: What forms of scriptural reading were now found to be hindered by the Langton–Saint Albans chapters? The answer is a mixture of political tension between dissent and established religion, a new epistemology, and an increasingly visible and central cultural practice, and it is best exemplified in the occasional biblical criticism of John Locke, perhaps the most famous of the modern chapter system's detractors.[18] Locke's attacks on existing biblical capitulation were not particularly new. He had been preceded by at least a half-century of fairly explicit argumentation that the modern chapters should be treated as accidental and improvable, either by a return to the past or by a newer model. What Locke supplied was a more fundamental grounding for this opinion, based not in the happenstance existence of manuscripts that suggested alternatives but instead in a thorough reconsideration of the purposes to which textual division might be put. For Locke, the central question was how the mind operated when engaged in continuous private reading. As he explained it, existing biblical chapters were at odds with both this mode of reading and the mental operations that subtended it.

Most of this argument emerged posthumously, as part of his project *A Paraphrase and Notes on the Epistles of St. Paul*, which was published in parts starting in 1705 before its final collected edition in 1707. Locke's prefatory essay was the final element to appear, and it contained his most explicit account of the textual divisions that the rest of the project sought to eliminate. Like Boyle before him, Locke asserted that many of the complexities of the Epistles were a result of the epistolary genre itself, in which the tricky rhetorical stances and wavering, inconsistent modes of address of Paul's communicative situations have outlived their original context. But there were also significant "external Causes" that exacerbated Paul's opacity:

> First, The dividing of them into Chapters and Verses, as we have done, whereby they are so chop'd and minc'd, and as they are now Printed, stand so broken and divided, that not only the Common People take the Verses usually for distinct Aphorisms, but even Men of more advanc'd Knowledge in reading them, lose very much of the strength and force of the Coherence, and the Light that depends on it. Our Minds are so weak and narrow, that they have need of all the helps and assistances can be procur'd, to lay before them undisturbedly, the Thread and Coherence of any Discourse; by which alone they are truly improv'd and lead into the Genuine Sense of the Author. . . . These Divisions also have given occasion to the reading these

Epistles by parcels and in scraps, which has farther confirm'd the Evil arising
from such partitions. And I doubt not but every one will confess it to be a
very unlikely way to come to the Understanding of any other Letters, to
read them Peicemeal, a Bit to day, and another Scrap to morrow, and so by
broken Intervals; Especially if the Pause and Cessation should be made as
the Chapters the Apostles Epistles are divided into do end sometimes in
the middle of a Discourse, and sometimes in the middle of a Sentence. It
cannot therefore but be wondred, that that should be permitted to be
done to Holy Writ, which would visibly disturb the Sense, and hinder
the Understanding of any other Book whatsoever. If *Tully's* Epistles were
so printed, and so used, I ask whether they would not be much harder
to be understood, less easy and less pleasant to be read by much than
now they are?[19]

This passage condenses several charges against chapters, fusing capitulation
and versification into one general category, while also separating out their respective deleterious effects. If the biblical verse promotes an aphoristic selec-
tivity that confirms bias and promotes sectarian reading, the chapter disrupts
overall sense, leaving the mind detached from authorial intent and grasping
after any other support it can find—which will inevitably be isolated sentences, read through the scrim of a preexisting prejudice. The chapter unmoors
us, and the verse acts as a delusive lifeline carrying readers away from our
proper anchor. That firm support is and can only be authorial intent. The essay's title is a dramatic declaration of Locke's ability to access it, its subtitle
veering close to necromancy: *An Essay for the Understanding of St. Paul's Epistles, By Consulting St. Paul Himself.*

The thinking here passes through three distinct phases, borrowing from
earlier charges made against chapters, while generalizing and thereby transforming them. First is the familiar argument that modern textual divisions are
belated dismemberments of what was once whole, entirely without authorial
sanction. But Locke continues: a textual division not produced by the author's
hand is highly likely to break a discourse into artificial units that are not sense
units. This is the accusation of clumsiness frequently lodged against the modern
chapters, but here read as a general likelihood of any system of segmentation
rather than a quality specific to the Langton–Saint Albans chapters. Locke's
tendency is to explain the observed deficiencies of the modern chapters as inevitable results of the act of capitulation rather than any particular set of flaws
that could be forgiven or corrected.[20] Here Locke's argument makes its final

turn, which is also a return to his original premise: insofar as these divisions break a discourse, they hinder our ability to access authorial intent, because authorial intent can be known only through what he calls "coherence": a slow temporal process of following a continuous, developing thought. Instead of a chain with links, Locke prefers the image of the "thread"—single, extended, uninterrupted. It echoes an argument pressed in *The Reasonableness of Christianity* (1695): "We must look into the drift of the Discourse, observe the coherence and connexion of the Parts, and see how it is consistent with it self, and other parts of Scripture; if we will conceive it right."[21] Continuity is the sign or guarantee of a thinking mind. It can be appreciated only by a reader able to match that continuity with patient and fluidly uninterrupted attentiveness.

This is a description both of an epistemology and of a particular practice: solitary, immersive reading.[22] The political and theological urgency of this complaint derives from an effort to halt sectarian uses of Scripture, to find some common ground—that is, Paul's original intent—by which the various interpretive gambits of theological dissent could be adjudicated.[23] But the argument rests on an ironic inversion. If private and untutored reading might be said to be a cause of the sectarian discord about which Locke worries, he nonetheless seeks to rescue it, in intensified form, as the only possibility for moving past that discord. The solution is not partial or morcellated reading— of which even reading in a liturgical setting would be one example—but the prolonged, unpunctuated comprehension that comes of an individual alone with a text. For Locke, chapters are the artifacts of communal approaches: citation, proscribed ritual segmentation, numbing serial interruptions. As such they vandalize scriptural coherence with ephemeral, distracting marks. Private reading, in this view, is inherently at odds with capitulation.

Locke's reasoning here has an austere consistency that, he realizes, can be enacted only through compromises; he admits defeat from the start. A Bible printed "as it should be, and as the several Parts of it were writ, in continued Discourses where the Argument is continued," he goes on to lament, would be greeted as "an Innovation, and a dangerous Change in the publishing those holy Books." Sheer habit would make it difficult to accept, and as for confirmed sectarians, they would be unlikely to welcome the change, as they "would most of them be immediately disarm'd of their great Magazine of Artillery wherewith they defend themselves . . . if the Holy Scripture were but laid before the Eyes of Christians in its due Connection and Consistency" in the form of an undivided text.[24] A nonsectarian text would be experienced only as the height of sectarianism. Failing that utopian solution, Locke turns to makeshifts:

paraphrases and resectioning. The paraphrase attempts to restore in miniature the discursive thread that the chapter disrupts; the resectioning attempts to treat the cultural addiction to reading in segments through replacement therapy, whereby more coherent divisions might wean a reader from the damaging effects of the current system's arbitrariness.

A numerical glance at the eventual work of the *Paraphrase and Notes* reveals what an amelioration to the Langton–Saint Albans scheme means. Compared with the existing system, Locke's new "sections," to use his deliberately neutral substitute term for chapters, are both more numerous and also more various in size. The modern system's attempt at uniformity is explicitly flouted in favor of a more supple model that can match the irregularity of Paul's thought and that permits subdivisions; these "sections" are often divided into subunits. The Epistle to the Galatians's divisions are expanded by Locke from six chapters to fourteen units; Ephesians from six to twelve. Some of these units are as small as a handful of verses, while his section 2 of 2 Corinthians gathers ninety-one verses, almost twice as long as the longest of the modern chapters.[25] This new rhythm is not meant to be contrapuntal so much as organically irregular, in the sense of owing as little as possible to mere quantitative consistency. The ironies of this project ramify: first, that this attempt at rationalization looks, in one respect at least, *more* irrational, its units exhibiting such a variety of sizes that the idea of a "section" itself seems to lack any formal identity; second, that his paraphrase is finally even more thoroughly fragmented than the usual biblical text it attempts to clarify—published in installments, offering divisions within divisions, presented in a page design that resembles medieval glosses more than a linear, unmarked text.[26] Lastly, one general irony lingers over them all, that such a prominent opponent of textual division would be reduced to grappling with his own method of segmentation.

For all Locke's reasoned doubts about capitulation, it seems to have been a compulsion he could not avoid. After his permanent retirement to Oates, the Essex estate of the Whig member of Parliament Sir Francis Masham and his intellectual wife Damaris, he seems to have become preoccupied with both the usual and ideal modes of reading and with formulating rules for reading's proper orientation.[27] This was the period that resulted in the *Paraphrase and Notes*, but just before that work began, in August 1701, he returned to *The Reasonableness of Christianity* to articulate its chapters. Harvard's Houghton Library owns Locke's copy of the unchaptered 1695 edition, in which he adds marginal Roman numerals to indicate chapter breaks, occasionally with short rubrics provided as well (figure 5.1).[28] The breaks coincide with those

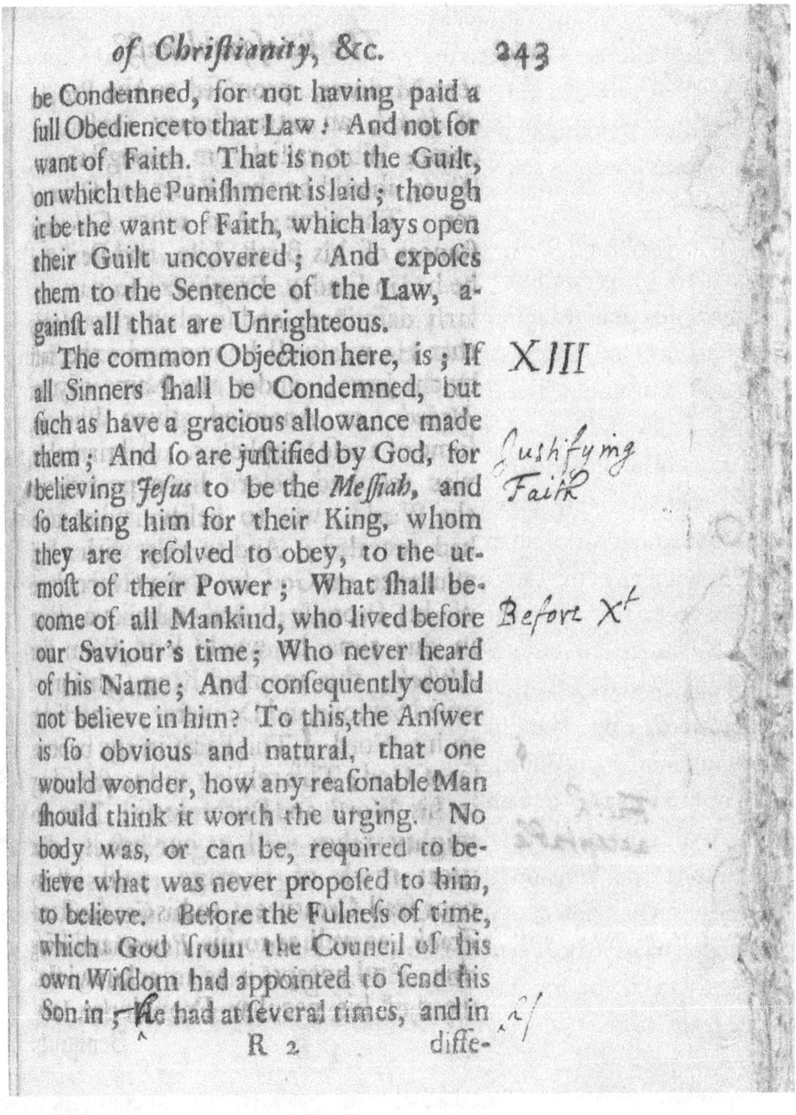

be Condemned, for not having paid a
full Obedience to that Law: And not for
want of Faith. That is not the Guilt,
on which the Puniſhment is laid; though
it be the want of Faith, which lays open
their Guilt uncovered; And expoſes
them to the Sentence of the Law, a-
gainſt all that are Unrighteous.

The common Objection here, is; If XIII
all Sinners ſhall be Condemned, but
ſuch as have a gracious allowance made
them; And ſo are juſtified by God, for *Juſtifying*
believing *Jeſus* to be the *Meſſiah*, and *Faith*
ſo taking him for their King, whom
they are reſolved to obey, to the ut-
moſt of their Power; What ſhall be-
come of all Mankind, who lived before *Before X^t*
our Saviour's time; Who never heard
of his Name; And conſequently could
not believe in him? To this, the Anſwer
is ſo obvious and natural, that one
would wonder, how any reaſonable Man
ſhould think it worth the urging. No
body was, or can be, required to believe what was never propoſed to him,
to believe. Before the Fulneſs of time,
which God from the Council of his
own Wiſdom had appointed to ſend his
Son in; He had at ſeveral times, and in
          R 2   diffe-

FIGURE 5.1 A sample of Locke's 1701 chaptering annotations in his copy of
The Reasonableness of Christianity (London, 1695).
Houghton Library *EC65 L7934 695ra. Courtesy of the Houghton Library, Harvard
University.

provided by Pierre Coste's 1696 French translation, but the brief rubrics of Locke's annotations are far from the long summary titles Coste had provided. It is as if the dream of a purely linear private reading, one that synchronizes with the linear thinking of the author, is just that, a dream—even when the author is one's own past self. Private reading is inexorably contaminated with caesuras.

Locke is significant in the history of the chapter because of his willingness to sketch out the grounds for an antichapter theory, and the extent to which those grounds depend upon private reading as the norm the chapter disrupts. He is less important as an actual influence. His conclusions, as he had anticipated, ran afoul of the chapter's embeddedness in biblical textual tradition specifically and literate culture more generally, and were critiqued from the start as historically naïve, overstated, and inconsistent. Robert Jenkin, one of Locke's frequent antagonists, insisted on a common-sense reading of chapters as essentially human things: necessary since antiquity "for the ease of the Reader, and for the Conveniency of citing in Authors," but fallible; the more useful the longer they have been accepted, regardless of their flaws; and in any case inevitable, even for their critics. "For if the Epistles must not be read by Chapters, much less by Verses; and if they may not be read in this manner," Jenkin argues indignantly, "why should they be at any time cited in such manner? Why did Mr. *Lock* divide them into Sections?"[29] Catching Locke out in this way was not a move limited to Jenkin. While agreeing in general with Locke's complaints against sectarian reading styles and their relation to textual division, the Swiss theologian and ex-Calvinist Jean Le Clerc nonetheless detected in Locke's argument a fantasy of a completely unmediated relation between reader and text for which his *Essay* itself served as contrary evidence, because Locke's analysis of textual division was itself derived from another source, and that source was, as Le Clerc dryly observed, Le Clerc himself.[30]

Responses like these outlined a situation in which biblical chapters were felt to be both theoretically indefensible and practically ineradicable. The historical consciousness of their very contingent medieval fabrication, the general effort to avoid sectarian hermeneutics, and the emphasis placed on private reading as the crucial scene of biblical consumption all led to a complicated stasis in eighteenth-century Bibles. For well over a century, chapters were flagged as unwelcome but insistent guests in a host text that had no way of refusing them, and every offered solution seemed inadequate.[31] When in the 1740s a project to replace the Authorized Version was mooted, its draft proposals hesitantly addressed divisions: "Some parts of Scripture supposed to be out of due place, may be better arranged. A more commodious Division may be made. Contents of chapters neither accurate clear nor full."[32] Yet the Authorized Version, with its stylistic distinctiveness and politically motivated centrality, loomed too large to be replaced, and as a result this historicist textualism could attach itself to no one major project. The result was a dispersal. As filtered through the influential work of Richard Simon, even relatively cheap Bibles reflected Spinoza's skeptical distinction between the physical text and its divine message, which meant that chapters had to be handled somehow—either explained, defended, debunked, altered, or replaced, options that were attempted in various combinations.[33] Locke's critique was diffused among many possible, equally impermanent solutions.

The prefaces of eighteenth-century English Bibles are rife with anxious speculation and strategizing on the matter of capitulation. For those translators and editors who agreed to retain the modern system, it required at the very least an apology as well as an explanation of their provenance, as if to acquit themselves against charges of naïvety and inoculate the reader against any excessive credulity in the system's significance. William Whiston's 1745 *Primitive New Testament* advertised in a title page that the "modern Distinctions of Chapters, and Verses, and Sentences, and Words, are retained, though not in the MS."[34] George Campbell's 1789 *Four Gospels* anxiously explained that the division into chapters "does not proceed from the inspired writers, but is a contrivance of a much later date."[35] Historicist apology goes only so far, and many editors contrived workarounds. Campbell simply listed all of the poor chaptering decisions made in the Gospels—including among them the familiar examples of the openings of Mark 5 and 9—as a way to indicate his awareness.[36] Philip Doddridge's 1740 *Family Expositor* footnoted unhappy chapter divisions, often waving away with one hand what the other hand had pointed out, as in this note to the midsentence transition between Luke 23 and 24: "Such *Divisions* are great Instances of Negligence in the Person by whom they were first made; but in a Work like this *Harmony*, they are less material, and hardly in some Cases avoidable."[37] Others used page design as a compromise, relegating chapter numbers to the margin in an effort to ease their eventual disappearance. Richard Wynne's 1764 New Testament declared its attempt to "rescue the Sacred Writings from the confusion into which they have been thrown by the modern division of them into Chapters and Verses," but did so not by eliminating them—thanks to their continued utility for citational purposes—but simply sidelining them in the margin "without making a new section at the beginning of every chapter, or breaking off the line at the end of every verse."[38] This was a generally recommended procedure; the clergyman and theorist of the picturesque William Gilpin applied his taste for removal and rearrangement to chapters in 1788, advising their detachment from the text and relegation to the margin, as they are, like a poacher on an estate, "unauthorized intruders."[39] A different approach was to bury them within other divisions, as if in a diversionary gambit: Jean Le Clerc's 1703 French translation of the New Testament recommended further subdivision of chapters, particularly into paragraphs, to reduce the likelihood that any chapter could be taken as offering a single argument or single event.[40] Edward Harwood's 1768 *Liberal Translation of the New Testament* did just that, explaining that the "old division of chapters and verses I have been persuaded, contrary to my own judgment, to retain, but I have everywhere signified to the reader, by the manner of *printing* and *punctuation*, when they are erroneous; and I have divided the whole into *sections*."[41] Often, as in Nathaniel Scarlett's 1798 New Testament, those sections received their own subtitles, while chapters were left without headings, as if they were a merely vestigial apparatus distant from any actual sense unit.[42]

This was moving rather far from Locke, certainly, as it depended on the multiplication of paratextual interventions—disclaimers, annotations, new divisions—rather than their elimination. Yet a solution that would eliminate or revise the modern chapters was hard to come by. When calls for a new capitulation were made, they were quickly hedged round with reservations. Anthony Blackwall's 1731 *The Sacred Classics Defended and Illustrated* insisted that the "most valuable book in the world is the worst divided; and is deformed and encumber'd with the most improper sections and pauses," and suggested that Langton's work was long due for a revision, but finally conceded that his divisions had to be retained in the most liturgically central places—the Psalms, the Gospels, the Epistles—to avoid disrupting Anglican tradition. This left Blackwall in the position of virtually every other eighteenth-century editor, cataloguing the modern system's curious decisions, such as the midsentence beginning of John 8, and suggesting modest alterations.[43] Perhaps the most Lockean of eighteenth-century Testaments, the *New Translation* of 1765, which combined Doddridge's translation with his paraphrases, eliminated all verse and chapter numeration, indicated chapters only by a marginal graphic mark, and used numbered lineation as its finding system. Its prefatory description of modern capitulation as "a barbarous innovation" that "almost everywhere disjoint or confound the sense" was, for its time, fairly orthodox, but its experimental, elegantly spare page design did not catch on.[44] The Lockean protest ended in a curious stalemate: chapters appeared ever more contingent and peculiar, their abstraction ever more distant from the text they divided, but their durable imperfections ended up demonstrating, if anything, the inevitability of textual division, the implausibility of a fantasy in which units could be wished away.

So the long period of disquiet around the Langton–Saint Albans chapters finally ebbed, having failed in the project of rationalizing or removing them; in the nineteenth century far fewer English-language Bibles bothered to explain their provenance or annotate their stranger aspects, thereby renaturalizing them. Yet the lasting effect of historical textualism in regard to chapters may have been outside Scripture. The consequence of this learned and often creative skepticism was to highlight the very quality—the alien abstractions of chapter division—that it critiqued, and in so doing perversely affirm its interest as an *effect*. By exploring the gap between the chapters as they existed and the biblical text's sense units, and insisting that this gap was not a proper scriptural effect, it turned that effect into a literary one—antique, and at times bizarre, but therefore perversely compelling. The historicist defamiliarization of the Bible, that is, helped make the abstracted quality of the medieval chapter available for a more generally aesthetic use in secular narratives.[45] In the end what a critical approach to textual division accomplished was to reveal the possibilities lurking in the unruliness of biblical chaptering.

A Schema of the Held Posture

No single comparison helped eighteenth-century novelists imagine and defend chapters, because the chapter could not be figured as any one thing, serving any one purpose, or looking any one way. Too many aspects of its existence cried out for attention—exactly the condition that had reduced biblical translators and editors to frustrated resignation to their continued existence: the chapter was for discontinuous access, citational reference, and liturgical exigency, not to mention readerly signposting, and each function insisted on its own importance, continuing to prop up the chapter even when other legs were knocked out from under it. In Fielding's influential discussion in *Joseph Andrews*, similitude falls into a winkingly self-aware confusion in the effort to account for the different component parts of the chapter. A chapter is first of all a break or white space—the inn or resting place between "Stages" of a journey; yet it has a title, which is an inscription over that inn's gate, "informing the Reader what Entertainment he is to expect"; and yet it is also something in itself, a patch of text, an experience bracketed by rests and advertised by titles that becomes, in the metaphor's final gesture, meat that a butcher has jointed, in a "great Help to both the Reader and the Carver," the substance that, one might presume, the inn serves its visitors.[46] Break, title, contents: the inn metaphor stretches to the point of incoherence in the effort to encompass it all. Is the actual substance of the chapter the journey that the chapter break at the inn interrupts for a rest, or is it the refreshment and entertainment provided at the inn itself, which its title—the sign over the inn's gate—has promised? Is that entertainment mere diversion (good talk at the inn, say) or nourishment (the meal served there)? How much autonomy does the reader have—is the decision to stop a fully free one, or is it dictated by the enforced passivity of the coach journey, the linearity of the narrative reading experience?[47]

That consciousness of the chapter as a compound element comprising halting (a break), marking (a title), and filling (a stretch of text) extended itself everywhere in the practice of the novel, particularly after Fielding's similes had made chaptering in novels so eminently discussable.[48] But the practice of chaptering in the decades around *Joseph Andrews* managed a more tacit synthesis than the unstable figure of the stage journey. In fact, eighteenth-century chapters tended to entwine two separate if related syntheses, whose braiding together contoured how the novelistic chapter, for a time at least, was both understood and habitually performed. The first of these two syntheses is a binary reflected in the tension between Fielding's metaphor and the form of the chapter in which it is discussed: *the opposition between the chapter as an articulation of a long temporal sequence and the chapter as a stand-alone entity defined by subject rather than sequence*. We can think of this as a binary between time and space: on the one hand, the chapter divides or cuts time into units; on the other, it is a spatial container, a volume filled with particular contents, a topos and not a slice of time. More prosaically, this binary is the opposition between the chapter's narrative and essayistic modes. If Fielding's inn figure imagined the chapter as inescapably temporal—a journey frequently interrupted, a trajectory that takes, and is made of, time—the particular chapter in which it occurs is labeled as a discursive, non-narrative unit, with the familiar and ancient deictic noun phrase "Of Divisions in Authors." One joke here is that narrative time has to stop in this particular chapter in order for Fielding to provide a set of metaphors for the narrative time of the chapter per se; the essayistic has its little, anachronistic triumph over the temporal. Topical chapters like these are the residual trace of the chapter's informational, indexical past, and as such they tend to be a relatively minor if recurrent part of a novel's texture, either dotted stochastically throughout or, as in Fielding's 1749 *Tom Jones*, assigned a particular recurrent place, such as the opening chapters of its eighteen books. In either case it is usually easily spotted and openly signaled. Take the five books of *Gargantua and Pantagruel*: of the total of 258 chapters, 210 are titled with the *comment*, or "how," form, which as we have already seen from Burgundian remediations promises a narrative mode, but 13 chapters are prefaced by the noun-phrase style that indicates an essayistic excursus, such as "Concerning the significance of the colors white and blue" (1.10). In sheerly quantitative terms, whether in Rabelais or Fielding or elsewhere, these topos chapters are a minority within prose fiction. But they bear a far greater importance conceptually, because the chapter is still largely conceived of as, in essence, a container for a particular subject. Here the rhetoric of *Tristram Shandy* is illustrative. When Tristram announces the plan to write a chapter in particular, it tends overwhelmingly to be a chapter *of* or a chapter *on*: "Have I not promised the world a chapter of knots? two chapters upon the right and wrong end of a woman? a chapter upon whiskers? a chapter upon wishes?—a chapter of noses?"[49] A chapter on chambermaids, on buttonholes, upon sash windows (to be found, we're informed, in the *Tristrapaedia*), green gowns, old hats, straight lines, Toby's modesty, sleep, pishes, Calais, and, as if to give this tendency its purest articulation, the "chapter of THINGS": the material is potentially infinite but the loosely genitive noun form consistent (*TS*, 269). It is a memory of the chapter's original indexical function, Sterne's homage to the encyclopedic discontinuity that the chapter had originally been tasked with organizing, and effective as an ongoing joke because the chapter's indexical function is so familiar still. The popular idea of the chapter, that is, as opposed to its usual novelistic reality, still emphasizes the topical over the temporal—but of course, very few of those promised topical chapters in *Tristram Shandy* are ever actually delivered, with the interesting exception, as we will see, of a chapter "on" chapters.

One binary between time and space, then, but a second between two kinds of time. The latter is a distinction between simultaneous but asynchronous temporalities: *the opposition between the chapter as a division of time within the story and the chapter as a division of readerly time, a unit of communication between narrator and reader that acknowledges, and sculpts, the time it takes to read.* How long does a chapter last? The question is susceptible to several different answers. Somewhere between a thousand and two thousand words? This is the norm, at least, of Fielding's own novels—and therefore a matter of some few minutes of reading time.[50] And yet also, in Fielding: something that might be less than an episode, perhaps, of story time, something to be described by terms evoking a certain limited duration—an event, an incident, an occurrence. There is a relation between these two registers but it is not rigid or formulaic, and it performs, in the eighteenth century at least, what Christina Lupton calls "temporal non-equivalence."[51] Named by Gunther Müller in 1948, we have here that old wedded pair narrative time (*erzählte Zeit*) and the time taken by narrating (*Erzählzeit*), dependent on each other but known best by their quarrelsome misalignment, their different scopes and intensities.[52] If both narrative and narrating time in the eighteenth-century novel chapter are shorter than they will later become, the reasons will vary depending on which time one wants to emphasize. Chapter brevity can function within eighteenth-century novels as both a story effect, which is to say a preference for the minuter transactions of daily life, and as a convenience within the time of narrating, as a helpful replacement for the turned-down corner or thumbed leaf of a solitary novel reader parceling out their own time in which to read. As with the first binary, self-conscious chapter titles will also play with this disjuncture between temporal orders. The title of chapter 10 of book 3 of Alain-René Lesage's novel *Gil Blas*'s first volume—"Which is no longer than the previous [Qui n'est pas plus long que le précédent]"—implicitly raises the question, Which duration is meant here?[53] Chapter 10 of book 9 of Lennox's *Female Quixote* is slightly more direct about the ambiguity: "A short Chapter indeed, but full of Matter."[54] Short, that is, for a reader; rather more crowded for the story. As for Fielding, in *Tom Jones* he will reduce this ambiguity by widening the difference: "My Reader then is not to be surprised, if in the Course of the Work, he shall find some Chapters very short, and others altogether as long; some that contain only the Time of a single Day, and others that comprise Years; in a word, if my History sometimes seems to stand still, and sometimes to fly."[55] The distinction remains salient, however, no matter how it is handled. Where it is most salient is with the alternation between readerly address, clustering at the beginnings of chapters and at times extending to titles and even epigraphs, and the stretch of plot narrated—a distinction that stands in for, and expresses, the narrated time/time of narrating binary.[56] Of course the distinction is not absolute, and in Sterne it is often violated on those occasions when his characters continue to operate and move during narratorial digressions; but it works nonetheless as a rule of thumb, and never more so than in the frame of the chapter, which is both an occasion for encapsulating a narrative unit and for resuming contact with a reader—resetting, that is, two interdependent times, that of story and that of communication.

What these two binaries produce, taken together, is a semantic field: a scheme of possible relations to the novelistic chapter in a particular era, the moment that lasts from the early picaresque to Fielding and Sterne. It is not that every chapter must touch on every possible relation here, but that each chapter in the period takes its bearings from the boundaries these binaries stake out. It can define its difference from other chapters among which it is set, however subtly, by recalibrating its place within this field of possibilities.

Such a chapter form is a complexly knotted series of relations or interdependencies. A chapter is an occasion to renew an ongoing, intermittent discourse with a reader, but that occasion is reciprocally dependent on the production of breaks or pauses, the falling into brief silences that allows a reader to escape from the very relation about to be renewed: the copulative and disjunctive, in a strained equilibrium. The chapter "on" or "of" something *gathers*; it understands itself as a volume measure, a container ("in which" or "containing," old titling conventions that remain pertinent) to hold contents that are taxonomically related; the chapter that narrates a single event or incident *selects*, holding up a single specimen plucked out of the stream of time on the basis of its stubborn peculiarity, its status as something "interesting"; yet a contrary pressure is always being exerted on each, the topos needing to finally instantiate itself in an illustrative or generative anecdote, the incident needing to classify itself as a *kind of* event that happens.[57] These chapters are delicate syntheses (figure 5.2), managing the pressures involved in inserting discontinuous impulses into the linearity of narrative.

While true in a general way, a description like the foregoing is also perhaps too neat. What we have here, perhaps more than an elegant double synthesis, is a kludge: a messy, makeshift assemblage meant to solve a problem, here the complex linkage of narrative and information, story time and reading time. To write a chapter with these multiple commitments requires no small amount of jostling. There is much to nod to, acknowledge, gesture toward, all while attending to the varied rhythm in which each particular solution must make sense in a series.[58] Resume a communicative relation to a reader, if only out of the awkwardness of restarting what has been paused. Provide something striking and singular, but in a way that is also categorizable. Mediate between the closed or counter-entropic sense of the form (*here* is where you will go to find *this* information) and its necessary incompletion (and yet there is more to come). And do all of it in a small space: the smaller-than-2000-word form. Like all such kludges, its various components have a tendency to fly apart. Never more so than in *Tristram Shandy*: the chapter-as-container becomes the two blank chapters of volume 9, empty jars waiting to be filled. The

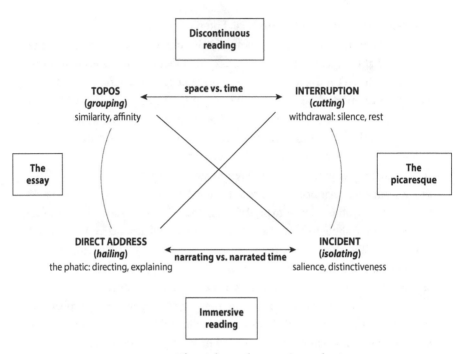

FIGURE 5.2 The eighteenth-century synthesis.

chapter-as-interruption becomes the single-sentence chapter, little more than an ejaculation bracketed by silence:

CHAP. XV.

——I'll put him, however, into breeches said my father,—let the world say what it will. (*TS*, 349)

Direct address, meanwhile, can take entire chapters, and not simply in Tristram's own voice; as in volume 3, a chapter can be a sermon, or even a delayed preface. An incident can shorten itself into the smallest of units—a gesture, an utterance. These are not simply Shandean fantasias; they are lurking possibilities in any novelistic chapter in the period, which from time to time in *Tristram Shandy* are allowed expression freed from their usual reciprocal obligations. Even in those isolated forms they point out, by way of contrast, the compromises the usual chapter is otherwise negotiating. Which is to say that, as a kludge, the eighteenth-century novelistic chapter lacks conceptual clarity.[59] Its most consistently identifiable feature is its brevity, but that tendency to conciseness only accentuates the multiple operations that have to share such crowded and trickily balanced parameters.

And yet, something to chapter style remains consistent, an image type that subtends its machinery. Finally it is Sterne who helps describe it, in the most completely self-conscious chapter of his century, *Tristram Shandy*'s "chapter upon chapters" in its fourth volume. This is the Sterne who is not violating the form so much as defending it, by providing a metaphor that would be less elaborate than Fielding's coach journey while also more attentive to the chapter's several balancing acts.[60] It begins with an action interrupted: Walter and Toby Shandy walking together down a staircase, Walter having just soothed his despair at how a pair of forceps has mutilated his infant son's nose by announcing his intention to name him Trismegistus, a great boon to counteract a great misfortune. The two brothers negotiate their peristaltic way down the set of stairs, pausing for Walter's self-pity to expend itself in his usual volubility, as he bemoans the "million to one" chance that befell his heir. They reach the staircase's first landing, and with it the break that produces the chapter upon chapters:

> It might have been worse, replied my uncle *Toby*—I don't comprehend, said my father—Suppose the hip had presented, replied my uncle *Toby*, as Dr. *Slop* foreboded.
>
> My father reflected half a minute—looked down—touched the middle of his forehead slightly with his finger—
>
> —True, said he. (*TS*, 224–25)

The break occurs midgesture, with what the theorist Viktor Shklovsky identified as Sterne's motif of the "posture," the bodily gesture momentarily frozen into an emblematic pose.[61] These postural moments are comic because narrative time stops to capture them, but also because, with Sterne's signature double temporality, the different time of the reader-narrator communication has not stopped, as if Walter must strain to hold his body in that posture while the narrator proceeds to speak over him. (Any pose or expression held too long undoes itself: a grin becomes a rictus, an embrace becomes a forcible restraint.) Walter's posture is expressive—it is an *attitude* struck, a relation *to* something, an attempt to perform meaning; its awkwardness comes from its unusual duration, the way that the chapter break transforms a gesture into a fermata. "Attitudes are nothing, madam," Tristram insists earlier in volume 4, "'tis the transition from one attitude to another—like the preparation and resolution of the discord into harmony, which is all in all" (*TS*, 221). The chapter as Sterne understands it is a particular posture taken in relation to the world, however antic or brooding, that exists in an uncomfortable double time—a posture captured both in its frozen form and, with all the comic strain and pathos of any such attempt, in the act of trying to hold itself while time passes. So the chapter's "attitude" is always brief, and yet somehow also stretched almost too long, as if bound to undo itself and become something else, but not quite yet. For this reason we might think of the novelistic chapter of Sterne's time as postural in essence: a tensely held expressive attitude trying the paradoxical task of simultaneously condensing and dilating time.

This particular chapter break, between the ninth and tenth chapters of volume 4, pauses the two brothers on the landing. The ensuing "chapter upon chapters" begins by launching into its metadescription:

> Is it not a shame to make two chapters of what passed in going down one pair of stairs? for we are got no further yet than to the first landing, and there are fifteen more steps down to the bottom; and for aught I know, as my father and my uncle *Toby* are in a talking humor, there may be as many chapters as steps;—let that be as it will, Sir, I can no more help it than my destiny:—A sudden impulse comes across me—drop the curtain, *Shandy*—I drop it—Strike a line here across the paper, *Tristram*—I strike it—and hey for a new chapter! (*TS*, 225)

Collapsed here in a brief span—the entire chapter is less than five hundred words, not unusual for Sterne—are all the parameters of the chapter's business as I have sketched them above. A direct address, introducing the chapter's topos (which happens here to be chapters themselves); narrating a small incident (the conversation on the stairs) that requires an interruption—not just the dropped curtain or line struck across the paper, but the splitting of the stairs into two, via a landing and the chapter break's white space: the strange parturition of the chapter, one becoming two, amid all the other obstetrical talk. This newborn chapter will then go on to mock any rule-based understanding of how division works ("the duce of any other rule have I to govern myself in this affair") and describe as "cold conceits" any of the usual understandings of what chapters do, that they "relieve the mind" or "are as necessary as the shifting of scenes"; and yet it will not offer its own explicit definition of chapters, and instead suggests reading Longinus without explaining why (*TS*, 225). But it is the staircase, in the stalled diegesis outside this chapter's parenthesis, with Walter and Toby themselves stuck halfway down, that surreptitiously becomes Sterne's actual definition, the unmentioned heart of the chapter upon chapters.

The staircase, unlike Fielding's more well-known comparisons, captures the chapter's doubled chronometry, that tension expressed by the simultaneous binaries of space versus time and narrated versus narrating times. Where the coach journey is strictly linear, starting and stopping, the staircase unpacks two complementary but opposed dimensions: it is both a *vertical* trope, expressing a linear movement—down the stairs go Walter and Toby, onward goes the narrative, however slowly—and a *horizontal* one, a structure of steps and landings, cutting or segmenting linearity into discrete stages. This is of course a strange inversion of a more conventional figuration of time, in which the horizontal signifies linear time and the vertical its depth or duration, an inversion that only adds to the funhouse mirror of Sterne's comparison. It is also a reimagining of textual space, the horizontality of the chapter break's white space on the page translated into a vertical passage up, down, or across it. Regardless of how we apportion these dimensions, Sterne has provided here a master image for textual division and how such divisions parse time's gravitational force. The chapter is a pause on a step or landing, a continuing motion or gesture caught midway, the awkwardness of stopping somewhere one is meant to keep traversing. (The discomfort of conversing down a staircase: the little vertigo of turning one's head to talk while being pulled downward, forward.) What is as yet purely ontological in Sterne's staircase image, however, will soon gather historical weight. The progression of "steps" acquires a vocabulary of related terms—stages, phases, periods—that can lock chapters into all possible historiographical scales and enable them therefore to express new kinds of collective temporal experiences. It does so first by one all-important and purely quantitative shift: as with other significant moments in its history, the chapter changes by becoming longer.

Falling and Holding in Equiano

This much is evident: the chapter within fictional narrative up to the late eighteenth century—at the moment of perhaps its greatest self-consciousness—is, however seemingly flippant or insouciant, very much a complexly crafted form, busy and tight. What looms next is a paradox. The more that narrative art begins to grapple with personal, experiential time under the conditions of domination and emancipation, particularly from the perspective of the liberation movements of the later part of the century, that chapter form loses definition. It slips into incoherence; it embraces arbitrariness, the very arbitrariness that Protestant scholars of the Bible had lamented and tried to resolve. Most visibly, it elongates. Stretching the chapter's length could have produced an ability to articulate the larger phases of a life, or at least the units of retrospective assessment into which a life could be parsed. This is not quite what happened. Instead, the late-eighteenth-century chapter refuses coherent shape, particularly the shape provided by the topos, by "aboutness." There is something like a law of the chapter's history operating here. The way the chapter develops in its ability to capture new kinds of narrative textures and subjects is to return to the power of arbitrariness—to derigidify, to exploit the possibilities of what can look like meaninglessness or carelessness. This often goes hand in hand with simple expansion in size; lengthening is an invitation to experimental kinds of imprecision.

Such pressures on the novelistic chapter may not be intrinsically or originally novelistic. Other narrative forms may be crucial to its changes, often in cross-fertilized relationships with novelistic norms. A key locus for the shift away from the short, postural chapter in the late eighteenth century is the autobiography of emancipation, particularly the early slave narrative. In Olaudah Equiano's *Interesting Narrative of the Life of Olaudah Equiano, or Gustavus Vassa, the African* (1789), the chapter has novelistic trappings but explodes that intricate equilibrium. Here one can see a new version of the chapter coming into being, one in which it imposes an entirely external grid onto a life story whose events only poorly fit such segmentation. In Equiano, the chapter works against narrative transitions: it obscures what we might take to be pivotal events, interrupts at moments aslant from the kinds of sense units that might seem natural, as if in full awareness of their own conceptual irrelevance, and evokes a time in which events lose their ability to cohere. Chapters are here rooms emptied of their usual purpose, things that maybe once made a certain sense but do so no longer; they are no good indexical guide other than to their inability to guide. There is something persistently alien about the map they provide—alien, that is, to the map we might want to make of Equiano's text; our desire to arrange his life along some linear grid is defeated by the usual textual signs of that grid.

To start with its most visible features: *The Interesting Narrative* is divided into twelve chapters, originally spread across two volumes. A dense paratextual apparatus announces them. Each chapter starts a new page and is prefaced by a summary list of contents, closer to an ancient argumentum, in lieu of a more traditional title; the table of contents at the beginning of the book offers as chapter titles an abbreviated form of that list. The system seems to exist for discontinuous access, but only at the level of particular events; the chapters are presented as a disconnected list of actions, as in the summary title for the ninth chapter:

> *The author arrives at Martinico—Meets with new difficulties—Gets to Montserrat, where he takes leave of his old master, and sails for England—Meets Capt. Pascal—Learns the French horn—Hires himself with Doctor Irving, where he learns to freshen sea water—Leaves the doctor, and goes a voyage to Turkey and Portugal; and afterwards goes a voyage to Grenada, and another to Jamaica—Returns to the Doctor, and they embark together on a voyage to the North Pole, with the Hon. Capt. Phipps—Some account of that voyage, and the dangers the author was in—He returns to England.*[62]

Here is a succession of actions without framing, either temporally or directionally, and therefore without a discernible center. The table of contents abbreviates it further into just first and last items, its most sensational element, the polar exploration, omitted entirely: "*The author arrives at Martinico—Meets with new difficulties, and sails for England.*" The summary of the eleventh chapter reaches almost two hundred words, but the table of contents—and this for a chapter that includes the origins and eventual failure of a Miskito Coast plantation Equiano had been hired to oversee—offers only: "*Picks up eleven miserable men at sea in returning to England from Spain*" (*IN*, 30).[63] We are evidently back to the question of "bad" titling practices, and again, the "bad" form has a particular intent: neither long nor short summary can offer a higher-order encapsulation. They both signal a time separated from meaningful succession, something accidental, aleatory. And yet also highly visible: the chapter insists on its presence through these peculiar paratexts at the same time that it cannot justify its own shape at any level of abstraction higher than a list of discrete actions. It is not a method of division or indexing at all common to those few slave narratives that preexisted Equiano's, nor to captivity narratives of the previous century, nor to fictional treatments in English of enslavement or colonization, including Behn's *Oroonoko* or Defoe's *Robinson Crusoe*, all of which are far less encumbered by paratext.[64] What it does resemble, however, is a convention associated with one particular novelistic subvariant, the naval picaresque—particularly Tobias Smollett's 1748 *Adventures of Roderick Random*, whose lengthy content summaries Francis Coventry had compared unfavorably to Fielding's playfully reticent titles. Equiano's adoption of this paratextual style is evidence both of the book's eagerness to engage an audience—it is clustered with readerly aids, framings, attestations—and a tendency toward novelization of the slave narrative that would become even more pronounced in the following century.[65] The summaries of *Roderick Random*, however, are briefer, and consistent between its table of contents and chapter openings. *The Interesting Narrative* provides both a distended and a highly distilled version, as if to emphasize that neither scale of summarizing a chapter, and perhaps no scale at all, is calibrated to a satisfactory whole: neither an episode, nor a topos, nor even a defined place or time.

Some of *The Interesting Narrative*'s other paratexts have received attention from scholars, including its frontispiece portrait of Equiano and its continually revised list of subscribers, but its chaptering method has been ignored, perhaps because of its apparent inadequacies.[66] Readers have instead preferred to read past it and apply their own temporal grid to Equiano's text, or to misread Equiano's divisions to fit them into some preferred time scheme. Richard Gough's 1789 review in the *Gentleman's Magazine* describes a simple two-part liberation narrative: "The first volume treats of the manners of his countrymen, and his own adventures till he obtained his freedom; the second, from that period to the present, is uninteresting; and his conversion to Methodism oversets the whole."[67] This is not only conceptually dubious, it is factually false: Equiano's manumission occurs in the text's second volume. Contemporary attempts to discern temporal patterns in the narrative are more sophisticated but no less untethered to its chapter divisions.[68] What they have in common is a commitment to, as Lisa Lowe puts it, a concept of transition-as-liberation, "a progressive development from one stage to another," a linear process whose discontinuities are signs of emancipation and some version of enfranchisement.[69] It is a way of reading Equiano, recurrently compelling but at odds with the text's own articulated divisions. Equiano's chapters seem so opposed to broader allegorical schemes that they have to fall out of any such reading, as if they are simply inapt, or inept. While recent readers of Equiano have become more attuned to the slippages in his narrative that mitigate against any moralizing linear progression, the structures they detect, of isolated instants and discontinuous episodes, are still inattentive to the text's own marked segmentations.[70]

What then are those periods Equiano gives us—what is a chapter in his life's narrative, what kind of time is it? Most obviously his chapters are capacious; they *last*, well beyond the limits of any episode or incident. *The Interesting Narrative*'s average chapter is 6,500 words long, easily three to four times the length of the ordinary novel chapter of his moment, so even his possible borrowing of a titling style from one fictional genre will not suffice to make his units seem conventional. Too much happens in each to adopt a single pose or gesture, and even the most memorable, pivotal, or emblematic moments of his narrative—his sale into slavery, his description of the Middle Passage, his presence at major naval battles of the Seven Years' War, the betrayal of one owner's promise of manumission, his purchase of his freedom in 1766, his conversion to Methodist Christianity—take a modest place, however uneasily, in each chapter's list of narrative items, for which Equiano has a consistently atomized vocabulary: events, scenes, incidents, occurrences, sufferings.[71] Chapters neither begin nor end with strongly marked moments or allegoriz-able shifts.[72] They tend to begin instead with a double-edged gesture of reset-ting through temporal-deictic markers like "now," "thus," "such": "I now totally lost the small remains of comfort I had enjoyed in conversing with my coun-trymen" (chapter 3); "Thus, at the moment I expected all my toils to end, was I plunged, as I supposed, in a new slavery" (chapter 5); "Every day now brought me nearer my freedom" (chapter 7); "Such were the various scenes to which I was a witness" (chapter 12) (IN, 62, 95, 131, 220). While resynchronizing a nar-rative clock, these opening clauses also point to stasis: the clock has reset but previous conditions linger, perdure. It is a catching of breath rather than a cleanly marked new phase. The "now" of the new chapter stretches to cover the previous chapter's conclusion, as if to mitigate any rupture. Not that the effort to produce disjuncture isn't present in the narrative: in fact *The Interest-ing Narrative* is dotted with farewells, the sheer rageful pleasure of departure, liberation experienced as leaving behind:

> With a light heart I bade Montserrat farewell, and never had my feet on it since; and with it I bade adieu to the sound of the cruel whip, and all other dreadful instruments of torture! adieu to the offensive sight of the violated chastity of the sable females, which has too often accosted my eyes! adieu to oppressions (although to me less severe than most of my countrymen!) and adieu to the angry howling dashing surfs!" (*IN*, 164)

This layered moment of *adieux* comes early in the ninth chapter, which ironizes its seemingly strong narrative beat by following it with a series of returns, like a tide washing back in. After travel to England and the Mediterranean from Nice to Smyrna, Equiano heads back again to the West Indies and a syntax of repetition: "I met once more with my former kind of West-India customers," he comments wryly (*IN*, 170); in Jamaica, there are again "a vast number of negroes here, whom I found, as usual, exceedingly imposed upon by the white people, and the slaves punished as in the other islands" (*IN*, 171).[73] Just as

Equiano's legal status as manumitted slave is never entirely safe, the frame of the chapter juxtaposes permanent departure with eventual return, offering simply too large a time span to accord any single impulse more than momentary effect.

Each chapter is therefore the signature of an inhabited or endured, rather than willed, time. The release of the chapter break cuts erratically and often incomprehensibly against the progression of events, while within chapters themselves an accumulation of survivals, efforts, and entropic reversals pile up, each new event partially swallowing what preceded it but never quite erasing it. It is the grammar of what Christina Sharpe has called the "long time/ the long shot, the residence time of Black life on the verge of and in death," elongation here doing something of the work of exposure, leaving individual will rawly vulnerable to repetition and reversal.[74] The chapter stretches, but also, in its non-Euclidian logic, develops folds, into which individually motivated phases or demarcations disappear.[75] The small moment of triumph— "I now entered upon a scene quite new to me, but full of hope" (*IN*, 164)—is, so to speak, tucked away in those folds. Seen from this perspective, the summary lists of *The Interesting Narrative*'s indexical apparatus are almost inevitable: what can a chapter be other than a list of its contents? The chapter as topos, the chapter "on" or "of," organizing and taxonomizing, vanishes from the field; the chapter as a single incident, isolated and bounded, disappears as well. With their erasure, something decisively shifts in the history of the form. The pressure not only of the biographical frame, but the biographical frame under conditions of domination, breaks the tenuous balance between topos and event that had, for a time at least, obtained in the chapter form of the century's fiction. Events do not stand out because they will be repeated, and the repetition is too unwilled and too long-term to be gathered into meaningful groupings. One segmenting practice has died; there will after this have to be other solutions.

Not that Equiano's chapters are self-conscious in a Sternean fashion about this breaking apart, but there is instead a melancholic awareness of timing mechanisms, more congenial than this stretched and vulnerable time, that are unavailable to him. Early in the narrative he offers a brief ethnography and poetics of Igbo public dance and its narrative forms. "The assembly is separated into four divisions, which dance either apart or in succession, and each with a character peculiar to itself," he explains: married men, married women, young men, and maidens. "Each represents some interesting scene of real life, such as a great achievement, domestic employment, a pathetic story, or some rural sport" (*IN*, 34). Social decorum and generational succession are reflected in a form with clearly marked, appropriate divisions between segments, with each segment reflecting both a particular genre and a single "scene" to instantiate it. "Interesting," but not to excess, nor in chaotic form; measured, bounded, evenly paced. Elsewhere he notes the Igbo calculation of the year, and how time calculations are the province of wise men, "for we called them Ah-affoe-way-cah, which signifies calculators, or yearly men" (*IN*, 42). There is throughout this description of Igbo life a tremendous attraction to the social and bodily harmonies of consensual, regular, embodied articulations of time, time as dance. Such time is magic, but grounding magic, the magic of homeostasis, self and world in agreement. It is why he is entranced, even amid the horror of the Middle Passage, by the shipboard operations of the quadrant. It is why, alongside the instruments of restraint and torture, what fixes his attention on entering his first owner's house is a watch hung on a chimney.[76] The calculations of time are magic even in these forms, but never again to be the magic of harmony. Either there are the abstractions of commodified time—the watch in the master's house; the labor-time erased when he bargains to purchase his freedom for the same price at which he was sold years previously—or the chaos of unmoored time that is what the chapter configures. No suns rise and set, no stars rotate, no bodies move, in rhythm with the time Equiano's chapters tell.

Of this time, unlike the different calculations of dances or watches or quadrants, there is not much to say; one simply waits it out. How then to describe the chapter in Equiano, or more bluntly, why bother to do so? The answer is its dramatic, seemingly deliberate insufficiency, the impossibility of finding a habitable place within it. It is the measure of unmeasured concatenation: the list, the leap or gap between items; there, but minimally, a chapter degree zero. Not only does Equiano's narrative break open the equilibrium of the chapter as a held pose, but it makes the chapter's primary rationale its very lack of one, and so renders it strangely mute. A dance like those he describes in Essaka is graceful and erect, but the "incidents" assembled in his chapters are more often sudden collapses, in fact experiences of falling, not being held nor being able to hold oneself, but falling into a "hold" nonetheless. Brought on board the ship that will take him from Africa, he faints. A ship is always is a place of unstable surfaces; "I myself," he relates, "one day fell headlong from the upper deck of the Aetna down the after-hold, when the ballast was out" (*IN*, 88). Uninjured by the fall, Equiano describes it as an instance of providence, but it opens up as well a temporal dimension not of linear movement but of porous surfaces—time is that which threatens to swallow you, into the "hold," whose slave-ship resonances scarcely needed underlining in this particular anecdote.[77] With the hold beneath you always, there is no way to find one's footing in time. Across these abysses of time's harm the chapter simply hovers, more or less shapeless, more or less incoherent, but present still. To have them at all, particularly in such a visibly marked way, was a decision Equiano made—and not a norm passively followed—to expose, bitterly or plangently, a desire for meaningful temporal division it could not satisfy. To say: a life cannot be measured this way, not this kind of life. To do so, the chapter will have to change yet again.

Chapter Contra Epoch in Goethe

Back to the novel, just a few years on, and to a text that looks at first glance nothing like *The Interesting Narrative*: Goethe's *Wilhelm Meisters Lehrjahre* (*Wilhelm Meister's Apprenticeship*), whose publication in four volumes from 1795 to 1796 presents a biographical narrative without almost any of the paratextual business that marks Equiano's story. Printed on high-quality paper with a newly designed typeface, the clean, proto-modernist "Unger-Fraktur," and with generous "leading," or space between text lines, the *Lehrjahre* was an art book, where the art resided in its spare design, its only adornment an expanded whiteness.[78] Each chapter is untitled, starting on a fresh page and untethered to any index or table, the headings chastely ordinal (figure 5.3). It is nothing like a reference book; the emphasis is on a stately linearity, with space to breathe and reflect. Within the novel itself, tabularized, indexed books are refused. His father asks Wilhelm to write up an account of his travels and provides "a systematic plan [*tabellarisches Schema*] of how to set it out"— something cross-referenced, labeled, synoptic.[79] When nothing of his travels, particularly his membership in a wandering theatrical troupe, seems appropriate for such a reference text, Wilhelm enlists the help of his fellow actor Laertes in concocting a fake, if appropriately tabulated, travelogue. It is sufficient to fool his father and his practical-minded friend Werner, but just a pastiche nonetheless, foreign in substance and design to Wilhelm's own narrative. In this novel—and perhaps in any novel at all, if Wilhelm's meditations on novel versus drama are indicative—we are in the realm of the syntagmatic rather than the paradigmatic, of *Nacheinander*, or succession, rather than *Nebeneinander*, or juxtaposed simultaneity; what Goethe referred to in a letter to Schiller as his novel's "progressive continuity" rather than "unity."[80] Reading *Hamlet*,

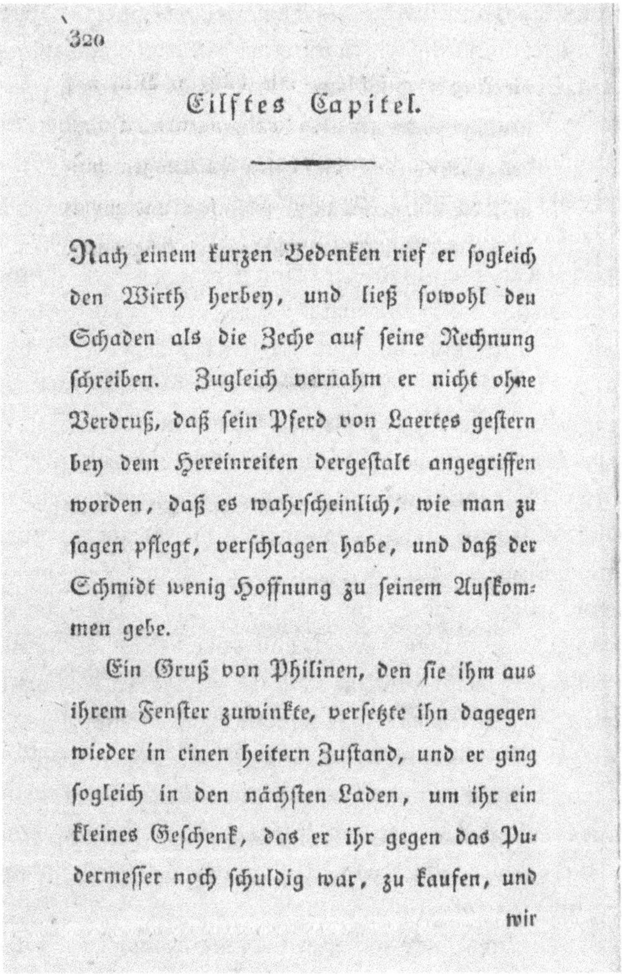

320

Eilftes Capitel.

———

Nach einem kurzen Bedenken rief er sogleich den Wirth herbey, und ließ sowohl den Schaden als die Zeche auf seine Rechnung schreiben. Zugleich vernahm er nicht ohne Verdruß, daß sein Pferd von Laertes gestern bey dem Hereinreiten dergestalt angegriffen worden, daß es wahrscheinlich, wie man zu sagen pflegt, verschlagen habe, und daß der Schmidt wenig Hoffnung zu seinem Aufkom- men gebe.

Ein Gruß von Philinen, den sie ihm aus ihrem Fenster zuwinkte, versetzte ihn dagegen wieder in einen heitern Zustand, und er ging sogleich in den nächsten Laden, um ihr ein kleines Geschenk, das er ihr gegen das Pu- dermesser noch schuldig war, zu kaufen, und

wir

FIGURE 5.3 The "short reflection," or *kurzen Bedenken,* of the newly spare, uncluttered apparatus of the chapter break in volume 1 of *Wilhelm Meister's Apprenticeship* (Berlin, 1795). Courtesy of the Rare Book and Manuscript Library, Columbia University.

Wilhelm complains to the director Serlo that he struggles to find "the structure of the whole [*Vorstellung des Ganzes*]" or any "overview [*Übersicht*]" (*WM*, 128). Such things are the province of tabular paratexts, but no such aid is provided by the *Lehrjahre* to the life path it depicts.

We are now fully in the world of the nonindexical chapter, seemingly liber- ated from its organizational function—although, as with Equiano, the lingering question is how this liberated manner of segmentation reflects the varieties of unfreedom from which the story's central figure attempts to detach himself. Even in their own time, *Wilhelm Meister*'s chapters seemed choppy, irregular, uncertainly related to the very idea of shape.[81] It was a critique sometimes articulated as a problem of subordination: Are these parts governed by any whole? The effect of the novel's chapters is that of a rule disobeyed or superseded; the question of what belongs to what radiates from them.[82] If a chapter no longer belongs to any indexical order, or any topical or essayistic constraint, what is it doing, to what does it refer? What are such chapters marking: moments, events, phases? *Wilhelm Meister*'s chapters are, as in so much of the eighteenth-century novelistic corpus I've considered earlier, generally subepisodic. Conversations, scenes, exchanges of letters, patterns of arrival and departure: chapter breaks interrupt them all, and often. Their joints do not even mark the line between event and consequence. Wilhelm's first dissipation with the theater troupe he joins is a typical minor disaster—the town guard is raised, and Wilhelm has to bribe them to avoid worse trouble—but this brief incident's chapter break falls after he has slept off the night's effects and woken to regret the whole business. The following chapter begins with the phrase "After short reflection [*Nach einem kurzen Bedenken*]"—a momentary hesitation, almost empty of both cognition and affect, really just a marshaling of inner forces before launching into the next series of events, which, after paying his landlord for the previous evening's damages, largely erases the previous evening's effects (*WM*, 71). It is a pause rather than a consequence, offering little resistance to the onrushing flow of action.

Simply put, the break here and elsewhere seems undermotivated, almost accidental. (Beware improvisation! Wilhelm lectures the troupe in one of his callower moments—decide on an appropriate *Szeneneinteilung*, or division of scenes, beforehand. Futile lament, and in any case inapplicable to the novel itself: a chapter is not a "scene.") The condition of the chapter in *Wilhelm Meister* is a state of uncertainty, evolving toward a newer practice, as a result of the untenability, by the late eighteenth century and within a different narrative form, of older syntheses such as the kludges of Sterne's practice. In the new life narrative that would come to be known as the *Bildungsroman*, brief narrative segments like the chapter collided more forcefully with the retrospective divisions into significant units that could articulate a life's growth stages. Textual caesuras and internally consistent, meaningful biographical phases do not

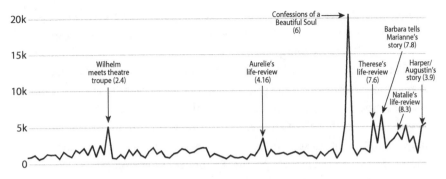

FIGURE 5.4 Section lengths in *Wilhelm Meister's Apprenticeship*.

line up, and the result is a confusing misalignment in the act of being slowly calibrated. Calibrated, in fact, across two different overlapping timelines: across the divide between pre- and post-revolutionary late-eighteenth-century history, and within *Wilhelm Meister* itself, where the traces of change to the chapter are evident. As so often, the key trace of that change is the simple growth in the size of the chapter.

The composition of the *Lehrjahre*, spread across eight books published in four two-book installments, is the story of two different procedures. From the first to the middle of the fifth book, Goethe was primarily revising his manuscript of the late 1770s and early 1780s, *Wilhelm Meister's Theatrical Mission*, and despite profound changes, he largely adhered to the general size of chapters from that earlier period—short bursts that hovered around a thousand words each.[83] After the middle of the fifth book, however, there was no more of the older manuscript to revise. Instead, a narrative solution to Wilhelm's story needed to be found, as well as a form in which to shape it. The result is, among other more visible changes to the elements of the novel that originate in the 1790s, a chapter form of greater amplitude (figure 5.4).

The difference is not thoroughly consistent, but it is marked, particularly after the experiment of book 6, the "Confessions of a Beautiful Soul," which is entirely unchaptered—an undivided personal narrative of more than twenty thousand words. Chapter lengths of several thousand words become frequent and cluster in the latter two books of the novel, as if the "Confessions" had prepared the way; the pattern is jumpier, more erratic, but tending to expansion. What has occurred? Certainly the sheer amount of plot business in books 7 and 8 is denser. The Society of the Tower has started not only to manage Wilhelm's future but to reveal the multiple interconnections already present in his past; events now do not flow in a quasi-picaresque linearity, but require retrospective explanation. There are things to wrap up, enigmas to be resolved, and this, one might think, takes time, which becomes busier, and textual space, which becomes more crowded.[84] Yet figure 5.4 suggests a slightly different correlation, and a slightly earlier genesis in the novel: with some regularity, the novel's longest chapters are those that are themselves biographical, but the biographies of *others*. Various figures step forward to review their life stories, and these moments are not marked by a chapter break; they conquer, or motivate, the chapters they occupy. Experiments with longer units admittedly begin prior to the break away from the *Theatrical Mission* material; the fourth chapter of book 2, in which Wilhelm first meets Laertes, Philine, and Mignon—a day of accidental beginnings, situated at an inn, as if a quasi-picaresque episode stuffed into a single unit larger than the picaresque norm—is the most salient example. But with Aurelie's life story in book 4, and then the dramatic example of the "Confessions," we see the novel's chapters becoming distended under the pressure of biographical summary. As with the several examples in the final two books, when a character seizes the opportunity to relate a life path, either their own or that of another, the usual rhythm of chapter breaks is in abeyance. Interruptions to these stories can occur (indeed, Aurelie pauses her story to let Mignon attack Wilhelm with requests, a pause pointedly not granted a chapter break) but not at the level of textual caesuras. Chapters lengthen: continuous attention must be paid. It isn't a matter of respecting the integrity of the novel form's old friend, the interpolated tale—in the *Wanderjahre*, for instance, some interpolated tales, such as "Who Is the Traitor?" or "The Man of Fifty Years," are interrupted by chapter breaks.[85] What seems instead to keep the chapter break at bay is a character's self-narration.

This expansion effect, the result of narration's temporary occupation by a capsule biography, suggests something about the relation between chapter and story world: the caesuras of capitulation are entirely external to the self-conceptions and life worlds of characters themselves. Chapter time is not their time. It is a grid applied on top of or over their experience, entirely extrinsic—the work only of the third-person narrator or implied author, a timing mechanism that cannot be naturalized within *erzählte Zeit*, and yet, without the metafictional reference to the chapter break so common in the novel form prior to the late eighteenth century, or even an indexical purpose, not simply explicable as just *Erzählzeit* either. It is a time that is imposed from elsewhere, and imposition is its signature. Its feel is that of something dissonant, out of sync with the temporal attunements of characters, which have a different vocabulary:

> What's the use of these wretched scribblings—they are not a stage [*Stufe*] toward anything (Wilhelm; *WM*, 46)

> Isn't the thing now to take the final step [*der letzte Schritt*] (Wilhelm; *WM*, 165)

> Had it not been for some unusual circumstances I would have remained at this stage [*Stufe*] (The Beautiful Soul; *WM*, 237)

> a moment is usually reached when it is at its zenith [*der höchsten Stufe*], its best, its greatest unity, well being, and effectiveness. Then personalities change (Abbé; *WM*, 208)

> when his development has reached a certain stage [*Grade*], it is advantageous for him to lose himself in a larger whole (Jarno; *WM*, 301)

A semantic cluster, articulating in closely adjacent ways the loose periodizations into which biographical memory falls: stages, levels, phases, and, notably, steps, the vertical ascent and the horizontal movement coinciding. But these "steps" are not quite the staircase units of Sterne, because they no longer modulate between psychological and textual units. There is no textual mark or hiatus adequate to express them. A chapter is not here a step or a stage. These divisional terms are all too profound; they are metamorphoses and liberations, hinges to open latent powers. They signify a time bent to individual aspiration, lives striated by metamorphoses. (No surprise that when Wilhelm collects his personal scroll, or *Lehrbrief*, produced by the Society of the Tower at his initiation, he mounts several steps to their makeshift altar.) "Life doesn't narrate itself, it is just lived": Gunther Müller's formulation, never less true than in the *Lehrjahre*, where life is always narrating its own phases.[86] As in Equiano we have a mismatch between a desire for significant units and the unit of the chapter, but in Goethe the chapter seems too evanescent to capture the duration of a life plan and its self-measurements. The idea of the biographical "period" conflicts with a time of short, contiguous moments.[87]

Nowhere is this distinction clearer than in the case of the most common term in Goethe for such personal time distinctions, the "epoch":

> Certainly, now, for me that time was a turning point [*Epoche*] (Wilhelm; *WM*, 14)

No occasion is more dangerous for a man than when external circumstances produce a serious change in his situation without his thoughts
or feelings being prepared for this. The result is change without change
[*Epoche ohne Epoche*] (*WM*, 170)

they for their part were of the opinion that this united effort was the har-
binger of a new era [*eine neue Epoche*] in the German theatre (*WM*, 188)

We are reaching a period [*Epoche*] it is not good to dwell on (Therese;
WM, 280)

A term in some semantic flux in the eighteenth and nineteenth centuries, *Epoche* combines the notion of period or time span with that of punctual change
or transition in an almost untranslatable manner; indeed, in Thomas Carlyle's
1824 translation, each of the above usages is simply rendered as "epoch." The
Greek *epochē* was a technical term from astronomy, signifying the zenith of an
orbital movement, the moment at which a star seems to halt in its course.
"Check" or "cessation" was already by the time of Plutarch its metaphorical
usage, and increasingly in Greek prose it could mean "suspension," which
brought it close to the sense of "period" or "term" that it increasingly carried
in western European languages during and after the Enlightenment, while also
retaining the sense of transition or "turning point" from the original astronomical sense.[88] Its frequent use within *Wilhelm Meister* is a symptom of the
desire, common to all its characters, to locate in the past the demarcation lines
by which time lurches from old to new, to write a stadial history of the self in
a schematic, almost tabular form.[89] It is a "neue Epoche," after all, that Goethe
is said to have proclaimed at Valmy in 1792, shortly before beginning work on
transforming the *Theatrical Mission* into the *Apprenticeship*.[90]

Yet—it should be stressed—neither Valmy nor the turning points or new
stages of the novel's characters, however truly epochal, were at all equivalent
to a new chapter. Epochs and their iterations, such as stages, eras, or periods,
are strong form-giving parameters, to which the shape of *Wilhelm Meister*'s
chapters, still at the novel's outset bearing a similarly diminutive size to earlier
eighteenth-century examples, cannot respond. Chapters seem partial, fleeting,
unhistorical even in the limited range of a personal history. But here we have
to consider something on the order of a dialectical, or at least ironic, inversion.
By virtue of what seems like its stubborn inability to synchronize with the
period indications of personal history, it is the chapter that starts to best indicate historical transition instead. I mean here not something recognizable

within the sphere of the novel itself, where "chapter" never attains the dignity of "epoch," and where when confronted with personal narrative the chapter break meekly waits for its conclusion; I mean in the necessary dilation of chapters because of their seemingly futile attempts to match the elongated epochs of characters, a dilation that itself is historical. They distend, and in so doing, themselves enter a new period.

For now, let us stick to numbers and dates. The leap Goethe takes between books 1–5 of the *Lehrjahre*—based on the material from the *Theatrical Mission*—and books 7–8 is more than a doubling of chapter size, from an average of roughly 1,300 to over 3,100 words, marked by the crucial intervention of book 6 and its biographical form. The last two books push outward the possible high end of chapter length and are also slightly less variable in chapter size, an upward normalization. Purely numerically, it is a distinct shift beyond the usual parameters of the eighteenth-century novel segment, not just in Fielding or Sterne or Goldsmith, but even *Candide*, or, closer to home, Wieland's *Agathon*—all those briefly held postures, those jeux d'esprit that knew enough not to overstay their welcome. It is, in its own way, evidence of a developmental step toward the more expansive, coming in the shift from early adulthood to middle age; time for Goethe has perhaps slowed, a rhythm of more rapid shifts decelerated. In the novel's own terms it is a departure, both decisive and unannounced, from the "piecemeal" [*stückweise*] kinds of narrative that both Wilhelm and Serlo lament to something less visibly or frequently morcellated.[91] What we might also recall here is that between one version of the chapter form and its newer, doubled shape there has been not only a personal transition but also a collective historical one, that of revolution—the early 1790s have occurred, and not only in the history of its composition but in its plot; as members of the Tower Society note in book 7, political upheaval is now threatening settled rule and private property. An epochal shift that in turn leaves its impress on *Wilhelm Meister* by forcing on the novel a temporality of epochs, stages, steps, eras: a time with fewer divisions and more consequential ones, thresholds you cross gravely, with a little appropriate awe.[92] "All transitions are crises [Alle Übergänge sind Krisen]," the narrator explains as Wilhelm reads his—seemingly unsegmented—*Lehrbrief* scroll, even as a chapter break, signaled by the Abbé telling him to stop reading it for now, halts its initial perusal (*WM*, 309). Mere chapters cannot match this weighty and ceremonial time, of course, but when characters attempt simply to articulate it, they delay the fall of the chapter break and its far less weighty interruption.

A triple turning point, then: a world-historical transition (the end of the ancien régime), a maturational transition (the end of youth), a career transition

Chapter Word Averages in Jane Austen

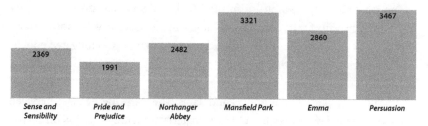

FIGURE 5.5 Jane Austen's chapter lengths and the epochal shift.

(running out of youthful material to revise), all reflected in the expansion of the chapter's parameters. There is, as it happens, another example of the same phenomenon, at almost the same moment, this time a shift visible within a career arc rather than a single novel, and that is the change in the shape of Jane Austen's chapters (figure 5.5). Seen in order of composition rather than publication, a trend appears. In Austen's case we have three novels whose initial versions were youthful compositions: *Sense and Sensibility*, *Pride and Prejudice*, and *Northanger Abbey*, productions of the late 1790s reworked for publication after an intervening decade and a half. As with the first five books of the *Lehrjahre*, these hew more closely to eighteenth-century novelistic chapter sizes even as they refuse some of the typical signs (chapter headings, narratorial self-reference to chapter breaks) of that fashion. As for the novels written entirely within Austen's busy and brief maturity of the 1810s—*Mansfield Park*, *Emma*, *Persuasion*—the chapters press upward in size, both floor and ceiling rising. The triple-digit-word-count chapter, like the conversational vignette with which *Pride and Prejudice* begins, recedes. The chapter over five thousand words, such as those that cluster near the end of *Persuasion*, so full of retrospect, reevaluation, and epochal consciousness—"It is a period, indeed! Eight years and a half is a period"—multiplies.[93] In between early and late styles, in both *Wilhelm Meister* and Austen's career alike, overlapping dislocations: revolution and war, detachment from home, aging, the accumulation of memory; and binding them all, a heightened sense of the gravity of transition, pushing outward the boundaries of the humbler units of the novel, toward something like what will be their nineteenth-century norms. In the history of the novelistic chapter, *Persuasion*, just like the latter books of *Wilhelm Meister*, has moved one step into a new era.

That swelling of the chapter, however clearly it marks a break with earlier eighteenth-century practice, is a complicated double gesture. As a response to the pressure of epochal-periodizing language, it is in one sense a move toward giving narrative units the weight of such momentous segmentations—the longer, one might say, the heavier. Epochs and phases are not brief, so chapters should not be either. In another sense, though, that chapter breaks do not generally interrupt biographical reflection in *Wilhelm Meister*, and thus inflate in size, actually reconfirms the stubborn otherness of the chapter within life narratives. Epochal transitions are not, finally, at all like the brief reflections of the chapter break, and the difference is not just one of intensity or stress, nor does the smaller unit nestle in the larger without friction. In parsing one's life into epochs or periods, one becomes known to oneself by seizing perspectival centrality: one divides in order to arrange in sequence and connect. It is the creation of what Goethe so pervasively called *Zusammenhang*, the discovery of an animating whole out of attention to component parts.[94] Most people, the Abbé sententiously remarks, are *formlos*, without form, and cannot give a shape or *Gestalt* to their own self, preferring instead a "loose and flabby substance" (*WM*, 351). But they seem to yearn otherwise: Wilhelm is entranced by the Hall of the Past in the Society's Tower, with its "regular spaces" decorated with "a splendid sequence of vivid representations, ranging from the first childish impulses ... to the calm, grave detachment of wise old age" (*WM*, 331). Regularization signifies control. An epoch, like these sequentialized paintings, has to be willed into being. To speak of it demonstrates an ability to anticipate, to either will the next step taken or just to know where one is stepping, and an ability to retrospectively demarcate what one has crossed, to make a strong shaping gesture. The Goethean chapter, on the other hand, descends irregularly and resists the ascription of meaning. Like the biblical chapters eighteenth-century editors lamented, it cannot quite be rationalized; like the chaotic mereology of Equiano's chapters, it speaks of a time structure that is not one's own, a fall rather than a step—a rhythm of dispossession, where what is dispossessed is mastery over time's rhythms. That is where the novelistic chapter ends the eighteenth century, no longer as a careful equilibrium between narrative and discourse, incident and topos, but as a rhythmic counterpoint to "meaningful" time: imposed, external, and inscrutable. Its paratextual function now almost entirely shorn away, the chapter can make sense only as a fractured rhythm out of one's control and unassimilable to the ways one might otherwise segment a life. To update the old astronomical metaphor: the chapter is that artificial light blinding us, in its frequency and glare, to the epochs of the stars, their disappearances and returns. To make this odd polyrhythm feel natural again will be the basis of many of the technical adaptations in the century to come.

6

The Repertoire of the Chapter
circa 1865 (the Tacit)

TOLSTOY—GASKELL

BY THE MIDDLE of the nineteenth century, silence descends upon the novel-istic chapter. This is of the order of vast but, to readers of fiction in any number of national or linguistic traditions, hardly controversial generalizations: the chapter no longer receives the playful, embarrassed, or self-ironizing com-mentary from within the narrative voice that had characterized so many of its uses in the previous century or two. The cluster of tropes that eighteenth-century authors attached to it—the inn, the milestone, the carved joint, the staircase—recedes in favor of a colorless, antifigurative familiarity. The chapter lands instead in a vacant middle ground, neither just an accidental property of textuality deserving a winking nod nor an openly acknowledged solicitation of readerly convenience, nor a property of time itself in any strong sense. Nor is it attached to the rationalizing schemes of the kind that would become more common in the following century, the organizational grids of, say, *Ulysses* or *Under the Volcano*. Chapter headings become shorter and more elliptical, when they don't vanish entirely; the interface function of the chapter becomes al-most solely implicit.[1] When it comes to the novel of the nineteenth century, particularly in its western European iterations, we are in the land of the tacit.

This does not mean, of course, that a common range of types and motiva-tions is absent from these nineteenth-century iterations. It means we are con-fronted with a landscape of unadvertised *techniques*: a variety of possible ap-proaches to the ordinary felt necessity of dividing narrative, none of which excludes any other or asserts a strong claim to be the correct, or necessary, way of performing the task. If anything, variety—the avoidance of any overly regular manner of handling the chapter break—precludes anything like a consistent, overarching rationale. A chapter break is not one kind of caesura; it is many possible kinds, yet all bounded by a family resemblance, a reassuringly limited and non-hierarchized set of recurrent moves, gestures, and cues. These are only very rarely occasions for virtuosity. Instead we have something like exhibitions of competence: the novelist's ability to display a wide range of possible chapter shapes, and manners of stitching the resulting fissures, without making any one of them too insistent. Such modesty is, of course, part of the general recessiveness of realist art: the masking of technical decisions.

What follows is an attempt to itemize some of the most common iterations of these techniques, through two novels published in the same decade: Tolstoy's *War and Peace* and Gaskell's *Wives and Daughters*.[2] These are novels in different languages, with distinct tonal palettes and thematic interests, and different processes of publication, that nonetheless share a great deal in their use of the chapter, both at the level of technical manipulation and in terms of its formal significance. At first glance this itemization will look like an account of craft labor, the humblest units of a novelist's art. What will be visible is a certain pleasure in slight experimentation, in variation, in appropriateness, something we might call *fit*. The wilder cuts of the chapter's earlier history are softened or tamed. Yet the results of this craft labor will end up having a perverse thematic resonance, by virtue of lightly undermining the obsessive concerns with time each novel exhibits. Modest as they may be, the chapters in each novel emerge as stubborn instruments of temporal ambivalence, existing to mark divisions of time while embodying a skepticism about those very divisions. They are constitutively fraught, as their regularity and innocuousness undercut the momentousness of transitions that both novels worry at and wonder about, while nonetheless expressing a lingering attachment to the psychological anchors of transition points that they are undermining. Both Tolstoy's and Gaskell's novels surface the question of time, to the point of having specific "ideas" about time. Within these novels is the form of the chapter, shaped in various but conventional ways; indeed, each could be taken as an anthology of chapter styles. The chapter form, in its variety, both collaborates with and resists those ideas about time, making it a source of something like a persistent, inescapable tension, a muted polyrhythm that will outlast the 1860s and become a signature of the novel.

Crossing the Berezina: *War and Peace*

The Tolstoyan character is restless. That restlessness can come in different keys (enthusiasm, irritability, emotional lability, physical clumsiness) and have different orientations (intellectual, spiritual, careerist), yet what it tends to share across these psychological types is a constantly alert inner attention to change, an awareness of transitions both as they loom and as they appear, however trickily, in hindsight. Transition seems unfathomable and irresistible both, taking on a nagging insolubility: what will I be afterwards? When did things become this way, why didn't I notice as they did? Before and after begin to seem irreconcilable to this Tolstoyan metacognition, their contiguity amounting to a mystery. Andrei, before the battle of Schongraben, thinks: "It's begun! Here it is! ... But where, then? How will my Toulon declare itself?"[3] Pierre, hesitating before proposing to Hélène: "I must inevitably cross it, but I can't, I can't" (*WP*, 213). Similarly, "the most complex and varied feelings" occupy him as he prepares for his Masonic initiation and what he believes will be the momentous transformation it will produce; this unstable combination of emotions will turn out to be the most intense phase of his Masonic life, over before that life even begins (*WP*, 355). As often as this attention is anticipatory it is retrospective, almost the necessary accompaniment of any strong sensation of presentness. So it is for Nikolai as he finds himself in Dolokhov's trap, gambling away his father's money in a single night: "Just now, when I came to this table, wishing to win a hundred roubles to buy that sewing box for mama's birthday and go home, I was so happy, so free, so cheerful! And I didn't realize then how happy I was! When did it end, and when did this new, terrible condition begin? What marked the change?" (*WP*, 339). Put another way, Tolstoy's characters are episodists: they recognize themselves as existing within particular episodes, and those episodes have an intensity, even an autonomy, that swallows longer kinds of diachronic thinking.[4] What concerns them about these episodes, however, is the mystery of the boundary lines that surround the episode in which they locate themselves. Inside an episode, it is hard to imagine any other episode at all, and any narrative that links them seems inaccessible, implausible. Yet somehow "now" emerged out of "before," and it will later pass into another "before." How could that have happened, how can it conceivably happen again? Is there a feeling of passing over a threshold, an event horizon or phase transition, and how can one notice it?

This aspect of Tolstoyan psychology jars against the novel's obsessive quarrel with periodization of any kind: "it is from the arbitrary division of continuous movement into discrete units that the greater part of human errors proceed" (*WP*, 821). It is the constant burden of the novel's essayistic sections to demonstrate a larger whole when a segment is in question, to prove any claim of disjuncture fallacious, any assertion of origin or conclusion blinkered. Division is error: "there is not and cannot be a beginning to any event, but one event always continuously follows another" (*WP*, 822). This is a postulate that is political—skeptical of any claims to the transformative power of particular events or acts—but ultimately metaphysical, even at one point mathematical, as in Tolstoy's notorious discussion of how calculus, specifically Leibniz's infinitesimals, solves Zeno's paradox and its false trap of analyzing continuity through discrete stages.[5] The decisive moment is never that. Nothing changes, unless it was already changing. A battle, an affair, a plan for personal advancement or social amelioration: these have preparations and effects much more diffuse than any beginning and ending. The threshold, rupture, or breach is a retrospective illusion, merely an arbitrarily selected portion of a larger process. Of the French retreat across the Berezina—a literal crossing taken to stand for a new, decisive phase of Russian triumph: "The French troops melted away in a mathematically regular progression. And the crossing of the Berezina, of which so much has been written, was only one of the intermediate steps in the destruction of the French army, and not at all a decisive episode in the campaign" (*WP*, 1096).

Whatever credence one wants to lend to this Tolstoyan narrative theory, let us be clear about two things, which together make Tolstoy's novel a key resource in the history of the chapter, in effect an anthology of the practice of chaptering. The first is the disjuncture, amounting to an ontological distinction, his theory opens up between narration and story world. Something that has no theoretical validity may still have great phenomenological purchase, and the novel's characters believe in, and hunt for, the very markers in time that the narrator insists on debunking. Searching for ways to distinguish episode from episode, these characters are met with lines that blur the closer they look at them. The result is a particular frustration that marks his characters' encounters with this epistemic impasse; they do not give up the search, but without a reliable means of distinguishing before from after they brood, are disappointed, feel unmoored; they are episodists without episodes. Between the narrator's austere theoretical insistence on continuity and his characters' compulsive search for units there is an impasse. The second is the implicit quarrel such a theory of temporal continuity bears toward the form in which it is written, a distinction here between narration and genre. *War and Peace* is self-evidently an elaborately segmented text. In its essentially final form, achieved in the fifth edition of 1886, it is scored by divisions between four *toma* ("books") and an epilogue, within which are seventeen *chasti* ("parts") and 361 untitled and unnamed chapters, the terminology and arrangement of which varied in earlier editions and would later give trouble to translators.[6] It was impossible for Tolstoy to detach himself from morcellation even while theorizing its falsity. The question may not be one of continuity versus segmentation, therefore, but the size of those segments and their manner of self-effacement. Segmentation creeps in where it is being refused, but in a minor mode. *War and Peace* describes lives lived with attention to an experience—the experience of transition—that the voice describing those lives insists is illusory, while nonetheless still arranging those lives into segments. It is a dynamic of skepticism and dependence.

What results is, perversely enough, an astonishing formal flexibility. If segments are arbitrary impositions upon the continuous flux of time, they can be handled in any way; no one model for the segment is owed any particular respect. Textual divisions, like the scenes they interrupt, come to seem fragmentary, inadequate to whatever broader processes they supposedly instantiate.[7] Tolstoy is free to use any technique that comes to hand to sculpt his narrative units because the narrative unit itself has for him no genuine reality. Thus his chaptering variety, scattershot and encyclopedic, by turns antique and ultracontemporary. It is the freedom of the performer who doesn't quite believe in the performance. The chapter becomes a peculiar novelistic compromise: too brief and partial to satisfy his characters as a thing in itself, too frequent and insistent and messily inconsistent to appease a narrator who sees in time a continuum and an inexorable flow. For whom could the chapters of *War and Peace* conceivably be valid experiences? Averaging a little more than 1,200 words, they are usually far too truncated to be scenes in and of themselves, and as subepisodic as any of the chapters in Caxton's *Morte*.[8] Without heads, or any pretense at tabularity or indexicality, their independent existence is reduced to the minimal sign of their number. They are tenuous, brief coagulations of something inevitably fluid, fleeting hallucinations of sameness set within flux. Their hallucination does not deceive the narrative voice's sober metaphysics. Their fleeting duration does not give his characters any completeness to grasp. It is a between time, deriving from neither the projections of characters nor the overarching design of omniscience, opportunistic and partial, yet therefore full of tactical ingenuity.

Weightier temporal markers descend from time to time, implanted already with varieties of credulousness and instability. Most famously, there is the great comet of 1812 that Pierre sees hanging over Moscow, having consoled Natasha after her aborted abduction by Anatole Kuragin:

> Almost in the middle of that sky, over Prechistensky Boulevard, stood the huge, bright comet of the year 1812—surrounded, strewn with stars on all sides, but different from them in its closeness to the earth, its white light and long, raised tail—that same comet which presaged, as they said, all sorts of horrors and the end of the world. But for Pierre this bright star with its long, luminous tail did not arouse any frightening feeling. On the contrary, Pierre, his eyes wet with tears, gazed joyfully at this bright star, which having flown with inexpressible speed through immeasurable space on its parabolic course, suddenly, like an arrow piercing the earth, seemed to have struck here its one chosen spot in the black sky and stopped, its tail raised energetically, its white light shining and playing among the countless other shimmering stars. It seemed to Pierre that this star answered fully to what was in his softened and encouraged soul, now blossoming into new life. (WP, 600)

That the comet feels transitional to Pierre, like the onset of a new era in his life, seems ratified by the powerfully closural position it is given, at the end of book 2 and at what is almost the novel's exact middle. This is, it would seem, truly marked time, vivid and collective and real. Yet it is riven with narratorial dubiety: the "as they said," "seemed to have struck," "seemed to Pierre" qualifications gently refuse the belief in this telling time by the heavens and the heart together that is otherwise given such patient attention. In terms of the novel's own time scheme, it is disruptively achronological. Although the comet's appearance must be set in February 1812, if one follows the calendrical markers that have been placed up to that point in part 5 of book 2 it must *also* be February 1811, the conclusion of a year's engagement between Natasha and Andrei— as if the comet's timing mechanism forced the narrative's compression of 1811 into 1812.[9] The comet accelerates time as it accelerates in space; it is, if accidentally, untimely. Finally, the comet is one of Tolstoy's several metaphors, if a privileged one, for the collision between continuity and segmentation; the comet only "seems" to have stopped, but is in fact in continuous if scarcely comprehensible motion, so that using it as a caesura or mark is itself of the nature of a human, perspectival illusion, the illusion of the *epochē*. As in other charged moments in which time seems to halt, an experiential register—surely something has ended and another thing begun!—collides with narratorial irony. All this, Pierre's love for Natasha, the falling away of his Masonic project, the French invasion, and more, has been long in preparation.

Yet neither continuity nor disjuncture can have absolute sway. In their midst are minor times, little evanescent articulations, that are not entirely available to experience nor wholly a theoretical construct, while being somehow both. They exist beneath notice: too humble to be theorized, too fleeting to be always felt by those living in them.[10] The language Tolstoy has for these times is scattered and hesitant. In describing the flanking maneuvers of the Russian army's pursuit of the retreating French, and arguing against its "invention" by a general or generals, some of that language appears: "this maneuver, just like the retreat from Fili, was never pictured by anyone in its entirety, but proceeded step by step, event by event, moment by moment [a shag za shagom, sobytiye za sobytiyem, mgnoveniye za mgnoveniyem], from a countless number of the most diverse conditions, and only presented itself in its entirety when it had been accomplished and become past" (*WP*, 988). No single register completely fits; neither the spatial and agentic (a step), the narratological (an event), or the temporal (a moment) can fully describe these minute and unnoticed components of the large processes that bring about change. Even separating out these aspects is arbitrary; only a supple, manifold attention, aware of the different dimensions to this minor time, could hope to capture it. This is the terrain of the Tolstoyan chapter, an in-between time that has many different signatures.

A Taxonomy of Chaptering Techniques

Hybrid as it must therefore be, *War and Peace* nonetheless contains a set of recognizable types of chapter break, each aimed at a distinct manipulation of narrative mechanics: some regulating the speed of plot (sudden accelerations, equally sudden suspensions), some adjusting the narratorial perspective, some attending to the coordination of plots or the synchronization of a plot to various extranarrative chronologies. What follows, then, is an attempt to gather these practices into five major categories, while acknowledging some of the many subtle variations within each group. They take their full significance, however, from their serial, rhythmic combination. Using *War and Peace* as the basis of this taxonomy reveals that there is no one characteristically "Tolstoyan" mode; they all have long, familiar novelistic afterlives, and what is most Tolstoyan, perhaps—as well as being most novelistic—is their multiplicity. The overall result is a narrative interruption that is diverse in its modes; that is occasionally, and only mildly, surprising; yet that is rarely jarring, while never falling into routine. There seems to be a pleasure taken in felicitous alternation, along with a compositional tact that ensures the felicity is never too marked. That tact is inseparable from the chapter's function, and not just for Tolstoy, but for an entire era of the chapter's history.

In tune with its technical syncretism, some of the novel's means of handling chapter breaks are "traditional" in the sense of deriving from the pre-novelistic practices we have already seen. The first such mode hearkens back to early Gospel capitulations: the *signal* or *incitation*. Here an action is divided at a moment precisely before its immediate onset; preparation is severed from action. The first sentence of such a chapter, operating like a herald, takes on a particular weight. There is a sense here of what Bachelard called the "supremacy of willed time over lived time," a dramatic summons marking off now from then and puncturing any passive sense of duration.[11] So, when a regiment quartered in Austria in the autumn of 1805 prepares itself to be inspected by Kutuzov:

"He's coming!" the signalman shouted just then. (*WP*, 116)

And the first words of the chapter in which Pierre fights his duel with Dolokhov, his wife Hélène's presumed lover:

"Well, begin!" said Dolokhov. (*WP*, 315)

Or when a convoy of Russian prisoners making its slow way west of Vyazma in October 1812, including Pierre and Platon Karataev, is ordered to make way for a passing French marshal:

"*À vos places!*" a voice suddenly cried. (*WP*, 1063)

Chapter openings like these resemble what Margaret Anne Doody has called the rhexis, or "Breaking Trope," the abrupt cut that signals a departure, for character and reader alike, from ordinary life.[12] But the effect of these cuts is evanescent: like the early Gospel chapters whose form they more closely echo, they are marks rather than initiations to a whole. The prisoner convoy shuffles off to the side of the road, the marshal appears bearing an expression inadvertently revealing compassion, and then the commotion passes. Yet minutes later, at the chapter's end, Karataev, too ill to continue walking, has been shot. The chapter's incitation—the marshal's arrival—has no real causal connection to its dark conclusion, other than perhaps distracting Pierre from his friend's

peril. Similarly, the chapter of Kutuzov's inspection continues past his departure, lingering in the details of the regiment's febrile collective mood. The incitation is not a prelude to a complete, or even easily comprehensible, experience; it reflects a concussive sort of time, one in which tedium, stasis, or
suffering is jolted out of preoccupation into some temporary outward attention. By severing preparation—Pierre's quarrel with Dolokhov, Karataev's
illness—from result, it renders the experience of the result as more convulsive,
less comprehensible, less casual or "natural." It is the chapter break as a minor
species of explosion.

Also recognizably pre-novelistic is our second category: placing a chapter
break at a *moment of threshold crossing*. In practice this is more of a "figure" of
chapter breaks than the previous category, because it is so often, as we will see,
enacted as a trope, centered on literal apertures and thresholds.[13] But it is also
reflective of a somewhat different temporality, a momentary stasis, hesitation,
taking stock; rather than a summons, it reflects a brief balking of the will before the new experience is initiated. Like the fifteenth-century *remaniements*
where this particular figure was frequent, Tolstoy's threshold crossings produce a momentary "before" tableau. The emphasis is here on final sentences
rather than initial ones, on the liminal state of "just prior to" rather than "now."
Thus, Pierre pausing at the entrance to the bedroom of his dying father at a
chapter ending:

> Pierre went through the door, stepping on the soft carpet, and noticed that
> the adjutant and the unknown lady, and some other servants—all came in
> after him, as if there was no longer any need to ask permission to enter that
> room. (*WP*, 79)

So Nikolai also pauses at a chapter break, before crossing from the nightmarish
hospital ward for enlisted men to the officers' ward; so too does Napoleon
pause, at another chapter break, before the Dorogomilovo gate to Moscow,
awaiting the delegation that will not come. At other times the chapter break
cuts at a different kind of threshold, such as the rising of the curtain before the
opera, where Natasha will find herself ensorcelled by theatricality and Anatole
both:

> As soon as the curtain rose, the boxes and parterre all fell silent, and all the
> men, old and young, in uniforms and tailcoats, all the women, in precious
> stones on bare bodies, with greedy curiosity turned their attention to the
> stage. Natasha also began to look. (*WP*, 560)

In this category of caesura, a momentary hush descends and dilates, marking
the gap between a physical action (opening a door, stepping through a passage,
watching a curtain rise) and the belated cognitive registration of what that act
has brought about. It has a tendency to catch characters at their most pitiful,
because it is the pity we feel for the before state—before an illusion has been
shattered, a trap has been sprung, an injury received, a burden placed, a
mistake made—that suffuses the narrative irony of these fleeting interstices.

Also oriented toward chapter endings, the third category—the *suspended
revelation*—enacts surprise rather than pity, and its concussiveness is longer
lasting, more clearly consequential. It is the most dramatic version of Tolstoy's
chapter breaks, although it is still curiously muffled. An instance: at the end of
a chapter devoted to the Rostov family's preparations for evacuating Moscow,
a caleche and wagon, carrying a wounded man and his attendants, approach
their courtyard, and a servant allows them to enter:

> "My masters won't say anything . . ." she said. But they had to avoid carrying
> him upstairs, and therefore the wounded man was taken to the wing and
> put in Mme Schoss's former room. This wounded man was Prince Andrei
> Bolkonsky. (*WP*, 857)

Later, at the end of 1812 and after Andrei's death, a chapter devoted to Natasha
and Princess Marya's slow rhythm of mourning ends in this way:

> Quickly and heedlessly, with a frightened look on her face, unconcerned
> with her, the maid Dunyasha came into the room.
> "Please go to your father, quickly," said Dunyasha, with a peculiar and
> animated expression. "A misfortune, about Pyotr Ilyich . . . a letter," she said
> with a sob. (*WP*, 1078)

The death of Natasha's younger brother Petya in a nighttime reconnaissance
mission is news the reader already possesses. The force of its revelation here
depends on its direct subversion of a different affect (excitement, sorrow, both
forms of complacency) that had prevailed in the chapter it ends and therefore
upends. Such a chapter concludes, that is, with its dominant mood revealed
retrospectively as having been a false state, as if to say: all along, *this* had been
the case! Characteristically, the following chapter performs a knight's move
away from the direct consequence of the revelation, opening out ("Moscow's
last day came," in the first instance [*WP*, 857]), or moving back slightly in time in
order to generalize ("Besides a general feeling of alienation from all people, Natasha experienced at that time a particular feeling of alienation from the persons

of her own family" [*WP*, 1078]). The revelation is cut off at the moment of its peak intensity, its beat punchy and abrupt; its percussiveness might remind listeners of late twentieth-century pop music of the gated reverb, the wave form that is artificially severed at the place where its intensity is greatest. While this version of caesura changes everything—although not always immediately—its first function is to burst the frame of the chapter itself. It comes from outside the chapter's boundaries and shows how permeable, how arbitrary and fragile, those boundaries had been.

These first three varieties can all be, in their own way, what we might call "strong" divisions. Either in their figuration or their tempo, they provide particularly marked transitions or vivid interruptions of ongoing actions. Not coincidentally, perhaps, these caesuras seem to have the oldest avatars, as if they are not quite native to the more-tacit ripples of novelistic chapter breaks but are derived from other generic rhythms. The remaining two categories are softer, subtler; they tend more frequently to interrupt ongoing actions with only the briefest of adjustments to continuous narration. They are less exuberant, perhaps, but more truly experimental, a testing out of the ways in which interrupted narrative can serve the goals of multiplot fiction rather than merely offer false segmentations of continuous time. We can distinguish them by referring to two different, if complementary, modes of marking time: tense and aspect.

"Tense" can be taken to mean, here following Wolfgang Klein, any adjustment to "the situation described by the sentence and some deictically given time-span."[14] The *tense uses* of the chapter, our fourth category, can be thought of then as its clock relations: its tendency to articulate, at its opening, the correspondence between a plot event or events and some shared chronology, or to adjust the temporal frame in which a plot event is being related, either by increasing or slackening the precision of the frame. At its simplest and most pervasive, a chapter's opening sentence is the most common moment to insert a chronological indication, a synchronization of the action to an implied narrative clock operating at various frames, from the historical frame of calendric time (years, seasons, dates) to the personal frame of daily time and its vaguer notations of the sequence of days, although these registers can sometimes be simultaneous:

On the twelfth of November, Kutuzov's active army, camped near Olmütz, was preparing to be reviewed the next day by two emperors—Russian and Austrian. (*WP*, 237)

After nine in the evening, Weyrother moved with his plans to Kutuzov's quarters, where a council of war was called. (*WP*, 260)

Natasha was sixteen, and it was the year 1809, the same she had counted up to on her fingers with Boris four years ago, after they had kissed. (*WP*, 448)

On the day after his son's departure, Prince Nikolai Andreevich summoned Princess Marya to him. (*WP*, 686)

On Saturday, the thirty-first of August, everything in the Rostovs' house seemed turned upside down. (*WP*, 852)

The chapter opening, in these cases, anchors narrative to chronology—not, as in earlier or more metafictional models, to the time of narratorial utterance (as in "we now return to," or "as was related previously"), but to an abstract temporal grid made up of a sequence of hours, days, months, years. Yet as much as these tense relations tether a single plot event to some abstract time, they just as often triangulate two plot strands to that same calendar, as a way to shift between plot strands while keeping them synchronized—the chapter break being, as Monica Fludernik has argued, the primary place for such shifts in prose fiction.[15] This is the chapter's "meanwhile" function. Clustering in first sentences of chapters, we have such synchronizations as:

Just as the sixth anglaise was being danced in the Rostovs' ballroom to the sounds of the weary, out-of-tune musicians and the weary servants and cooks were preparing supper, Count Bezukhov had his sixth stroke. (*WP*, 70)

While this was going on in Petersburg, the French had already passed Smolensk and were moving closer and closer to Moscow. (*WP*, 709)

Taken together, these are all modulations of *temporal location*—they ask: *when* did this occur, and in relation to what other occurrences? They establish the chapter break as a moment for time reckoning, including a reckoning with the peculiar incommensurability of events that are nonetheless simultaneous.[16]

The chapter's tense relations also can modulate the *speed* of narration. Specifically, they can be used to accelerate or delay narrative time by shifting from—to use Gérard Genette's terms—scene to summary, or vice versa.[17] While those shifts do not exclusively occur at the chapter break, that is their most frequent, even privileged, position. The shift from iterative summary to particular scene usually takes the form of a calendrical indication, however vague, tethered to a preterite verb, however buried in participle clauses:

> One evening, when the old countess, sighing and groaning, in nightcap and bed jacket, without false curls and with one poor little knot of hair sticking out from under the white cotton cap, was bowing to the ground on the rug as she said her evening prayers, her door creaked and Natasha came running in, her bare feet in slippers, also in her bed jacket and her hair in curling papers. (*WP*, 450)

The reverse, however, is usually established via temporal adverbials:

> After the sovereign's departure from Moscow, Moscow life flowed on in its former, habitual way, and the course of that life was so habitual that it was hard to remember the recent days of patriotic rapture and enthusiasm, and it was hard to believe that Russia was actually in danger and that the members of the English Club were at the same time sons of the fatherland, ready for any sacrifice for its sake. (*WP*, 745)

These can, but do not necessarily, shuffle between plot strands, but their primary work is to shift between registers of narrative momentum; and they do so through the clock mechanisms that accumulate at the start of chapters. Nor are these speed shifts exclusively forward in their orientation. Often they involve both a shift to summary, and a move slightly backward in time, in order to establish the general conditions that obtained in the previous scene. For instance, after Andrei's first encounter with the reformer Speransky, the next chapter opens with a vaguer assessment of the disposition that had made the meeting so peculiarly stimulating:

> During the initial time of his stay in Petersburg, Prince Andrei felt that his whole way of thinking, developed in his solitary life, was completely overshadowed by the petty cares that consumed him in Petersburg. (*WP*, 431)

Or, after the pivotal flirtation between Anatole and Natasha at the opera, the chapter break returns us to a more general prior time, to synchronize the preceding scene within a vaguer, if ominous, "situation":

> Anatole Kuragin was living in Moscow because his father had sent him away from Petersburg, where he spent over twenty thousand a year in cash and the same amount in debts. (*WP*, 567)

This particular subvariant is more generally telling in relation to the tense relations of the chapter break. By moving out of a scene (Natasha's fall into seduction during a theatrical performance) in order to establish a vague temporal
situation for that scene (the broader time of Anatole's aimless exile in Moscow), the break *reduces* the narrative tension, both by shifting out of the scene's
suffocating intensity and by locating that tension in a bounded past. It is as if
to say: this was a particular, temporary moment, it will soon be over. These
tense indications function, that is, as a minor relief, providing the security of
knowing where (because when) we are, and reestablishing the abstract perspective of chronology in which every moment will have its end. They are
reminders of the persistence and reliability of an external world, and of the
inexorable directionality of time. Yet these shifts offer only minor relief after
all; they are, one might say, "weak" chapter boundaries, easily passed over or
ignored, lodged in grammatical structures rather than given any dramatization.
Their indicia are semantically and syntactically subtle, even banal. It was, after
all, such an ordinary novelistic clock resetting ("La marquise sortit à cinq heu-
res") that, André Breton's legend has it, so offended the tastes of Paul Valéry.[18]
Yet they allow the novelist to synchronize the various clocks in the narrative's
world, and by doing so, remind us that what passes over the chapter break is,
as always, time.

If, however, many of these tense relations seem neutral—as neutral as a
calendar can be—the chapter break is just as frequently used to shift the orientation point of this chronology. We can call this final category the *aspect relations* of the chapter break: its alteration, subtle or dramatic, of the "point of
view" through which a set of circumstances is considered. Grammatical aspect
has usually a complex relation to the boundedness of time, to whether an action has been concluded or is ongoing, but more generally is a set of "different
ways 'to view' or 'to present' one and the same situation."[19] There are many
ways in which aspect can be modulated at the chapter break, but all of them
perform a shift in the perspective governing a continuing situation. In narrative terms, this can mean that the chapter break is a primary occasion for adjustments to the modes of third-person narration. In Tolstoy, it most often
involves moving from conditions of immediacy (focalized on a character) to
the broader, vaguer perspective of a categorical statement about, or a bird's-eye
view of, the events that had before the chapter break seemed suffocatingly
urgent. At Schongraben, his first battle, Nikolai ends up fleeing into bushes to
escape a solitary charging French soldier, an almost hallucinatory experience

of disorientation; nothing has gone as expected, nothing makes any sense. Broken off as bullets whistle past him, the next chapter begins by placing his reaction within a broader process:

> The infantry regiments, caught unawares in the woods, ran out of the woods, and, companies mixing with other companies, retreated in disordered crowds. (*WP*, 190)

In a less perilous vein, an early segment of the novel's long opening scene at Anna Scherer's Petersburg salon is presented from Pierre's point of view, as he waits impatiently to participate in the intelligent exchanges he expects to find there. His perspective is self-involved, out of sync; he lacks the tactical peripheral vision to behave with the restrained wit that the salon's habitués perform out of habit. The chapter break, however, mildly jolts us out of his consciousness and into a general view:

> Anna Pavlovna's soirée got going. The spindles on all sides hummed evenly and ceaselessly. (*WP*, 11)

These chapter breaks are in the mode of epistemic corrections. They move from what a character cannot see, and the stifling intensity of that ignorance, to a historical retrospect, wiser if wryly detached. It is the location for omniscience to assert its privileges. They can just as often take the form of aphoristic or essayistic remarks, an even stronger aspectual shift, such as this chapter opening following the previous chapter's transcription of a strongly worded letter from Bagration to the Tsar's adviser Arakcheev:

> Among the innumerable subdivisions that can be made in the phenomena of life, one can subdivide them all into those in which content predominates and those in which form predominates. (*WP*, 705)

As has long been noted, these transitions cluster in the novel's 1812 sections, when an emerging sense of the novel as an "epic" form necessitated a rhythm of philosophical digressions, but in subtler manner they are found throughout.[20] It is of course a mode common to a wide variety of nineteenth-century narrative styles, from Hugo to Balzac to Eliot.[21] What it trains a reader to expect is a readjustment of focus after the chapter caesura, a rhythm of detachment from the immersiveness and partiality of a single viewpoint.

I use the term "detachment" because it is not merely an epistemic issue but also one of mood: the chapter break's aspectual shifts tend overwhelmingly to insert a more ironized, even dissociative external attention, to allow a metacognitive dilution of affect to occur. Andrei's first anguished conversation with Pierre, started in the novel's fifth chapter, is interrupted by the chapter break, after which:

> There was the rustle of a woman's dress in the next room. Prince Andrei shook himself as if coming to his senses, and his face took on the same expression it had had in Anna Pavlovna's drawing room. (*WP*, 25)

A reverie of Nikolai's, produced by Natasha's precocious if unpolished singing—"It's all nonsense! One can kill, and steal, and still be happy!"—is similarly interrupted, even chastened:

> It was long since Rostov had experienced such enjoyment from music as on that day. But as soon as Natasha had finished her *barcarolle*, reality again reminded him of itself. (*WP*, 343)

If the effect of the aspectual shift could be summarized, it would be as *the reassertion of an outward focus*. This can be motivated within the narrative, by the rustle of a dress, the end of a song, the faintest of modifications of tone in a social setting, or more bluntly executed by the insertion of narratorial comment; its modes, and the force of its arrival, have perhaps more variance than any other technique of the chapter break. Its affective dimension, however— its rebuke to intense preoccupation—is perhaps the most consistent.

It has more notoriety within literary criticism than other kinds of caesura, perhaps because free indirect discourse, that most celebrated of novelistic techniques, is often implicated in the aspectual shifts of chapter breaks. D. A. Miller has noted an instance in *Emma* in which the same sentence ("Emma could not forgive her") concludes one chapter and begins the next, the first in free indirect discourse, the second in "mere omniscient narration, more remote in its detachment, and less engagé in its impersonality."[22] This is perhaps an extreme instance of the chapter break's tendency to enact a more or less tactful withdrawal from the fever of absorption, its intensities and blinkered obsessions, in favor of a move outward—up, and, in a sense, away. This need not involve a change of scene or any temporal disjuncture, nor does it require the shift to absolute omniscience, although the stronger versions of this shift can do so. It is something more like a rapid change in attitude, or altitude. Across the cut of the chapter break it can offer a sardonic or patronizing backward glance, but one not always entirely distinct from a nostalgia for the nerviness of personhood it has surmounted. So *The Wind in the Willows*: "Such a rich chapter it had been, when one came to look back on it all!"[23]

TABLE 6.1 The repertoire of chapter rationales in the nineteenth century

Type	Place of Emphasis	Affect	Temporal Orientation	Force
1. Incitation or signal	Opening sentence(s)	Concussiveness/ alertness	"Now"	Strong
2. Threshold crossing	Closing sentence(s)	Pity/foreboding	"Just before"	Varies
3. Suspended revelation	Closing sentence(s)	Surprise	"All along"	Strong
4. Tense relations (the "clock")	Opening sentence(s)	Relief/ reassurance	"Meanwhile"/ "at that time"	Weak
5. Aspect relations ("point of view")	Opening sentence(s)	Detachment	"But, in reality . . ."	Varies

These five categories of chapter rationale are a repertoire rather than a hierarchy. Table 6.1 shows them to be interdependent and yet moderately diverse, a taxonomy of techniques whose virtuosity resides both in the variations with which they can be deployed and in the rhythm in which they are distributed. These methods of placing boundaries in the midst of continuous action are ad hoc rather than systemic. What they lack, and what Tolstoy's narration and characters both in their ways pursue, is a binding theory; they reveal no continuous logic of progression, and no sequence of emblematic eras or moments. These novelistic chapters cannot provide a means of organizing a life. They seem to belong to the realm of minor affects: changes, but survivable ones; erratic fluctuations, but within a band of the vaguely expected. They are steps (*shagy*), events (*sobytiya*), or moments (*mgnoveniya*) too random to belong to any eschatology, however utopian or doom-ridden, to which one might attach fears or hopes. We can take them as instead offering a stubbornly secular comfort amid bigger cataclysms and stronger endings: in this sort of life, for the most part, nothing lasts for long, but no change is too large for us. Call it the background time of realism: the pensive, slightly tranquilized alertness of the middle view.

Wave Succeeding Wave: *Wives and Daughters*

Meanwhile—or, at that time—in July 1865, only months after the first portions of *War and Peace* had appeared in the *Russian Messenger*, Gaskell's *Wives and Daughters* was in the middle of its own serial run in the *Cornhill Magazine* and nearing a pivotal narrative juncture. Roger Hamley, younger son of a declining Tory squire, is preparing to leave on a scientific research expedition to Africa that will take him away for many months. Before he does so, however, he plans to make a marriage proposal. It will be to Cynthia Kirkpatrick, the alluring and mercurial stepsister to Molly Gibson, the quieter, steadier young woman who is the novel's central consciousness and who herself nourishes a half-acknowledged love for Roger. The installment's first chapter ends with Roger riding to the Gibson house and a lightly ironized direct narration of his thoughts, which for a naturalist involve an oddly indulgent series of figurations: "he called her a star, a flower, a nymph, a witch, an angel, or a mermaid, a nightingale, a siren, as one or another of her attributes rose up before him."[24]

The subsequent chapter, "A Lover's Mistake," relocates to the house he will enter, and cuts from the looseness of desire's logic to a distanced terseness.

> It was afternoon. Molly had gone out for a walk. Mrs Gibson had been paying some calls. Lady Cynthia had declined accompanying either. (*WD*, 370)

Innocuous as it is, the transition here manages to encapsulate all five of the rationales that *War and Peace* employs. The staccato summons of "It was afternoon" decisively moves us to a distanced, abstract perspective—an *aspect* shift away from Roger's consciousness—while also acting as a herald or *incitation*, a signal that some event has just begun, that attention now has to be paid. The temporal reminder of "afternoon" is of course also a *tense* relation, synchronizing Roger's imminent arrival with the "meanwhile" activity, unaware and habitual, of the women in the Gibson house, who do not expect him. There is a revelation that the previous chapter has left *suspended*—that Roger has made the decision to propose—and, finally, the chapter starts with a double series of *threshold crossings*: Molly will walk out of house just before Roger will enter it; she will as a result return only a brief time later to find that the event is already in process, the mistiming of their exits and entries encapsulating Molly's misfortune in this, her first love.

All of which is to say that Gaskell's use of the chapter break here is particularly deft, not only for its terrifically condensed multiple registers but also for its sheer tact. There is the abrupt shift in syntactical cadence that occurs as the unit of the sentence passes through the force field of the chapter break, yet otherwise there is no machinery that might make this deftness more noticeable. This is the novelistic chapter in its paradoxically tacit glory, humming along in its varied, coordinated rhythms so smoothly that it need not even be noticed. It would be worth pausing, then, to applaud Gaskell's craft, particularly the way that the rationales Tolstoy moves between in successive chapters are here, with impressive simplicity, entwined in one. Yet it would be wrong to say that this is Gaskell's craft, exactly, for the reason that this chapter division was not her choice.

In the manuscript, held at the John Rylands Library, there is no indication of the chapter division here, aside from the fact that "It was afternoon" starts a new paragraph. In fact, at almost no point in the *Wives and Daughters* manuscript does Gaskell indicate the start of a new chapter, let alone anything like a chapter heading. The novel was, apparently, written as a continuous, undivided narrative, as in a garment weaving where any cutting to size would be done only later and delegated to someone else.[25] In its published state, *Wives and Daughters* is multiply partitioned; it was first published in eighteen serial installments, arriving once a month from August 1864 to January 1866 in the pages of the *Cornhill,* with each separate installment further subdivided into anywhere from two to five titled chapters; only upon completion of the serial run would a volume edition be issued, with the chapters intact. The practice was common in Gaskell's time, particularly as serial novels migrated from the stand-alone pamphlet-sized installments more popular in the 1840s to insertion in the general-interest magazines of the 1860s. Yet all this division, into chapters and monthly portions, seems not to have been Gaskell's labor. We have here a strange return to the chapter's initial material situation: the post-composition insertion by editorial hands of breaks and labels.

We return, then, to a collaborative series of acts. In the manuscript, chapters are either entirely unmarked or indicated by an ad hoc collection of editorial insertions, such as double slash marks, lines drawn across the page, or the scrawl of a name (figure 6.1). As with Caxton's chaptering of the *Morte,* such divisions would have had to attend to a complicatedly braided set of concerns both quantitative and qualitative: casting-off estimates to adhere to the proscribed length of serial numbers, which was only very slightly flexible; the convention that each number would include at least two, and potentially as many as five, chapters; locating appropriate places within the narrative, small junctures of transition or pause, to sufficiently motivate these divisions; making sure those divisions did not produce chapter lengths that were far outside the norm.[26] Chapter headings themselves would then later have to be supplied as well, necessitating another interpretive act. That this was more normally authorial rather than editorial work in the nineteenth century does not erase the fact that the chapter was still susceptible to editorial management. Insofar as it was understood both as an aspect of page design and as a tool for readerly

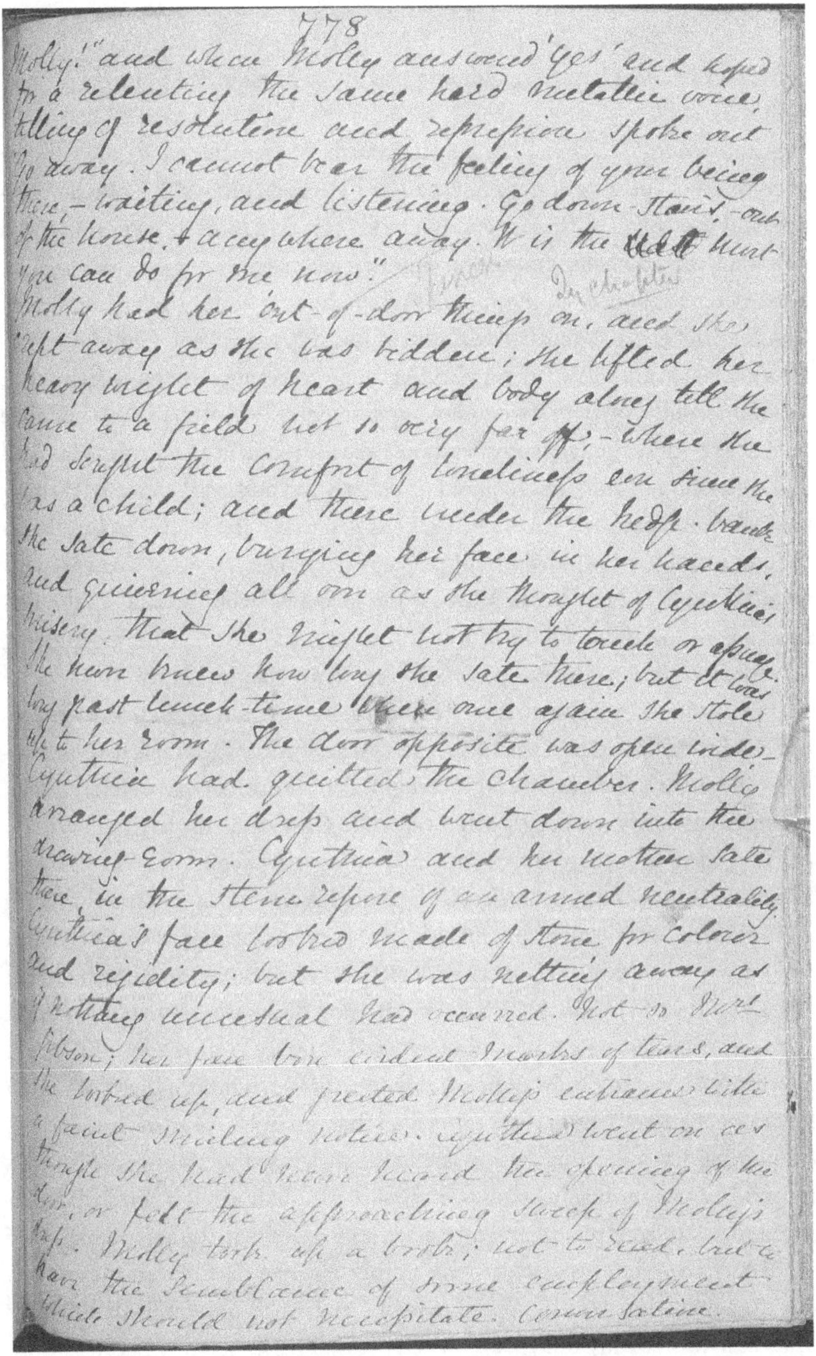

Molly." and when Molly answered 'yes' and hoped
in a relenting the same hard metallic voice,
telling of resolution and repulsion spoke out
"Go away. I cannot bear the feeling of your being
there — waiting, and listening. Go down stairs — out
of the house, & anywhere away. It is the best thing
you can do for me now."

Molly had her out-of-door things on, and she
crept away as she was bidden; she lifted her
heavy weight of heart and body along till she
came to a field not so very far off; — where she
had sought the comfort of loneliness ever since she
was a child; and there under the hedge-branch
she sate down, burying her face in her hands,
and grieving all over as she thought of Cynthia's
misery, that she might not try to touch or assuage.
She never knew how long she sate there; but it was
long past lunch-time when once again she stole
up to her room. The door opposite was open inside —
Cynthia had quitted the chamber. Molly
arranged her dress and went down into the
drawing room. Cynthia and her mother sate
there, in the stern repose of an armed neutrality.
Cynthia's face looked made of stone for colour
and rigidity; but she was netting away as
if nothing unusual had occurred. Not so Mrs
Gibson; her face bore evident marks of tears, and
she looked up, and greeted Molly's entrance with
a faint smiling notice. Cynthia went on as
though she had never heard the opening of the
door, or felt the approaching sweep of Molly's
dress. Molly took up a book; not to read, but to
have the semblance of some employment
which should not necessitate conversation.

FIGURE 6.1 The editorial insertions at the start of chapter 51 in the manuscript
of *Wives and Daughters*, seemingly marked twice: once with a slash mark and a
name, and again with "*Li chapter*."
John Rylands Library English MS 877, volume 2, n637. Copyright of The University of
Manchester.

convenience, the chapter remained potentially outside the purview of pure authorial "style."

Although the *Wives and Daughters* manuscript provides a rare late glimpse of editorial chaptering, it does not seem to have been unique in Gaskell's practice, and the collaborations involved could include figures more familiar, and powerful, than the anonymous *Cornhill* staff who segmented it.[27] Her habit of delegating chapter dividing seems to have begun under the editorship of Charles Dickens, particularly with the publication of "Lizzie Leigh" in Dickens's journal *Household Words* in 1850. Surviving correspondence reveals a dance of editorial authority and solicitude around the question of chapters, which are treated as both secondary considerations, a matter for editorial pragmatics, and also a question of craft that required discretion and authorial consent. Writing to Gaskell in February that year, Dickens discussed the matter of providing chapter divisions and serial installments, reassuring her that, of the work as it stood, "I think I would break it where you propose," while adding, of the story's as-yet unwritten conclusion, that if it were to go longer than expected, "I would divide it, with your permission into two chapters more."[28]

The permission seems to have been granted here, but as their working relationship continued into the 1850s, the exact nature of Dickens's responsibility as chapter divider became more fraught. Dickens reveals himself to be keen to retain authority over segmentation, while Gaskell seems to have partially resisted the potentially interventionist energy his segmentation implied. When it came to the appearance in *Household Words* four years later of *North and South*, matters were more difficult than they had been in 1850. Dickens at first presented his editorial offices with tactical mildness, as a mere facilitation: "Do not put yourself out at all, as to the division of the story into parts. I think you had far better write it in your own way. When we come to get a little of it into type, I have no doubt of being able to make such little suggestions as to breaks of chapters, as will carry us over all that, easily."[29] As an indication that chaptering decisions might occur late in the process of serial publication, this is useful information; as an instance of editorial solicitude, it is somewhat disingenuous. Dickens placed great stress on his expertise in the segmentation of serial narrative, and this extended not simply to the serial numbers themselves but to the chapters within them. He seems, in fact, to have considered these units as symbiotically linked, and when pressed on it, his tone became more peremptory. Gaskell, for her part, seems to have implicitly accepted Dickens's authority in the matter of serial divisions, but was more cautious about the chapter divisions within them. Four months later he wrote to outline a plan of where *North and South*'s serial breaks should fall, adding that these numbers "would sometimes require to be again divided into two chapters, and would sometimes want a word or two of conclusion. If you would be content to leave this to me, I could make those arrangements of the text without much difficulty."[30] This was a sneakily buried addendum: Dickens was now arrogating to himself the right to compose chapter-ending sentences, to sculpt a break rather than merely insert one. Gaskell must have demurred. Two weeks later Dickens wrote with an ambiguous retraction: "Nor had I any ambition to interpose my own words of conclusion to any of the divisions. I merely wished to smooth everything for you as much as I possibly could, and to present any little harassing necessities in their easiest light."[31] The vague but charged line between segmentation and composition had been crossed, however, and Gaskell would keep up her guard, possibly with a tactical silence. A month later Dickens rather testily complained that "I do not understand whether you permit me to divide the story into chapters," reminding Gaskell with shaming obviousness that a serial number does, after all, have to begin with a new chapter in any case.[32] Yet despite this outbreak of impatience, he later returned to a tactful diffidence as a way to defuse Gaskell's objections, writing that once a portion of the novel was in type, "I will merely divide it into chapters."[33] "Merely" dividing, "little" suggestions, "a word or two" added: the diminutives seem to perversely emphasize the importance Dickens placed on the segmentation over which Gaskell had largely, but not completely, disowned responsibility.

These exchanges illustrate the confusing middle ground chapters continued to occupy. Chapters were a weaker "internal" beat to the serial installment's stronger rhythm, but of course both would coincide at the beginnings and endings of each installment. Chapters could come late enough in the publication process—including after typesetting—to seem merely paratextual, but maintained a compositional urgency requiring forethought and expertise. Mechanical enough to be shaped by editors, they yet remain largely if not entirely an authorial prerogative, neither quite "writing" nor entirely *mise en page*. The record of Gaskell's refusal and occasional resumption of chaptering suggests an even more curious lesson: chaptering could be delegated because the function of the chapter was understood as a matter of vague aesthetic consensus rather than any deeply individual creativity. The chapter "worked" if it felt generally, and generically, appropriate. Insofar as it articulated novelistic time, the chapter needed to feel as familiar and innocuous as the everydayness the novel was meant to reflect—precisely *not* strange, *not* remarkable. The labor could be outsourced; editors could take their turn in attempting the deftness that the author had refused.

Yet, admitting all that, why refuse in the first place? The reason—as Dickens evidenced by his persistent linking of the chapter to the serial number while yet belittling the labor of chaptering, and as Gaskell seems to have known well enough to have carefully guarded some of her right of refusal to his decisions— is that the chapter is a means of temporal measurement at a scale more intimate, and less immediately tied to format, than the serial number, and dividing time in this way, or at all, clearly spurred in Gaskell a lasting ambivalence. She was used to writing in long stretches in which segmenting narrative time was simply avoided, deferring the matter to editorial control, as if this was the best way to cope with a matter—the divisibility of her fictional world's time—that she neither entirely believed in nor could dispense with.[34] As with Tolstoy, a deep commitment to temporal continuity conflicted with a recognition that segmentation was at the very least a lived experience, however illusory, that had to be itself represented, and even, in the case of the reader, provided. Unlike Tolstoy, that conflict was managed by a sometimes uneasy division of labor, postponing the question of chaptering to later editing while reserving the right to intervene. Even in the case of *Wives and Daughters*, Gaskell was capable of sudden isolated bursts of decisiveness when it came to chaptering. The manuscript includes one somewhat confident, somewhat beseeching instruction in her hand, set within a couple of lines' worth of white space: "Please, end of a chapter" (figure 6.2).

The placement of that particular, isolated insertion, somewhere between a polite request and a command, helps open out what is at stake in this deferral and occasional resumption of authority over segmentation. Its function is to conclude a chapter in which two tenuously related events are occurring simultaneously. The aging Squire Hamley, a Tory whose grip on his property is being loosened by debt, ventures out to visit a dying tenant, Old Silas, in a feudal ritual that Silas, at least, treats as such. During the squire's visit, Silas informs him that workmen hired by the Cumnor family, the squire's far richer and newer Whig rivals, have been working on the boundary between the estates, pulling up for fuel gorse and brush that belong to the Hamley property and, as a result, slowly removing the covers necessary for fox hunting. The scene is situated both in a deep time—a feudal tradition, the rituals associated with death in a rural community—and a very shallow one, comprising the squire's mounting anger at the Cumnor ascendancy, which is in any case a displaced reaction to his own family troubles. The squire leaves Silas to find

FIGURE 6.2 "Please, end of a chapter": Gaskell's request/instruction for what would become the break between chapters 30 and 31 of *Wives and Daughters*. John Rylands Library English MS 877, volume 2, n113. Copyright of The University of Manchester.

Mr. Preston, the Cumnor land agent, at the works where the spoliation is occurring. An argument ensues, saved from becoming violent only by the arrival
of the squire's son Roger. The squire, in fact, may not have survived any further
anger, such is his constitution. Yet as Roger leads his father away from the
scene of the quarrel, a child arrives to tell them that Silas is in his final crisis
and has requested the squire to come attend it. Gaskell wrote her instructions
to the editors after one final sentence: "So they went to the cottage, the squire
speaking never a word, but suddenly feeling as if lifted out of a whirlwind and
set down in a still and awful place" (*WD*, 341).

In one sense this is a strong ending, and its strength would seem to motivate
Gaskell's unusual direction. Death intervenes to disrupt and conclude a scene,
the end of which is perceived by the squire itself as a "lifting" and "setting," a
forcible relocation. The chapter conclusion, that is, is naturalized within the
scene; it ends because the squire feels it to have ended. And yet, as the subsequent chapter begins, this "strong" beat is revealed to be a temporary sensation,
weak if not virtually nonexistent. Silas drops out of the narrative entirely, his
death unnarrated. The deep time of feudal ritual drops away. Where the next
chapter picks up is again with the shallow time, the preoccupation that the
Hamleys are beginning to have with the Cumnors and their proxies—a preoccupation that is complicated, in Roger's case, by Mr. Preston's realization that
they are rivals for Cynthia Kirkpatrick's affection. If the previous chapter ends
with the priority of the inexorable and traditional over surface battles—as if
to present a closural "perspective"—when the next chapter resumes, that perspective has vanished. Silas's death and its "still and awful" aura is a moment
only, the sensation it offers of a lasting shift merely a fleeting interruption.
Faced with that death and its claims, the narrative simply *proceeds*, with the
world of emergent, developing, and inconclusive, if not even minor,
struggles.

Gaskell's isolated instruction, then, pays homage to Silas and his death
while highlighting how swiftly that homage is rendered moot. Given her habitual avoidance of divisions while writing, it is perhaps symptomatic that
her one explicit attempt to segment *Wives and Daughters* reflects this ambivalence even more starkly than many of the suture points fashioned by her editors. It is foundational for Gaskell: her novel is committed, quite openly, to a
minimally articulated time, to continuity and even flow, to experiences of
gradual, organic, even repetitive change, to refusing divisibility.[35] It is a time
associated with private, domestic, female life, one so sensitive to the minutest

of fluctuations, alongside the massively persistent conditions that underlie them—socially enforced helplessness, disenfranchisement from virtually any possible choice in the achievement of one's desires, or even the ability to articulate them—that any division of time into "events" or "phases" would seem delusional. The paradigmatic experience the novel records is almost completely resistant to segmentation: Molly Gibson's chronic condition, that of *waiting*. And yet: what anyone can recognize as the novel's seamlessness, its resistance to time that seems marked with boundaries, is shot through with a yearning for the discrete event. Indivisible time can offer homeostatic comfort—isolation from shock, a recognition of how slowly change develops—but it is itself also a mode of suppressed panic, the claustrophobia produced by the potentially interminable. And indeed every state in *Wives and Daughters* threatens to become endless. On the unhappiness occasioned by her father's marriage, Molly protests: "I don't see any end to it" (*WD*, 135). Comforting the squire after the death of his eldest son, this is what Molly senses: "Time had never seemed so without measure" (*WD*, 552). Even into late adolescence, Molly bears memories of a long childhood evening spent among strangers at the Cumnor estate—the novel's first scene—and the Cumnor drawing room, "an interminable place of pacing" that "had haunted her dreams" (*WD*, 615). What often seems like a situation of ontological security can become the very threat from which one would want a refuge.

The point of the foregoing is not simply to recharacterize the conflicted tonality of Gaskell's last novel, which has been amply discussed elsewhere.[36] It is that the chapter break is the pressure point where this contradiction makes itself most acutely felt. It bears the full weight of Gaskell's ambivalence, because it ruptures what should be a continuous flow, and thus distorts the experience of time that Molly Gibson inhabits, yet can be so minor a caesura, so diffident and forgettable, that it can express something of the mingled disbelief in, and hope for, stronger transitions. It is flexible, potentially locatable almost anywhere, unsystematic, more evanescent and minor than the serial break within which it fits and with which it sometimes coincides—and as such, can express both a fleeting hope (will something change?) and its denial (nothing much likely can, or will). And the final expression of Gaskell's ambivalence is her almost total refusal to locate them herself. By ceding control over them, by returning the chapter to its initial historical condition as a post-compositional, editorial insertion, she places herself in Molly's position, removing her control over the ruptures in time that she cannot entirely credit in any case. It is a deliberate passivity that is inescapably, as *Wives and Daughters* insists, a gendered way of being in the world: an attunement to the interminable that defers transition to others because transition can only come from without, as a shock or a gift. (Or, as in her struggles with Dickens, an insistence one could refuse or cannily delay.) In this deferral, though, is a paradoxical strength. By not shaping her own chapters, by not writing *in* chapters, Gaskell makes their construal as event-based, strong narrative units virtually impossible. She therefore gives chapters their proper novelistic significance, which is as a time so weakly bounded and contingent that it can exist only as a failed analogy, labeled à la Magritte: this is not an episode.[37]

Which is to say that the anti-episodic quality of *Wives and Daughters'* chapters is the purpose, and not simply the outcome, of Gaskell's unusual relinquishment of control over them. A return to the serial number that was marked in the manuscript by "Please, end of a chapter" will help reveal the constraints within which Gaskell compelled the anonymous capitulators to operate. Her explicit instruction ended the first chapter of the novel's eleventh serial installment, creating a unit of around 3,500 words, a length well within her own, and her period's, norms. The next chapter begins, as we have seen, with a perspective shift that is also a return to the preoccupation of the previous one after a transient interruption (of Old Silas's impending death) that is not mentioned again. Yet if, as they surely did, the *Cornhill's* editors had an eye on the appropriate remaining length necessary to fill out the installment, they would have projected something like another 9,000 or so words left to them for the month's copy. It would have been open to them to produce out of that amount three more chapters—the four-chapter installment was not unusual for the novel, and indeed the very next installment would have that many—or only two. The problem confronting them, however, was that those 9,000 words contained nothing like a "scene" or "event" long enough to form a chapter of its own.

Let us look at what exactly faced them and conjecture as to their thinking. They might have first determined the end of the installment at the moment when Molly first hears from her stepmother of Roger Hamley's impending departure for his African research expedition, a shock that she characteristically hides, although the manuscript bears no marks at this point. It would have likely seemed appropriate by virtue of its strong narrative beat and its sufficient distance from the installment's beginning. Between "Please, end of a chapter" and that moment, however, Gaskell's text offers only a series of fluctuations—of location, time, and perspective—that sit uncomfortably between

scene and summary, both too brief in duration to be the former and too medi-
tative in texture to be the latter:

1. An analysis of Mr. Preston's resentments toward the Hamleys and Tory
   interests in general, combined with a glance at his rising reputation
   since having succeeded the Cumnors' prior agent
2. A description of Molly's growing despondency in regard to Roger's
   attachment to Cynthia
3. A turn to Roger's concerns over his brother Osborne's estrangement
   from their father, which leads him to suggest—in a conversation "one
   day" (WD, 347) with the squire—that he will somehow find enough
   money to resume the drainage schemes that his father had been forced
   to abandon
4. An ensuing conversation, "one evening" (WD, 350), between Roger
   and Osborne in which Roger offers to arrange a second, English
   wedding between Osborne and his secret French wife, in order to
   ensure that Osborne's will is not contested
5. A visit "one day" (WD, 354) of one of the Cumnor family, Lady
   Harriet, to her former governess, Mrs. Gibson, now Molly's stepmother, from which Molly is deliberately excluded, and during which
   Lady Harriet announces that Roger has been awarded the research
   grant that will take him to Africa
6. A brief exchange that night in which Mrs. Gibson passes on that news
   to Molly and her father, unaware of its impact on them both.

These are intertwined strands that are less "events" than the potential, incipient germs of events. They are multifocal, loosely related, and set within a calendrical scheme that is thoroughly hazy. They modulate between the iterative
and gradual—deepening gloom, growing concern—and encounters that do
not direct or change those gradual processes so much as instantiate them. This
is, of course, typical of the novel's texture, its blurring of scene and summary,
once and often. Where, then, to insert a break here?

Perhaps the most obvious candidate would be right before the start of Lady
Harriet's visit, the longest continuous quasi-scene of this stretch. Indeed, it is
prefaced by a transition from the Hamleys to the Cumnors that actually theo-
rizes the local, repetitive oscillations the novel knows as change:

But as wave succeeds to wave, so interest succeeds to interest. The family, as
they were called, came down for their autumn sojourn at the Towers; and

again the house was full of visitors, and the Towers' servants, and carriages, and liveries were seen in the two streets of Hollingford, just as they might have been seen for scores of autumns past.

So runs the round of life from day to day. (*WD*, 353)

"Succession" is prioritized to something like "transition": a partially overlapping periodicity that erodes any stronger punctual temporality. But the *Cornhill* editors did not choose this moment, despite both its more flagrant scene shift and its placement almost perfectly between the end of the number's first chapter and the end of the installment. Instead, chapter 32 begins immediately after Roger's short conversation with his father—so immediately, in fact, that it starts with Roger's plans on how to find the money he has just promised his father. The caesura is an enjambment, placed between a "scene" of sorts, however fleeting, and its consequence, rather than between scenes, perspective shifts, or plot strands. The choice means that chapter 32 will be considerably (60 percent) longer than the others in the serial number, distending the chapter form rather than maintaining consistency.

Again, as with the Langton–Saint Albans chapters that received so much withering commentary in later centuries, we have a "bad" or at least puzzling chaptering decision. The temptation, here as before, is to explain it as an effect of haste, sloppiness, incomprehension. What is curious, however, is that this particular caesura is harder to discern than the option I've outlined above; it requires a certain work, a certain gaze, to locate a break precisely here rather than elsewhere. That gaze would seem to be one that sought to avoid anything like the cleanly episodic. The result is best encapsulated by chapter 32's tellingly indistinct title, "Coming Events": a tag that does not refer to a particular character, nor a specific event, nor even a series of events that actually occur— merely their collective *potential* to occur, their looming but vague incipience. The editors who placed the break here have both discovered and in part created Gaskell's rhythm, a segmenting so stubbornly aslant of strongly marked beats that scenes and episodes dissolve into the irregular regularity of waves, breaks that only body forth the slow, massive continuity from which they come.

"Bad," perhaps, but also well done, or done according to an idea. The familiar chapter-break rationales of the nineteenth century create a vague consensus that the units they shape should not reflect completed actions or episodic wholeness; in the case of *Wives and Daughters*, these norms were already clear enough that its editors could use them even when other, "stronger" narrative beats were possible. There is in this sense something potentially untethered about the novelistic chapter in this period. It seems here linked to no other kind of time, whether personal and agentic—the path from intent to action to consequence—or impersonal and communal, as in clock or calendrical time. This was not always the case; as my following chapter will argue, at least one tether remained prevalent. But in Tolstoy and Gaskell both, something deeply characteristic about the novelistic chapter is markedly present: a deliberate offhandedness in regard to its construction, a carefulness, in various ways, to appear indistinct, and so to ensure that their chapters do not harden into anything like a regular, forceful measure. The form becomes a tool for undoing the grander kinds of divisions and periodicities.

7

The Days of our Novelistic Lives (the Circadian)

DICKENS — ELIOT — MCGREGOR

IT IS A TECHNIQUE with many avatars: the use of daily time to structure a narrative. There is Attic tragedy, famously limited to what Aristotle called "a single revolution of the sun, or thereabouts."[1] At another extreme both historically and aesthetically there is Christian Marclay's 2010 *The Clock*, the twenty-four-hour montage film in which the timepieces visible in every scene precisely synchronize scenic presentation with viewing time, in the process swallowing—or becoming—narrative. But the practice is more commonly associated with internal divisions. At the end of ancient textual units, for example, sleep often descends. The Alexandrian scribes who segmented the Homeric epics into twenty-four books often chose the descent of "sweet sleep" as a convenient place to make their divisions.[2] The practice was retained in mock-epic; Apuleius's Lucius, having gone without the satiation of heroic dining, turns in at the end of book 1 of *The Golden Ass*: "So, not before time, I escaped from this tiresome old man and the interrogation plus starvation that was his idea of entertainment; and weighed down, not with food but sleep, having dined solely on conversation, I went back to my room and surrendered myself to the repose that I was longing for."[3] It is not the only occasion Apuleius will have to conclude an internal division with the end of one of Lucius's days.[4] In this way he gestures to the epic day as *kairos*—its status as the unit of significant and appropriate action, watched over by the gods, whose slumber matches that of the epic heroes, and marked by ritual observances—while emptying it. We may live in days, but they are not like the full, awful days of epic action.

The epic heroes, Auerbach observed, "wake every morning as if it were the first day of their lives."[5] Their kairotic days are ceremonial, replete, strongly collective, and unique. Not so, however, with the chronological dailiness of the novel, where the boundary between days also marks the interruptions inevitable in a form that cannot be consumed in a single sitting, but with a very different tonality. Ordinary circadian rhythms depicted by novels often align with the boundaries of textual segments as if to invite us to sleep as well, to put the book down and relinquish its hold on us, thereby tying the necessary ephemerality of our reading—doomed to be interrupted by boredom, disgust, arousal, duties or pleasures, any kind of inattention—to the ephemeral itself, to the *day* and its rhythms. Novel reading is always in part a negotiation, or timing exercise, with sleep. It is an utterly unsurprising fact about human physiology and its relation to any aesthetic experience that demands more than a few hours of our time. That fact is registered by a particular formal mechanism that develops gradually in the history of fiction: the coordination of novel chapters with the time span of the day. But here the merely physiological fact acquires a new dimension. By affiliating its internal divisions with diurnal boundaries, the novel asks: What is possible, or even thinkable, within the frame of the day? What is thinkable within a unit—the chapter—that is limited to it? How does that frame coexist with other, larger ones?[6]

The linkage between a chapter and a day, or the idea of a chapter as a record of a single day, is long and goes back at least as far as Gellius's *Attic Nights*.[7] We have seen it already in examples as different as the Langton–Saint Albans system of biblical capitulation and Pym's *Excellent Women*. It recurs in scattered times and places, from Sade's *120 Days of Sodom* to Iris Murdoch's *The Word Child*. What follows, however, is a study of how the day, particularly in its linked solar and physiological manifestations, becomes prominent in the segmenting design of the novel in a specific place and time: the nineteenth century in Britain. Here it is that, pervasively and innocuously, circadian rhythms become storytelling rhythms, notably through the calibration of the frame of the chapter with the duration of a day. This is at once a peculiar, historically bounded choice and a response to the static inevitability that reading a novel will, with very few exceptions, take more than one of the days of its readers. It is also a design that rarely achieves salience. Like our days themselves, the pattern is so repetitive that it is more ground than figure, and as with our days, it is a patterning perhaps best known by simply counting them. But to say that, with remarkable frequency, the nineteenth-century British novel chapter *equals a day* will mean that these chapters are naturalized, even regularized; and that to naturalize the chapter in this way, to make the day the below-threshold, basal time of the novel, is a way of denaturalizing other times. Bakhtin on the static time of the nineteenth-century provincial town: "A day is just a day, a year is just a year—a life is just life."[8] But to make the day primary, as the diurnal chapter does, is to throw into question the meaning of the larger frames, from a year to a life, that it punctuates.

A Day in the Dickensian Life

An initial example, from an unexpected source: Dickens. Unexpected, because few novelists have been more associated with impatient refusals of the circadian. A noted insomniac, Dickens's incessant energy seemed to flout the day's ordinary rhythms. "The first ray of light which illumines the gloom": that opening phrase of what would be his initial novel-length production imagines a burst of energy that scarcely ever flags; Pickwick, that notorious early riser, seems to be living in a permanent morning light all his own.[9] Yet even in Dickens's restless world the diurnal makes its insistent mark. Sleep intervenes; his world's energy is afforded the usual caesura to replenish itself. And the place for those caesuras is at a chapter's end. A cento of nocturnal reflections from *David Copperfield*'s chapter-ending paragraphs:

> I remember how the solemn feeling with which I at length turned my eyes away, yielded to the sensation of gratitude and rest which the sight of the white-curtained bed—and how much more the lying softly down upon it, nestling in the snow-white sheets!—inspired. I remembered how I thought of all the solitary places under the night sky where I had slept, and how I prayed that I might never be houseless any more, and never forget the houseless. I remember how I seemed to float, then, down the melancholy glory of that track upon the sea, away into the world of darkness.[10]

> Here, among pillows enough for six, I soon fell asleep in a blissful condition, and dreamed of ancient Rome, Steerforth, and friendship, until the early morning coaches, rumbling out of the archway underneath, made me dream of thunder and the gods. (*DC*, 298)

> But, as I fell asleep, I could not forget that she was still there looking, "Is it really, though? I want to know;" and when I awoke in the night, I found that I was uneasily asking all sorts of people in my dreams whether it really was or not—without knowing what I meant. (*DC*, 306)

Poor Traddles! I knew enough of Mr Micawber by this time, to foresee that he might be expected, to recover the blow; but my night's rest was sorely distressed by thoughts of Traddles, and of the curate's daughter, who was one of ten, down in Devonshire, and who was such a dear girl, and who would wait for Traddles (ominous praise!) until she was sixty, or any age that could be mentioned. (*DC*, 436–37)

From the perspective of chapter endings, *David Copperfield* can read like a record of beds, all of them temporary. (A way of putting it: the number of beds slept in that add up to a life.) The elemental rituals and sensations of sleep's onset—nestling, floating, dissolving—suspend the day's action without entirely closing it off. Comfort alternates with the persistence of a vaguely troubled consciousness as the day's vivid jumble yields to its distilled afterimages and diffused echoes. At its close, the day *coagulates*.

These represent the commonest form of chapter framing in *Copperfield*, and they define a modestly elastic narrative clock that subtends both plotlines and serial numbers alike. The above examples come from chapter endings within serial numbers and not the numbers' conclusions, which tend toward more decisive or surprising gestures (Aunt Betsey's bankruptcy, Dora's death). Matching these sleep endings are frequent matitudinal chapter openings:

On going down in the morning ... (*DC*, 210)

When I awoke in the morning ... (*DC*, 350)

I mentioned to Mr Spenlow in the morning ... (*DC*, 437)

I received one morning by the post ... (*DC*, 707)

Within larger episodic developments, diurnal time pulses, quietly but discernibly, through the chapter. The pattern is frequent enough to be clear, but not so frequent as to become mechanical: by a conservative count, thirty-four of the novel's sixty-four chapters involve a reference, at their start or end, to the morning's first actions or the night's last thoughts before sleep. It is a novel, after all, that begins with a birth at midnight and ends as the narrator's "lamp burns low" deep in the night (*DC*, 882). But the chapter is the day's primary register; it is within chapters that a day in the Dickensian life takes place.

The diurnal-chapter relation, however, does not possess any chronological or calendrical precision. *David Copperfield* is a novel generally absent of dates, its days instead succeeding each other in a loose and unspecified linearity. Nor is it pitched with explicit reference to clock time; a vaguer circadian impulse, solar and physiological, still dictates the texture of that relation. The civil day yields to the solar circuit. If the time of industrial work discipline matters here, it is perhaps only in the implicit scenario of the reader, whose presumed evening leisure to read—work discipline's necessary complement, limited to the hour or so when consciousness slows before sleep—is the silent partner of the novel's circadian oscillations, which tame or naturalize that industrial exigency, dissolving clock time into a broader ontology of dailiness.[11] Of course, whether Victorian novel reading did usually occur right before sleep is hard to gauge. The available evidence suggests that for much of the century bedtime reading would have been difficult, even dangerous.[12] But historical prevalence need not dictate a particular literary rhetoric, and the chapter ending situated at day's end is a gesture to exactly that situation: reading as the day's last act, before we let one day blur into the next. The end of day may not have actually been the ideal or even frequent timing for novel reading, but it is the experiential frame novel chapters like these prefer to imagine, one oriented toward the gentled worries and jumbled, persistent retrospects of sleep, the moment when the will gives way and rests. The empirical time of reading and the aesthetic time of narrative arrive at a satisfyingly comfortable concord at a chapter's end, where a reader's work-disciplined rest matches David's retreat into sleep.[13] Close of chapter, close of day; tomorrow there will be more.

Copperfield is emblematic for a history of the chapter because it marks a shift in Dickens's career from treating the chapter with playful homage—as reflected in the deliberately antique garrulousness of the chapter heads in *Pickwick* or *Oliver Twist*—to a newer, quieter method that ties the chapter, pervasively if tacitly, to diurnal time. The day, that is, resanctions an old form. The chapter is given weight, or seriousness, by becoming allied with the recurrence of day and night, an ontological fact that cuts through plot events and the agential attitudes, such as plans, projects, or desires, that make up plot or, as it has been called in *David Copperfield*, destiny.[14] So sleep becomes a primary figure of chapter closing, rather than the narratorial incursions ("now leave we," "as the next chapter will show") that had so often marked it before.[15] The diurnal frame in Dickens's more mature work is pressing enough that it even leaves its mark where the action of the chapter breaks off prior to nighttime. Take the chapter in which David says what will be his final farewell (and a chapter ending is a kind of farewell) to his mother upon departing for school: rather than concluding on the receding image of his mother holding up his half-brother as Barkis's cart ambles off, the chapter's final paragraph accelerates to thoughts of how future sleep will recall that image: "So I lost her. So I saw her afterwards, in my sleep at school—a silent presence near my bed—looking at me with the same intent face—holding up her baby in her arms" (*DC*, 133). It is almost a direction—when you, too, sleep, and it will be soon, this is what you will remember of all this—but inferred only. Where chapter breaks had previously been an occasion for clusters of narratorial comment and direction, the suturing of story world and reader that the nineteenth-century chapter performs is an alignment of times, a synchronization of light. The reader no longer primarily inhabits a communicative relation; instead, reader and story share a temporal rhythm.

What this feels like, at each end-of-day chapter envoi of David's story, is something softly settling. There is no absolute break, only the draining of detail into a condensed, static tableau: what we still see when we close our eyes. It is not the experience itself that lapses at these chapter breaks, but the acute and bewildering consciousness of the experience as it happens. Alertness lulls into a semi-inert quiescence, and as a result, an afterimage settles into place; an emergency, in which something can still be done, vanishes into a trace, something to be read or pondered. (Another chapter-ending sentence: "The snow had covered our late footprints; my new track was the only one to be seen; and even that began to die away (it snowed so fast) as I looked back over my shoulder" [*DC*, 595].) *David Copperfield*'s diurnal chapter frames do not exist solely to suture the reader's leisure time to a story rhythm marked by turning in, nestling under, or drifting off. They also put this synchronization to use as occasions for a continually renewed perspectival shift, away from agential personhood and toward a third-person haven of reflection. Presence, its responsibilities and calamities, is relieved at these rhythmic intervals by a partial or temporary absence, a shift to what persists or lingers—what of our experience will continue, and also what in that experience survives or subtends our troubles.

Shklovsky called these "false endings," a turning away to an impersonal surround such as the quality of light or the weather.[16] Think of it as a minor dissociativeness. A later chapter ending, set not in bed but at a day's end nonetheless: "I was thinking of all that had been said. My mind was still running on some of the expressions used. 'There can be no disparity in marriage like unsuitability of mind and purpose.' 'The first mistaken impulses of an undisciplined heart.' 'My love was founded on a rock.' But we were at home; and the trodden leaves were lying under-foot, and the autumn wind was blowing" (*DC*, 671). The seeming inconsequence of the items that follow the closural "but"—to be at home and therefore partly insulated from the autumnal desolations around him—express a gradual detachment, from active first-person *thought*, which is here starting to run in an automatic series of repetitions, through the second-person "at home," to a widened third-person appreciation of enduring, and more slowly shifting, *conditions*. While not literally a chapter ending in sleep, it performs the same movement: moving down, into the self, its solitary and increasingly dissociated ruminations, and at the same time moving up, toward a depersonalized register, where everything is seen from a distance. The mental camera dollies back.

Chapter breaks like these perform a tonal resolution from what Yi-Ping Ong has described as "deliberative reflection" into "imaginative reflection": the taking up of a "state of reflective, imaginative suspension that is proximate to and yet discontinuous with the condition for the exercise of self-knowledge through agential choice."[17] Life as a *problem* for introspection, one characterized by duties and decisions, yields to a more static appreciation of life as a *situation* for aesthetic appreciation, seen from a perspective from which no decision can take place—the self as seen by the non-self. And yet that de-perspectival perspective cannot take hold for long, because it is assigned a time, is rooted in daily temporality: evening, the close of day and the loosening of consciousness.[18] It is constantly dissolved by the hiatus of sleep, as mirrored in the chapter break, after which the urgency of life as a problem reemerges with daylight. As the reader approaches the chapter's caesura, the narrative offers us a model for detaching from a world, or at least—given that the world, and the novel, will continue after that caesura—what John Plotz calls "semi-detachment."[19] That detachment manages to reconcile, or settle into temporary alignment, the difference between past and future, or between what Reinhart Koselleck called the "space of experience" (*Erfahrungsraum*) and a "horizon of expectation" (*Erwartunghorizont*); it is an occasion to register change, but only while change itself is in abeyance, stilled by the recurrent, ordinary intervals of rest.[20]

The coziness of these moments, tinged by a gratitude and relief born out of an experience of how precarious such coziness can be; their preoccupation with the repetitions of dreams; the metalepses in which narratorial retrospection pushes experience backward in order to move plot forward; the mixture of regret and pleasure in reviewing the day's actions at its close: these are Dickensian chapter signatures.[21] But they are also very much of their particular aesthetic moment, in which the ordinary Victorian novelistic chapter takes its shape, frequently if not exclusively, from the curve of a day's energy, the rising and falling of light. This is the naturalization of the novelistic chapter, the way it vanishes—as an occasion for metafictional play, for ironic comment, or any self-consciously elegant shaping—into the mundane repetitions of a sequence of days. We might also think of this, as the next section will demonstrate, as the chapter's regularization, its submitting to an external logic of loose quantitative sameness. But in so receding, the chapter does perhaps even more significant work, by making the day itself into an experiential frame indispensable to the period's fiction, even if an experiential frame that overlaps and competes with other, broader frames. Where do we live? The Victorian chapter says: first, and perhaps above all, in days.

The 3,600-Word Form (Counting I)

The relationship between what is "natural"—which is to say, ontologically given, existing in negotiation with our fluctuating awareness of it—and what is "regular," or objectively, measurably alike, is in the case of the day not entirely simple. Days are more or less like one another. Some days are longer than others. These are only partially conflicting claims; a phenomenological elasticity, but of a modest or bounded sort, is a core aspect of diurnal experience. It means that thinking together both durational sameness and durational variation are essential to the temporal frame of the day. One way to convey that relationship is through the kairotic days of epic or tragedy: impossibly dense, pivotal days that are somehow nonetheless—as registered by the tight unity of tragic action, or the ceremonial and collective rituals of nightfall in epic— just days still, as if picked out of a stream of undistinguished days in order to be transfigured by an extraordinary event.

Another way would be to stitch this relationship between objective sameness and subjective variation to a preexisting formal pattern, one that both possessed a vaguely appropriate size and could violate that boundary without necessarily becoming something else—a form whose sequentiality could express not kairotic distinctiveness but chronological accumulation, where some items in the chain could bulge out more than the rest without rupturing its linkages. Meaning, of course, the chapter. The effects on the time unit and the textual unit would be reciprocal: an ontology of dailiness would emphasize repetition over uniqueness, while the chapter itself would change to reflect its alignment with the day, both in thematic terms and quantitatively. It would become streamlined, less variable; it would also, perhaps, become slightly larger, in order to encompass, more than single actions, something like a collection of events within a revolution of the sun.

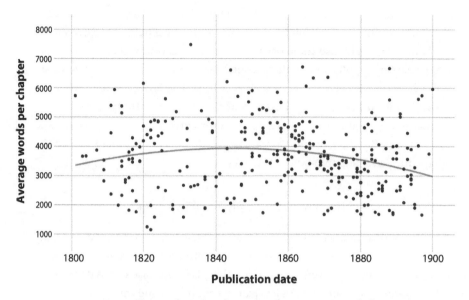

FIGURE 7.1 Chapter lengths in nineteenth-century British fiction.

This, at least, is the premise behind figure 7.1, a quantitative snapshot of the nineteenth-century British novelistic chapter. Pictured here is a survey of average chapter word counts per novel, compiled from three hundred novels dating from 1801 to 1900, where word counts are used as the most neutral method of measurement. The corpus is the collection formerly known as the Chadwyck-Healey database of nineteenth-century fiction, expanded by fifty more novels in order to fill out certain subgenres and decades; chapter word counts were extracted using the "Chapterize" script written by Jonathan Reeve.[22] The trendline of this survey displays a gradual and slight expansion in chapter size by the middle of the century, to almost 4,000 words—more than six times larger than the Caxton-Malory model—before a somewhat accelerated late-century shortening. All told, however, the century's average novelistic chapter was 3,600 words, a size that would have been utterly conventional at any point in the period. Of course that number itself—3,600 words—is inert. It cannot tell us what is usually narrated within that span; and it certainly cannot tell us the full range of possible contents within such a limit. Nor is it sufficient in itself to explain the difference in narrative terms between this unit of novelistic manufacture and the 600-word chapters of Caxton's *Morte*, or, say, the shorter chapters of *Tom Jones* (averaging a little over 1,600), *The Vicar of Wakefield*, or *Pride and Prejudice* (both of them slightly under

2,000). The increase in size can perhaps be explained with reference to Ted Underwood's argument that literary time, from the eighteenth to the twentieth century, slows to a "scale of minutes" rather than a "scale of days"; if the day is a predominant temporal frame for the chapter, chapters would therefore become longer as they brake into that new, more dilated pace.[23] Whatever the cause of the chapter's expansion, within the nineteenth century we have an image of relative stability, suggesting a vague consensus about the appropriate length or duration of the novelistic chapter that held for a century.

In another sense, the 3,600-word chapter scarcely exists. It is a quantitative construct, a way to bridge such outliers as Benjamin Disraeli's 1833 *The Wondrous Tale of Alroy* (almost 7,500 words per chapter) and his 1837 *Venetia* (at 1,884 words per chapter, more concise than early Austen). Even within particular authors' careers there is rarely a quantitative signature. That 3,600-word norm can seem more artificial still when compared with the even more wild deviances of particular chapters: over 20,000-word chapters can be found in Amelia Opie's 1804 *Adeline Mowbray*, Samuel Warren's 1841 *Ten Thousand a-Year*, and George Meredith's 1856 *The Shaving of Shagpat*; or, on the other side, the 208-word chapter in Thomas Hardy's 1872 *Under the Greenwood Tree*, or the literally lapidary 44-word chapter "The Narrative of the Tombstone" in Wilkie Collins's 1859–60 *The Woman in White*. These are the outer boundaries. The 3,600-word figure is only a norm in a very loose sense; the nineteenth-century chapter is capable of tolerating extremes, a pliant, ductile form with just enough stiffness to resist being bent out of recognition. If the figure has a meaning for us, it is as a point of balance that ensures that the departures from its invisible norm are felt *as* departures—as deliberate alterations to a rhythm. We must be careful, then, not to ascribe too much consistency to the 3,600-word chapter. It is a perspectival focal point, as illusory and helpful in organizing our expectations as, say, our default sense that each of our days will last as long as the others. It signals a modestly capacious size—certainly much greater than the size of internal units in earlier fiction—that possesses a regular irregularity. Each chapter can be shorter or longer than the ones it follows or precedes, on occasion by significant amounts, but they are all finally the same—that is, all referable to a vague experiential standard that remains largely intact across the century.

Such data pose one immediate question: What forces held that norm stable, both from outside the story world and from within it? Let us look first at the possible material or format constraints upon chapter size. A sensible hypothesis would be that if the average word count of a chapter is a dependent variable, the demands of serialization would be at least one independent variable, if only because of the sameness—in terms of page counts—required by serial installments: thirty-two octavo pages, the post-*Pickwick* norm for stand-alone numbers; something a bit less, on the order of twenty-five to twenty-eight pages, for magazine installments such as those run by the *Cornhill*. This would have meant a fairly well-defined amount of text—roughly speaking, 15,000 words in the stand-alone format—in which a certain number of chapters, usually three, would have had to be apportioned.[24] The temptation to regularity of chapters would seem to be far greater in that format than the unrestricted, or at least far less restricted, world of the three-volume novel. Taking a wide historical survey of the two competing formats, from 1832 and the serialization of Frederick Marryat's *Peter Simple* in his *Metropolitan Magazine* to 1900, by which point multivolume publication had ceased, the results suggest otherwise (figure 7.2). The trend line for volume publication is remarkably consistent across the entire period of Victorian fiction, hovering near 4,000 words per chapter, while that for serial publication rises and declines. During the period from 1850 to 1870, however, when general-interest periodicals such as the *Cornhill* gained prominence, serialized chapters essentially matched the chapter sizes of the period's three-volume, or "triple-decker," novels. Is this perhaps an illusion of calculating averages? Is it possible that the constrained size of serial numbers, which would have produced a more limited range of chapter lengths, simply arrives, by an alchemy that could scarcely have been fully conscious, at the same mean as a more widely *variable* practice of chapter lengths in three-volume format, where no such constraint existed?

The answer suggested here is only a very partial and limited yes. At the historical edges, novels published in volume form display a slightly larger range between largest and smallest chapters than do their serialized counterparts (figure 7.3). But in the century's middle decades, almost no telling difference emerges. The serialized chapter is neither significantly different in *average* size, nor significantly more *variable* in size, than the chapter published in volumes. The 3,600-word norm into which the nineteenth-century novel divided itself was, it seems reasonable to conclude, not a variable purely dependent on the demands or opportunities of format. The norm floats free of any extrinsic obligations or any rules, quantified and enforced in any explicit way, for how long a novelistic chapter should be. It could only have been self-imposed; "short" and "long" chapters balancing each other, with a rough equivalency, to arrive at a similar, and remarkably long-lasting, mean. It is a form that seems

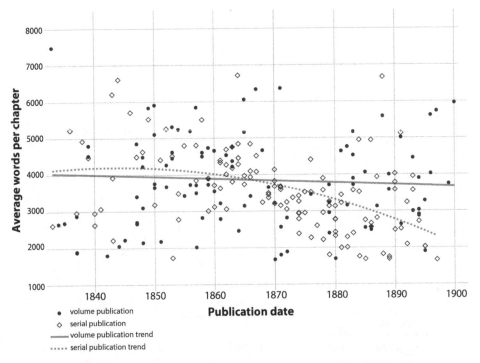

FIGURE 7.2 Chapter lengths in British fiction, 1832–1900: serial versus volume publication.

to arise out of itself, as if in an unexpressed concord with a notion of general suitability—in that sense, a true "norm."

Put more simply, if it was not externally imposed by publication format, the shape of the novelistic chapter must instead have been a response to shared internal, or narrative, time values: to the ways in which narration is divided, according to which clocks its rhythms are timed. Here the narrated day returns to help explain both the overall consistency, and moderate flexibility, of the period's chapters. The chapter of nineteenth-century fiction lives in constantly close proximity to the diurnal event. The 3,600-word norm is an impalpable consensus, an unarticulated general expectation, that derives its sense of a generally appropriate *size* from the general appropriateness of the day's *duration* as its motivation, its narrative spur. Considered again in the aggregate, the period's fiction displays obvious signs of such design. A 2018 study by Jonathan Reeve looked at the opening and closing paragraphs of chapters in a corpus of several thousand English-language novels to determine words distinctively found in each category. The results indicate a heavy diurnal bias to both ends

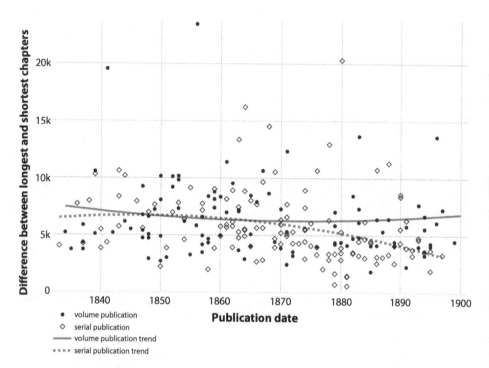

FIGURE 7.3 Chapter length range in British fiction, 1832–1900: serial versus volume publication.

of the chapter, as well as a tilt from neutral scene-setting indications in the former to a more psychologized timescape in the latter. Among the distinctive words in opening paragraphs were "morning," "early," "breakfast," and "awoke," alongside seasons and names of months, as if a narrative clock has just been set. Closing paragraphs were populated with "asleep," "sank," "withdrew," "homeward," and "farewell," as well as a series of verb forms associated with actions having concluded or not yet begun, with outcomes or reactions, such as "thanked," "wept," "parted," "prayed." These closing paragraphs were also dotted with the reflexive terms in which story time and reading time are sutured: "page" and, of course, "chapter."[25] It is worth pausing to note that these chapter-bracketing terms do their temporal work in a strictly "natural" fashion, observing patterns of celestial motion and human rituals oriented around sunlight; the abstractions of clock time are absent from Reeve's lists, which are both more social and more strictly physiological.

But to isolate first and last paragraphs, however suggestive the results, might still mean underplaying the impress of the day upon novelistic chapters. Even where opening paragraphs are devoted to more discursive tasks—character analysis, broad reflection, summaries of adjacent plotlines—a descent back into diurnal time, keyed usually to mornings, tends to be a delayed necessity. Take *David Copperfield*'s chapter 21, which begins with the lengthy introduction of Steerforth's enigmatic, intimidating manservant Littimer and David's attempt to account for the unease Littimer's disdainful reticence evokes. The opening paragraphs develop, in a sketch-like fashion, a persona, one that mediates between a particular mystery (what is the nature of the services Littimer performs for Steerforth?) and a general, comic social type (the servant whose haughtiness exceeds that of his master); as such it is pictorial rather than narrative. Yet the action of the chapter, however delayed by these initial considerations, begins with Littimer's matitudinal appearance, "in my room in the morning before I was up," revealed by David's drawing aside the bed curtains (*DC*, 307). Littimer may have been present to David before this initial scene, but to tread upon the scenic world of the novel, to become part of its representational universe, it is the proper custom to enter in the morning. Effects of delay like these reinforce rather than disrupt the chapter's usual diurnal manners. The statistical evidence can therefore confirm a couple of general premises: the day is closely correlated to the shape of the nineteenth-century novelistic chapter. And that day—the day of Victorian fiction—stretches from rising to rest, or dawn to dark, with an almost archaic simplicity.[26]

Scheduling the Novel:
The Case of *Middlemarch* (Counting II)

So far I have counted words in chapters computationally, in order to provide a broad picture of the parallels between the signature of the nineteenth-century chapter's formal elasticity and that of the experiential frame, the day, with which it is so often paired, and to argue for the shaping effect of the latter upon the former. To this I want to add a more focused consideration of how days and chapters coincide rhythmically across a novel's span, given the imperfect nature of that match. Not every chapter, in even the most regular of novels, lasts for a day of story time. The responsiveness of the chapter to diurnal time is partial, or syncopated, and that syncopation requires a different kind of quantitative gaze. Where I turn now is to a noncomputational—I might even call it an artisanal—approach to counting: counting days alongside chapters.[27] My aim here is to think more phenomenologically about how these two kinds of temporal segmentation interact in a reading. It is also to enter more deliberately into the counting logic common to both days and chapters. Counting is, after all, the simplest, most primal way of understanding duration: one, and then the next, and then another. It enforces boundaries; it opens up spaces, even very narrow ones; it habituates us to a certain span of our attention. And counting is in one sense what both days and chapters are for: they are numerical phenomena, both ordinal and cardinal. The presence of one implies a sequence into which it fits—as if, like our days, every chapter is Chapter the Next, at least until Chapter the Last.

Slow, noncomputational counting will also help reveal the characteristic deictic formulae by which days and chapters coincide—a *rhetoric* of the day— as well as help us develop a picture of how nineteenth-century novels describe those periods and their boundaries, which means a *poetics* of the day. One further way to conceptualize what follows is to say that it will track the novel's internal scheduling. I use "schedule" here because the idea of synchronization it encapsulates has its roots in material acts of dividing; the Latin *sceda* developed to mean a papyrus leaf or sheet, and the Middle English *cedule* followed by denoting a small written document. The evolution of the term into meaning a timetable, or indeed any appropriate slotting of events, reminds us how dividing time and dividing text are mutually implicated. The root act of dividing or splintering common to "schedule" and *sceda* serves also as a reminder that what we are counting are acts of slicing: the creation of units, whether chapters or days.

First, then, on counting fictional days. Perhaps only *Tom Jones*, among novels in English at least, advertises its ratio of days to chapters, by indicating in all but its initial volume, both in its table of contents and at each internal "book" division, the amount of narrated time—calculated in varying units, but most often in days—each book contains. Outside of Fielding, one has to count oneself. To take up, then, one of Victorian fiction's paradigmatic examples, an assertion: *Middlemarch* contains 146 days of narrated action. It is a deceptively simple statement, evoking the naïve heresy of trying to count Lady Macbeth's children, or the kind of equally naïve empiricism that George Eliot herself might have critiqued. In his 1675 *Traité du poème épique*, René Le Bossu argued that the *Iliad* narrated 47 days, but rarely since then has quantification of this kind, oriented toward the diegetic world of the text, passed for analysis.[28] The act of counting *Middlemarch*'s days—if not the figure of 146, to which I am only mildly committed and which could, like Le Bossu's calculation, be contested by a moderately different sum—is ultimately in the service of arguing that temporal measurements are key to the novel's formal practices of binding individual and collective experiences; that what goes into counting days—segmenting the flow of experience, placing boundaries—is a perceptual act foundational to both the psychologies depicted, and the reading experience demanded, by fictional realism in Eliot's time. More immediately, however, the counting act attunes a reader to the habitual means by which division occurs.

At this point some accounting, or explaining the method behind the counting, is necessary. Arriving at 146 days requires surprisingly little, for the most part, in the way of hermeneutic deftness. Eliot's novel is generally lucid about and attentive to beginnings and endings of days, particularly their beginnings. My counting method employed one framing rule: to include only narrated action—not, that is, narratorial divagations, and not any specified amounts of elapsed unnarrated time (such as, for instance, the specification in chapter 31 of Rosamond's uneasiness after "ten days" of Lydgate's absence).[29] *Middlemarch*'s diurnal boundaries are most commonly noted in the form of innocuous adverbial phrases that, in combination with a preterite verb, establish a fictional presentness.[30] The most frequent such phrases involve the word "day" itself: "the next day" (25 instances) and "one day" (19 instances):

Before he left the next day it had been decided that the marriage should take place within six weeks. (*M*, 51)

But Fred did not go to Stone Court the next day, for reasons that were quite peremptory. (*M*, 259)

And the next day Sir James complied at once with her request that he would drive her to Lowick. (*M*, 492)

But the next day she carried out her plan of writing to Sir Godwin Lydgate. (*M*, 657)

She one day communicated this piece of knowledge to Mrs. Farebrother, who did not fail to tell her son of it . . . (*M*, 263)

"I shall like so much to know your family," she said one day, when the wedding-journey was being discussed. (*M*, 355)

One day that she went to Freshitt to fulfil her promise of staying all night and seeing baby washed, Mrs. Cadwallader came to dine, the Rector being gone on a fishing excursion. (*M*, 548)

Following these in frequency are "the next morning" (12 instances), "one morning" (10), "one evening" (8), "on the morrow" (5), and "the morning after" (4). Sequence clearly matters here—the linking of one unit to the next—and there is a decisive preference in favor of daylight's initiation of a new unit. Occasionally other forms of daily time are noted, such as "at breakfast" (*M*, 652); less commonly there are indications of weekly reckoning—such as "on the following Friday" (*M*, 178)—although these usually follow a prior indication of a diurnal boundary more specifically pointed toward either a sequence of days or the dawn of day. Clock indications, such as "at half-past one," are less common (*M*, 123). Eliot's time markers function as *breaks* rather than markers tied to either a calendrical or twenty-four-hour grid.[31] Instead there is morning, afternoon, evening: the three canonical hours of nineteenth-century novelistic time.

These are *Middlemarch*'s explicit diurnal indications, clustering often but not exclusively at chapter beginnings and endings, as we shall see below, and easy enough to note and count. At other times, however, less explicit signals do the same work. Some diurnal transitions are as minor as the deictic "now," dropping us into a scene:

> Mrs. Bulstrode now felt that she had a serious duty before her, and she soon managed to arrange a *tête-à-tête* with Lydgate . . . (*M*, 298)

> The group I am moving towards is at Caleb Garth's breakfast-table in the large parlor where the maps and desk were: father, mother, and five of the children. Mary was just now at home waiting for a situation . . . (*M*, 399)

There are also completely unmarked transitions, where only the subtle swoop from a narratorial present tense to the past tense of the scene, a preterite of small actions, summons us to a new day. Although only a few instances offer any substantial ambiguity, this is where some judgment is called for in the counting procedure. One such example: "The subject of the chaplaincy came up at Mr. Vincy's table when Lydgate was dining there, and the family connection with Mr. Bulstrode did not, he observed, prevent some freedom of remark even on the part of the host himself" (*M*, 156). The descent of the narration into a scenic present occurs without explicit indication, only through the temporal-adverbial phrase "when Lydgate was dining there." Often that shift occurs through a negation or exception, the coordinating conjunction "but" working as an implicit temporal deixis, shifting the narrative from summary to scene: "Aunt Bulstrode was again spurred to anxiety; but this time she addressed herself to her brother, going to the warehouse expressly to avoid Miss Vincy's volatility" (*M*, 346).

Thus, 146 days. "One" day, the "next" day: these narrative situations pluck an instance out of a stream without any strong claims to distinctiveness or importance; it is *chronos* and not *kairos* that is suggested. Where "one day" bears an affinity to the unplaceable fairy-tale invocation "once upon a time," "next day" returns us to a sequential timescape, if one still vague enough to retain the naïve presentness of the "one." Together there is a compromise between unit and chain. The temporal-adverbial phrases that do this constant innocuous work therefore function more modestly than the signals— "suddenly," "just at that moment," and the like—that Bakhtin saw as crucial to the "adventure-time" of ancient Greek prose romance.[32] A different way to say this is that the diurnal or solar boundary in *Middlemarch* is only loosely related to, while not completely independent of, any calendrical index. That frame has some reasonable precision, at least as far as its overall scope: the novel's present action begins on September 30, 1829, when Sir James Chettham comes to dine with the Brookes and Dorothea accepts the bequest of a ring and bracelet of her mother's. ("What a wonderful little almanac you are, Celia!" Dorothea exclaims when she is reminded that exactly six months have elapsed since the April 1 date when Mr. Brooke had first given them the jewels [*M*, 11]. Like Dorothea, the novel is generally unconcerned with such calendrical specifics.) It ends more vaguely in May of 1832, although the novel's epilogue extends our information virtually until the moment of publication. *Middlemarch*'s main time scheme, then, covers roughly 1,000 days of elapsed time, of which our 146 have been selected for narrative representation—something like 15 percent.[33]

Not all days are equal, of course, even among this select 15 percent. Here we might introduce our second temporal unit, the chapter, to start to parse a rhythmic relationship between the two. *Middlemarch*'s days tend to observe the textual divisions of monthly part (or "book") and chapter; with only one exception, the day that bridges books seven and eight, each part begins with a new day. Eliot is reluctant to let a textual break interrupt a diurnal span, particularly the break between serial parts. But not completely: there are 18 narrated days that take more than one chapter to narrate. These 18 "peak days," as they might be called, stretch from two to four chapters, and if we want to find a gravitational pull within the complete set of 146, that would be our first subset to investigate. We can then further identify a core segment within this subset, because there are three sequential pairs of peak days in the novel: multiple-chapter days that are in immediate diegetic sequence. The first involves Ladislaw's disastrous decision to visit a Sunday service at Lowick despite Casaubon's interdiction, which leads to Casaubon's request to Dorothea to do whatever he asks of her after his death. The second centers on the rapid decline and death of Raffles in Bulstrode's care. The third, a six-chapter dilation, is a peak indeed, spanning Dorothea's attempts to reconcile Rosamond and Lydgate and Rosamond's admission to Dorothea of Ladislaw's love for her. These three pairs of peak days, the periods of longest uninterrupted presentness in the novel, all involve middle-of-the-night activity: an agonized marital conversation, a death, a breakdown. They are days unnaturally elongated and joined, sleepless and blurred. This then would be an initial observation: Eliot's refusal, except under extraordinary or emergency circumstances, to let the narrated day transgress the boundaries of the chapter, and in those few cases to depict the unnatural wakefulness of the action, the transgression of the day/night boundary, as narrative motivation. Maintaining the integrity of time segments—the interval between chapters, the caesura of sleep between days—is what *Middlemarch* otherwise, and largely, prefers. A circadian rhythm dominates.

If we move to charting the evolving relation, across the novel's eight parts, of that circadian rhythm and its alignment with chapters, we might further uncover the quality of that dominance. Figure 7.4 compares the number of chapters and the number of represented days by part. The result is a picture, from a distance, of a timing relationship that operates in a roughly circular fashion. With 146 days in 86 chapters, it is a relationship that moves through stages. *Middlemarch*'s first and last books offer a rhythm in which the number of narrated days roughly equals the number of chapters; in each there is also a high proportion of chapters that restrict themselves to a single day's action. However, in the novel's middle, and particularly its late middle—when plot complexity has reached its maximum, when the number of interrelationships being tracked is at its presumed height, before any resolutions are in view—this rhythm is thrown off, the relation between day and chapter pried apart. Chapters become temporally capacious, their boundaries porous. In books five through seven the number of single-day chapters declines to a minimum, while the number of narrated days balloons. Days begin to hurry; not quite as sealed off from each other, they encapsulate briefer events that are less apt to extend to the close of the day's human activity. Their frames, that is—waking and rest—become weaker indices of significance. The path of narrative energy no longer so neatly adheres to the path of the sun. Then, with the gradual resolutions of books seven and eight, the novel's temporal rhythm returns to its outset, and the boundaries of the day and the chapter begin to cohere once

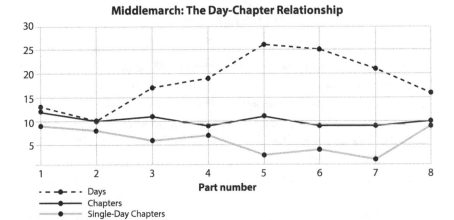

FIGURE 7.4 The day-chapter relationship in *Middlemarch*, by serial part.

more, as if *Middlemarch*'s dominant chord has been resolved back into the tonic.

The chapter, that is, works here through a partial, syncopated responsiveness to diurnal time; its attunement to the day's parameters is more sensitive at the novel's outset and resolution. This pattern can be thought of as a polyrhythm, but ultimately a closed or resolved polyrhythm, one that enacts a drama of disruption to and restoration of a circadian consonance that ties story time to reading time. The day finally triumphs; its patterning resumes, its distention subsides. It is a process that the cognitive theorist John Michon has called "tuning": the reflexive activity of matching events in the outside world with inner or mental events, and thereby keeping them roughly synchronous, through the mediation of a "base" time that becomes the barely recognized pulse of consciousness.[34] That base time, in the realist fiction of the nineteenth century, is the day. Such a base time is not inevitably novelistic; Shklovsky argued that the day-night cycle, as a compositional fact, scarcely exists in *Don Quixote*, while Barthes described the haiku's intimate relation with the semantic "boxes" or "thresholds" of the day.[35] But it is in Eliot's moment compellingly so. It attunes story time, or *erzählte Zeit*, to *Erzählzeit*, the necessarily interrupted time of our reading, through its syncopated relationship with the chapter and its caesuras. And that base time of the day provides the backdrop to, and possibly places a limit on, other time scales of human experience. So much a little rudimentary counting can reveal. The question now is what kinds of meanings or experiences the day can contain.

Day, Chapter, Epoch

Day and chapter: as an account of time's measurements in nineteenth-century British fiction, it is a somewhat parsimonious list.[36] To flesh out the importance of the question of temporal units in Victorian realist narrative it is necessary, particularly in *Middlemarch*, to add to it the Goethean concept of the epoch. An "epoch" in Eliot measures a particular kind of biographical self-understanding, and is employed with considerable frequency in the novel's close third-person or free indirect style when characters assess their pasts. Upon her meeting Lydgate, "Rosamond could not doubt that this was the great epoch of her life" (*M*, 118). After her first marital battle with Casaubon, Dorothea "remembered it to the last with the vividness with which we all remember epochs in our experience when some dear expectation dies, or some new motive is born" (*M*, 211). Phrases, all of them, that would not have been out of place in *Wilhelm Meister*, or at least Carlyle's translation of it. "Epoch" performs here the same work as the adverbial phrase "one day" or a chapter break: it denotes a boundary that also implies a unit, either by way of beginning or ending. In Eliot, it points to the psychological tendency to recall transitions, and demarcate major units, in a personal history. The transitional definition of the epoch—its earlier sense, to use Hans Blumenberg's terms, as a "point" of disjuncture—is particularly strong here, more marked than the durative quality of the biographical phase it nonetheless produces.[37] And these biographical segments marked by the violence of their onset, these "epochs," are of course broader than days, while their relationship with chapters is undefined. A new day or chapter can *indicate* the transition of an epoch, but the epoch generally floats free of these units.

The day-chapter-epoch triad seems potentially isomorphic, either a nested relationship or a hierarchical one, but in practice the alignments and scalar differences are loose and complex.[38] These categories are capable of some occasional equilibrium or overlap, but they speak to competing orders of time. There are 146 days, 86 chapters, many personal epochs—likely fewer on a per-person basis, but divided among so many characters in *Middlemarch*, who could possibly count them, and how could they be counted? What is key is that while each of these temporal forms contours experience differently, it is the interrelations and misalignments between diurnal time, biographical time, and textual (or format) time that will help us best describe the sense of being in the world, a more diffuse and more outwardly attuned state than mere consciousness, toward which *Middlemarch*'s realism is aimed. How one occupies the world in

Middlemarch—what kinds of attention we give it, where we pitch our concern—depends in large measure on which of these temporal units we take to be governing, or bounding, any particular experience, and how that governing unit inflects the others.[39] This should come as no surprise in a novel so attuned to the ironies and mysteries of measurement and scale. "The little waves make the large ones, and are of the same pattern," Ladislaw thinks to himself, with the logic of Mandelbrot's fractals (*M*, 461); Eliot's narrator seems to disagree, insisting on how seeing things "in their larger, quieter masses" alters any judgment we might make from within smaller frames (*M*, 762). Day-chapter-epoch is a triad where the units are in an unstable relation to each other. What is generically crucial, however, is that the realist writer feels herself, at least in Eliot's time, obliged to juggle all three. That volatile compound is one of *Middlemarch*'s formal signatures and perhaps one of the formal signatures of Victorian domestic realism more broadly.

First, then, the day. With the relative salience of *Middlemarch*'s "day" markers in mind—their insistence on light as a condition over other indices, such as clock or calendrical time—we might recall James Clerk Maxwell's claim that *Middlemarch* "is, and is intended to be, a solar myth from beginning to end," a claim perhaps less unwarranted than it first seems.[40] The reason for the novel's foregrounding of daylight is not, however, mythic in Maxwell's sense, nor is it merely a matter of evoking a rural and technologically backward recent past without gas-lit interiors and the social habits that come from them. It is to produce the temporal mood of the "day," as backdrop to other temporal moods. The day is *Middlemarch*'s temporal grounding. "But even when we are talking and meditating about the earth's orbit and the solar system," the narrator reminds us, "what we feel and adjust our movements to is the stable earth and the changing day" (*M*, 525). The stability of those changes, however, provides room for two very different tensions. The first is something like a lack of tension. This is the register of everydayness that brings Eliot so close to something like bovarysm: the Rosamond who learns of a marriage composed of "everyday details which must be lived slowly from hour to hour, not floated through with a rapid selection of favourable aspects" (*M*, 661); the plot of constant small deferrals and dispersions, as of Mayor Vincy deciding not to dissuade Lydgate from marrying his daughter, because "in the earlier half of the day there was business," while "in the later there was dinner, wine, whist, and general satisfaction," producing a daily scheme in which "the hours were each leaving their little deposit and gradually forming the final reason for inaction, namely, that action was too late" (*M*, 346). In the reduction of the "everyday" to the repetitions of "every day," we discover the tension of no tension, a pallid dailiness looking helplessly for relief.

But this is not the only mood of diurnal time. The other is expressed by the resoluteness of Dorothea "waked to a new condition" after a night of despair, asking herself: "What should I do—how should I act now, this very day if I could clutch my pain, and compel it to silence, and think of those three!" The narrator follows: "What she would resolve to do that day did not yet seem quite clear, but something that she could achieve stirred her as with an approaching murmur that would soon gather distinctness" (M, 787–89). This diurnal time is close to Aristotle's "single revolution of the sun," the unit of kairotic, or even tragic, time—what Ricoeur calls "the world in which it is 'time to' do something, where 'now' signifies 'now that.'"[41] The day in its urgent sense is offered, frequently in the novel's closing sections, as the necessary counterpoint to the absence of tension in the everyday; not every day, but *this* day, now, the particular day as the inverse of the everyday. It can have the connotation of coming due, either of debt or of guilt ("to-day," we read of Bulstrode, "a repentance had come which was of a bitterer flavour," [M, 620]), or of resolute but limited action ("To-day," we read of Dorothea, "was to be spent quite differently. What was to be done in the village?" [M, 805]), but either way it is a climactic sense of dailiness here, veering close to the melodramatic. The day, that is, provides either a sense of repetition—this day is like every other—or a powerful but also temporary, and in that sense delusive, sense of absolute difference: this day is like no other.[42] Daily time in this emergency sense translates a highly limited agency, by virtue of gender norms or the complexity of social life more broadly, into the willingness to do the limited thing the day permits—the action sufficient unto the day only.[43]

If the day is natural in *Middlemarch*, that is, it is so not merely atmospherically but because of its persuasive dualism: either nothing, or everything; sameness, or radical difference. That persuasiveness is checked, however, by the realist notation of time that, by situating these days, enumerating them in various ways, provides alternatives. How, for instance, to believe in the absolute priority of the novel's 3, or 18, peak days when there are 146 worthy of narration? The novel's 1,000 elapsed days, blank to narrative recall but implicit nonetheless, are also relevant; those 1,000 environing days exert an invisible gravitational pressure in *Middlemarch*, and they pose an invitation to reconsider which days might really matter, or if days are the only unit that matters. Here a different span comes to seemingly unknot the tangle between the urgent and the repetitive day and the lingering crisis of temporal confidence, the tug between absolute repetition and sudden singularity, they create. In fact, if living in days produces either dull passivity or the emergencies of sudden difference, it is living in epochs that is the far commoner way Eliot's characters narrate themselves.

By "living in epochs" I mean the effort to determine *the moment of bio-graphical history in which one lives*: to construct an elongated "now" (certainly longer than the now-time of a day) that differs from some equally constructed "then" time. It is an effort, that is, to detect transitions, subtler than those of light and dark, and more decisive. These moments of epoch detection are metaphorically rich insofar as they draw upon, and also cancel, images of the diurnal transitions from which they differ. Take, for instance, Dorothea in Rome:

> However, Dorothea was crying, and if she had been required to state the cause, she could only have done so in some such general words as I have already used: to have been driven to be more particular would have been like trying to give a history of the lights and shadows, for that new real future which was replacing the imaginary drew its material from the endless minutiae by which her view of Mr. Casaubon and her wifely relation, now that she was married to him, was gradually changing with the secret motion of a watch-hand from what it had been in her maiden dream. (*M*, 194)

A "history of the lights and shadows," the task of the old public sundial, yields to the watch hand (which may not necessarily here have yet acquired its companion, the minute hand), both being slight catachreses for an even more gradual—or to use the terminology of nineteenth-century experimental psychology, "just noticeable"—temporal difference. We might be reminded here of Lydgate's search for the "delicate poise and transition" between health and disease; the poise that is also transition, of course, being the original semantic knot of "epoch" (*M*, 165)

What matters here is that unlike the "natural" boundaries of day and night, these constructed boundaries are impossible to fix while being virtually irresistible. Caught in a span whose accretions defy comprehension, Eliot's characters wonder: When did this really begin? At what point did better yield to worse, then to now? It is a question of ontological location: Where (or, when) am I now? If the "day" is the sign of the temporal span whose inevitability veers wildly from inconsequential to paramount, the "epoch" is the sign of the fruitless desire to live in a bounded span that is defeated by its always-dissolving limits—the desire for a tauter span that slips out of our grasp. No insignificant nightmare of *Middlemarch* is the defeat of this impulse. Dorothea has here, after all, just been confronted by a Rome whose "suppressed transitions which unite all contrasts" are the historical analogue to her own inability to separate then and now (*M*, 193). Ladislaw will later playfully refer to this as Rome's way of preventing one from thinking of history as "a set of box-like partitions without vital connection," but the lack of any partitions evidently creates panic (*M*, 212). It is a personal crisis of periodization: the lack of faith that these temporal constructs truly obtain for more than a moment's intense, and credulous, attention.

If I have stressed the untenability of the "epoch," it is because its moments of possibility seem to be undone both by theoretical doubt (surely these boundaries don't really exist) and ethical imperatives (nor should they). Bulstrode's pivotal self-reflection turns on an evocation, and then a dismantling, of distinct periods of his past: "That was the happiest time of his life," an only seemingly innocuous phrase, precedes "the moment of transition," a passive voice that prefers sudden visitation to responsibility; "the fact [of his fraudulent suppression of his stepdaughter's existence, ensuring his inheritance of his wife's fortune] was broken into little sequences, each justified as it came by reasonings which seemed to prove it righteous," a partitioning that is a dark parody of Humean skepticism about causality (*M*, 618). If there is anything consoling in the lesson that the boundaries of biographical time seal us off from our deeds, it is that those boundaries never obtain for long, even in our reflections; the harder we look at them, the more out of focus they become. A general lesson, however, might run as follows: diurnal time spans are too strong—so strong as to compel us to the despair of their continual recurrence, or to limit our scope to that which is sufficient unto the day—while the epoch, as a temporal unit, is only an object of desire, never a thing in the world. In a general way, this gap between the dreary, or alarming, strength of diurnal recurrence and the allure of biographical periodization is in line with a familiar reading of *Middlemarch*: time defeats the projects, either retrospective or prospective, of its characters. We tend to thematize this dynamic as "failure"; we describe its temporality as "everydayness." But there remains the textual time of the chapter, with its curiously oblique relationship to the diurnal and the epochal.

Oblique because, to some fairly significant extent, Eliot understood the chapter as operating under a material quantitative pressure: the need to keep each of her serial installments roughly equivalent in size. The "Quarry" for *Middlemarch*—the small notebook that, starting in late 1868, Eliot used to plan her novel and store research relevant to it—contains lists of chapters with capsule summaries and manuscript page counts. The balancing act here is between tracking plot and text length together:

Middlemarch. Part I. Miss Brooke. Decr.

Chapter 1 The two sisters pp 1–13

2 Mr Casaubon & Sir James come to dine. 13–23

3 The two suitors persevere 23–36

4 Dorothea's eyes opened. A letter arrives 36–45

5 Mr Casaubon accepted 45–57

6 Mrs Cadwallader informed, & Sir James 57–70

7 Dorothea reads with Mr Casaubon 70–75

8 Sir James appeals to the Rector 75–82

9 Dorothea sees Lowick, & Will Ladislaw 82–92

10 The marriage approaching, & at a party 92–103

11 Lydgate talked of at Fred Vincy's breakfast

12 Rosamond & Fred ride to Stone Court & Mr
Featherstone asks for something awkward.
Ms. 134 pp.[44]

The page counts are not consistently noted throughout, and as these summaries progress their frequency diminishes, although the totals by part remain. There is an effort, that is, at vague material uniformity. There is also a corresponding effort at something like narrative granularity: the sculpting of units defined by particular verbs, although such verbs vary from the dynamic and discrete (to arrive, to appeal, to see, to ride) to the participial and imperfective (to be approaching) to the stative (to persevere). Objects of these verbs receive as much attention as their agents: characters are informed, are talked of, have their eyes opened. All of which means that the purely scenic cannot entirely dictate how these chapters will operate. Nor can even a single day entirely capture some of the longer processes intended here; a marriage "approaching" will spread beyond that limit. In the notebook's later summaries, even verbs recede:

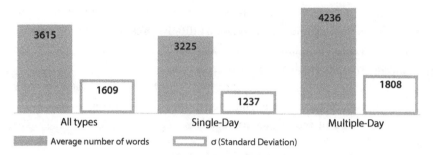

FIGURE 7.5 The effect of the day on chapter lengths in *Middlemarch*.

Part VIII. February

Sunset & Sunrise.

Ch. 72 Dorothea wants to help Lydgate—.

73 Lydgate's first anguish

74 Mrs Bulstrode learns her sorrow

75 Rosamond & Lydgate

76 Lydgate & Dorothea.

77 Dorothea, Rosamond & Will Ladislaw

78 Will & Rosamond [interlineated, underscored: 79]

afterwards Will & Lydgate[45]

Eliot is feeling here for a unit that can be at once larger than a single action, smaller than a biographical period or phase, incompletely but residually tethered to daily time, and capable of a certain limited collectivity, as often expressed by the "and" ligatures connecting the individuals here. External pressures—the period of the day, the limits of a particular scene, the climaxes of individual revelations or epochal turning points, and the demands of reasonably consistent lengths—each moderate the other. The chapter's formal signature could be expressed as a negotiation. Like the solar days of *Middlemarch* it narrates, no excessive precision regulates it; it has no minute hand.

Call this, then, *weakly bounded time*: a "span" without climaxes or strong transitions, with a tenuous and provisional hold on significance. Some of that negotiated flexibility can be revealed simply by returning to word counts, as a proxy for Eliot's own manuscript page counts (figure 7.5). By this calculation, Eliot's chapters reveal a contained responsiveness to diurnal time. It is perhaps not surprising that chapter lengths expand to accommodate multiple days of narrative, both in absolute terms and in terms of greater variability; but this distention is only moderate, not far from of the norms of chapter length in Eliot's time, nor differentiating these chapters in any dramatic way from those that adhere to single days or scenes. As a temporal unit, the chapter is flexible, but bounded; capacious, within limits.

A compromise formation like this exerts a special pressure on the syntax around chapter thresholds. *Middlemarch*'s chapter-closing sentences are marked by a balance between progressive and perfect verb forms, suggesting an interim boundary only: temporary halts, as these examples suggest, within ongoing processes.

> Celia had become less afraid of "saying things" to Dorothea since this engagement: cleverness seemed to her more pitiable than ever. (*M*, 82)

> Thus Mr. Casaubon remained proudly, bitterly silent. But he had forbidden Will to come to Lowick Manor, and he was mentally preparing other measures of frustration. (*M*, 377)

> He wished to excuse everything in her if he could—but it was inevitable that in that excusing mood he should think of her as if she were an animal of another and feebler species. Nevertheless she had mastered him. (*M*, 667)

The two different verb forms tend actually to become chiasmatic; the perfect forms here, indicating the closure of a scene ("Nevertheless she had mastered him," "Cleverness seemed . . . more pitiable"), promise a continuation, more of the same; the progressives, however, promise conclusion ("was mentally preparing" will be swiftly succeeded by the results of the preparation). "Once" and "again" blur. It is a contrast of tenses similar to what Sarah Allison has called Eliot's "commentative clauses" that join to a past-tense statement of a fictional particular a relative clause offering a present-tense, reflective specification of that statement; both the perfect-progressive mix of these chapter conclusions and the past-present combination of the commentative clause fuse what is true in a single instance with what has long been, or will continue to be, true.[46] On a scale above that of syntax, chapter frames tend to ironize even fairly strong actions. Take chapter 18, which moves relentlessly toward a decisive action—Lydgate's simultaneously reluctant and defiant vote for Tyke as chaplain of the new fever hospital—and then veers away in its final four paragraphs to Lydgate's low estimate of Farebrother's willpower. Or chapter 4, which, while almost concluding on another decisive action—Mr. Brooke's delivery of Casaubon's letter of proposal to Dorothea— finishes instead on Brooke's characteristically indolent perplexity before the question of female motivation. Eliot's chapters end often on aphoristic reflections, but those aphorisms are just as often inconsequent, aslant of, or curiously unresponsive to the actions they conclude.

Inconsequent, but not therefore inconsequential. Actions end (a vote is taken, a proposal is accepted), but the frames of the chapter, from the famous epigraphs to the weak finality of each chapter's reflections (so often a reflection by a character *not* involved in the main action of the chapter), point toward something one might instead call lingering: a diffuse consequentiality. Not as strong as the boundaries of the "day" nor as delusive as the boundaries of the epoch, the chapter negotiates between them by providing an image, particularly in the novel's middle sections, of porous and provisional but still bounded temporal spans. This extradiegetic span can merge with a diurnal one, as in the single-day chapters that cluster at the novel's beginning and end, but it is not "natural"; nor is it mythical or allegorical, as epochs strain to be. It is arranged, within a loose but still vaguely felt paradigm of appropriate size and shape, entirely above the consciousness of characters, although it is responsive to them, usually in groups. Neither wholly impersonal and public like the "day" nor intimately personal like the epoch, chapter time is, perhaps, something like an image of *weak collective time*—a confluence of personal and impersonal timing mechanisms. A chapter is a posing of the problem of how time could be spanned, how a "now" could be constructed, with respect to both individual and group, slightly outside the agency of any one inhabitant.

This in-between time is more difficult to characterize than its diurnal or biographical counterparts, but the state it produces is as metaphysically modest as the chapter is in fictional prose innocuous: something like *ongoing preoccupation*. As with her characters, so with her readers: in *Middlemarch*, we are above all preoccupied. That sense of only temporary pause, a small provisional bracket around a long unspooling set of processes, engenders an attunement to the world that is both bound to it and less than intent about any one portion of it.[47] Thinking collectively in *Middlemarch* is as much a temporal as a spatial matter, and it is the unambitious register of preoccupation and its flexible and provisional time spans as expressed by the chapter that mark in Eliot the limits of our ability to live and think collectively.

The Chronocommunity

The torque of the chapter upon the days it narrates could be phrased as two complementary lessons. The day is the time we have in common. The chapter is the way of demonstrating how little we know that commonness, that community—how strange and provisional it is, how often unavailable to us, how little it is amenable to individual will; it is not a community *for* something, it is a shared experience that is not quite an experience of sharing. We know we live in days. We do not know how those days can be chapters, because they are not chapters for any one person in particular. A chapter is a grouping in time, a chronocommunity, that consists of members unaware of the grouping they exist in; it is an asynchronous synchronicity. For a history of the chapter, a broader lesson still would be that whenever the chapter takes on the shape of a natural unit of time, it is inevitably reflecting on collective experience. That experience turns out to be a species of impossibility: collective, but not experience; experience, but not collective. What it has in common is time.

Even well past the norms of Victorian realism, narratives that set out to reflect on communal life will often have recourse to the technique of chronocommunity, in which textual segments are aligned with either abstract or natural times or both together to depict lives related, however faintly, by unwilled synchronicities. Here, however, the choice of natural time span may be much broader than the day. Jon McGregor's 2017 novel *Reservoir 13*—a twenty-first-century version of *Middlemarch*, a story of a small, unnamed Peak District village under pressure from an emergency produced by arrivals from outside the village as well as from slower historical mutations, and told through multiple perspectives—starts with the disappearance of a thirteen-year-old girl whose family had been holidaying in the area. What follows are thirteen chapters, each covering exactly a year of time, starting at the new year's first midnight. "At midnight when the year turned" begins all but the first and last chapters, and also starts the second paragraph of the first chapter.[48] Each chapter-year contains either twelve or thirteen paragraphs covering roughly a month's time.[49] Spatially, the novel never travels outside the village's rural surround; temporally, it gathers disparate experiences into textual units representing calendrical slices. The result is an expansion of the more familiar novelistic day-chapter into a unit that flirts with the chronicle form, narrated in an unplaceable collective voice.

McGregor's scheme throws off the synchronization between the diurnal time of reading and the diurnal time of the chapter, but deliberately accentuates something else that is incipient in versions of that synchronization like Eliot's: the inevitable ironizing of the "scene" when set within a chapter frame attached to natural time. The collectivity of the time segment brackets, even swallows, the individuality of the scene. His month-paragraphs always include something like a scene of sorts, each of them a ritardando of the more liquid summary time of the passing seasons; these scenes can be both intense and inner directed, involving the smallest of gestures, as well as the interpretive and affective ripples those gestures can create. (Water—streams, filled quarries, floods, and the titular reservoirs—is the novel's master image for time's flow.) *Reservoir 13* is not, or not exactly, antipsychological. And yet, these scenes have a brevity and only accidental singularity within longer-term cyclical processes and collective rituals, as if to say: so many little scenes are happening at the same time, *in* the same time, without any reference to one another other *than* that same time.

McGregor's chapters nestle their scenes among a narration of yearly rituals: the natural or agricultural (days lengthening or shortening, the mating of foxes or bats, spring lambing, heather burning, grass cutting, the yellowing of primroses, and the coming up of nettles); the cultural (Bonfire Night, well dressing, a yearly cricket match against a rival town, the Christmas pantomime, the ends of school terms, the Remembrance Day gathering at the memorial to a downed Lancaster bomber); and those that mediate between the two, such as the twice-yearly changing of the clocks, or the phantom aging of Becky Shaw, the missing girl, each time the police update her computer-generated image. Of the furtive liaisons of Gordon Jackson, the local seducer, the coolly distant narrative voice says more than once: "There was a pattern but it was never routine" (*R*, 82). Every chapter, that is, tells the same story: the tensile thinness of a sociality rooted just in synchronicity. When you share a time, what is it you share?

McGregor's typical paragraph-months may expand the temporal frame from a day, but they are also are severe compressions, hard and jagged, of the workings of Victorian chapters:

> By April the first swallows were seen and the walkers were back on the hills. At the heronry high in the trees above the quarry there was a persistent unsettledness of wings. Night came down. At the allotments the water was turned back on for the year and Clive was the first to get his hose hooked up, the silvery water skidding across the ground before seeping into the cracks. There was blasting again at the quarry, and when the first siren came everyone ignored the long rising wail. The second siren came a few minutes later, and anyone with washing on the line was quick to bring it inside. The third siren went and the birds flung themselves up from the trees in the quarry and scattered, and the air stilled for a moment before the deep thudding crack thundered out through the ground and was gone. At the first

all-clear the birds settled in the trees. At the second the workers in the quarry went back. In the village the windows were kept closed for a few hours more until the dust had cleared. At the river the keeper dropped the cage of sample bottles into the water from the footbridge by the weir. Always the same spot, at the same time of day, on the same day of the month. Meanwhile there were two chaps who looked like they were scouting for fishing spots, and he wanted a word. He passed Irene on her way up to the church with two bags full of flowers. When she got there she heard singing from the vestry, and it kept on while she gathered the vases. She wasn't much of a judge but it was quite a piece of singing. Took a few moments to realize it was the vicar, because you didn't hear her singing like that in a morning service. She didn't recognize the tune and she could barely make out the words but there was something capturing about it. The high bright windows and the dust in the air and the smell of wood polish and Irene standing there with her arms full of flowers not wanting to move. (*R*, 79–80)

Here as elsewhere McGregor exploits the lack in English verbs of simple perfective or imperfective aspects: "there was" or "there were," his favorite clausal underpinnings, negotiate between a "persistent unsettledness of wings" and "two chaps" looking for fishing spots. The terseness of "night came down" acts as a false specification: it refers to no particular night, as if to say "night, now as always, came down." The scene here—a day of quarry blasting—arises out of repetition and is itself repetitive. *Once* is continually embedded in *repeatedly*. Yet marking this flow of the singular out of the iterative is a series of segmenting notations, and these timing mechanisms are what create an attenuated togetherness out of isolation. The five timed signals coming from the quarry blasting elicit differently united responses; the return of the swallows matches the return of the walkers; the keeper's monthly routine brushes him against the town; church song is overheard. These are not really interactions. They are co-occupations, coordinated without consciousness, of an elastic moment, produced by rhythmic scoring.

At the heart of prose like this is the existential predication: there was blasting, there were two chaps. "In June the evenings were open and clear. The sun didn't set so much as drift into the distance, leaving a trail of midsummer light that seemed to linger until morning. There was a reluctance to sleep. There was talk" (*R*, 223). Such constructions present the standpoint of the chapter as an exterior observation of what once (for a specified period of time) was—a general, enveloping condition organized around no particular act and no individual consciousness. Beneath all the many things there were, there was a day, *there was a time*. McGregor's chapters do not immediately read as particularly Victorian; in their deliberate, even flagrant repetitiveness, their obvious reference to a consistent design, they seem closer to modernist experiments.[50] But while his version of the Victorian chapter-day form has widened its measure from the diurnal to the annual and regularized even further its rhythm, it has left intact that form's significance: to imagine collectivities that exist simply by virtue of occupying the same time, and to imagine therefore the nonpurposiveness of such collectivities, their resistance to any projects, demands, desires. Here, perhaps, the effort to narrate the limits to collectivity in an alienated modernity finds in the chapter an apt means to express being together as merely a co-timing, responsive to no particular intention, alien to our actions, our reasons, our tragedies. The narrative voice alone can think what might only become apparent later to the characters who inhabit a chapter: then, we were together.

8

The Poignancy of Sequence
(the Antique-Diminutive)

MACHADO—B. S. JOHNSON—VARDA

THE NINETEENTH-CENTURY novelistic chapter was soberly conventional yet flexible, regularly irregular, tethered to human times yet partially detached from them, and above all unobtrusive, so common and yet unregulated as to present the fantasy of normality without norms, form without formulas. To a very large degree—it is the argument of part III of this book—that tacitness, and its usual operations, remains the default mode for prose fiction. But not everywhere or in every instance, and not even always in the nineteenth century itself, when in one place in particular the fictional chapter acquired something that ran against its usual course, and that disturbed its perceived ubiquity and universality: a lineage. That place is Rio de Janeiro in the 1880s and 1890s, in the mature work of Joaquim Maria Machado de Assis. In Machado's fiction after the famous midcareer shift inaugurated by *Memórias póstumas de Brás Cubas* (*Posthumous Memoirs of Brás Cubas*, 1881), the chapter—perhaps uniquely among nineteenth-century fictions—does not have to be observed by a trained eye; it is what *marks* these novels, to even the most superficial glance. The mark operates visually, through the chapters' extreme and consistent brevity; textually, through the constant reference to their construction by Machado's narrators; and conceptually, through the invention, and citation, of a tradition of chaptering that leapfrogs over the tacit consensus of nineteenth-century practice back to eighteenth-century European examples.

Above all, Machado's units are conspicuous. His condensed chapters and self-referential titles make his segmentation salient; they say, *something is being done here, and it is being done according to a recipe, a plan, which is worth noticing.*

That plan is itself often the "topic" of these chapters. In a representative moment from *Quincas Borba* (1891), brevity, self-reference, and cited lineage are combined to negate the idea of the chapter's commonplace, neutral availability; it is no longer a tool to be used but a determinate concept that constrains. The novel's hapless protagonist Rubião, whose succession to an unexpected inheritance has made him the prey of speculators, has been befriended by the politically ambitious and unscrupulous Dr. Camacho, who inveigles Rubião into funding an opposition newspaper. When Rubião suggests a slight change in wording to an editorial, Camacho agrees in order to flatter his benefactor. And indeed Rubião feels the elation of authorship. There follows a fantasia on chaptering that interrupts—and the chapter in Machado is always an interruption—Rubião's pleased self-contemplation.

The next chapter, the novel's 113th, opens with a counterfactual in a novel without chapter titles, and reads in its entirety:

> Here's where I would have liked to have followed the method used in so many other books—all of them old—where the subject matter of the chapter is summed up: "How this came about and more to that effect." There's Bernardim Ribeiro, there are other wonderful books. Of those in foreign tongues, without going back to Cervantes or Rabelais, we have enough with Fielding and Smollett, many of whose chapters get read only through their summaries. Pick up *Tom Jones*, Book IV, Chapter I, and read this title: *Containing five pages of paper*. It's clear, it's simple, it deceives no one. They're five sheets of paper, that's all. Anyone who doesn't want to read it doesn't, and for the one who does read it, the author concludes obsequiously: "And now, without any further preface, I proceed to our next chapter."[1]

Tradition not only licenses but actually speaks for the author, who employs Fielding's transition as a password or incantation. The chapter is thematically empty aside from this invocation of tradition; its emptiness underlined by its reference to a potential title in a novel that has no chapter titles, it tells us nothing more of Borba's mental state. Nothing happens, that is, other than the device of the chapter break itself.

The next chapter, scarcely any longer, returns to Rubião's pleasure and tells us what follows: a delusion that he has authored everything he's ever read. But Machado's narrator reflects that there is a "gap" (*um abysmo*) between the small pleasure and the enormous delusion—a leap in a mental process that would not only be tedious to narrate but necessarily exceed Fielding's five pages. Here the tradition of chaptering is cited to enforce a brevity that prevents the description of any complex chain of events or thoughts in a single chapter, which balks Machado from narrating it at all. The chapter frame has compelled his silence. "The best thing is to leave it this way: For a few moments Rubião felt he was the author of many works by other people." Chapters can make note of gaps but not fill them, because the chapter tradition precludes it. In fact, as we will see, Machado's chapters often attempt a strange chiasmus, in which they come to signify "gaps" or *abismos* even more than the literal gaps between them, which must be taken instead as including all the unarticulated matter the chapters have leapt over. Of course this obedience to precedent, so well advertised, is also so extreme as to become a violation of precedent. Far from Fielding's five pages, the very next chapter consists of one sentence: "On the other hand, I don't know if all of the next chapter could be contained in a title" (*QB*, 160).

Three chapters of *Quincas Borba*, then, of 122, 144, and 15 words. Closer in size to Fielding than, say, Hugo or Dickens, but exaggeratedly so. Something so distinctly short runs the risk, when set against the usual chapters of his time, of turning form back into formula. The stuttering, fractured rhythm is foregrounded, while the narrative material is swallowed into obscurity; this quick succession of units can only talk about itself, by insisting upon its—as we're told, lamentably imperfect—adherence to an established model. Or by joking: when Brás Cubas insists that his story has no "visible joints, nothing to upset the reader's calm attention—not a thing," it can only be taken as denying, as he might say, the nose on his own face.[2] If there is a gap in Rubião's thinking that escapes narration here, there is also, quite obviously, a gap in literary history that is tactically omitted: the moderately lengthy, unobtrusive chaptering of the novel of Machado's own century, a chaptering that he had himself practiced up to the writing of the *Memórias póstumas* a decade prior. The result is a characteristic triad. Conspicuousness, brevity, and venerable precedent are conceptually tied in Machado, as if to demonstrate that to make the novelistic chapter a marked *thing*, it must be made both *diminutive* and *antique*. Its vivid presence, that is, depends upon it being something easily graspable and redolent of age—a small valuable object held delicately in the hand, turned to various lights for inspection and comment.

There is affection and constraint mingled in this grasp. The rebellion against the chapter's existing norms is violent—to the extent of forcing this shy form into the spotlight—yet also muted, because it cherishes one particular version of those norms so openly as to seem more devoted than hostile.[3] This example from *Quincas Borba* is a clue to Machado's place within the history of the chapter: he identifies the European novel with chaptering per se, then locates a particular strand of chaptering as an internal dissidence against this larger identification as a way to carve out a compromise position, one that can belong but at a distance. It is Machado's way, and if it has no immediate predecessors, it ends up producing a lineage of its own, one that crosses barriers of language and medium, in which the naturalized, tacit chapter form is replaced by something more fragmented, more self-conscious, more self-referential—and yet still, technically and in its own self-declared fashion, traditionally a chapter. It will reappear in the mid-twentieth century in Britain, with the oddly traditionalist experimentalism of B. S. Johnson, and in France, in the chaptered, formally bookish early films of Agnès Varda. Brevity, self-reference, conspicuousness: this triad is an incomplete apostasy, full of misgiving and baffled affection for the traditional chapter form it undoes. The characters that shelter within these chapters are themselves minor, marginal figures—the feckless, the hopeless, the deceived, the mad, the stricken, the prematurely disappointed and irremediably solitary—as if the restricted ambit of these chapters can fit no bigger lives than those who, out of failure or refusal, belong to no collective. The question being asked, despite the different circumstances and with widely varying inflections, is: How is time segmented when broader, more generous collective temporal experiences are unlikely or undesirable? What value does the antique gesture of the chapter break then have?

Machado's Betweenness

The feel and function of a chapter shift when it is written as etiquette to be observed punctiliously, even flagrantly, rather than a repertoire of common procedures followed implicitly. "Very conventional, much taken with formalisms," as Antonio Candido has described his social persona, Machado in his work is continually fascinated with performances of adherence to a rule—not just form's constraint, but the desire to signal that one has been constrained, whether to attract sympathy for the sacrifice, or praise for the flair, with which the regulated act was performed.[4] If for the social superior this attitude might be experienced as unfreedom's sublation into freedom purely by the relish taken in compliance, it is shared with a difference by the *agregado*, or factotum, Machado's recurrent figure, who as Roberto Schwarz has argued "takes his love of formalities to its ultimate conclusion, which is disbelief in the forms themselves."[5] The *agregado* bustles about, explains his performance as it goes on, has no repose. He must not only obey norms but show he is doing so competently and willingly; everything is done adverbially. José Dias, the Santiago family's *agregado* in *Dom Casmurro* (1899), speaks in superlatives; he does not perform a duty, but instead "a *most* unpleasant duty."[6] Nothing is done but it is done excessively; which is to say, it is never done naïvely. Schwarz famously identified this figure—the dependent, or the freely unfree worker, bound not by law but by an inside-outside relationship to a family, neither owner nor slave but implicated in each position—both as the distinctively Brazilian image of the nineteenth-century bourgeois order and as the correlative to Machado's own fictional form, which reworks the *agregado*'s anxious formalities into its antic citation of novelistic norms.[7]

What Machado abandons about the chapter, then, is its tact. A compliance that goes to great lengths, if in a small compass, to point out the rules it is obeying is cunningly tactless—it cannot be accused of rule breaking, but it raises the possibility of a skepticism about the rules being obeyed, one that could be leveled at their source, their applicability, or their sanity. Nowhere is this adroit tactlessness more evident than in the diminutive size of Machado's mature chapters. It is clearly a choice, made at one moment and then adhered to for the rest of his career. In his early work—the romantic novels that owed a clear debt to José de Alencar, such as *Ressurreição* (*Resurrection*, 1872), *A Mão e a luva* (*The Hand and the Glove*, 1874), and *Helena* (1876)—average chapter lengths are fairly conventional for the genre, between 1,500 and 2,000 words. The transitional *Iaiá Garcia* (1878) comes even closer to length norms in Alencar's fiction, with an average of over 3,000 words—a figure that, as we have seen, is also, if coincidentally, the contemporary British norm.[8] After that, from the *Posthumous Memoirs of Brás Cubas* to *Esaú e Jacó* (1904), a drastic curtailing (figure 8.1). The simple metric of the word count reaffirms the famous "Machadian turning point," and demonstrates at least one significant modality in which it occurred.[9] The number of chapters in each of the later novels now reaches triple digits. These new micro-units are accompanied (with the exception of *Quincas Borba*) by chapter heads that keep up a running commentary directed at the reader. This diminutiveness permits a resurrection of the chapter's ancient task of managing discontinuous access; readers of Machado are often encouraged to follow cross-references, such as "Nhonhô, the future university graduate of Chapter VI" (*PM*, 139) or "the *cocadas* song which I mentioned in Chapter 18" (*Dom*, 120). It also has a material, even tactile reality; given their size, Machado's chapters are often limited to a single page, indeed are linked to the page by design. A former typesetter's apprentice,

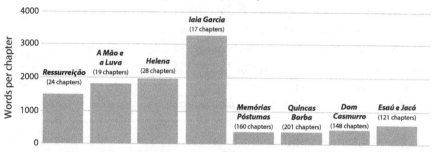

FIGURE 8.1 Chapter values in Machado's novels, 1872–1904.

Machado seems to have either permitted or even insisted that each chapter of the *Posthumous Memoirs*, for instance, began on a new page, a practice that not only was contrary to his eighteenth-century models but, given the size of his chapters, tied the chapter to the page in a direct way—a chapter becomes a leaf, a distinct physical unit, so that to move from chapter to chapter one must make a manual gesture.[10] The chapters become quasi-autonomous by virtue of their brevity and material isolation, bound to each other only at the margins. At their extremes, they achieve lapidary condensation, as in this cento of complete chapters from the mid-career novels:

> But that same man who rejoiced at the departure of his rival was soon to commit . . . No, I won't recount it on this page; let this chapter serve as a respite for my vexation. A callous, low act, with no possible explanation . . . I repeat, I won't speak of it on this page. (*PM*, 203; chapter 102)

> But, either I am very much mistaken, or I have just written a useless chapter. (*PM*, 255; chapter 136)

> The lady reader, who is my friend and has opened this book with the idea of relaxing between yesterday's cavatina and today's waltz, would like to close it in a hurry now that she sees we are skirting an abyss . . . Don't do it my dear; I'll wheel about. (*Dom*, 225; chapter 119)

> "It's clear to me," Dr. Falcão was thinking on the way out. "That man was the lover of this fellow's wife." (*QB*, 259; chapter 186)

Neither scenes, incitations, decisions, or even acts, these shortest of the short chapters are more often evasions, things not said, confrontations avoided.

There is a trick here, but one that works by laying bare the ruse rather than hiding it: Machado's brazenly peculiar microsegmentation presents itself as an act of traditional compliance while violating the norms of its own day. If initially Machado had shaped his chapters much like the romantic novels of his youth—a moderate amplitude, capable of some internal plot development and diegetic duration—now his chapters differ wildly from the ascendant naturalism of the 1880s and 1890s. Compared to that school's lengthy, development-heavy chapters, such as those of José Maria de Eço de Queirós, Machado's obsessively punctuated novels make a fuss over their difference; rather than Queriós's occasional ten-thousand-word units, there is instead a flaunted short-windedness. The norm breaking, however, has identity papers. In the prefatory note to *Posthumous Memoirs*, the flourishing of those papers has the mark of a defiant nonapology: "This is, it's true, a diffuse work, in which I, Brás Cubas, if I have adopted the free form of a Sterne or a Xavier de Maistre, may have added a few grumbles of pessimism" (*PM*, 3).[11] There is the note here of the superior whom the guard didn't recognize: *these* credentials, surely, must impress.

So the violation of the short digressive chapters is excused by a reference to a tradition, one whose laissez-passer has an antiquarian piquancy; a ruling-class erudition licenses disruptive conduct that would otherwise need significant explanation. Some ironies ramify here. The first is that the traditionalism feels radically modern, as if its century-old guarantors are just a convenient mask for a contemporary and experimental mode of discontinuity.[12] But others await. "Free form" (*fórma livre*), by which Brás seems to mean a procedure not wedded to plot or even sequential temporality, must submit to a different and even more vivid restriction: that of the constant chapter divisions or cuts, whose rhythm—tied as it is to the page—is more regular and more peremptory than the usual novelistic chapter. And the work's "diffuseness," or wandering quality, must submit to a regime of morcellation that parcels out the diffuse into small discrete chunks; it will not spread so much as stop and start. This identification of the chapter with a particular lineage, in fact, reduces its freedom, even if it makes its oddity, with a certain hauteur, permissible. The "Sternean" chapter is in Machado the sign of constraint's vanishing into a yet firmer constraint. It has strong norms: it must be short; it must be discursive; it must be thoroughly self-conscious, even self-annotating; it must avoid the banalities of sequence matching causality. It must be recognizably itself, which is to say, look like the family—something the chapter-as-usual is under no particular obligation to do.

The chapter becomes a particular kind of thing in Machado, distinctive and affiliative rather than neutral, and as such it makes demands. Here the note of the *agregado* returns to inflect much of the self-reference around these chapters. Even Brás Cubas occasionally feels the chapter's obligations: "If I refrain from narrating the endearments, the kisses, the admiration, the blessings, it is because, should I do so, the chapter would never end, and end it must" (*PM*, 29–30). So with Bento Santiago, aka Dom Casmurro: "It was not yet the moment of our farewell; that took place on the night before I left, in a way that demands a special chapter" (*Dom*, 102). When the chapter is invoked it is often a matter of the inflexibility or limits it places on behavior: "Ah! I am not going to tell the story of the seminary; one chapter would not be enough" (*Dom*, 106). "These are too many questions for just one chapter" (*QB*, 195). "If Aires followed his inclinations, and I his, neither he would continue to walk, nor I would start this chapter."[13] The question of what is right, what is permissible, what is appropriate tends to cluster around these discursive moments, as if the chapter produces a performance anxiety prompted by its severe constriction. Do your job and get out before you've worn out your welcome; never be tedious; know that your allotted time is brief. These are the dependent's concerns. Not that the dependent's aims are entirely frustrated; it is more a question of knowing how best to use the short span to accomplish a surreptitious goal.

And yet the master too resides in these small forms, the same master figure whose waving of Sterne and de Maistre is supposed to allay any suspicions. Just as often as the chapter expresses an anxious obligation produced by its austerity, it can serve to exhibit the opposite, a performance of leisured indulgence. "Long chapters are better suited for ponderous readers," Brás Cubas tell us; "and we are not much for folios, but rather duodecimos, with little text, broad margins, an elegant type, gilt edges, and illustrations" (*PM*, 65). Occasionally these miniature chapters, like the famous seventh chapter of *Posthumous Memoirs* ("Delirium"), dilate just slightly so as to achieve an excerptible, self-contained brilliance—the chapter as star turn, ready for anthologization. A relation is forged between the chapter and other small forms for the exhibition of mastery and connoisseurship: the vignette, the *crônica*, the brilliant little sketch, what Schwarz has described as "petulant, cosmopolitan pirouettes" in which a witty freedom is the keynote.[14] These set-piece chapters are slight and knowing violations of various norms; they press toward detachability from the host narrative as if they are almost interpolated tales, and they flirt with non-narrative forms like the essay or the epigram by becoming *topical*. Here highly complex effects of tone can ensue. "The Whip," chapter 68 of *Posthumous Memoirs*, is one such vignette: in it Brás's aimless flânerie is caught by the following object lesson: "a negro was whipping another in the square." It turns out to be his boyhood slave Prudêncio—whom Brás had himself once ridden as a horse in play, and whipped with a switch—now freed, whipping his own slave as a punishment for laziness. Brás requests him to stop and Prudencio agrees, saying: "Master's word is an order" (Nhonhô manda, não pede). Upon which Brás leaves and ruminates: "I went on my way, unfurling countless reflections, which I'm afraid I have forgotten entirely; they would have made for a good chapter, perhaps a cheerful one. I like cheerful chapters; I have a weakness for them." And indeed the chapter now takes a consolatory tone that belies his claim to have forgotten his reflections: Brás marvels at how Prudêncio has found a way to pay back, "with steep interest," the debt of trauma he'd accrued out of his former abuse at Brás's hands. So the chapter ends: "See how clever the rascal was!" (PM, 148–49).

The moral question posed by this little object lesson is immanent to the question of chaptering, and could be put as follows: How self-contained is this moment? On the one hand, we have a seemingly endless and causal series of violent exploitations. Master whips slave, who becomes a master who whips slaves; it is not so much a dialectic as an infinitely extendable procedure, resolving nothing. To add an abyssal depth to this causal chain, Brás informs us at the chapter's outset that he is in Valongo, pointedly not bothering to add that this was the site of Rio's entrepôt and market for slaves prior to 1831. This is the *narrative* potential of the chapter, its ability as a syntagm to isolate one moment within a temporal and historical process. Yet Brás's self-reference to the chapter as a chapter ("I like cheerful chapters") mobilizes an antinarrative topicality, a form of abstract thought and moralizing that generalizes out of the temporal process and in fact closes it down. Brás offers instead a "philosophical" or paradigmatic lesson: see how old pain is canceled by inverted repetition of the traumatic event! Prudêncio's public Fort/da game speaks to the resilient ingenuity of human compensations rather than any specific series of events— neither Brás's own treatment, which has now been canceled like repaid debt, nor slavery per se, which becomes merely an occasion through which to observe how humans work through their former powerlessness. Rather than guilt or implication, Brás can feel the detached relish appropriate to arriving near to an epigram—because the chapter, as all chapters must, closes. Indeed, after this scene Prudêncio vanishes from the novel. To use one of Schwarz's terms, the chapter *dismisses*.[15] Masters like chapters as much as dependents; they like how they end, wave something away.

The dependent anticipates, and maneuvers around, the break or interruption; the master manipulates it. The Machadian chapter manages therefore to hold in tension a social disjuncture. The mulatto grandchild of a slave and also founder and first president of the Academia Brasileira de Letras, Machado might have been expected to savor this ambiguity.[16] Both anxious subordination and insouciant privilege prefer to live in the chapter's small spaces, and in their own ways experience them as offering opportunities for a constrained daring—as long as both observe a general rule above all, which is to always be conscious of those spaces, always speak of them. *Capítulo* is, as it happens, one of his novels' most common words.[17] It is invoked as explanation, in celebration, and in a spirit of propitiation or apology; the chapter offers its opportunities, like a jealous deity, only if it is publicly paid homage. After all, as much as the chapter originates from Machado's garrulous and urbane narrators, from Brás Cubas or Bento Santiago or Counselor Aires, it also comes from outside them, is imposed on their experience over their heads, as a requirement, perhaps the most pressing requirement of their narratorial task. It is appropriate for the show-offy, elegant social world of these narrators, designed to entertain and not tire, to exhibit a character's formal etiquette, their wide culture, their acquaintance with fashionably antique and foreign rhetorical modes and occasions. And yet the chapter shapes them as much as they shape it; it speaks to a rhythm of interruption and deflection of purpose that they finally cannot quite control, and that they only mimic as a brave attempt to hide their fundamental powerlessness. However hard these narrators work to fashion the chapter through what Schwarz identified as the class privileges of caprice (*capricho*) and volubility (*volubilidade*), the numbing onslaught of short chapters, a break on virtually every page, evokes an imposed necessity with which even the wildest caprice cannot quite keep pace.

What must be obeyed—if also opportunistically exploited—is the cut, the gap. It is the chapter break, its interruptive and dispersive force, that is really most conspicuous in Machado; an overproduction of chapters is finally an overproduction of gaps. Perhaps the most paradigmatic chapter title in his work: "Now a Leap" (*EJ*, 52). The gap, or *salto*, occasions the other two elements of Machado's formal triad: its constant presence, never deferred for any long stretch, must be explained, alluded to, excused, made self-referential; and it is most often excused by precedent, by its pre-nineteenth-century lineage. Understood as a practice of frequent interruption per se, the lineage is more than just Sternean, however many other Sternean tricks a novel like

Posthumous Memoirs deploys. It is wider than that, a severe discipline of brevity and fracture that encompasses both Fielding and Sterne along with Rabelais, Ribeiro, and Cervantes, one that gives the eccentricity of Machado's gap the patina of age. Such an excuse might be needed because the gap, like a deity whose laughter is the outward sign of a threat, is in Machado primarily a negation. Each new chapter is a swerve away from, a correction to, or refusal of, what preceded it—as exemplified in the two consecutive chapter heads in *Posthumous Memoirs*: "Sad, but Short" and "Short, but Happy" (*PM*, 66–68).[18] Often enough that negation is simply a stop, putting an end to a chain of action or thought that might, given more amplitude, have led somewhere. Aposiopesis is the governing rhetorical figure of Machado's chapter endings, even when they do not (as seventeen chapters in *Posthumous Memoirs* do) end in an ellipsis. The breakings off are tonally more abrupt than gentle, more like quick caesuras than slow diminuendos; as with the unpredictably truncated sessions—the *pierres de rebut* ("chipped" or "scrap" stones)—of Lacanian psychoanalysis, they emphasize that interpretive solutions to what has transpired occur in the gaps rather than in the units themselves.[19] The gap is not just a hiatus but where content is located.

It leaves the units themselves in the curious position of narrating evasions, failed confrontations, events that do not happen. No duration or metamorphosis can occur within them. Even, or especially, when they mimic contemporary fictional norms: in *Dom Casmurro*, the arousal of Bento's suspicions of his wife Capitú and friend Escobar, and his doubts about the paternity of his son Ezekiel, can never quite be explained within a causally sequential frame, despite the use of temporal-deictic gestures common to the realist chapter. Chapter 130 of the novel, "One Day," is even a dark joke at the expense of the diurnal chapter frame.[20] "One day Capitú wanted to know what made me so silent and gloomy," it begins, and if Bento refuses to answer her, his refusal leads not only to no climactic or even particularly typical event, but instead produces confusion about how the days of his jealousy relate to one another sequentially:

> Pardon me, but this chapter ought to have been preceded by another, in which I would have told an incident that occurred a few weeks before, two months after Sancha had gone away. I will write it. I could place it ahead of this one before sending the book to the printer, but it is too great a nuisance to have to change the page numbers. Let it go right here; after that the narration will proceed as it should right to the end. Besides, it is short. (*Dom*, 237).

After which, the following chapter, "Anterior to the Anterior," narrates a scene with a perplexing relation to the nonscene of the "one day": a dinner in which Capitú remarks that Ezekiel's eyes have an expression that resembles both her father's and Escobar's. As Bento narrates it, that comment fails to even activate his suspicion in the moment; quite the opposite, in fact, as he replies that his son's eyes resemble his mother's for beauty, Capitú smiles modestly, and he finds her demureness so charming that he covers her face with kisses. Did her comment activate anything, then? Where is the link between that day and the "one day," other than in the gap or leap between them in which diegetic time is momentarily reversed? Nothing happens in these chapter-days, that is, other than what is happening all the time.[21] The day is almost too *long* to possess meaning in Machado; development, experiential amplitude, can only happen invisibly, in the interstices. The dreamlike slowness of diegetic time is cut by the hyperrhythmia of the chapter breaks. The relation between size and significance, as paradigmatically expressed in the elongated multichapter "peak days" of *Middlemarch*'s crisis moments, is reversed so firmly as to be snapped. In which case, better to be brief.

Such a procedure does not mean that Machado's short chapters are simple; they are melismatic, a single syllable gliding through multiple tones. Few catalysts, or nuclei, or quilting points are given, but plenty of hesitation and states of abeyance. What they tend to describe is the feeling of betweenness. It is not the chapter break that is between experiences in Machado but the chapter itself, an interstice as thin as the page to which it is often limited, that is between twin abyssal and inarticulable experiences. So they are instead forms of interim time: intercalations within long ongoing processes, either of relief, or insight, or madness; temporary escapes from, or evasions of, broader logics and the undertow of causality pulling his characters toward fates they will not want to meet. Holding off experience—trying to come to some temporary compromise with it—is their primary modality, a dwelling in the brief and delusive spaces of rest before the next leap, cut, or gap. If there is a characteristic action in Machado's plots, it is compromise in the interests of delay, pusillanimity in the face of dangerous or unappealing binaries. Brás Cubas and his adulterous lover Virgília try to somehow preserve their liaison without rupturing her marriage or his comfort. Bento Santiago seeks to live with suspicions of his wife's fidelity without either confirming them or doubting his own logic. In *Esau and Jacob* the mechanism becomes almost allegorical: two twins love the same young woman, who loves them both; caught in an intolerable suspense before a choice that can only be catastrophic, the solution to which everyone connives is to wait, hope it resolves by itself, and in the meantime beguile and distract as temporary forms of relief. In this spirit *Esau and Jacob* mentions the parable of the old man longing for death who nonetheless, upon seeing it coming in the door, "turned his head away and hummed a nursery song, to deceive her and live" (*EJ*, 226). The impasses are almost unendurable, but preferable to their resolution. This is the fate of betweenness, to know its own brevity but to try various ways to suppress that knowledge.

So the antique, eighteenth-century, ludic, or Shandean chapter—pick your adjective—has changed its tonality, and if in Machado it comes dressed like its model, it speaks with a different voice. Where it was perhaps once an expression of free inquiry, or the mind's liberty to range over its associative links rather any strict dependence on empirical reality, in Machado's hands it speaks to the unhappy desire to remain deadlocked. Maybe, at times, it offers some fleeting relief. In *Quincas Borba*, the Bovaryesque Dona Sofia Palha—Rubião's unrequited love, herself infatuated with the rakish Carlos Maria—falls one rainy day into a fit of regretful longing. Images of formerly potential lovers oppress her during the day's "closed atmosphere" (*QB*, 223). Across the break between chapters 159 and 160, however, the sun appears. Chapter 160 in its entirety:

> At that point the rain let up for a bit, and a ray of sunshine managed to break through the mist—one of those damp rays that seem to be coming from weeping eyes. Sofia thought she could still go out. She was anxious to see things, to have a ride, to shake off that torpor, and she hoped the sun would sweep away the rain and take charge of earth and sky. But the great star perceived that her intention was to turn it into the lantern of Diogenes and it told the damp ray: "Come back, come back to my bosom, chaste and virtuous ray. You're not going to lead her where her desire wants to take her. Let her love if she feels like it. Let her answer love notes—if she receives them and doesn't burn them—don't you be a torch for her, light of my bosom, child of my entrails, ray, brother of my rays . . ."
>
> And the ray obeyed, retreating into the central focus, a bit startled at the fear of the sun, who has seen so many ordinary and extraordinary things. Then the veil of clouds grew thick and dark again, and the rain began to fall in buckets once more. (*QB*, 223–24)

A short chapter, as usual, for the shortest of breaks in the emotional weather between dark confinements—a break that changes nothing, an intercalation that goes nowhere. Would Sofia even want it to? Machado's characters are half in love with the constraints they lament. So with Machado himself. The only lasting relief to this loathed stuckness that fears its own end—a deeply historical experience, coming from the precipice of a change, where the past cannot be idealized nor its elimination desired—is to make that constrained life always visible, to exhibit it openly. All those short chapters: little boxes of time without transformation, holding off the transformations to come.

Minding the Gap in B. S. Johnson

In 1964, shortly after the publication of *Albert Angelo*, his second novel, the British experimentalist B. S. Johnson wrote to his friend Anthony Smith to defend certain choices of form and format. *Albert Angelo* was notorious for having a hole cut in its pages, revealing three lines of text two leaves farther on, as well as a host of other unique typographical and stylistic devices, including its organization in a five-part structure whose titles mimicked sonata form ("Exposition," "Development," "Coda"). Smith had evidently written to applaud at least one distinctive choice, the novel's lack of ordinary chapters, while lodging reservations about the book's outlandish fragmentation. Johnson replied with a defense that, after the example of Machado, will seem familiar:

> Neither Tom [Eliot] nor Hemingway nor myself invented the fragmentary method, of course: if I got it from anywhere it was from the SATYRICON, which I think extremely funny, and which is of course in fragments because that's how the ms. has come down to us. Not to deny chapters absolutely: I can see some subjects which would require exactly their formal shape and counterpointing. But as a convention, no, I agree, in most cases in our time they're out.[22]

The defense via antiquarianism performs here exactly the task it did for Machado, which is to chart a narrow course between that which is unlicensed by prior practice and that which is unthinkingly habitual. Fragmentation has precedent, but has not hardened into something rote; insofar as any formal divisions exist "as a convention," they must be excised, but anticonventionality does not imply any radical futurism. The backward leap just has to be considered, appropriate. Fragmentation is defined through chapters, but chaptering-as-usual must be repudiated.

What has changed from Machado to Johnson is the social tonality of antiquarianism. Machado offers a genteel and disembodied bookishness—the

bachelor-narrator citing Sterne and de Maistre to disarm the cruder expectations of readers and flourish, even if with reserves of irony, the bona fides of
an ownership class—that in Johnson has turned material, and even artisanal.
Petronius's "fragments" are not the result of deliberate design but the state of
the surviving manuscripts, something imposed by the accidental properties
of paper. In adopting the Satyricon's adventitiously fragmented shape, Johnson
will have to trust to more direct means than time. Pages will have to be stamped
and punctured. The book will have to be torn apart at the spine and rebuilt.
Craft labor, with an accompanying ethic of forthrightness and muscularity,
enters the tradition of chaptering. Albert Angelo's protagonist, while working
as a supply teacher in proletarian London schools, tries to self-train as an ar-
chitect, and slips into critiquing modern construction to his students while
thinking: "form should be honest, should be honestly exposed."[23]

Which means that if in Machado we can speak of chapters as a kind of
formal "thing," in Johnson they take a further step into thingness. Most famously, in The Unfortunates (1969), the chapter is literally artifactual. The work
that he is most associated with—and which gained him some measure of
countercultural fame—The Unfortunates pushes chaptering beyond its limits,
into an indeterminate space between segment and whole, by providing chapters
material independence. The novel is twenty-seven separate, unbound "sections"
held by a box, the sections arranged in a (mostly) random order and easily
rearranged to suit any personal shuffling or bibliomantic procedure. The sections range from a single page to twelve pages. The story these twenty-seven
units tell is a reasonably linear one in its broadest sense, narrating an event in
the present (the narrator visits Nottingham to report a football match), which
occasions memories of the past (the death from cancer of the narrator's friend
Tony Tillinghast, who had for a time lived in Nottingham). But without a
material binding, this back-and-forth between past and present is fractured
into shards to be arranged in any of a staggering 1.55112×10^{25} possible sjuzhet
combinations.[24] What makes a chapter for Johnson, every bit as much as its
textual composition, is its physical construction; if Machado's chapters have
the self-conscious elegance of an object held to the light, in The Unfortunates, the
chapter can actually be so held—in fact, must be. It is a made thing.

What to call these things, however, becomes rather more convoluted. In
the instructions to the reader pasted inside the box, they are called "sections,"
as they are both in the script Johnson wrote for the 1969 BBC promotional
film about the novel and in the introduction to the 1973 collection of his nonfic-
tion, Aren't You Rather Young to be Writing Your Memoirs?[25] Advance publicity

for the novel tended to do the same.[26] Importantly, "sections" had precedent; Johnson's lodestar and mentor Samuel Beckett had used it to describe the segments of *Murphy* (1938) in the novel's metanarrative cross-referencing.[27] Yet other terms hovered. Reviewers, although they tended to respect "sections," played in various ways with "leaves" as an appropriate term.[28] Following this bibliographic logic, Johnson also used "signatures," at least partially to liberate his units from the leaf or page; here he had in mind the example of Marc Saporta's 1963 *Composition No. 1*, an unbound stack of leaves in which, no matter the order in which they are placed, every leaf runs onto every other one. Saporta's method, Johnson explained to Bernard Bergonzi, "seems to impose another arbitrary unit—the page and what type can be fitted onto it—on the material," whereas the "separate signatures" of *The Unfortunates* could hold "whatever length the material dictates."[29] This despite the fact that six of the novel's twenty-seven units are single leaves and not, properly speaking, signatures at all. "Chapters," however, were present from the start. A sympathetic piece from the *Guardian* referred to the novel as "a boxful of unbound chapters," and indeed subsequent criticism has continued to use "chapters" ever since.[30] Johnson, however, shied away from it. Part of his reason, as the book's design made clear, was the connotation of *sequence* attached to "chapter," one that "section" lacked. A perhaps more deeply embedded problem lay outside the immediate challenge of the novel's material, and speaks to the technical/ artisanal rhetoric with which Johnson approached his units.

For Johnson, his artistic idea, or *donnée*—to write a novel in which present-day action would be interspersed with recollections, coming in an aleatory fashion, of a dead friend—was a puzzle of engineering.

> The main technical problem with *The Unfortunates* was the randomness of the material. That is, the memories of Tony and the routine football reporting, the past and the present, interwove in a completely random manner, without chronology. This is the way the mind works, my mind anyway . . . This randomness was directly in conflict with the technological fact of the bound book: for the bound book imposes an order, a fixed page order, on the material. I think I went some way towards solving this problem by writing the book in sections and having those sections not bound together but loose in a box . . . The point of this device was that, apart from the first and last sections which were marked as such, the other sections arrived in the reader's hands in a random order: he could read them in any order he liked.[31]

I will turn to the specific rationale later, but what is important to note first is the ethos of the proceeding. The creation of the right aesthetic form is a "technical problem" inherent to a stubborn object (the book) that will not satisfy a particular requirement; the solution inheres in fashioning the proper contrivance. It is skilled handicraft, the overcoming of recalcitrant material through practical ingenuity. The deliberately petit-bourgeois rhetoric here is, characteristically for Johnson, at once modest and swaggering, reducing an enormous question of industrial design to the scale of a clever individual modification to a preexisting technology, as if to say: here is a book I made, really just a box with unbound contents; it is a useful thing, and, if you're so inclined, beautiful because useful. Yet the carefully delimited scope of the "technical problem" works—if, perhaps, with a touch of anxiety—to obscure a formal or aesthetic problem that Johnson confronted repeatedly.

The difference between Johnson's artisanal labor and Machado's ironic haute-bourgeois homage could be derived from any number of geographical or personal factors, but also from a historical matter that I want to suggest provokes both the substance of Johnson's "solution" and the ethos with which it is described: between Machado and Johnson lies modernism, and it is modernism, at least the anglophone modernism with which Johnson was most familiar, that posed a problem for capitulation even deeper than the specific dilemma of the subject of *The Unfortunates*. It is a problem that dogged him throughout his career and led to the fabulation of many different "devices," if none so dramatic as the unbound sections in a box. The modernist chapter is the formal problem of Johnson's career, and the unbound "section" is one of its possible solutions. It might also be said, however—to push slightly aside the purely technical emphasis of Johnson's self-description—that the solution involved rediscovering, in his own terms, what had already been Machado's procedure before modernism had even created the problem.

Both in literary-historical terms and in those of Johnson's personal mythology, that problem could be expressed by two names that stood for opposing possibilities: Joyce and Beckett. Put baldly, the high modernist novel pulled the chapter in two complementary but divergent directions: toward isolation or reification, each chapter becoming its own world (*Ulysses*), or toward elimination (*Molloy, Malone meurt, L'innommable*). The excluded middle here is the nineteenth-century chapter, with its careful equipoise between subordination to the sequencing of plot and small individual distinctions, its muted transitions, its alignment via diurnal time to rhythms of reading, its moderate and flexible length—a synthesis between the discontinuous and the flowing.[32]

Instead the modernist chapter moves to totalization or disappearance, to either multiplying distinct worlds or vanishing into the terrain of one world. Fredric Jameson has read the Joycean chapter as the "ratification" of the chapter form—that is, elevating it from its subordinate role and in the process achieving something like reification: each chapter in *Ulysses* is "a complete unit, the very sign of completeness as such, which on the one hand approaches the luminous abstraction of the Platonic idea, while on the other it begins to portend the dialectical category of totality."[33] From a dependent clause, that is, to a sentence: each chapter will have its own distinct governing rules and procedures. Naturally, perhaps, a terminological problem arises, for these new chapters are not quite "chapters" in their traditional sense as interruptive segments.[34] For those unwilling to reify the chapter in this way, one could, in the mode of Proust or Beckett, dispense with chapters entirely. Unit and whole part ways.

Few examples are quite as pure as *Ulysses* or *Molloy*, but the modernist binary exerted a torque in two directions, between autonomous units and their disappearance (figure 8.2). Both options pull away from the novelistic synthesis in which distinct units are nonetheless inserted into, and linked by, a linear progression—a "tabularity," to use Barthes's terms, that is "vectorized," subordinated to temporal sequence.[35] Split apart in this way, the older novelistic chapter was understood now as a degraded form—too automatic or "conventional," insufficiently theorized, mass-produced, even remedial. The new units, or absent units, are reverse images of the Machadian chapter: innovative (rather than self-consciously antique), elongated (even up to the length of the entire work), and absent Machado's self-commentary. Up to *The Unfortunates*, Johnson wavered between the two modernist poles, which were for him under the stars of Joyce and Beckett respectively. *Travelling People* (1963) opted first for *Ulysses*-style autonomization, its method being, in Johnson's later words, "eight separate styles or conventions for nine chapters; the first and last chapters sharing one style in order to give the book cyclical unity within the motif announced by its title and epigraph."[36] A year later, *Albert Angelo* turned to sonata form to provide external scaffolding for its five "parts," although here too the attempt is made to generate distinct styles for each unit: one chapter includes a long section in double-column format, while the chapter titled "Disintegration" is almost entirely in direct address by an implied-authorial voice that insists on its nonfictionality.

For his next novel, Johnson turned to the other extreme. *Trawl* (1966) is devoted to continuity, from its *mise en page*—a narrow text block with no

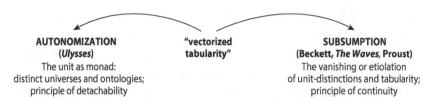

AUTONOMIZATION	"vectorized	SUBSUMPTION
(*Ulysses*)	tabularity"	(Beckett, *The Waves*, Proust)
The unit as monad:		The vanishing or etiolation
distinct universes and ontologies;		of unit-distinctions and tabularity;
principle of detachability		principle of continuity

FIGURE 8.2 Two paths for the modernist chapter.

paragraph indentations, stretching for pages without any interruption—to its narrative method, interior monologue from start to finish. Indeed, the scattered experimentation of his first two novels is entirely restrained in favor of a consistency that is new for Johnson, as if the shift away from segmentation demanded absolute procedural regularity.[37] The story of a three-week voyage on a deep-sea trawler heading to the Barents Sea to chase cod, the novel is invested in isolation, both physical and psychological; it is an experiment, on the protagonist-narrator's part, meant to summon up memories in order to achieve therapeutic catharsis, and on the author's part, to find a realist frame that might accommodate an unsegmented method. Days and nights blur on the northern sea, past and present merge, and only one external timing mechanism is allowed to fracture the even progression of time: the noise produced by the movement of the ship's towing block, working just above his cabin: "So every two hours or so, or two and a half, or sometimes longer, at the intuition of the skipper, CRAANGK! the towing block goes against my head, it seems, even inside my head, sometimes, it seems" (*T*, 8).[38]

Trawl speaks to a certain seasickness of Johnson's own career thus far, its yawing between two kinds of rhythms, the novel of autonomous segments (and heterogeneous styles) and the novel of unsegmented flow (and stylistic consistency). The presence of the towing block, though, allegorizes a self-consciousness about how either of these efforts is brought into being, and signals the beginning of an end to this stylistic oscillation. The towing block's noise is what starts *Trawl*—the first external stimulus noted, like the raising of the conductor's baton—and its dismantling by the crew will signal the end of the voyage and the end of the novel; it is a source of irritation, admiration, dependency. It makes its noise six times across irregular intervals, almost as if it has taken upon itself the function of chaptering this short novel when chapters themselves are absent. With almost too-perfect coincidence, its noises tend to appear during sleep, as a distant (and somewhat insomniac) echo of the diurnal breaks of nineteenth-century chapters. It is also, importantly, a *device*—an industrial contrivance. "It's a German invention, says Jack. You just pull this lever and your trawl comes free. It keeps the warps free of the screw aft, until you want to haul" (*T*, 148). Simple, even rudimentary—a matter of elementary hydraulics and the multiplication of human force, the pulled lever—it efficiently performs a complex act. What is introduced into Johnson's work here is the idea that a mechanical device, a designed thing, might break the impasse between modernism's two ideals of segmentation and open the path toward a method, even ideology, of narrative composition. A love of the mechanical object opens Johnson to raptures, extending to the trawler itself: "Certainly she has no conventional beauties, for me, which is to the good: she has a very narrow beam for her length, for her less than eight hundred tons, but function, function, function! The whole ship is dedication to the concept of function and that is what makes her so beautiful to me" (*T*, 137).

It is an almost pretheoretical image, this idea of the purely functional design, arising out of a world of active and practical men engaged in a robustly manual, three-dimensional pursuit. Which is to say that a certain class solidarity, however fantasmatic, frees Johnson to espouse the device as such—and through this idea of the practical device, licenses him to return in *The Unfortunates* to that abjected form, the chapter, and remake it by giving it a new kind of objecthood. In the act of transforming industrial device to literary device, however, the artisanal makes its return. The writer becomes the tinkerer, more *ingénieur* than genius, trying to make the right tool to solve a problem.[39] Johnson's device of the separate sections of *The Unfortunates* keeps the impress of handicraft, even if the novel's actual publication involved considerable industrial perplexities.[40] And like a handmade device, the resulting chapters are small—adapted to the hand—and made according to an old technological recipe: the box and the bound "signature," or the codex and the page, the tree trunk (*caudex*) and its leaves. The ideology here is oriented toward innovation ("it's a German invention") but is at the same time almost archaic in its simplicity and haptic responsiveness—modernism, but with its gaze turned backward. It is a circuitous route, that is, for Johnson to arrive at a strikingly similar solution to that of Machado.

When we return to *The Unfortunates*, then, we find a version of the Machadian chapter's formal triad, but pushed in the direction of even greater explicitness because of its enhanced status as a device (figure 8.3). A complex formal *idea*, that is, becomes a *thing*. Johnson's chapters, embodied in the shape of the twenty-seven separate signatures or leaves, are short; so conspicuous as to be the novel's central feature, even its "gist"; and, via their small-batch

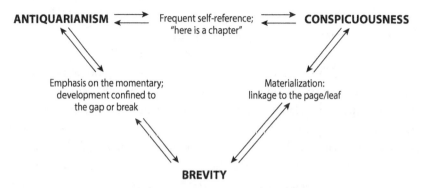

FIGURE 8.3 The antique-diminutive model.

production that exuded artisanal effort, an image of antique methods, even a certain artifactual fragility that arises when the detached page or small sheaf of pages becomes a basal unit.[41] Indeed, when the novel's Hungarian version had to be published in bound form for economic reasons, Johnson lamented in a special introduction for that edition that its readers would miss "the physical feel, disintegrative, frail, of this novel in its original format."[42] But the novel's objecthood intensifies the other two sides of this triangle. Self-reference becomes explicit procedural guidance, as in the instructions to the reader pasted inside the box. The gap between units is pushed to a limit, as each gap threatens to become an aporia: which section should come next? The Machadian chapter had a ghostly, incomplete thingness, but the artifactuality of Johnson's version pushes the triad of this chapter form into an exaggerated relation to its own design.

The thingness of these chapters, their status as mechanical contrivances, has several consequences. Here Sianne Ngai's work offers a useful paradigm: as the artistic idea becomes a thing, the literary "device" reified even into a physical one, a crisis of evaluation arises. Namely, aren't Johnson's chapters just a gimmick? Ngai has emphasized the gimmick's dual status as idea and thing, as manifested in a negative judgement that is only partially entranced, but more pervasively disquieted, by the reification and commodification implied in that relationship.[43] And as it happens, reviews of *The Unfortunates* reflected exactly this suspicion. Stephen Wall's review for the *Observer* was titled "Curious Box of Tricks"; Richard Holmes in *The Times* referred to its "paperchase device"; in a more sympathetic piece in the *Guardian*, summarizing the book's initial reception, Hugh Hebert referred to the suspicion that the book was "a bit of a literary swindle."[44] Not that this sense was limited to 1969; as late as 2004, Frank Kermode argued that Johnson's "tricks simply prompt one to ask what the point of this sort of innovation really is."[45] As Ngai has demonstrated, the reified idea, as a "trick" or gimmick, leads to a discourse of value in which the primary attitude is the feeling of having been fooled, particularly by a disproportion of labor and time. Johnson's labor-saving device could be taken to cleverly pass off the labor burden—that of finding the connection between chapters—to the reader. For us, the actual work; for Johnson, simply a pair of scissors. The class dynamic here is apparent: Johnson's artisanal manipulations are rejected for their clumsy, obvious, even lazy attempt to get one over on the consumer. Johnson, Wall commented in a headmasterish admonition, suffers by comparison with writers like Robbe-Grillet or Sarraute "who really have done their theoretical homework."[46]

Yet the unease provoked by Johnson's "box of tricks" isn't simply about the transformation of idea into thing. Its dialectical counterpart is as true here if less evident, and more consequential for a history of the novel: Johnson has also turned a thing (the chapter) into an *idea*. The infusing of a conventional, tacit container like the chapter with theoretical heft—as implied by its physical manifestation, its new status as a device or trick, the discourse necessary to explain its function—is perhaps an even more serious transgression than commodification. At one level this is yet another symptom of what might be taken for tactless lower-middle-class effrontery, a bumptious striving that speaks far too much and far too loudly about something that does not deserve the fuss. Certainly the antitheoretical bias of mid-century British letters had Johnson caught, between those who saw his experiments as cheap trickery and those like Wall who felt he was not of the stature—as his metaphor reveals, did not have the education—to have the right to experiment. Whether he was seen as too aggressively theoretical or lacking the proper credentials to theorize, the suspicion lingered that his devices were a conman's ruse to disguise what he really wanted, which was to return to an ordinary, middlebrow chaptering method while claiming the mantle of innovation: to have his cake and eat it. This latter doubt, as we will shortly see, was not far off the mark. To these critiques, however explicitly they were voiced, Johnson had ready responses. The first was a reversed accusation of bad manners and bad faith. As he writes in *Albert Angelo*, in defense of his typographical innovations: "To dismiss such critiques as gimmicks, or to refuse to take them seriously, is crassly to miss the point" (*AA*, 176). The second was strikingly similar to Machado's: to align himself with an alternative lineage, one that included, as he wrote in a 1962

THE POIGNANCY OF SEQUENCE 265

article on Beckett, "Petronius, Rabelais, Cervantes, Nashe, Burton, and Sterne," one that was pointedly not the Leavisite great tradition and that was at once more bawdy, more formally adventurous, and more international.

All of this explains what licensed Johnson's experiment in *The Unfortunates*, either in his own mind or for his sympathizers, and how those justifications produced wariness or disdain. But it does not yet articulate why he would care at all—why recovering the chapter, the humble segment, from the rupture that modernism had performed on it mattered to him, why segmentation was his besetting technical dilemma. Why this formal issue, both abstruse and all too practical? Machado had reversed the usual nineteenth-century synthesis in which the transition from one chapter to the next must keep in productive, rhythmic tension the distinctness of each unit as well as its place within a meaningful, governing temporal order; instead, in Machado's version, temporal progression is reduced to the silence of gaps, and the chapters themselves speak to an always-doomed desire to stay rooted in time. This is a tension between unit and flow, however, that the modernist chapter had evacuated by privileging one at the expense of the other. Time becomes full, either in the plenitude of the moment or in the overwhelming rush of duration. As himself a (late) modernist committed to the ideal of stylistic evolution, Johnson could not return to the nineteenth-century model, not even in the mode of reversal; that way was barred to him. Yet the usual modernist models, via either Joyce or Beckett, failed him as well, because they could not properly express the experience of *acknowledging temporal flow while vainly attempting to resist it, an attempt that is under no illusion about its efficacy.* A desire, that is, not to progress—time holds neither plenitude nor promise, only the very limited and fragile ability to occupy moments that are always rapidly fraying at their edges into a void. Here again the gap matters. It is in *The Unfortunates* the abyss into which all light is pulled.

This speaks not only to the novel's subject matter—an elegy for a friend who died young—but also to a broader historical conjecture, a faithlessness in the postwar future that read to Johnson only as the erasure of his own class. As many of the testimonies assembled in Jonathan Coe's biography attest, Johnson's working-class identification, rather than revolutionary or forward-looking, was itself essentially elegiac.[47] So his modernist experimentalism is neither joyous nor wildly ambitious, but a series of practical, device-based efforts at local problem-solving, a temporarily effective jury-rigging that promises no lasting solution, nothing that can be reused—a nontransformative version of labor as (both psychic and economic) maintenance, one that expressed a militant, if at the same time wistful, identification with proletarian piecework. It is an identification that was not entirely secure and in any case saw as yet no way forward.[48] So while *The Unfortunates* in particular wears the costume of what Umberto Eco in 1963 called the "open work," the ludic chance-based artform designed to refashion our perceptual habits and to produce a spirit of discovery aimed toward an as-yet unexplored and indefinite future, its formally radical costume disguises an aim to seal that future off instead, to keep the present intact, for as long as possible, which is not long at all.[49] It is a balked, unhappy love of the chapter that *The Unfortunates* offers, one that forces a hypertrophy of its function, amounting to exploding it, in order to save it as an image of temporary refuge.

In this sense the accusations of trickery come close to the mark. Like any good magic trick, *The Unfortunates* works by way of cunning substitution, claiming to offer one thing and in fact smuggling in quite another. What it waves before the audience is what Johnson called "randomness," in the spirit of Eco's *opera aperta*, a freedom to remake sequence. What it actually provides is an experience of gaps in which sequence, the forward drag of linear time, is only provisionally fended off. The confusion has often stemmed from Johnson's use of the word "random," a term repeated in the novel's instructions: "Apart from the first and last sections (which are marked as such) the other twenty-five sections are intended to be read in random order. If readers prefer not to accept the random order in which they receive the novel, then they may re-arrange the sections into any other random order before reading." Already "random" is under some stress: a reader's rearrangement could be, to a greater or lesser extent, a *choice* rather than a random procedure, something Johnson tactically, or tactfully, omits. In fact, for the bound Hungarian edition, he recommended cutting out of the book a prefatory list of the printer's ornaments that begin each chapter, further cutting that list into strips, and drawing these strips out of a hat—or, failing that, "bowls, saucepans, eggboxes, wastebins," or even "that old-fashioned but still-to-be-found piece known in English as a *po, jerry,* or *pisspot*"—to achieve the true randomness the bound version had thwarted (*U*, xi).[50] Stressing that procedure of choice-avoidance mattered because of what Johnson insisted was the "randomness" of the material—both the randomness of the mind's workings (the unpredictability of the ways in which he would be reminded of Tony, and which moments from Tony's life would be accessed), and the randomness of fate itself, in which Johnson included the cancer that killed his friend. Here we come close to a central instability in Johnson's usage. To be "random" can mean a result achieved without direct purpose, accidental, aleatory—the strips drawn from the hat, the sections shuffled like cards: Johnson's "formal" usage. Yet that sense fits poorly with the cognitive or physical meanings of the term adduced as correlatives to the form. It is hard to say that being reminded of Tony when revisiting the scene of many of their interactions is in this sense accidental or random; it might have been repressed or beneath conscious-ness, but the mechanisms of his memories rising to the surface are hardly unknowable. Neither is cancer in this sense random, particularly if taken as a special instance of a wider case of mortality in general—nothing more cer-tain, nothing more causal, than the "disintegration" of the body that preoc-cupied Johnson throughout his career. Randomness, however, promises that the next event, the next section pulled from the hat, the next thought, cannot be derived from the previous one: sequence cannot be taken as a causal pat-tern. As a principle of cognitive processing or bodily change this is perhaps dubious, and the odd fit of the term with the phenomena that supposedly inspired Johnson's experiment might make us wonder if "randomness" really is at stake. But purely as a formal principle it could be taken to be more achievable. This is the feat the "trick" seems to promise: to suppress sequence or linearity, and thus causality.

Critical opinion has been divided about the extent to which the novel succeeds, or could possibly succeed, at this goal.[51] But is it indeed the goal? To understand it as such means privileging the *sjuzhet* or reader's arrange-ment of the novel's units, however haphazard or careful their selection pro-cess: the novel in this conception *is* the order, any of the enormous number of possible orders, in which it is read, which implies that the novel's *fabula* or story-chronology is either irrelevant or impossible to reconstruct. Tell-ingly, on this last matter opinion differs.[52] But perhaps Johnson's own "ran-domness" rhetoric has dissuaded any attempt to determine whether the novel's *fabula* can be reconstituted, because in fact it is entirely possible to map. What is shown in tables 8.1 and 8.2 is—at least by the standards of Johnson's official line about the novel—a heresy, although perhaps also the occulted content of the form's "trick": a list, in order of *fabula* chronology, of the novel's sections, with attention to the various internal timing nota-tions that permit this order to be uncovered. The open secret is that discov-ering this order is easy.

Arranging the sections in this *fabula* order violates Johnson's design in one respect. By indicating two sections as "FIRST" and "LAST," Johnson places the action of one day—the visit to Nottingham to report on a football

TABLE 8.1 Chronology and temporal indications in *The Unfortunates*: biographical frame

Section Opening	BSJ: Partner	Tony: Institution	Tony: Illness	BSJ: Writing Project	Tony: Location	Tony/June: Child
"That was the first time"		University		Student magazine	Nottingham	
"Up there, yes, the high mast"	Wendy	University		Student magazine	Nottingham	
"His dog, or his parents' dog"	Wendy	University		Poetry	Ewell, London	
"The opera singer"	Singer	University		Novel "in mind"	Ewell, London	
"The estate"		University			Nottingham "estate"	
"Then he was doing research"		Postgrad		Poetry	Nottingham outskirts	
"Again the house"		Postgrad		Novel 1 (working)	Nottingham outskirts	June pregnant
"I had a lovely flat then"		Postgrad	Headaches/flu?	Novel 1 (finished)	Visit to London	
"Southwell"		Training college			Lincoln	
"Just as it seemed"		Liverpool University	Cancer discovered	Novel 1 (pub party)	Lincoln–Chester	Birth
"For recuperation"	Pre-Ginnie		First treatment over	Novel 2 (working)	Brighton	"Baby's cot"
"That short occasion"			"Ill at ease"	Novel 2 (working)	Hove	
"Sometime that summer"	Ginnie (new)		More surgery	Novel 2 (typescript)	Brighton–Chester	
"At least once he visited us"	Ginnie		"A little slower"		Last visit to London	
"Then they had moved"	Ginnie	Liverpool University	Tumor regrown	Novel 2 (pub party)	Chester	"Walking now"
"So he came to his parents"	Ginnie		Given six weeks		Brighton	Too big for cot
"June rang on the Saturday"	Ginnie		Death		Brighton	
"We were late for the funeral"	Ginnie		Burial		Brighton	

TABLE 8.2 Chronology and temporal indications in *The Unfortunates*: diurnal frame

Section Opening	Main Action	Clock Time Indications
"But I know this city!" ["FIRST"]	Exit from station	"A quarter past twelve"
"Cast parapet"	Walk from station along trolley wires	
"This poky lane"	Walk past Council House, buys and eats ham	
"Yates's is friendly"	To Yates's bar, sips marsala	"Ten to one"
"Here comes the main course"	Disappointing lunch at Yates's	
"Time!"	Bus to the ground	"It's after two"
"The pitch worn, the worn patches"	Football match and phoned-in report	Phones in story "by five"
"Away from the ground"	Sherries in pub	Misses 17:55 train
"Paper, yes, Chelsea result" ["LAST"]	To station, evening meal on return train ride	Starts "thirteen minutes to wait" for 19:00 train

match—as the novel's base time, the hook from which all flashbacks hang.[53] But bracketing these designations, and placing the "first" and "last" chapters of Johnson's sketchily outlined *sjuzhet* within a chronological order, reveals several things. First, that the work of arranging the sections into chronological order is not only fairly simple but amply provisioned by the novel's own procedure. It is as if the sections invite the reconstruction that their material form seems to frustrate; the stochastic workings of *sjuzhet*, in this sense, are disclosed as the necessary dialectical counterpart of the *fabula*, the "other" it exists to elicit by, and not despite, a process of obscuring it. As the narrative voice muses: "how the mind arranges itself, tries to sort things into orders, is perturbed if things are not sorted, are not in the right order, nags away" (*U*, "Southwell," 1). It is not simply internal event clues that point to this reconstruction—of which more in a moment—but the novel's constant recourse to ordinal language and its role in establishing sequences.

"Tony came up to stay with me, the first time" (*U*, "I had a lovely flat," 1)

"For the first time he looked really ill" (*U*, "Then they had moved," 3)

"the first recuperation" (*U*, "Sometime that summer," 1)

"the paperback edition of the first one had come out" (*U*, "Then they had moved," 6) "the first year I knew Tony was also the year of that love, for Wendy, which ruined love for me for years after" (*U*, "His dog," 1)

"after the first treatment" (*U*, "For recuperation," 1)

"his mind had come back and they had talked very seriously about everything, for the first time had talked about death." (*U*, "June rang on the Saturday," 1)

If Johnson's official procedure places the word "FIRST" as the novel's opening, its *fabula* begins in a similarly ordinal way, but referring now to diegetic time rather than reading sequence: "That was the first time, that must have been the first time, yes" (*U*, "That was the first time," 1). Each section is carefully attuned to *series*: their inception, the ordering of items within them, the trajectories implied by each. A "first," after all, requires a "next."[54]

Along with this notation of initiating moments is a layering of multiple timing mechanisms, not all of which are in use in every chapter, but which, like a logic puzzle, are perfectly sufficient to line up the sections chronologically, to file them in correct tabular vectorality.[55] As noted in tables 8.1 and 8.2, those include (but are not limited to) trajectories such as Johnson's romantic history; the institutional stages of Tony's academic career; the progression of Johnson's writing projects; the pregnancy, birth, and growth of Tony and his wife June's child; Tony and June's geographical movements (from gradual post-university independence to a return to his parents' home in the final stages of his illness); and the progression of Tony's cancer. All of them, in various ways, indices of a seemingly inevitable, step-by-step, steady bourgeoisification and its equally inexorable, if more sudden, undoing. These take over for any calendrical notations, which are never fuller than seasonal or a vague reference to a number of years that had passed. Meanwhile, within the base time of Johnson's trip to Nottingham, clock time and a linked sequence of actions (arrival, transportation to the ground, the match, return) are easily discernible. Insofar as the narrative voice occasionally expresses uncertainty about memory, those uncertainties turn out to be irrelevant for the ordering of the sections, even if they render details within those sections—exactly what season an event occurred, say, or who was present at it—slightly hazy. Recourse to the basic scaffolding of the novel's personal timetables, and their overlapping or coincidence, keeps the train cars in proper order: "the first year I knew Tony was also the year of that love, for Wendy" (*U*, "His dog," 1). What these sequential notations do is to communicate across sections. The opening

clauses of one such section—"Sometime that summer, during the first recuperation, there was another visit, I went down to Brighton again"—may express one kind of uncertainty ("sometime") but index a "first" recuperation
that refers back to the section "For recuperation"; "another" places it subse-
quently to the visit that other section had narrated; and "Brighton again" dou-
bly sutures the section to others sections that transpire there. It is, as a puzzle
maker might say, all there.

If I have gone on at length to demonstrate the solution to what I am also
insisting is an easy challenge, it is because the ease of the solution is precisely
the point: the task, or "trick," of the novel's disintegrative form is to both obscure *and highlight* the forward pull of temporal sequence. *Sjuzhet* saws apart
the woman in the box so that we will look for the whole person, the *fabula*, that
the box's delusive proportions hide. In this sense chronology is not the form's
impossibility, or its illicit temptation, but its very purpose—to experience it
while holding it at bay. This is the work of the "section," to throw sequence into
relief while offering a terribly fragile refuge from it. What tables 8.1 and 8.2 also
suggest is that the two modes of temporal organization he uses, one in the
novel's base time and one in its flashback moments, are the two intertwined
modalities of the nineteenth-century chapter, but detached from each other as
if into newly distinct species. In the former, a return of the chapter's relationship
to diurnal time: a shaping by biological processes (walking, eating, urinating)
and mundane daily tasks (the job of writing up the match), framed by the path
of the sun, which is here indicated by clock time. In the latter, a different chro-
nocollectivity: the interweaving and overlapping of biographical benchmarks,
such as the waxing and waning of romantic relations, career advances, reproduction, disease, changes known by and to others, all of them seen through the
small lens of the social occasion—the visit, the trip to the pub, the drive to the
local attraction, the long talk, that one time, on the sofa. Yet in each part of the
novel there is a central section in which the different aspects to these temporalities combine in heightened form to a point of acute pleasure or pain. In the
diurnal frame, the long chapter of the football match, where the physical pur-
posiveness of the game, the relentless winding down of the game's clock, and
the relation between time and labor are all condensed. In the analeptic frame,
the section "Just as it seemed," which presents the discovery of Tony's cancer,
the birth of his child, and his belated success at finding academic employment
as all coinciding: an unbearable collision of distinct timetables.

The sections are then an acute decomposition of the nineteenth-century
chapter's formal synthesis, in the effort to reconstitute it in altered form—one

that, just as with Machado, places a new burden on the chapter break. The break or gap, accentuated by its unbound physical quality, becomes both an abyss and a protective barrier, the threat of linear sequence and the very provisional abeyance into which that sequence can be stilled. The line that segments in order to protect: it is an image that fascinated Johnson, as instanced by the description of Tony's radiation treatments, defined as "a square, the top line of which crossed his upper lip, to the bottom of his ribs, taking in the arm on the side the lump was . . . if one single cell escaped to another part of the body, by insinuating itself into the bloodstream, then it would grow and multiply there too" (*U*, "Just as it seemed," 8). In affective terms this meant an extraordinary heightening, amounting to the novel's dominant note, of poignancy.[56] In "Southwell," which occurs prior to Tony's illness, Johnson, Tony, and June drive to Southwell Minster for a summer day's outing. Intimations of loss to come loom; Tony and June have moved to Lincoln, where he will receive his diagnosis. On that day, however, nothing is yet lost. But the section's final sentence produces exactly the sense of held breath before a coming catastrophe that casts the entire occasion in a different light:

> We had a drink in a pub somewhere, near a new bridge here, on the way back, it was dark by then, though summer, and in the car park there was some incident, I think someone was backing into Tony's path, and he kept going, they both kept going, and I was supposed to be the one looking out for a learner, but I could not reach the brake as it was the other side of Tony, farther from me, and all I could do was to push the horn button, to touch the horn ring, did it have one, that model, and the other man stopped in time. (*U*, "Southwell," 3)

Stopped in time: it is what the sections do, perhaps all they can do. The averted minor disaster, however, only summons up the major disaster to come as the novel's relentless *fabula* unfolds. This is the tension of the gap, and it is the very tension of the novel's poignancy. We might think of poignancy as follows: *the sensation of an end indefinitely, but only temporarily, held off*. It is where *The Unfortunates*' sections lead us; it is the forward momentum that they at once hold us back from and expose us to. It is not, of course, sustainable, any more than is a held note. In the teeth of the modernist examples he otherwise venerated, Johnson retains the old, abjected chapter, shorn of its name and reduced to a fragile, pamphlet-sized object, to express a hopeless if also radical preservationism. A melancholy purpose: to keep something going—a life, a form, a moment—just a little longer.

Varda on the Cusp

Machado and Johnson, however distinct in mood, social tonality, geography, and history, together give us a formula: one future for the novelistic chapter is turning backward, to the small, even fugitive, times of its earliest novelistic forms, and then in various ways flaunting that backwardness and that brevity. As a future within novels that kind of chapter time has a recurrent allure but is always, and from the start, a minority option. The most compelling horizon of that future may not have been novelistic at all; it may be that the chapter's entrance into cinema, its life outside of the book, is where the antique-diminutive chapter model made its most significant mark.

The model here, almost concurrent with Johnson, is the early films of Agnès Varda, particularly *Cléo de 5 à 7* (1962). Segmenting was a field of experimentation for Varda from the beginning of her career: her first feature, *La pointe courte* (1955), was constructed in two distinct sequences that she conceived of as "chapters," alternately focused on a "private" narrative, a married couple in crisis, and a "public" one, a fishing village engaged in a collective struggle for survival, even if these sections are unmarked as such. The short quasi-documentary *L'opéra-Mouffe* (1958) gives segments a more literal presence, as the film's nine sections are separated by handwritten cards bearing song titles, each announcing a topical shift.[57] *Cléo*, however, brought her segmenting imagination into yet starker visibility. The film presents ninety minutes of one afternoon's existence for its title character, divided into thirteen "chapters." The chapters are labeled as such—each begins with a superimposed title giving the chapter number and a title made up of a character's name and the exact time in which the chapter takes place (as in its first: "Chapitre I: Cléo de 17 h. 05 à 17 h. 08"). The chapters contain on average a little over five minutes of time each, with the exception—on which more later—of a final, fifteen-minute chapter. *Cléo* is perhaps the first literally chaptered film, all the more so because its chapters are not derived from preexisting literary material that is being faithfully restored or mimicked, as in the section cards in Stanley Kubrick's 1975 *Barry Lyndon*. Varda's are by contrast entirely self-generated. Nor do they, like the twelve titled "tableaux" of Jean-Luc Godard's *Vivre sa vie*, which premiered the same month as *Cléo*, avoid the term "chapter" by referencing another plastic art form. What is being adapted in *Cléo*, and assimilated to filmic possibility, is specifically the novelistic chapter.

The primary possibility offered by this remediation is its capacity to precisely align diegetic time with the time of the viewer. If the loose synchronization between reading time and diegetic time was one of the novelistic chapter's hall-marks—as in the day/chapter dyad of the nineteenth century—*Cléo* gives us a down-to-the-minute equivalence: what Cléo does in her ninety minutes we watch for ninety minutes, and each chapter will align a several-minute stretch between protagonist and viewer. More precisely, then—as indicated for us by the chapter headings—what Cléo experiences in five minutes will take five minutes of our own time. Clock time, or objective time, marks us as much as, and in the same way, it marks the story universe. To achieve this coordination, however, Varda inevitably has to produce chapters in a Machadian vein: di-minutive, highly conspicuous (thanks to their unfamiliarity in film), and self-consciously citational, insofar as the very deployment of the word *chapitre* refers to a literary tradition exterior to the world the film depicts, which is a world of urban consumerism, pop music, the visual arts, and postcolonial war—a world, that is, in which the novelistic is imposed only from the outside, by the hand of the filmmaker. In that very distance resides Varda's justification for being so interested in the chapter form: just as *Cléo*'s chapters align our temporality with the film's story world, they simultaneously mark the distance between an objective, shared time and the times its characters are capable of inhabiting. We are synchronized with Cléo's afternoon but not necessarily her consciousness. The chapters flaunt their very imperfection in articulating her sense of her own time, and as a result have a diminutive, old-fashioned, slightly ominous presence.

Varda, of course, was not motivated by Machado's chapters, if she even knew of him; in fact, her sense of the chapter came from entirely elsewhere. In inter-views she would cite Faulkner's *The Wild Palms* (1939) as one inspiration, pre-cisely for its mode of what I have earlier called modernist autonomization: Faulkner's chapters alternate between, and therefore seal off from each other, two different plots.[58] At other moments she seems to have been thinking of Brechtian title cards, referring to the interruption of segment titles as affording a similar *Verfremdungseffekt*: "The spectators could, if they wanted to, identify with Cléo, or they could simply tell themselves it was the story of a beautiful young blonde who dies and be moved by that," Varda asserted in 1965. "On the other hand I voluntarily created distance by cutting the film into chapters with the time of the day indicated."[59] Autonomous worlds, alienation effects: as inspirations these do not belong to the line of chaptering, beginning with Machado, that I have been sketching. Yet the result converges. Perhaps a film could do no other; its chapters will have to be brief if it is to have many at all, and given the prevalent cinematic ideology of continuity, its interruptions conspicuous. But as so often in the history of the chapter, intent and effect are not to be neatly connected. In the process of constructing filmic analogues to Faulknerian compartmentalization or Brechtian distancation, Varda produced recognizably Machadian units—small fragments, cutting through and around the "caprice" of an elusive and not-always-sympathetic central figure, that concentrate on the temporal cut or gap, the sign of an inability to connect subjective time to its objective, or even just collective, counterparts.

Cléo is also, like *The Unfortunates*, a formally experimental narrative centering on a cancer diagnosis, a *Bildungsroman* on its way to being cut short.[60] Cléo Victoire is a pop singer, known for a handful of singles that play on the radio, who in June 1961 is awaiting test results from a biopsy. The film tracks her from 5:00 to 6:30 p.m. on the day the results are due, starting with an appointment with a tarot reader—who seems to confirm that she has cancer—and wending through a series of brief interactions that take her through several Parisian neighborhoods, all marked by panicked impatience, as they are finally inadequate distractions from her imminent confrontation with mortality: visits to two separate cafés; shopping for a hat; a rehearsal; a visit to a friend, an artists' model, and her filmmaker boyfriend; a fortuitous encounter in a park with a stranger, a soldier on leave from Algeria named Antoine, with whom she quickly forms a bond; a bus ride with him to the hospital to receive her test results. The film's "episodes" are for the most part minor and fleeting, and Cléo tends to flee from them. What subtends them all is the looming pull of an inexorable *fabula*, just as in Johnson's novel: a merciless linearity toward death. The work of chapters within this frame, however, is a vivid contrast to Johnson's detached sections. Whereas *The Unfortunates'* segmentations violated that linearity and sought its disarrangement—if only to demonstrate how finally impossible any escape from it might be—*Cléo's* chapters interrupt filmic continuity in order to insist upon linearity. There will be no *fabula/sjuzhet* games here; plot runs in almost perfect lockstep with filmic duration, or as Varda later put it, the film takes place in a present tense with a "real" duration.[61] Varda, in fact, filmed in the order of her screenplay, refusing to mix story and plot even in her shooting schedule—ostensibly to provide assistance to Corinne Marchand, her Cléo, but also, it seems, as part of the film's rigid commitment to linear time.[62] Scenes were shot at the exact time of day indicated by the screenplay, at the same time of year: late afternoon, late June and early July. Although natural light was part of the nouvelle vague's aesthetic and a necessary cost saving, this realism of lighting conditions—to capture 6:00 p.m. sunlight on an early summer afternoon rather than simply 5:30—presents a devotion to moment-to-moment linearity so uncompromising it could function only beneath the threshold of a viewer's consciousness.[63] Story time equals plot time equals running time (with filming time mimicking this order): it is a temporal juggling feat. Such a daunting task leads, inevitably, to some minor lapses. At the end of the film's seventh chapter, labeled as occurring from 5:38 to 5:45, a clock on the corner of the Boulevard Raspail and the Rue Delambre enters the frame as Cléo approaches the Dôme café, reading 5:50. Actual run times of the chapters are close but not identical to the durations signaled in the chapter headings—off generally by less than half a minute, enough to provide a sense of slight elasticity but not to be otherwise noticeable.[64] These slight asynchronicities, however, only reinforce the strenuous effort at keeping times in alignment.

What in practice synchronizes all these times that are supposed to be running simultaneously is the *cut*. The film's first words—"Coupez, mademoiselle"—are uttered by the tarot reader Madame Irma to Cléo; and if Cléo will go on to draw from two cut decks fourteen cards for Irma to interpret, it is perhaps meant to underline that the film's fourteen units, an untitled five-minute prologue and thirteen chapters, are tied to the filmic cut.[65] Each chapter opening is tied to a cut, but not to an accompanying title card—instead, the titles are superimposed immediately following a more ordinary, often quite inconspicuous, cut. The chapters are assimilated to the cut in a way that at least partially naturalizes them, so that cinematic time can continue even as the chapter title arrives and recedes. The cut is not a pause, then, but a minor percussion or swiftly passing marker, like the bus-stop signs that articulate, while only mildly interrupting, Cléo's bus journey from the Parc Montsouris to the Salpêtrière at the film's end. On the rare occasions that Varda gives us a more marked cut, such as when in the pivotal seventh chapter Cléo draws a black curtain—which fills the screen—behind which she changes into the black dress that will signify her emancipation from object-image to disillusioned viewer of the scene around her, that cut is not aligned with a chapter break. The chapter cut is instead the regularly irregular descent of an objective time inserted into, or superimposed on, the subjective flow that is oriented around Cléo and her afternoon, split as it is between her aimless, impulsive behavior and the dread that is its motor. The "caprice" with which her hangers-on charge her—"Caprice, caprice, vous n'avez que ce mot à la bouche, mais c'est vous qui faites de moi une capricieuse," she bitterly reproaches her songwriter Bob ("Caprice, caprice, that's the only word you say, but you're the one who makes me capricious")—is not what gives the chapters their shape (*C*, 59). Nor do whatever stronger transformations occur in Cléo's consciousness. *Cléo's* chapters are not in that sense Cléo's chapters; they are temporal divisions that abstractly mark and enumerate, or "score," her anxious ninety minutes and its jumpy rhythms. Some synchronization between objective and subjective time is possible: when Cléo descends Madame Irma's staircase at the start of chapter 1, the rhythm of her footsteps matches the tempo of the clock that had been ticking during the tarot reading as well as the music playing over her descent. It is rare, and ominous. The chapter breaks tend to be more oblique, unpredictable, discreet, and asynchronous with her actions.

This is, if anything, highly traditional chaptering, by which I mean highly novelistic. Indeed, Valerie Orpen has suggested that Varda borrowed the symmetrical thirteen-chapter design, with its climactic seventh chapter, from Zola's 1876 *L'Assommoir*.[66] Numeration aside, the usual framing of Varda's chapter-opening cuts belongs securely to a broader nineteenth-century tradition. They tend to fall into two categories, neither of which excludes the other: shifts in point of view, and articulations of a scenic shift through a threshold crossing, whether a door opened or closed or a staircase mounted or descended (figure 8.4). And yet: while the names in the chapter title seem to indicate a change in the film's focal consciousness, and the doors opened at a chapter's opening seem to promise a key scenic shift, neither of these reorientations in fact is very durable. Point of view is never as consistent within a chapter as its title promises, even if Varda argued in her screenplay's preface that these names "color" the units they preface (*C*, 8).[67] And few chapters remain in a single place; the threshold crossed, as in chapter 8, which begins with Cléo's entry into the Dôme, is just as quickly recrossed. We are back in the world of the chapter as *incitation*, not shapely whole. Chapters have within them very little distinct stylistic, scenic, perspectival, or episodic consistency. Little episodes exist, such as the parodically antique-romantic visit of Cléo's perfunctory lover José, but they come and go within a chapter rather than characterizing the chapter as a whole.[68] Varda did insist that the eighth chapter was conceived as "a little documentary," and—somewhat inaccurately—that the twelfth was filmed in one shot, "like a deep breath" (*C*, 63, 89) but these are both exceptions and back-formations attempting to give her chapter form an aesthetic clarity it otherwise seems to intentionally lack.[69] The chapters are no more and no less than, in Varda's own words, "slices of time that mark contractions and distentions of time."[70]

What makes this tradition odd, or conspicuous, is how that novelistic quality cuts against filmic norms. Take David Bordwell's uncontroversial claim that

FIGURE 8.4 The two distinct, if overlapping, modes of *Cléo*'s chapter breaks. *Top*, the point-of-view shift: Cléo's duenna Angèle (Dominique Davray) sighing and rolling her eyes at the supposed theatrics of Cléo (Corinne Marchand), who, weeping, has turned away from the camera toward a mirror. *Bottom*, the threshold crossing: Angèle opens the door to admit the songwriter Bob (Michel Legrand) to Cléo's flat, the chapter title vanishing as the doorway's aperture widens. *Cléo from 5 to 7*, directed by Agnès Varda (Athos Films, 1962).

one cinematic norm, the Hollywood style, contains only two kinds of segments: the scene and the montage.[71] An analogy to the novel is clear, with
"summary" standing in for montage. *Cléo's* chapters are neither. Varda's commitment to continuous, linear time rules out montage, and as for scenes, one
of Varda's accomplishments in *Cléo* is to produce a texture that is either *all*
scene, or *no* scene at all; to use Christian Metz's terms, the film occupies an
undecidable middle ground between two kinds of narrative syntagmas, the
scene and the episodic sequence.[72] Certainly, however one conceptualizes
Cléo's scenes, their existence in relation to chapters is anything but isometric.
Chapters can contain multiple small scenes (as in chapter 3, which moves from
the lulling consumerism of a hat shop to the brusque, jarring tonalities of a cab
ride), while longer scenes, such as the leisurely, tentative, almost pastoral conversation between Cléo and Antoine, the solider on leave whom she meets in
the Parc Montsouris, are interrupted by a chapter break. That a chapter cannot
quite align with ordinary cinematic grammar may simply be part of Varda's
pervasive literariness. One could understand it with reference to the larger
category that she coined as *cinécriture*: a totalizing conception of "style," in
which every aspect of the film can be considered as intentional and interrelated, which brought every aesthetic choice under the category of "writing"—
and which, importantly enough, made an analogy between cinematic processes like framing and editing and textual stylistic choices such as "type des
mots, fréquence des adverbes, alinéas, parenthèses, chapitres continuant le
sens du récit ou le contrariant, etc." (vocabulary, the frequency of adverbs,
paragraph indentations, parentheses, chapters that continue the narrative tone
or work against it, etc.").[73] Certainly the chapter titles, which seem to speak in
a different medium than the images upon which they are layered, insist upon
an authorial voice, perhaps even an authorial plan, which within the film is
knowable only in the occult table of contents of Madame Irma's fourteen tarot
cards.[74] Yet the peculiarly uncomfortable fit these chapters have in relation to
Varda's medium is not just a backward-looking bookishness. It is a turn to the
novelistic chapter format that performs one gesture—cinematizing it, which
means making a chapter duration precisely measurable in clock time in a way
that is identical to the time of the viewer—in order to accomplish what is almost the reverse goal: finding a way, within a medium given to continuous
temporality, to imagine a stilled, or stuck, time. The chapter has to be "timed"
in order to drain it of time.

This is all very abstract, and perhaps best understood by enumerating the
ordinary ways in which *Cléo* periodizes itself, biographically, culturally, and

historically. At whatever scale one wants to use, Varda's film situates itself in the midst of a duration—a *situation*—that feels simultaneously as if it must soon, and yet will never, conclude. It is a thematic winkingly suggested by the film's title itself, a slang term for the time of day appropriate for an extramarital dalliance or discreet affair. In biographical terms it is of course mortality, the film's *donnée*, that grounds this feeling: Cléo is the maiden in the grasp of an inconceivable, all-too-common death. It is also her fame, upon which she relies implicitly while also doubting its resilience. Cléo worries that she is disrespected by her coterie, treated as childish or ignorant or lacking taste, untalented and unloved. Fashion beckons and threatens; rejecting a song Bob plays for her, she tells him it isn't contemporary enough, yet when her friend Dorothée blithely proclaims that the streets around the Gare Montparnasse should be renamed for living celebrities—Piaf, Bardot, Aznavour—Cléo responds that, for her, such recognition is already too late. There is a culture-industry hum that proceeds in the film's background, whether in the form of the snatches of song that Cléo sings, or hears on the radio, or plays on the Dôme café's jukebox, or in the advertisements for films that paper the streetscapes through which Varda's documentary gaze travels. Adjacent to it, almost its inevitable counterpart, is the Algerian War. Cléo hears news of the trial of the April 1961 putschists on a taxi radio and as part of a conversation among strangers at the Dôme; it is the violent unrest to which Antoine will return, and which buzzes in the Parisian air. In all of this there is a postwar mood of impossible but still palpable infinitude. The conjunction in which Cléo dwells, the pointless restlessness of fashion, the invisible omnipresence of futile colonial war, the cancer that is gestating "dans le ventre," or "in my belly," as she confesses to Dorothée: this all seems to stretch on to a temporal horizon, its inevitable end that is yet impossible to think through.

This is, to use a term Varda provides in the preface to her screenplay, the tempo of the film's "violon"—its melody, the stretching and suspension of time that tends toward the future but whose resolution feels infinitely, if either sweetly or unbearably, suspended. It is a kind of waiting, whether anticipatory or fearful. So Antoine comments to Cléo: "Vous avez l'air d'attendre quelque chose, pas quelqu'un" (You seem to be waiting for something, not someone) (*C*, 90). Then there is the second element of the film's syncopation, what Varda calls its "métronome," the repetitive beat that segments it (*C*, 9). The metronome is clock time, the sudden and seemingly arbitrary cut, the chapter break.[75] What the chapter break provides is a sign of measurable, in fact (as in the titles) already-measured, duration, cutting into an experience of a measureless time. Throughout Cléo's afternoon the question of how long an experience actually lasts repeatedly makes itself felt. It can be heard in her two utterances to Antoine, as she thinks of the time they have before he has to catch his train back to his unit: "Il nous reste si peu de temps," and then, less than a minute later, "On a tout le temps" (We have so little time; we have plenty of time) (C, 102–3). It can be heard just after the film's central event, her rehearsal of Bob's composition "Sans toi," whose elegiac tone leaves her almost prostrated with grief. When the lyricist Plumitif boasts that the song will transform the music business, Cléo responds bitterly: "Mais qu'est-ce que c'est qu'une chanson? Combien de temps dure-t-elle?" (But isn't it only a song? How long does it last?) (C, 59). It is a culture-industry question with an imponderable, even abyssal, range of answers. Literally: the song lasts a little over two minutes, as it happens, a small miniature episode set within the film's seventh chapter and, if pivotal to it, not even close to exhausting what that chapter depicts. Tactically: it is a move in the game of artistic contemporaneity that Bob and Plumitif have committed themselves to playing, dated almost from the minute of its release and doomed to be supplanted by another hit. Ontologically: longer, perhaps, than Cléo herself; the song is likely to outlive her, become her own elegy; yet there is also felt here the promise the song holds out, that one can dwell in it, somehow, permanently—or at least just a little longer. Compared to an experience like "Sans toi," the duration of a chapter can seem lifeless or mechanical, because its title matter-of-factly answers the question: this chapter will take three, five, eight minutes.

As Varda's comparison to the metronome suggests, that is exactly the chapter break's ostensible function: to perform a regular recurrence of abstract, even meaningless transition, perhaps even to empty transition out of any supposed agency or content. It is why the chapters are linked to clock time; it is why the titles do not even receive a title card, but are merely superimposed upon a cut; it is why they are linked to so few strong plot "beats," to the extent that Cléo possesses such things. Which returns us to the film's situational dynamic, its postwar tension between a threatening dynamism and a feeling of stasis. What Cléo narrates is a series of overlapping transitional moments that are experienced nonetheless as a feeling of being caught rather than a passage through to something new. It is a fact that suffuses the film's orientation in time and space both. As Antoine reminds Cléo shortly after introducing himself, it is June 21, the summer solstice, the longest day of the year. (To which Cléo, possessed by the spirit of Bergsonian durée, jokes mordantly: "Le plus long, c'est bien vrai," or "the longest day, that's for sure" [C, 87].) Spring is shifting to summer, the northern hemisphere has begun its slow tilt away from the sun; as in the ancient astronomical term, the solstice is an "epoch," the moment when an elliptical orbit reverses its direction. It is therefore also, as Antoine innocently remarks only to be rebuked by Cléo, the day the sun leaves Gemini to enter Cancer. This conversation occurs in the Parc Mont-souris, location of the observatory—which Cléo passes in the taxi on her way in—where the Paris meridian, which lasted until the adoption of Greenwich Mean Time, was established in 1667.[76] It is a way of noting that the film exists in what might be called time and space degree zero. Or: it occupies a cusp, a space of transition—a series of them, in different frames from the personal to the national-collective.

The cusp, in turn, becomes here a place of stasis, something that envelops rather than moves. And it is here, in the film's concluding chapters, that the empty objectivity of its timing mechanism starts to gently shift. In chapter 12, Cléo admits her fear of her probable diagnosis. "Et puis tout ça, moi . . ." Cléo sighs—a gesture to a condition ("all this"), that, as she fingers Antoine's army jacket, clearly takes in more than just her own situation. "Eh bien voilà," Antoine responds tenderly, "on est deux dans une bulle": "well, here we are, both in the same spot, the same 'bubble'" (C, 92).[77] A predicament and a fragile refuge both, this bubble, the distended moment holding them in place before some transfor-mation; and the location, therefore, of safety as much as of an almost unbearable anxiety. It is at this point past 6 p.m., but the afternoon on June 21 fades very slowly, and when they rise from their park bench, they will enter the film's lon-gest and final chapter, whose duration (fifteen minutes, or as the title to chap-ter 13 has it, "Cléo et Antoine de 18 h. 15 à 18 h. 30") is twice that of the norm Varda had established previously, almost as if she has allowed her characters to will that distention. A tremendous retardation of time, set within Cléo's very linear move-ment, is imaginatively underway. Minutes later, after their bus ride to Salpêtrière, Cléo will have her diagnosis confirmed, if with a brusque evasiveness, by her doctor: two months of radiation treatments await, and why, his manner suggests, would she have expected anything different? When Antoine says he is sorry to be leaving like this and would prefer to stay with her, Cléo responds in that new temporal spirit: "Vous y êtes" (You are) (C, 107). What is now expands into a stillness that has detached itself from what will be, as the camera holds them both in the film's long final shot, one that only concludes with—in a final descent of objective time—the chime of a nearby bell tolling half-past six.

There is a whisper of deixis to Cléo's phrase, picking up perhaps on An-toine's deictic "voilà": the pointing to the present (on, in which, concerning), as if to say "here you are, here we are," that is the traditional work of the chapter heading and that Varda replaces with her more literal clock-time indications, pointing to and dwelling in the unit of time they share. It is what Varda's medium, accentuated by those frequent clock-time references, makes so palpable: the referent to the deixis here has to be time, not space. Cléo and Antoine, that is, have together subjectivized, and given some existential density to, the very brief unit in which they are situated.[78] It is stasis still, certainly, the stasis before the forecasted but still inconceivable change to come; but a stasis that is now at least partially willed, self-aware. Where it was previously the task of the film's chapters to synchronize running time and the objective time of Cléo's afternoon, now we are given something like a synchronization of subjective durations: the final chapter elongates, and its protagonist seems to have produced that elongation herself. This is not particularly or profoundly transformational, this final alignment of *durée* as well as *temps*. In saying so I am departing somewhat from the consensus on *Cléo*, which views it as the story of a transformation of consciousness, from Cléo as the passive object of an objectifying and even self-objectifying gaze to a seizing—through the crucible of chapter 7, the film's midpoint, when she accepts the cancer diagnosis yet to come—of the right to see.[79] What robs Cléo's poignant deixis of its transformational potential is its very temporal limitation: the place and time she points to will, rapidly, end. The fifteen-minute final chapter, so much more open to *durée* than its earlier counterparts, is still in the end just as much a closed form as the five- or seven-minute chapter. But its slightly expanded parameters have allowed the moment to breathe, even to seem to stop. Call this a prying open of the possibilities of stasis, and how to live with it, rather than a radical shift; in this, Varda stays true to the limited, minor quality of the novelistic chapter's promised transitions.

In all of these examples—Machado, Johnson, and Varda—the self-conscious adaptation of an earlier model of novelistic chaptering bears a wry, detached relation to the meliorist optimism that had previously inflected the chapter's shape: that marking of stages on life's way which promised a partial cancellation of the past, a space to assess and settle, and an equally partial new beginning, often enough in fact a new dawn. Adapted to a different kind of modernity—in Johnson's and Varda's case, a postwar order of delusive security masking reckonings to come—chaptering became more of a temporary bulwark against sharper dislocations, something defensive and not wholly satisfying, minor transitions to guard against both desired and feared major ones. Perhaps there is something to the coincidence that *The Posthumous Memoirs of Brás*

Cubas, *The Unfortunates*, and *Cléo de 5 à 7*, these three instances of formal experimentation around the chapter, are elegies, written by, for, and about the
dead or dying? In a situation like this, the antique art of the chapter takes on
a certain ironic significance.

A final image from *Cléo* might express this difference. Cléo takes a taxi to
the Parc Montsouris in the film's eleventh chapter, one she shares with Dorothée for a time. It is a few minutes after 6 p.m., the afternoon sunlight softened.
Alone after Dorothée departs, the taxi proceeds down the avenue René Coty
toward the park, the camera situated in Cléo's perspective, looking out over
the driver's shoulder as the tree-lined avenue passes. An instrumental version
of "Sans toi" begins, piano alone at first, strings coming in later to swell the
theme's minor chords. The driver turns back and asks, "Et maintenant?" (And
now?). Cléo replies "Tout droit" (Straight ahead). Only seconds later, another
question and answer: "Et maintenant?" "Encore tout droit." The arrow of time
is linear and forward, inexorably, down the long straight avenue, ultimately to
the doctor and her test results, and at this point Cléo has left everyone behind:
the monitory, unsympathetic Angèle; the useless José; the cynical and perhaps
even parasitic Bob and Plumitif. Dorothée has just run up a staircase to the rue
des Artistes, her back to Cléo, the last of the film's farewells and its only fond
one. (Again the staircase: Dorothée's life, at least, has several more phases to
come.) Like the superimposed grid of chapter titles that keeps an objective
"now" in the forefront of our awareness, the driver's request—what now?—
has only one answer: forward, as there is no way to stop or go back. But in
twice interrupting what seems like a reverie of Cléo's, the driver's "maintenant"
actually seems to allow the moment to expand, gives it some weight, as a recognition of what in this now has not yet happened, and a permission to stay
there for just a moment. This is, as in Johnson, the art of the chapter as necessarily an art of poignancy. To say as much demonstrates the chapter's appeal
as well as its limited horizon, a limitation that is both its subject and its enabling
condition. Now, that is all that a chapter can do.

The Future of a Convention (1970–)

UWE JOHNSON—EGAN—KRASZNAHORKAI

ONE LAST BREAK, then, one final lurch: into the broad present day, when to speak of the chapter, as I've done, can seem like no more than a pedant's obsession.

So first, a vignette of chapter pedantry, from the concluding volume of Uwe Johnson's 1970–83 *Jahrestage* (*Anniversaries*), taken from its protagonist Gesine Cresspahl's memories of her secondary schooling in the German Democratic Republic of the early 1950s. As Gesine relates it, her German class has been taken over for the year by a student teacher, Mathias Weserich, a war veteran whose prosthetic leg and facial reconstructive surgery are somehow less notable to his students than the excruciatingly deliberate tempo of his instruction. Weserich sets his class a single text, Theodor Fontane's 1882 novella *Schach von Wuthenow*. As the book has a little over a hundred mimeographed pages, his students expect to be done with it reasonably soon. Instead, Weserich lingers over questions of historical detail and narrative craft: about the precise social geography of Fontane's Berlin; the etymology of the street names it mentions; the exact shape and use of the objects that appear in its descriptions and metaphors; who narrates the tale, how they come by their information, how they introduce the tale's characters. Three weeks of instruction, at four German classes per week, are needed for the first six pages; almost two months pass before the second chapter can be started. It takes just as long for Weserich's students to come to terms with the discomfort of this intensely decelerated attention. And then:

> Two weeks of class on the riddle: Why did Fontane give titles to his chapters here, unlike in *Under the Pear Tree* only three years earlier, or *Count*

Petöfy one year after *Schach*? What is a title. It is placed at the top (but why are paintings signed at the bottom or the side?); it indicates what is to follow. It's a courtesy to the reader, who at the end of a chapter is invited to take a breath and then know in advance where the voyage is going—to Sala Tarone, to Tempelhof, or Wuthenow. Yes, and is it supposed to whet our appetite? Such writers do exist, but we are dealing with Fontane here. A title is a milestone along the path: Wanderer, after twelve miles you will be in Jerichow. A sign at the edge of town—when a stranger reads "Gneez" it doesn't tell him very much at first, but once he's entered that city he knows where he is. A title as a warning. As an ornament, accompanying the old-time fashions of Berlin in 1806. Perhaps. The question remains: What is a title?[1]

These East German teens are rediscovering what they didn't know needed discovering at all: a capsule history of chaptering and its by-now ancient justifications. The chapter title as index, as aeration, as advertisement, as milestone, as commentary, all appear in this classroom's collective thinking. The voices of chaptering, ancient and modern, are summoned up at once, speaking over one another, placing their slightly different emphases and arguing their slightly different perspectives, as if to say, chapters exist *so that*—well, so that many things. So that it may be at once clear what is to be sought (*quaerere*) and found (*invenire*); so that the reader may thus be usefully guided; that by all meanes the reader might be holpen; to inform the Reader what Entertainment he is to expect, which if he likes not, he may travel on to the next; that chapters relieve the mind—that they assist—or impose upon the imagination; that it is only out of consideration for the reader, who is always keeping an eye out for places to pause, for caesuras and new beginnings, that I have divided into several chapters what in my own conscientious authorial opinion can really lay no claim to such segmentation. And so on. Herr Weserich's students know all this somehow, and also don't know it. It has had to be made clear.

It is, this small moment from Johnson's four-volume novel, a miniature recapitulation of the history my book has been exploring. It also illustrates the chapter's postwar odor of obsolescence. The chapter title, the chapter break, these are embarrassingly primitive technologies of narrative, like a hydraulic power that, however common, we should have dispensed with by now. If Gesine will come to believe, from a different country and a much later phase of her life, that Weserich "had taught us how to read," something or many things have been signaled as finished: the fanatically close attention to narrative imagination that Weserich demonstrated; the bourgeois realism that Fontane exemplified; and any interest at all in what now seem like antiquated literary devices.[2] There have been innumerable transitions in the collective life around Gesine by the time that year of German classes occurs, transitions that left their marks on her teacher's body, but no one, now, is encouraged to think very hard about how transitions are managed.

And yet: what's on view here is also a cunningly adaptive reuse of that obsolete device. Weserich asks his students to ponder chapter titles in a novel without traditional chapter titles, but not a novel without chapters of a kind.[3] *Jahrestage* is divided into 367 units, each titled by a date, from August 21, 1967, to August 20, 1968, aside from one undated prologue. The units literalize the nineteenth-century novel's diurnality, but in fact explode the calendrical frame: while each unit gestures to the contents of that day's edition of the *New York Times*, and narrates Gesine's daily activities in the New York of that epochal year, the units also pivot to episodes—some momentary, some quite prolonged—in the past of Gesine and her family, from the 1920s to the 1950s, a period that takes her home territory of Mecklenburg across multiple devastations. Each "day" of these chapters, in its carefully noted late-1960s present, is capable of widening to swallow weeks and months of historical memory. The academic year of Weserich's teaching, for instance, is condensed within the chapter of August 2, 1968, which begins with the *Times* noting Soviet-Czechoslovakian tensions and the excessive Manhattan heat of the previous month. These are, in one sense, not chapters; at least, not named as such. Yet they take the logic of the novelistic chapter of the previous century to an extreme. Their diurnal frame and quasi-episodic content strain against each other in a friction between different tempos that is continually readjusted, and entirely flexible, within the mechanistic given of their date-titles. Personal time and collective time are braided in multiple ways through the rubric of the calendrical date, which is both public (as attested by that day's edition of the newspaper) and private (the ordinariness of everyday activities, and the ineluctable privacy of recollections, that occur on that date). This is, to use a word to which I've often had recourse, a syncopation, not at all unfamiliar from the chapter's history, however unusual the manner of its arrangement. It is a solution—unprecedented and not meant to be reproduced—to the question of what a chapter might now be, in the wake of total war. It is also embarrassed of itself; only in the short anecdote of Herr Weserich's pedagogy is its relation to the history of literary technique even tacitly broached. As distinctive as Johnson's chapter form may be, it is also characteristic of a historical moment:

the chapter is disavowed in name, yet survives in alternate guises. Might this be how a convention endures? And might that now be the purpose of the chapter itself: to demonstrate the sheer ability to endure, to survive past all kinds of changes?

Make no mistake: in the literary novel of the second half of the twentieth century, chapters are embarrassing. We know this because they become increasingly recessive, when they have not entirely vanished. The designation "chapter" becomes a rarity within fiction, even as the term lingers as the almost inevitable label, in critical or even casual practice, for the units that themselves avoid it. Simple numeration, or even a printer's device or blank space, replaces the chapter head almost as a matter of course, not to speak of the other paratextual possibilities, such as the epigraph, that are even less likely to interrupt prose narrative. The possibilities for signaling and spacing units of prose are profoundly more varied than in the consensus chaptering pattern of nineteenth-century novelistic practice, and it might seem that virtually any conceivable arrangement of visual and textual cues can now be discovered in postwar fiction, such as the breathless text blocks of Thomas Bernhard, or—to choose a few quite different examples of postwar fiction—the neo-traditional epigraphed, numbered chapters of Alejo Carpentier's 1956 *Los pasos perdidos*; the small set of rubrics ("Cities and eyes," "Cities and names," "Cities and desire"), repeated with incantatory irregularity, inside of nine large units in Italo Calvino's 1972 *Le città invisibili*; or the exuberantly hypersegmented labeling, made up of mock-mythic chapter titles and quasi-journalistic paragraph rubrics, of Fran Ross's 1974 *Oreo*. (As Mathias Weserich asks: What is a title?) Even within a single author's career, techniques vary: W. G. Sebald, for instance, employed titled units indexed to a table of contents (*Vertigo*, 1990); Roman numerals instead of titles, but with a prefatory table of summarizing subheads (*The Rings of Saturn*, 1995); and simple asterisks as a divider, a last discreet trace of segmentation (*Austerlitz*, 2001): a stochastic series of differences, in which each text has to find its own unique compromise with the need for internal division. But what all these possibilities share—even at the margins of experimentation, from the compulsively ruptured to the monumentally continuous—is their disavowal: a refusal, not just of the name "chapter," but of the conventionality upon which novelistic chaptering tended to rely for its justification.

Refusing the chapter is actually a matter of differentiation along multiple axes. There are distinctions of media in play: a refusal of the "tabularity" common to mass-media formats, with their devotion to paratextual apparatuses such as the headline, the dek, even the chyron, as well as the electronic editions of novels where "chapters" can often be forcibly reapplied, in the metadata of their digital indices, to novels whose print editions carry no such label.[4] A novel without such conventional segments can distinguish itself as comparatively *demanding*, where what it demands is uninterrupted consumption, a continuity of texture that sets itself against the contemporary attention economy. This is, as Christian Vandendorpe has noted, not just a media distinction but also one of cultural status; "high" here is signaled by the unsegmented, sparely segmented, or idiosyncratically segmented, "low" by a consistent and culturally familiar practice of morcellation.[5] It is a dynamic familiar from recent decades of Hollywood film: as David Bordwell has argued, the accelerated cut rate of mainstream film—from eight to eleven seconds per shot prior to 1960 down to three to six seconds by the late 1990s—creates a situation in which independent or auteurist cinema distinguishes itself by prolonged shot durations; Mark Goble has argued that among these practices of resistance to the faster tempo of the cut is an aesthetic devotion to slow motion.[6] As in film, this is in prose fiction a status differentiation tied to genre and the presumed maturity of a genre's audience. Genre fiction is more likely to be chaptered in a traditional fashion—numbered, regularly sized, possibly even titled— whereas literary fiction, as a marketing category, is bound by nothing so much as its avoidance of such arrangements, unless that arrangement can be, as it is in *Jahrestage*, reinvented with reference to some other structure. The "chapter book" is, after all, for younger readers only. The hierarchy of value that prefers the unsegmented or peculiarly segmented text is also, always, a judgment of reading competency—and more bluntly, of age. Ordinary chaptering has taken on the connotation of the remedial.

Not that these social differentiations are commonly voiced, on those rare occasions when chaptering is even mentioned. Instead the explicit logic tends to stand on a surprisingly literalist foundation: that chapters are not real-world entities. In an interview following the publication of his 2012 novel *Umbrella*, Will Self offered a fairly blunt version of this line of reasoning: "The modernist aspects of it [*Umbrella*] include the refusal to accept the arbitrary divisions of chapters and line breaks. I wrote it like that because life doesn't resolve itself into chapters, nor is it punctuated by line breaks."[7] Life is not divided into chapters: this is true, but only in a banal way. And it may mean different things: we might just as well think of the pauseless temporality of late capitalism as the supposedly unbroken stream of human consciousness.[8] In any case, Self here confuses the artifactuality of the chapter—its status as a made thing, a *form*—with what he takes to be its essential falsity of segmentation in relation to our mental lives. Whatever one might think about the "arbitrariness" of form, the latter claim, at least from the perspective of cognitive science, is demonstrably untrue. Our comprehension of time is continually and inescapably punctuated and divided, not only in retrospect but in the very moments of its formation. As Vilém Flusser put it: everything stutters.[9] Whether the inescapable periodicity of how we process time is well or poorly expressed by the chapter form is a question Self does not take up, partly because he is committed to an unexamined idea of consciousness as constituted by a "continuous present," but partly because "chapters and line breaks" here are really just convenient stand-ins for a formal conventionality that has to be always refused in a game of distinction among genres and readers.

Above all, this embarrassment, or disavowal, constitutes a paradox: the chapter is obsolete, too rote now to pulse with reality; and yet so difficult to erase, still so functional, that it must be serving a purpose, perhaps even its oldest purposes still. It can be bent, tweaked, distended, sneered at, abbreviated, subjected to external systems, pressed into allegories; yet it persists, with massive continuities. Why, if the novel form itself is premised upon its almost infinite formal elasticity, do such things as chapters survive; why is that convention—or any convention at all—so tenacious? So one might ask, in a frustrated or merely curious tone. As Self's interview suggests, so novelists *do* ask. "Convention" tends to imply constraining habit or unthinking repetition, the thing we no longer need do once we realize we are doing it. But it can also reflect something closer to durability: the persistence of infrastructure, which can support many disparate uses, many different kinds of traffic. When it comes to the novel of our own time, after all—not to speak of human subjects in general—survivability is itself a value. And we might be able to detect that more open, or less frustrated, relation to the chapter's conventionality in some of the ways it has most recently been reimagined, as an enduring kind of time measurement when time seems resistant to any measure.

What if the chapter could persist in a less embarrassed mode, perhaps with reference to other media, as a part of the inescapable discontinuities of any form or format? The chapter might then no longer be just a residue of the novel's past, but precisely that aspect of its form that brings novels into contact with other ways—residual, emergent, dominant and not-quite-yet-dominant ways—we now experience any of the arts of duration. Which is to say that, seen from the angle of a media history of the present, the chapter might oddly be reimagined as the novel's most *contemporary* formal feature.

To come clean: these hesitant formulations are also ways of describing Jennifer Egan's 2010 *A Visit from the Goon Squad*, one of the more sustained attempts of recent decades to rethink the future of the chapter in a way that is neither dismissive nor half-ashamed. In one sense, these chapters are deeply traditional: the novel's first unit was initially published independently as a magazine story, and its thirteen titled and numbered units are each focalized through a different character at different moments in historical time from the early 1970s into the 2020s, as if *Goon Squad* could be considered an example of that very American form, the short-story cycle.[10] Told out of linear order and with slightly different stylistic approaches, each unit can seem polished and distinct. In crucial ways, however, the units push against any such storylike isolation. Egan herself refers to them in interviews as "chapters," and also has described the novel's genesis—as a single story that engendered sequels, thus turning units into chapters—as modeled on a differently traditional form: the record album. *Goon Squad*'s chapters are divided into A and B sections, and in length and tone Egan seems to be striving for effects of contrast and variation that are more common to the pop or rock album than a collection of related stories. The album is, in fact, her primary way of thinking through interstitial experience, or the experience of interruption. "Our perception of time is full of all these gaps," she explained in a 2010 interview. "That really interests me, and I think it informed the fragmented structure of the book."[11] The album, then, is the chapter's master referent, a vocabulary for her characters' obsessions with their unaccountably segmented lives—"I want to know what happened between A and B," one asks—by translating across media.[12]

Like the chapter break, the album produces a comfortingly familiar sensation of transition: the audible crackle of an experience in abeyance for a moment, an almost below-threshold, ambient sound signifying the pulse of time beneath, or within, experience. It is much younger than the chapter, of course, but the phenomenology—the experience of the gap—is strikingly similar. The specter of technological obsolescence, however, inflects this similarity. The LP, despite its small nostalgic boom of the early twenty-first century, is a relic of an age before music's dematerialization into bits stored in clouds and algorithmically dictated streaming services. So, perhaps, the novel as well, its bookish heft vanishing into the infinite scroll of internet content. It is for this reason that Ivan Kreilkamp has described *Goon Squad* as a novel whose very subject is the "late stage of the novel form," a meditation on its own belatedness, displaced onto the demise of the music industry that is the novel's ostensible topic.[13] If recorded music in physical form and the printed novel are both soon to be part of the material clutter of a vanished cultural system, then their twinned practices of segmentation—the song, the chapter—are visible only insofar as one catches them marching off into collective memory.

Within that elegiac structure, however, is one surprise. *Goon Squad*'s chapters take many different generic forms, but its penultimate chapter is derived from a different medium: a PowerPoint presentation, taking that obsolescence as its subject. Titled "Great Rock and Roll Pauses," it is ascribed to Alison Blake, the twelve-year-old daughter of Sasha, the protagonist of the novel's first chapter, and set in the American southwest at some point in the 2020s. It is Egan's experiment with narrative after the novel, and therefore, and centrally, narrative *after the chapter*, taking the shape of what Egan would later call "a pixelated/pointillist form" of "discrete units with no real continuity between them."[14] This later description of the technical challenge Egan set herself is, however, slightly misleading. Certainly each PowerPoint slide can seem both atomized and completely standardized, its rectangular shape offering none of the moderately flexible amplitude of the chapter; and the border of the slide—its complete vanishing with the click or swipe that, like a turn of the page, moves a viewer to the next—seems harder, less porous, than the white space between chapters. Yet despite the format's strongly bounded segments, a narrative emerges from the presentation chapter: a young girl's acute registration of twenty-four hours in the life of her family, itself an atomized unit in an ecologically precarious near future, with the psychological stresses produced by her father's work as a physician for illegal migrants and her older brother Lincoln's autism. Alison's narrative is an elegantly nested double movement, in fact, mapping one small interpersonal adjustment—her father's angry impatience with her brother's obsessiveness shifting into an apologetic reentry to parental engagement—onto a larger history of her family, whose contingent origins she traces back to some of the events the novel has already described in earlier chapters. This pointillist chapter in a non-novelistic format is in fact the segment of the novel most interested in discovering continuities, not only in what it narrates but in how it sutures together both disparate moments from the larger narrative within which it is set and disparate moments in technological history.

Just as Sterne had done, that is, Egan here writes a chapter on chapters, through a transhistorical and multimedia history of segmentation. Much like *Tristram Shandy*, it employs blank slides as self-commentary. ("I see a lot of white," her mother comments of the slides. "Where does the writing come in?" [*GS*, 253]) Its implicit and explicit numeration—slides about her mother titled "Annoying Habit #48" and "Annoying Habit #92," referring to an absent but presumably thorough index Alison compiles—gestures toward the ordinal position within which the chapter itself fits, which happens to be a twelfth chapter for a twelve-year-old. Its boxes and arrows, the typical infrastructure of the PowerPoint interface, show how experiences can be both sealed off from and linked to each other in a seriality that is, theoretically at least, infinite: if the rock album's A and B sides are an image of completion, like alpha and omega, the PowerPoint's numeration trails off much less conclusively; there can always be one more number, one more slide. Ostensibly these slides worry at the segments that make up a family, from the smaller worlds of particular relationships that compose a family's affective Venn diagram to the physical walls between bedrooms that are themselves, by nocturnal knocking patterns, used as communicative media. But they are also interested in the media history of segmentation, such as her mother's collages of found objects—and, most centrally, her brother Lincoln's chief interest, the pursuit that gives the chapter its title and its purpose: his deep interest in silences in popular music. Everywhere Alison looks, in every medium, there is a practice of pause and connection across pause. The PowerPoint slides she uses are not the negation of these practices but merely their spatialized arrangement in a format whose possibilities she exploits as self-expression.[15] What Alison is after, that is, is the same thing as her brother: how to understand the feeling of time passing, a feeling that is shaped by media.

Lincoln, as recorded by Alison, listens compulsively to rock music, but only for the pauses within it. "Hey dad, there's a partial silence at the end of 'Fly Like an Eagle,' with a sort of rushing sound in the background that I think is supposed to be the wind, or maybe time rushing past!" (*GS*, 249). On Jimi Hendrix's "Foxey Lady": "But this one isn't total silence, we can hear Jimi breathing in the background" (*GS*, 244). Or, on Garbage's 1995 "Supervixen": "This one is unique, because the pauses happen when there's *no rest in the music* . . . It sounds like there's a gap in the recording, but it's intentional!" (*GS*, 276). While her father worries that this listening habit is maladaptive behavior, her mother insists that it "connects him to the world," the connection happening, that is, in the interstices (*GS*, 277). If the pause can seem like autistic noncommunication, it is actually better understood as the subtlest and most finely modulated of communications, words for those with ears to hear them. Alison's presentation ends, in fact, in a series of four quantitative graphs charting pauses within songs over almost a half century, the last chart of which is called "The Persistence of Pauses over Time" (figure 9.1). Part of the effect of these

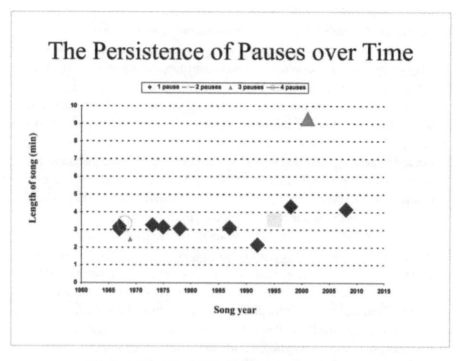

FIGURE 9.1 The final slide of Egan's PowerPoint chapter.
A Visit from the Goon Squad (New York: Anchor, 2010) page 308.

last graphs is to evoke the sound of the not said as well as the not sung; their very existence is, as Kreilkamp notes, an act of recompense from father to son, the visible outcome of the father's belated participation in his son's eccentric interest.[16] Seen from the perspective of the novel form within which they are set, however, a transmedial history of segmentation arises: the digital units of PowerPoint slides link back to the three-to-five-minute units of recorded pop music, which itself is inserted into the far more ancient segmentation practice of the chapter. It is a continuum with differences that offers Egan's own segmented narrative a future by giving these newer practices a past. The novel may be dying, may already have died without our noticing, or may limp on in some antiquated state. But the novelistic effect of the periodic, not entirely predictably spaced, elastic, and suggestive pause persists, and by persisting in different and newer media ratifies the seemingly anti-modernist chaptered form that Egan insisted on maintaining in her novel.

Goon Squad offers us technological figurations for the chapter, but these remain figurations only, bound by the book that describes them—no actual

THE FUTURE OF A CONVENTION 295

music, no actual digital file of slides. Not so in László Krasznahorkai's 2019 *Chasing Homer* (*Mindig Homérosznak*), in which the chapter achieves an almost total independence from the book itself, disappearing into a digital infrastructure, and in the process literalizing many of the chapter's historical logics. The short, elusive story of an unspecified creature in perpetual flight from some unnamed killers, making their way down the Dalmatian coast to a final refuge on the island of Mljet—the purported location of Homer's Ogygia, the home of Calypso—unspools through twenty miniature units: nineteen numbered and titled chapters and one prefatory "Abstract." Each of these units begins with a QR code that, when activated by smartphone, takes the reader to a website where a different track of percussion for each chapter, scored by the Hungarian free jazz drummer Szilveszter Miklós, waits to be played. The method brilliantly synthesizes the double face that Egan juggled with her album/slide pairing: the QR code is at once the most up-to-date aspect of the novel, pointing us out to the digital infrastructure needed to read it (the smartphone, the website), and also an antiquarian gesture, hearkening back to the chapter-opening woodcuts and scribal devices that dot the chapter's history within books. Above all, Krasznahorkai's method achieves an almost total exteriorization of the chapter: its emancipation from the book, its only remaining residue the QR code waiting to take a reader to other media. Here the chapter is not a lingering, useless convention of narrative but the very force of technological disruption itself.

By this emancipation, Krasznahorkai does not merely literalize the alien syncopation of chapter time, he *physicalizes* it. Within his text, the emphasis is on the relentless continuity of total anxiety. Sentences expand to take up entire chapters in breathless accumulations of clauses: neither the narrator nor the reader can stop. The narrative voice insists that there is no time to think anything over when survival is in question, no time to sleep, in fact no time at all, at least if time were a property of distinct periods: "you might be aware that all of this could merit serious consideration, were there enough time for consideration between two instants, but there isn't any, because there's nothing between two instants, because from one instant to the next, such a focused state of being remains uninterrupted, nonstop, ongoing, it's not even worth speaking of instants, especially not of *two* instants, moreover two *successive* instants, how ridiculous . . ."[17] Fear is propulsive and seamless, an Augustinian durationless present. But the chapter frame descends onto this absolute continuity to disrupt it, entirely from the outside—a literal "outside," exterior to the book itself. It is a clumsy haptic process: open phone camera and focus on code, put book down, click on link to website, click on play button, adjust volume. One has to manipulate it. And what emerges from this digital fumbling are Miklós's rhythmically unstable compositions: traditional drums crashing in and out of recognizable meter, sounds of tearing and metallic stress, strings tuning and detuning, all of it a foregrounding of time itself, each chapter track a distinct experience of time coagulating and then dissolving. The duration of the chapter track seems to bear no relation to the length of the chapter text; its task is to segment and disrupt, syncopate so as to completely estrange. The narrating creature in flight cannot hear it. The book cannot enclose it, and can only direct one to it. It is a purely exterior time, entirely denaturalized, now living in digital space and attached to the novel by only the thinnest of mediations, the graphic element of the QR code.

Is this a way for the chapter to survive? In one sense, Krasznahorkai's chapter time seems vastly more fragile. It depends on a series of infrastructural platforms—all the digital code behind or within the phone camera, the existence of the publisher's website, the digital tracks of music uploaded to it—that are far more brittle than the printed book. How much longer will it be possible to read *Chasing Homer* this way? Perhaps not very long at all. But neither Egan nor Krasznahorkai is exactly elegiac. They may denaturalize chapter time by tying it to other media, by making it feel thoroughly mediated and in that sense more ephemeral. But this does not mean the end of the chapter; it may instead mean a return to its origins as a kind of estrangement, the oldest forms of the chapter convention reasserting themselves. Chapter time again here seems imposed from the outside, an alien or abstract insertion into or onto the times we think we live in, no longer nestled between, say, the day and the epoch, no longer the familiar and gently percussive framework of the way we might structure our lives, our stories, our pasts in some kind of semicollective way. This shift does not rob the chapter of its role; it gives it a new prominence. Now, perhaps, spread across different media that weave in and out of the format of the book, the chapter can express the disjuncture of time itself, our inability to synchronize with any of the rhythms—biological, cultural-economic, political, planetary—we live among but cannot manipulate. A chapter is not a convention because it is unthinking. It is a convention because it is constructed. A chapter is a time we have to make; there are many ways to make it. It is given to us to do so. That is its demand, and its promise.

ACKNOWLEDGMENTS

IN WRITING this book about the measurement of time, I have never stopped measuring the time it has taken to write it; like Anne Elliot, but with an even longer duration in mind, I can say now that it has been a period, indeed. That period would never have ended without the help of so many, over so many years, who read or heard parts of this book, offered hints or correctives, pointed me to avenues I hadn't seen, and provided sustaining encouragement. Within my institutional home at Columbia University, Denise Cruz, Joe Howley, Eleanor Johnson, Sharon Marcus, Edward Mendelson, Dorothea von Mücke, and Dennis Tenen dispensed counsel and knowledge at crucial junctures. I owe a debt to conversations and correspondence with Paul Davis, Frances Ferguson, Marcie Frank, Matthew Garrett, Rae Greiner, Claire Jarvis, Ivan Kreilkamp, David Kurnick, Tara Menon, John Plotz, Leah Price, Sophie Ratcliffe, Paul Saenger, Alex Woloch, and Connie Zhu. The assistance of Olga Fostiy, Jessica Monaco, Alexandra Owens, Jonathan Reeve, and Milan Terlunen is all over these pages. A fellowship from the Heyman Center for the Humanities allowed me the necessary time to push the book to its final stages and the communal support to imagine its eventual audience. Portions of this book were presented at Ohio State, Oklahoma State, Princeton, Wesleyan, Chicago, Berkeley, Johns Hopkins, Harvard, McGill, Yale, Indiana, Stanford, Oxford, Cambridge, and the University of Pennsylvania; I thank those audiences for their questions and observations, which helped refine my work. At Princeton University Press, Hanne Winarsky helped conjure the book's possibility; Alison MacKeen kept it alive with wise guidance; and without Anne Savarese's patience, tact, and acumen it could not have been completed. The Press's anonymous readers were crucial in helping me to see both what this book did and what it did not want to do. Long ago, in another world, David Levine asked a question that puzzled me; this book is my way of answering. Amy Jakobson then helped me knit the personal to the intellectual, and convinced me that my answer, when it came, would matter. Finally, throughout the often-burdened years spent on this work, countless students in my Literature Humanities classrooms contributed more than they can have known to the thoughts collected here.

Earlier versions of my thinking have appeared in a few venues: as "Trollope's Chapters" (*Literature Compass* 7, no. 9 [September 2010]: 855–60); "The Chapter: A History" (*New Yorker*, October 29, 2014); and "Chapter Heads" (pp. 151–64 in *Book Parts*, edited by Dennis Duncan and Adam Smyth [Oxford, 2019]). My thanks to the editorial work of Lauren Goodlad, Sasha Weiss, Dennis Duncan, and Adam Smyth respectively for giving me space to work through the problems I had set myself in a study of the chapter.

For Stephen, Isobel, and Penelope: the time it took me to write this book was a chapter we lived together, and for me the happiest one yet; your joy and wit and kindness, above all your love for each other, made everything else possible. For Kathleen: you know best what retentive feelings, over many chapters, can create. If every day I write the book, in our shared life it's always Chapter Two.

NOTES

Ante Chapter

1. W. James, "World of Pure Experience," 47.

2. Winnicott, "Parent-Infant Relationship."

3. H. James, *Ambassadors*, 470.

4. A list of some of those occasions might start with the Civil War, as in James Garfield's 1880 letter: "The public debt is now so well secured, and the rate of annual interest has been so reduced by refunding, that right economy in expenditures, and the faithful application of our surplus revenues to the payment of the principal of the debt will gradually, but certainly, free the people from its burdens, and close with honor the financial chapter of the war" (Garfield, "Letter Accepting the Nomination," 784). Or Reconstruction, when Woodrow Wilson spoke at Arlington National Cemetery in 1914 on a new memorial sponsored by the Daughters of the Confederacy: "My privilege is this, ladies and gentlemen: To declare this chapter in the history of the United States closed and ended, and I bid you turn with me with your faces to the future, quickened by the memories of the past, but with nothing to do with the contests of the past, knowing, as we have shed our blood upon opposite sides, we now face and admire one another" (Wilson, "Closing a Chapter," 78). Or the New Deal, in Franklin Roosevelt's 1936 State of the Union address: "In March, 1933, I appealed to the Congress of the United States and to the people of the United States in a new effort to restore power to those to whom it rightfully belonged. The response to that appeal resulted in the writing of a new chapter in the history of popular government" (quoted in Hiltzik, *New Deal*, 343). And the Nixon pardon, in Gerald Ford's September 1974 address: "My conscience tells me clearly and certainly that I cannot prolong the bad dreams that continue to reopen a chapter that is closed" (quoted in Crain, *Ford Presidency*, 62). Or the evacuation of the Saigon embassy, in Ford's April 1975 statement: "This action closes a chapter in the American experience" (*Public Papers of the Presidents*, 605). The fall of the Berlin Wall, in George H. W. Bush's 1989 Thanksgiving address: "This is not the end of the book of history, but it's a joyful end to one of history's saddest chapters" (quoted in Schlesinger, *White House Ghosts*, 376). The reopening of relations with Cuba, in Barack Obama's weekly address on February 20, 2016: "When Michelle and I go to Havana next month, it will be the first visit of a U.S. president to Cuba in nearly 90 years. And it builds on the decision I made more than a year ago to begin a new chapter in our relationship with the people of Cuba" (Obama, "Weekly Address").

5. The former is from Obama's 2009 address to the United Nations, as quoted in Sheila Croucher's *Globalization and Belonging* (p. 198). The latter is from Donald Trump's 2017 State of the Union address ("Remarks by President Trump").

6. I have been influenced here and elsewhere by Lisa Baraitser's account in *Enduring Time* of the dulled breath-holding of contemporary duration, of living in a caesura that seems to be endless.

7. De Quincey, *Autobiographical Sketches*, 27.

8. Flusser, "End of History," 147.

9. Gissing, *New Grub Street*, 81.

10. E. Taylor, *View of the Harbour*, 61.

Chapter 1

1. "There are countless forms of narrative in the world": Barthes, "Structural Analysis of Narrative," 79.

2. These characteristics—the two-column format, the lack of a capitula list, the presence of chapter numbers dividing the text according to the new system of division associated with Parisian universities, which would become the universally accepted system—mark this Bible from Bologna as part of the varied but nonetheless broadly consistent category of the "Paris Bible." These were texts largely meant for consultation, more portable than ceremonial, oriented toward "textual clarity and easily locatable textual divisions." See Poleg, *Approaching the Bible*, 108–9. Chapter division—how and where the text was divided—was therefore essential to the definition of the Paris Bible tradition; see Light, "Bible and the Individual," 233–34.

3. Genette, *Paratexts*, 300–308.

4. See Rodolphe Gasché's account of Kantian "form" in *The Idea of Form*, pp. 184–85.

5. So Frances Ferguson, writing on what might be "form" within prose fiction, refuses to grant that the chapter can be a form; she treats it as "less the novel's defining formal feature than as a divisional marker. Even though the chapter becomes a widely used novelistic unit, it is closer, in my view, to the comma and the period and other formal markers of the units of thought than it is to a formal feature that can detach itself from such markers of thought" (Ferguson, "Jane Austen," 159).

6. Kramnick and Nersessian, "Form and Explanation."

7. Gasché, *Idea of Form*, 179.

8. Two examples are preeminent: Georges Mathieu's *Changer de chapitre dans "Les misérables,"* which offers a lengthy theoretical introduction attempting a wide canvass of the chapter's fictional terrain, and Ugo Dionne's even more synthetic *La voie aux chapitres*. Some other examples: Philip Stevick's *The Chapter in Fiction*, which, while concentrating on English fiction, understands the chapter as a "cadence" and suggests that some roots for fictional practice exist in Homer, the Bible, and rhetorical theory; Marshall Brown's "Plan vs Plot," which argues, apropos of English fiction, that the "plan" of chapter divisions can indicate a network of symmetries that sits alongside and possibly undermines the developmental logic of plot. Also: Huber, "Kapitel"; Dürrenmatt, "Problème de division"; Fink, "Evolution of Order"; Haber, "Chapter-Tags"; Schultze, "Chapter in *Anna Karenina*"; Sultana, "Chapter- and Volume-Division." For a study of

chaptering in scientific treatises from antiquity to the eighteenth century, see *Pieces and Parts in Scientific Texts*, edited by Florence Bretelle-Establet and Stéphane Schmitt.

9. Da, "Lao She," 286. Mathieu uses the term "adequation" for this function of the chapter; see *Changer de chapitre*, 45.

10. Brontë, *Jane Eyre*, 111.

11. H. James, *Complete Notebooks*, 122, 162, 503.

12. See Lennard, "Mark, Space, Axis, Function."

13. A comparison raised, but rejected, by Jan Mieszkowski, in relation to the sentence (*Crises of the Sentence*, 134).

14. For the history of the summary–scene dynamic in fiction, which overlaps unpredictably with the chapter, see Brian Gingrich's *Pace of Fiction*.

15. L. Sterne, *Tristram Shandy*, 84.

16. Newtson and Engquist, "Perceptual Organization," 439.

17. See, e.g., Bower, Black, and Turner, "Scripts in Memory"; Lehnert, "Plot Units"; Zacks et al., "Event Perception."

18. This is not to deny that some of the more particular results of EST are potentially suggestive for a history of the chapter. Some important findings include the contention that spatial and temporal indicators in a text are often identified as event boundaries, which will be relevant for chaptering techniques as early as the thirteenth century. See Speer and Zacks, "Temporal Changes"; Zacks, Speer, and Reynolds, "Segmentation in Reading"; Ezzyat and Davachi, "What Constitutes an Episode."

19. The sense in which I use the term "virtual" here is that of Michael Clune: "The virtual work of art is a kind of thinking, a kind of tinkering, a kind of engineering. Its autonomy is that of thought moving in the space between reality and desire" (*Writing against Time*, 140).

20. Proust, "'Style' de Flaubert," 84. Proust wrote here in response to Albert Thibaudet's critique of Flaubert's style from a few months earlier in "Réflexions sur la littérature."

21. Not, that is, what seems to be suggested by Proust's description, a "slug," or blank line of print. For an analysis of the functional difference between slug and chapter break, and a brief history of the former, see Samuel Delany's 1978 critical study *The American Shore*, pp. 59–61.

22. On the subject of navigation devices like the chapter, Johanna Drucker writes: "The familiarity of conventions causes them to become invisible, and obscures their origin within activity.... Recovering the dynamic principles that gave rise to these formats reminds us that graphical elements are not arbitrary or decorative, but serve as functional cognitive guides" (Drucker, *SpecLab*, 172). As inarguable as this is—and as important to keep in mind—the insight must be paired with its opposite: the strange efficacy of the convention's invisibility.

23. Genette, *Paratexts*, 13.

24. Dionne, *Voie aux chapitres*, 11.

25. Here I am using Sandra Macpherson's deliberately minimalist definition of form as "nothing more—and nothing less—than the shape matter (whether a poem or a tree) takes" ("Little Formalism," 390).

26. Kundera, *Art of the Novel*, 89–90.

27. Fielding, *Amelia*, 91.

28. Haywood, *Miss Betsy Thoughtless*, 13, 48, 66, 126, 158, 221.

29. Genette, *Narrative Discourse*, 257; Fludernik, "Metanarrative and Metafictional Commentary," 24.

30. On "figure" and "ground," see William Hanks's "Indexical Ground of Deictic Reference." On temporal and spatial blurring, see Stephen Levinson's *Pragmatics*, p. 85.

31. Grimmelshausen, *Adventurous Simplicissimus*, 18; Kafka, *Trial*, 35.

32. See, e.g., Yem, "Inordinate Number of Words."

33. Gaskell, *North and South*, 317.

34. Levin, *Power of Blackness*, 28.

35. I borrow the orthopedic metaphor from Warren Chappell and Robert Bringhurst: "The codex does for the text what the alphabet does for the language. It *articulates* it—just the way the joints articulate the hand" (*Short History*, 39). The escalator metaphor is from Tom McCarthy: "You think of an escalator as one object, a looped, moving bracelet, but in fact it's made of loads of individual, separate steps woven together into one smooth system. Articulated" (*Remainder*, 16).

36. Here of course the Chinese novel is an illustrative exception, where a base-ten tradition of chapter totals (100 or 120) and internal plot symmetries expressed within those totals (such as 20-80-20) is generically normative; perhaps the paradigmatical example is the 100-chapter *Honglou meng* (*Story of the Stone*). The absence of such a tradition in Western prose fiction suggests a different origin story for the Western fictional chapter. See Plaks, "Shui-hu Chuan"; also Plaks, "Leaving the Garden."

37. "I feel it is destined to have 12 chapters and nothing more or less will satisfy me," Lowry wrote in a letter, explaining the number's several, syncretic resonances; yet some embarrassment about this unusual numerology lingers, as he also comments that "all this is not important at all to an understanding of the book; I just mention it in passing to hint that, as Henry James says, 'There are depths'" (Lowry, *Selected Letters*, 65–66).

38. See Oberrheinische Revolutionär, *Buchli der hundert Capiteln*.

39. Pound, *Pound/Joyce*, 157.

40. As Johanna Drucker has pointed out, digitization projects in XML format, which is structured as a series of nested hierarchies, faced a dilemma with chaptered codices: "Did one chunk a text into chapters or into pages? One could not do both, since one chapter might end and another begin on the same page, in which case the two systems would conflict with each other" (Drucker, *SpecLab*, 13). The nonisomorphic operation of the chapter cannot be entirely captured by hierarchical systems, particularly the way chapters interrupt other articulations of the text.

41. Ricoeur, *Time and Narrative*, 84.

42. These are all vocabularies arising from placing rhythm at the center of analysis. Take Hegel's discussion, in the second volume of his lectures on aesthetics, of musical time, in which "interruption" is the means by which the self becomes present to itself amid "indeterminate continuity and unpunctuated duration" (*Aesthetics*, 913–14). Or Barthes: "There is no rhythm as such: all rhythm is *cultural*. . . . [T]he function of all rhythm is either to excite or to calm the body . . . to assimilate the body to a nature, to reconcile it, to put an end to its separation, to *unsever* it" (*Preparation of the Novel*, 25).

43. Freeman, *Time Binds*, 3–4; Muñoz, *Cruising Utopia*, 22–32.

44. As Dennis Tenen reminds us, "written language and music notation are digital systems par excellence, having the property of reducing the undifferentiated analog input (human thought) into discrete semantic units (text or musical notation)" (*Plain Text*, 186).

45. Two notable exceptions: first, Leah Price, who has explored how Victorian accounts of interrupted reading often occasion sex—or violence—in *How to Do Things with Books in Victorian Britain*. Second, John Plotz, whose account of "semi-detachment" bears closely on how the Victorian "episode" and its periodic conclusions occasions a partly immersed, partly detached readerly participation (Plotz, *Semi-Detached*). By way of contrast, the most careful and exhaustive list of the mental activities involved in reading—recently compiled by Joshua Landy in *How to Do Things with Fictions* (p. 155)—omits temporary suspension (putting the book down) and resumption (picking it back up again).

46. A point made clearly by Natalie Phillips, who describes the chapter as "the basal unit" of attention in eighteenth-century fiction, its breaks permitting "an apportionment of focus" (*Distraction*, 91).

47. Nancy, *Listening*, 9–16.

48. L. Sterne, *Tristram Shandy*, 225.

49. Mann, *Doctor Faustus*, 120.

50. Such language is still employed by writers and book designers. Take the comments by the children's author Ellen Raskin upon her acceptance of the 1979 Newbery Award: "I plan for margins wide enough for the hands to hold, typographic variations for the eyes to rest, decorative breaks for the mind to breathe" ("Newbery Award Acceptance Material," 387).

51. See Drucker, "Reading Interface," 217.

52. I borrow the term "internal bracketing" from Erving Goffman, who explains it as temporary pauses or "time-outs" permitted by a given activity that has a different set of "external" brackets. Goffman's primary examples are sports—tennis, he comments, has "more time-out than time-in"—although his example of an activity that lacks internal bracketing is worth quoting in full: "Sexual interaction is practically all time-in, nature herself being accorded the sole right to establish rest periods between acts" (*Frame Analysis*, 260).

53. This is explicitly argued by Giorgio Agamben in his *Idea of Prose*, pp. 39–41. For more on the borderless, unarticulated quality of prose, see Jeffrey Kittay and Wlad Godzich's *Emergence of Prose*, p. 171.

54. The comparison is Bachelard's:

> Indeed, beating time does not work like duration but like a signal. It brings coincidences close together; it brings together the different rhythms in instants that are always notable ones. Moreover, conductors' actions are far more effective than would be the action of a well-regulated mechanism. They are truly masters of movement and pace rather than the dispensers of pure duration. They manage not just duration but breathing, and it is here that the values of intensity take precedence over those of duration. Conductors must often let the sound die away of itself rather than stifle it. They measure the outpouring of sound in terms of the physical control that first produces it. They also overlay one register on another and control rhythmic correlation. (*Dialectic of Duration*, 116–17)

55. Whether Homeric book divisions are Alexandrian in origin and whether they were inspired by the average storage capacity of a single scroll remain contentious questions. Frederick

Kenyon argued decades ago that Alexandrian scrolls were too large for one Homeric book, and that therefore the origin of the divisions may be older—or for another purpose, that of comfortable recitation length (Kenyon, "Book Divisions," 68–69; *Books and Readers*, 17). For a nonmaterial explanation of the Homeric divisions, see Bruce Heiden's "The Placement of 'Book Divisions' in the Iliad."

56. The *tuppu*-chapter comparison "readily suggests itself": Hallo, "Viewpoints in Cuneiform Literature." See also Wiseman, "Books," 33.

57. Mak, *How the Page Matters*, 12.

58. I borrow the terms from Jerome McGann in *The Textual Condition*.

59. Goffman, *Frame Analysis*, 251–52.

60. On tabularity and textual linearity: Vandendorpe, *From Papyrus to Hypertext*. On the "discontinuous" and the "flowing": Barthes, *Preparation of the Novel*, 18.

61. Dionne charts this process—the replacement of an indexical motive to chapters by a "literary" one—by the gradual shortening of chapter titles. True as this is, one point of interest would be the cases where chapter titles remain long, as part of an (ironic, affectionate) homage to this earlier function. See *Voie aux chapitres*, 382.

62. Stallybrass, "Books and Scrolls," 44.

63. Evidently we prefer greater exactness to greater durability. James O'Donnell notes as much when he claims that citation by page number is "bound to disappear" (*Avatars of the Word*, 59).

64. J. Sterne, *MP3*, 15.

65. See Wai Chee Dimock on a key irony of a temporally elongated literary history: it is a recognition of sequence that in many ways—by discovering persistence, anachronistic recurrences, and long periods of stasis—will violate strict sequentiality (Dimock, "Nonbiological Clock").

66. Several scholars have recently questioned the temporal concepts organizing literary history—as Eric Hayot puts it, "a strong unstated theory of the era" has supported "the intimacies of literary criticism"—and have suggested other possibilities: Wai Chee Dimock has mooted "deep time," while Katie Trumpener has offered the "chronotope, the annal, the paradigm shift, the episteme" as more promising possibilities than the "period." See Hayot, "Against Periodization," 742; Dimock, *Through Other Continents*; Trumpener, "In the Grid," 354.

67. Columella, *On Agriculture*, 171. As Pierre Petitmengin argues in his survey of chapter lists in antiquity, Columella is perhaps unique in having composed his own list ("*Capitula* païens et chrétiens," 497). On the placement of that list in the manuscript tradition of *De re rustica*—after book 11—and its operation within "the most consultable classical text to have come down to us," see John Henderson's "Columella's Living Hedge," pp. 111–12).

68. Gellius, *Attic Nights*, 1:xxxvi–xxxvii.

69. Cassiodorus, *Institutions*, 115, 124.

70. Translation by Philipp Rosemann in *The Story of a Great Medieval Book*, p. 25. Latin terms from the original text (Lombard, *Sententiae*, 4).

71. *Geneva Bible*, v.

72. Fielding, *Joseph Andrews*, 90.

73. *History of Charlotte Summers*, 68.

74. Fielding, *Joseph Andrews*, 90.

75. Genette, for instance, ascribes to the medieval period the characteristic "noun clause" style of chapter heading, which had been employed since late antiquity. Guglielmo Cavallo argues that the "systematic use of auxiliary devices to facilitate reading and consultation developed starting in the 13th century, particularly in the West, e.g. division of the work into chapters and paragraphs, the use of titles—often penned in red—for the individual chapters, the distinction between major and minor initials, systems for linking comments to the main text, and indices." The stress here is on "systematic": it is characteristic to feel that if chapters themselves are not new, something about their *quality* must be new. See Genette, *Paratexts*, 300; Cavallo, "On Rolls," 18.

76. See Macpherson, "Little Formalism," 387.

77. I owe a debt to Jonathan Kramnick's thinking on the subject of cognitive literary theory, particularly his insistence on disambiguating "design" and "function," often confused in the application of cognitive theory to literary form. See Kramnick, "Against Literary Darwinism," 329.

78. Berger, *G.*, 137.

79. Pym, *Excellent Women*, 75. Subsequent references will be given parenthetically in the text, using the abbreviation *EW*.

80. Without taking a stance on paraphrase as a literary-critical tool in general, a study of the chapter like this one finds itself in an ambivalent position in regard to paraphrase: it is necessary, but usually in order to reveal its very insufficiency. What "happens" in a chapter, particularly but not exclusively in a novelistic chapter, is an incomplete account of its operations, for the simple—but highly consequential—reason that chapters are not wholes, but rather segments, segments that often (as in this example from Pym) thematize their incompletion or partiality. They do not, to put it differently, fully tell their own story. My thinking about paraphrase owes a debt to Patrick Fessenbecker's "In Defense of Paraphrase."

81. "Mood" is, in contemporary theories of affect, a word both inescapable and persistently opaque. My use of "mood" here borrows from two strains of thinking visible in the complex deployment of this word among affect theorists. The first strain positions mood as a mediating force between the poles of the emotion/affect dichotomy; neither wholly a collective flow nor a purely embodied, perspectival stance, mood is, to use terms from Branka Arsic's reading of Emerson's moods, "relational" or "medial," a bridge between the two, or a muddying of that clean distinction. Arsic's reading of "mood" comes close, to my mind, to the Heideggerian notion of *Stimmung* or "attunement," as in the work of Jonathan Flatley, who has most recently tried to connect mood to the projects of affect theory. The tricky negotiation between inside and outside is an important part of the framing of Pym's chapter. The second strain is a sense that "mood" is a state that foregrounds its own temporality: it is always somehow *about* the conditions of its fragile persistence. So "moody" can mean fickle, changeable, emotionally labile; yet many affect theorists describe "mood" as a particularly durable state. Teresa Brennan defines moods as "longer-lasting affective constellations"; Rita Felski and Susan Fraiman describe how "instead of flowing, a mood lingers, tarries, settles in, accumulates, sticks around." The point for me is not whether mood is fleeting or durable, but that it seems bound to a sense of its own duration, which it inevitably brings into question—much, as in my reading of Pym here, as the chapter does. A mood, put another way, is always about its uncertain length. See Arsic, *On Leaving*, 135–38; Flatley, *Affective Mapping*, 19–24; Brennan, *Transmission of Affect*, 6; Felski and Fraiman, "Introduction," v.

82. I use here the term adopted by Seymour Chatman—from Roland Barthes's term "noyaux," or "cardinal functions"—for "narrative moments that give rise to cruxes in the direction taken by events," as opposed to "satellites" (Barthes's "catalystes"), which "entail no choice, but are solely the workings-out of the choices made at the kernels." See Chatman, *Story and Discourse*, 53–54; Barthes, "Structural Analysis of Narrative," 93–94.

83. Pym, *Jane and Prudence*, 126; *Less than Angels*, 64–65.

84. See Nancy, *Listening*, 17. Of further use to me has been Vincent Barletta's account of rhythm as a "stoppage of flow," a form-giving halt to the vortex of time that is how we know time in *Rhythm*, pp. 1–20.

85. I am borrowing these terms from Johanna Drucker (*SpecLab*, 50).

86. Forster, *Aspects of the Novel*, 29.

87. Two similar articulations: Carla Hesse's argument that books have a "mode of temporality"; Mark McGurl's that a physical book is "a box of time." See Hesse, "Books in Time," 27; McGurl, *Everything and Less*, 20.

Chapter 2

1. See Mattingly, "Lex Repetundarum." For a broader discussion of the fragments' legal context as well as the epigraphical complexities of their reconstruction, see Andrew Lintott's *Judicial Reform and Land Reform in the Roman Republic*.

2. I discuss the tablet briefly in the context of the history of the chapter heading paratext in "Chapter Heads."

3. See the conjectural figures and details in Harold Mattingly's "The Two Republican Laws of the *Tabula Bembina*." M. H. Crawford asserts that no known later legal tablets used its wide format, in all likelihood because it would have been less easily legible (*Roman Statutes*, 1:24).

4. See Butler, "Cicero's *Capita*," 83.

5. Crawford, *Roman Statutes*, 1:24.

6. Mattingly, "Two Republican Laws," 139.

7. Transcriptions and translations from Crawford (*Roman Statutes*, 1:67–73, 87–93).

8. On the traditional syntax of the heading, which he terms "elliptical rhematic titles," see Georges Mathieu's "Esquisse d'une poétique de la table des matières," p. 473.

9. Crawford surmises that numbering may have occurred first in book form rather than inscribed tablets (*Roman Statutes*, 1:25).

10. The headings, respectively, of 2.24, 1.23, 9.4, and 10.4 (Gellius, *Attic Nights*, 1:104–5, 202–3; 2:160–61, 228–29).

11. Joseph Howley has recently explored this aspect of Gellius's headings, describing the different ways any given heading in the *Attic Nights* "flirts intentionally with the problem of its own usability, demonstrating a wide variation in reliability and reflexivity that should keep a reader on his toes" (*Aulus Gellius*, 52). Howley's argument turns on the Gellian virtue of *inlecebra* (seduction, enticement), for which the headings act as training or simulation.

12. I take the term "topography" here from Matthijs Wibier's "Topography of the Law Book."

13. As, for instance, in 2.15 of the *Attic Nights*: "Thus in chapter seven [kapite VII] of the Julian law priority in assuming the emblems of power is given . . ." (1.162–63).

14. See Petitmengin, "*Capitula* païens et chrétiens," 500–505.

15. This is the argument of Leofranc Holford-Strevens in relation to Gellius's headings (*Aulus Gellius*, 29).

16. Gellius, *Attic Nights*, 1:xxxvi–xxxvii. Largus declares in his preface (*Compositiones*, 5) that he has laid out and numbered his text "quo facilius quod quaeretur inveniatur" (so that what is sought should more easily be found). The Largus-Gellius echo is noted by Andrew Riggsby in "Guides to the Wor(l)d," pp. 90–92.

17. Howley argues for some characteristically Gellian slyness here: what a reader seeks, so Gellius implies, may not be what that reader actually finds (*Aulus Gellius*, 55).

18. Isidore of Seville, *Etymologies*, 52. Robert Weber preferred the Greek terms "kephalaia" or—better yet—*komma* as referents for the marginal "K," given how often the units marked by the letter were small, although as we will see the size of a "chapter," whether caput or kephalaion, could vary enormously; see Weber, "Lettre greque K."

19. Such, at least, is Butler's surmise; see "Cicero's *Capita*," 92–97. Parkes offers the standard view, that the fragment's use of the "K" mark indicates a text "prepared by a teacher, or student, as a practice text by way of introduction to forensic oratory." See Parkes, *Pause and Effect*, 12.

20. Pompeius, "Commentum *Artis* Donati," 133. Translation mine.

21. This is the argument made by Marguerite Harl in her study of the chaptering of Origen's *Peri archon*; Harl insists that the chapter headings of antiquity do not gesture toward the "plan" of a work so much as help with facilitating the reading, and remembrance, of an otherwise unarticulated text. See "*Περί ἀρχῶν* d'Origène."

22. Book 11, 2.27–28 of Quintilian's *Institutio oratoria* (227–29).

23. Gregory of Nyssa, *De hominis opificio*, 127–28.

24. Howley, *Aulus Gellius*, 59–60.

25. Pliny the Elder, *Natural History*, 20–21.

26. A. Doody, *Pliny's Encyclopedia*. A sensible defense of the use of "table of contents" is that of Joseph Howley, who defines it as a "list whose defining feature is that it reflects the sequence of the text itself" ("Tables of Contents," 68).

27. Aude Doody suggests some possible explanations of this irony: as a joke at his own expense; as a way to indicate the novelty of his list; and as a joke with a certain twist, indicating that sequential reading is still the procedure Pliny expects his readers to follow (*Pliny's Encyclopedia*, 95–96).

28. See Blair, *Too Much to Know*, 18.

29. Riggsby, "Guides to the Wor(l)d," 94.

30. See Aude Doody's *Pliny's Encyclopedia* (101–9) for an extensive survey of these choices. For more on early printed editions, see Doody's "Finding Facts in Pliny's Encyclopedia" and Martin Davies's "Making Sense of Pliny in the Quattrocento."

31. Isidore of Seville, *Etymologies*, 142.

32. Gesner, *Scriptores rei rusticae*, xxiv.

33. Riggsby writes of the "ferocious acts of compression" of the early lists ("Guides to the Wor(l)d," 101).

34. Georges Mathieu has described the difference between the "table" and the "sommaire" as the difference between a flattened, tabular anaphora (the heading as facilitating rapid access, or *quaerere*) and a panoramic vision of the text that suggests thickness or depth (the heading as inciting interest, performing its analytic condensation, or *invenire*). Of course the

heading often, as in Gellius, exhibited both qualities at once. See Mathieu, "Esquisse d'une poétique," 450.

35. See Cicero, *De inventione*, 298–99 (2.45).

36. See Cicero, 186–87, 342–43, respectively (2.7 and 2.58).

37. See Butler's "Cicero's *Capita*" (81–86), where the argument is developed in detail.

38. Tantalizingly, the same ambiguity attends a very early use of the Greek term "kephalaia": the *Belopoiika* (On artillery) of Philo of Byzantium, one of the few extant parts of his third-century BCE compilation *Mechanike syntaxis* (Compendium of mechanics). Here too "kephalaia" seems capable of referring both to general "main topics" and, as a more specific referent, to the text's divisions. See Philo of Byzantium, *Belopoiika*, 21, 25.

39. See Schröder's *Titel und Text*, pp. 323–26, for a full discussion of the lexical history related to chapter headings. For further discussion, see also: Petitmengin ("*Capitula* païens et chrétiens," 492–95) and Jean Vezin's "La division en paragraphes dans les manuscrits de la basse antiquité et du haut moyen age," pp. 41–51.

40. See Frontinus, *Strategemata*, 2, 30, 70, 91.

41. See the analysis of the extant table by Jeremiah Coogan in "Transforming Textuality."

42. From M. Edwards, *Neoplatonic Saints*, 53.

43. For surmises on Porphyry's description, see Paul Henry's *Les états du texte de Plotin*, p. 15, and Anthony Grafton and Megan Williams's *Christianity and the Transformation of the Book*, p. 227.

44. Priscian, *Institutiones grammaticae*, 3; Cassiodorus, *Institutions*, 117. And yet later, writing on the Solomonic books, Cassiodorus uses "capitula" to refer to the same feature. The semantic confusion here is explored by Francis Witty in "Book Terms in the Vivarium Translations."

45. Jerome, *Commentariorum in Isaiah prophetam*, 570.

46. My reading here is indebted to the picture offered by Megan Williams in *The Monk and the Book: Jerome and the Making of Christian Scholarship* (Chicago: University of Chicago Press, 2006), pp. 112–13.

47. Jerome, *Commentariorum in Isaiah prophetam*, 21–22.

48. See Paolo Evaristo Arns, who suggests "beginning" as a translation for "capitulum" in *La technique du livre d'après Saint Jérôme*, pp. 113–14. Henri-Irénée Marrou, in a similar spirit, reads ancient chapter divisions as notes rather than divisions per se, calling them "un relevé de *notabilia varia*"; see "Division en chapitres," 247.

49. *Confessions* 8.12. Original text: Augustine, *Confessions*, ed. O'Donnell, 101. Translation: Augustine, *Confessions*, trans. Chadwick, 153.

50. Codex it no doubt was, given the sacralized *sortes Virgilianae* he enacts here; see Stock, *Augustine the Reader*, 345. That *codicem* could also mean "scripture" is simply because such texts in Augustine's time came primarily in codices; see Louis Holtz, "Mots latin," 111. For the centrality of the codex to scenes of conversion in Augustine, see Jager's *Book of the Heart* pp. 35–36. As for the lack of chapters in the codex Augustine consulted here, that conjecture can be based on the fact that early division systems were limited to the Gospels and Acts—a story to be told in the subsequent chapter of this book.

51. Notably, the *Confessions* itself was not initially chaptered; the current chapters seem to date from the Amerbach edition of the text, published in Basle in 1506. See Augustine, *Confessions* (ed. O'Donnell), lxi.

52. See *Confessions* 8.8: "The heat of my passion took my attention away from him as he contemplated my condition in astonished silence [abripuit me ab illo aestus meus, cum taceret attonitus me intuens]" (*Confessions*, trans. Chadwick, 146; original in O'Donnell, ed., 97). On the *arripio/abripio* echo here, see Stock (*Augustine the Reader*, 103). On *aperui* and the codex, see Jager (*Book of the Heart*, 36). Louis Holtz stresses that *aperire*, "to open," is a verb in Augustine associated with codices to the exclusion of any other format ("Mots latin," 110).

53. *Confessions* 3.8. Original in O'Donnell, ed., 30; Chadwick trans., 47.

54. Cassiodorus, *Institutions*, 154 (1.23).

55. On the *Literal Commentary*, see Michael Gorman's "Chapter Headings for Saint Augustine's *De Genesi ad litteram*"; on the *City of God*, see Marrou ("Division en chapitres," 236).

56. See Lambot, "Lettre inedité."

57. Original in Lambot, 113; translation in *Letters 1*–29**, 15.

58. See Lambot, "Lettre inedité," 117; Marrou, "Division en chapitres," 237–42.

59. Here the question of Firmus's identity is somewhat helpful: although initially identified as a priest, subsequent work has made clear that he was unbaptized—and that the twenty-two books of the *City of God* were presumably sent as part of an effort to persuade him to take that decisive step. With this particular purpose in mind, the function of the breviculus becomes clearer: it is an aid for the untutored, segmenting and labeling in the interest of inviting the reader inside. See van Oort, *Jerusalem and Babylon*, 173–75.

60. On Augustine's particular kind of "bookishness," see Gillian Clark's "City of Books." For the influence of Augustine's segmentations on a much later moment—the arrangement of medieval German books—see Nigel Palmer's "Kapitel und Buch."

61. Here I am indebted to Greg Woolf's account of the *instrumentum domesticum*, the set of epigrammatic, usually humble texts on mass-produced objects that, as a labeling practice, co-existed with and possibly nourished the more book-oriented labeling devices of the same period; see Woolf, "Literacy or Literacies."

62. Here the history of the chapter intersects with the ongoing debate over the birth and triumph of the codex in Western antiquity, particularly the role of discontinuous reading in its replacement of the scroll. One traditional account ascribes the success of the codex to the ways in which it permits a more segmented reading; but, as Eva Mroczek has recently argued, the cultural use of formats does not necessarily follow from our speculative reconstruction of a format's tendencies—it might even, for instance, be possible to say that the codex encouraged a continuous reading that the scroll had made difficult. See Mroczek, "Thinking Digitally." For a succinct articulation of the more traditional account, see Roger Chartier's "Languages, Books, and Reading from the Printed Word to the Digital Text." As the debate has evolved, the adoption of the codex has come to be explained as less a monocausal phenomenon, driven by ideology or technology alone or in some seamless collaboration, than a multifaceted shift in sociocultural attitudes and cognitive habits, oriented around the ways in which interruption is solicited, managed, and performed, and what kinds of interruptive reading were pivotal to particular reading communities. Key sources here include Roger Bagnall's *Early Christian Books in Egypt* and William Johnson's *Readers and Reading Culture in the High Roman Empire*. Finding devices, and their prevalence in codices, have long been thought to have played a role in this momentous shift—but capitulation, at least, is not native to the codex, complicating this narrative.

63. On the Greek literary prose text, and its "impression of uninterrupted succession, of a coherent whole," see William Johnson's "Toward a Sociology of Reading in Classical Antiquity" (p. 609).

64. Recent scholarship on Arrian's work tends to imagine a more active role—reworking, arranging, editing—than the prefatory letter admits; see Hershbell, "Stoicism of Epictetus." Yet the arranging of the collected discourses is often read as strangely disordered, without a clear didactic plan or comprehensible order; see Epictetus, *Entretiens*, xx–xxii.

65. Epictetus, *Discourses*, ed. Dobbin, 65, 128, 145. Dobbin prefers "On Self-Sufficiency" to Arrian's title for 1.17, "Concerning the Necessity of Logic"; see 161.

66. Howley, *Aulus Gellius*, 56–57.

67. See Souilhé, *Entretiens*, xxiii–xxviii.

68. Hadot, *Philosophy as a Way of Life*, 191.

69. Epictetus, *Discourses*, trans. Head. Subsequent references will be given parenthetically in the text with the abbreviation *D*.

70. So Hadot: "The work, even if it is apparently theoretical and systematic, is written not so much to inform the reader of a doctrinal content but to form him, to make him traverse a certain itinerary in the course of which he will make spiritual progress" (*Philosophy as a Way of Life*, 64).

71. See A. A. Long, "Stoic Psychology," 581.

72. Rhythmic tension is an important aspect of Stoic training, as Hadot noted with his description of Epictetus's "percussive rhetoric" (*Philosophy as a Way of Life*, 59).

73. I use "preconception" throughout here, but Michael Frede, who has written extensively on Stoic cognition, prefers "anticipation" to stress the "antecedent" quality of these concepts— we have them *before* the perceptions to which they are attached. See Frede, "Stoic Epistemology," 319.

74. See Sandbach, "Ennoia and Prolepsis," 27. Other useful general studies of Epictetus's "preconceptions" include Henry Dyson's *Prolepsis and Ennoia in the Early Stoa* and A. A. Long's *Stoic Studies*.

75. As A. A. Long and D. N. Sedley argue, this way of explaining the failure of preconceptions—their incorrect application to certain particulars—is a way for Epictetus to retain the idea that preconceptions are communally shared while allowing for their occasional failure. See *Hellenistic Philosophers*, 253.

76. Sandbach wryly comments that such a preconception, arrived at through subsequent study, would not be a preconception at all ("Ennoia and Prolepsis," 36).

77. Hadot is here an invaluable guide, particularly his accounts of Stoic "attention" and the present moment as the span in which attention operates (*Philosophy as a Way of Life*, 269–77).

78. Howley too reads Arrian's headings as a doubling, or reflection, of the teaching environment they describe (*Aulus Gellius*, 59). My emphasis here is perhaps one step more abstract: in so doing, they serve to theorize the presuppositions of that teaching environment, and thereby theorize their own function of prefacing, or labeling, experiences.

79. On "the symbolic qualities of inscriptional forms," see Stephanie Ann Frampton's *Empire of Letters* (p. 167).

Chapter 3

1. See Saenger ("Early Printed Page") for the prehistory of Estienne's verse numeration.

2. The work of the Pericope Group has been an invaluable guide for my inquiry here, insofar as the Group combines the methods of biblical paleography with an interest in what we might call literary form. See, e.g., Korpel, "Series Pericope."

3. On the repertoire of *notae* in Vivarian texts, see James Halporn's "Methods of Reference in Cassiodorus."

4. For a provocative unsettling of the general consensus that Christian use of the codex spurred the eventual demise of the scroll in the Mediterranean basin, see Benjamin Harnett's recent use of "diffusion of innovations theory" to account for the archeological data; Harnett situates the Christian communities as "early adopters," whose role would be therefore be less crucial, and less innovative, than previously argued. See Harnett, "Diffusion of the Codex."

5. Even this seemingly modest claim is potentially controversial. Frederic Kenyon stressed the threefold advantages of the codex: its greater comprehensiveness, its greater durability, and its increased convenience for reference or nonlinear access. Eric Turner placed the stress on comprehensiveness; R. W. McCutcheon has more recently emphasized the codex's greater openness to the advent of punctuation of various kinds, which is to say, reference aids. See Kenyon, *Books and Readers*, 113–15; Turner, *Typology of the Early Codex*, 82–95; McCutcheon, "Silent Reading in Antiquity." But others stress that the practical reasoning behind these opinions is a backward-formed technological determinism, and that in any case practical considerations would have been insufficient by themselves to account for Christian adoption of the codex unless joined to ideological motives: either to differentiate the sect from Judaism, or to preserve a memory of the "notebooks" of the early evangelists, or, by enabling the collection of the canonical Gospels in one volume, thereby ensure their status. See Roberts and Skeat, *Birth of the Codex*, 54–61; Skeat, "Christian Codex"; Mroczek, "Thinking Digitally."

6. See Grafton and Williams (*Transformation of the Book*) for a detailed argument as to the scope, and long-lasting influence, of the Caesarea library's work on textual configuration and segmentation.

7. Eusebius of Caesarea, *Histoire ecclésiastique*, vol. 1, *Sources Chrétiennes* 31: vii; vol. 4, *Sources Chrétiennes* 73: 111.

8. Relevant examples include Diodorus Siculus's *Historical Library* and Dionysus of Halicarnassus's *Roman Antiquities*, both of them first-century BCE texts that seem to have been furnished from their initial publication with prefatory summary lists that bear a similar syntactical form to that of the *Ecclesiastical History*. See Irigoin, "Titres, sous-titres et sommaires," 130.

9. See Blomkvist, *Euthalian Traditions*.

10. Translation from Barnes, *Constantine and Eusebius*, 121–22. Greek from *Novum Testamentum Graece*, 84*–85*.

11. Barnes, *Constantine and Eusebius*, 344.

12. Barnes, 121.

13. The search for textual monads is a recurrent, possibly inevitable feature of modern attempts to study the synoptic "problem"—that is, to determine what the sources were that the synoptic Gospels shared, and how they were elaborated into their final forms. The classic

statement of the problem, by Rudolf Bultmann, posited that the "aim of form-criticism is to determine the original form of a piece of narrative, a dominical saying or parable. In the process we learn to distinguish secondary additions and forms" (*Synoptic Tradition*, 6). The aim is to clear away later accretions, down to the original, coherent object, even if that object, the famous *Quelle* of the Gospels, can be only a hypothesis. As critiqued by Werner Kelber, what buttresses Bultmann's influential method is an idea of "pure form," an original monad (likely a "saying" or transcribed utterance) that develops later elaborations, just as biological simplicity evolves into complexity—a unidirectional process that ignores much of how the transmission of narrative, particularly from oral to written traditions, actually operates. See Kelber, *Oral and the Written Gospel*, 6.

14. There is some evidence that both Vaticanus and Codex Sinaiticus were produced in the same location, as a scribal hand has been identified as common to both. T. C. Skeat argues for Caesarea as their shared place of origin, and for Eusebius as the figure responsible, identifying both texts as attempts to fill the order Constantine sent him, soon after 330, for fifty copies of the Bible for use in Constantinople. See Skeat, "Codex Sinaiticus." J. N. Birdsall offers a note of caution, characterizing the evidence for such a confident attribution as scanty; see Birdsall, "New Testament Text," 359.

15. Metzger, *Text of the New Testament*, 22–23; Lake, *Text of the New Testament*, 52. There is evidence that an Old Latin set of capitula may date from the third century and be associated with Saint Cyprian; H.A.G. Houghton has called these "the earliest set of New Testament chapter divisions known to survive in any language" ("Chapter Divisions," 337–38; De Bruyne, "Quelques documents nouveaux."

16. McArthur, "Earliest Divisions"; Metzger, *Manuscripts of the Greek Bible*, 40–41.

17. Pisano, "Text of the New Testament," 27; Skeat, "Codex Sinaiticus," 601.

18. Read from the digital facsimile available at DigiVatLib, the Vatican Library's digital image library: https://digi.vatlib.it/view/MSS_Vat.gr.1209.

19. McArthur, "Earliest Divisions," 270.

20. This is the surmise of Philip Carrington, although it requires him, in the case of Mark, to discard the Passion narrative from his plan for a yearly cycle of readings based on Vaticanus's roughly 50 remaining units; and it makes less sense in the other Gospels—such as Matthew, with 170 such units in Vaticanus. See Carrington, *According to Mark*, 346.

21. Citation is McArthur's guess: see "Earliest Divisions," 271.

22. Skeat, "Provenance of the Codex Alexandrinus"; McKendrick, "Codex Alexandrinus."

23. W. Smith, *Gospels in Codex Alexandrinus*, 156–62; Goswell, "Early Readers of the Gospels," 136–39.

24. For the multiple solicitations of Gospel segmentations, particularly between first-time readers and rereaders, see Wierusz Kowalski ("Découpage du texte évangélique").

25. The circumstantial evidence for Eusebian influence has in fact led some to suggest Eusebius as the system's creator; see Barnes (*Constantine and Eusebius*, 124). For an argument that the divisions predate Eusebius, see von Soden (*Schriften des Neuen Testaments*, 426–32).

26. J. Edwards, "Hermeneutical Significance," 424.

27. Carrington, *According to Mark*, 346. Kurt and Barbara Aland concur with the lectionary hypothesis; see *The Text of the New Testament*, p. 252. For a concise account disagreeing with these explanations, see Edwards ("Hermeneutical Significance," 416–17).

28. As read from *The Codex Alexandrinus (Royal MS. 1 D V-VIII) in Reduced Photographic Facsimile*, and the digital photographs on the British Library website: Royal MS 1 D VIII, British Library Digitised Manuscripts, https://www.bl.uk/manuscripts/FullDisplay.aspx?ref=Royal _MS_1_d_viii. The translations here are mine; references to the number of each kephalaion are in brackets.

29. Not all readers of Alexandrinus would concur. James Edwards reads the kephalaia as oriented around Jesus's actions, despite his absence from the *titloi*, and as thereby observing a logic that is "not only Christological, but Incarnational"; Greg Goswell reads them as emphasizing miracles over discourse, or Jesus the healer rather than Christ the redeemer, reflecting a homiletic emphasis on moral exemplars rather than theological concepts. See J. Edwards, "Hermeneutical Significance," 426; Goswell, "Early Readers of the Gospels," 169, 173–74.

30. See von Soden, *Schriften des Neuen Testaments*, 423–44.

31. The possible ambiguity as to what counts as a beginning to an event—when one shifts from "preproceeding" to "proceeding"—is explored by Goffman in relation to events that are not yet formalized—such as, for instance, parties. See *Frame Analysis*, 262–63.

32. R. Fowler, *Let the Reader Understand*, 117. See also Black (*Sentence Conjunctions*, 111–14) for a description of the multiple possible shadings with which *kai* expresses continuity.

33. Read from *Codex Amiatinus*, 60. Translation mine. The history of Amiatinus's capitulation is complex; the list of headings for Mark, which parallels that of the Books of Kells and Durrow and seems to be of Insular origin, does not always match the marginal numeration in the text itself, which seems to have Italian provenance. In this particular case, however—capitulum 14 of its text of Mark—heading and marginal numeration match. See Verey, "Northumbrian Text Family," 110–13. The tendency of Amiatinus's Gospel headings to avoid the usual noun phrase in favor of intact sentences with a variety of syntactical structures has been taken to argue for a single author; see Meyvaert, "Bede's *Capitula lectionum*," 353.

34. Bultmann, *Synoptic Tradition*, 214.

35. See Edwards, on the general rule that a miracle in Alexandrinus must commence a new unit: "This rule is adhered to so rigidly that coherent narratives are sometimes disrupted" (J. Edwards, "Hermeneutical Significance," 419).

36. "Closing brackets seem to perform less work, perhaps reflecting the fact that it is probably much easier on the whole to terminate the influence of a frame than to establish it" (Goffman, *Frame Analysis*, 256).

37. de Bruyne, *Summaries, Divisions, and Rubrics*, 421, 512.

38. Admittedly with some minor exceptions; one moment in Genesis and one in Job differ in their contemporary chaptering from the thirteenth-century version, which was not fixed in every detail until the late sixteenth century. See Saenger and Bruck, "Anglo-Hebraic Origins," 182.

39. Ferruolo, "*Parisius-Paradisus*," 23.

40. On the varieties of *lectura* and *reportatio*, see Mariken Teeuwen's *Vocabulary of Intellectual Life in the Middle Ages*, pp. 292–97, 333–35. On the teaching environment more generally, see Beryl Smalley's *Study of the Bible in the Middle Ages*, pp. 222–24.

41. For the early thirteenth-century milieu around citation, see Carruthers (*Book of Memory*, 101–3, 188) and Light ("Bible and the Individual," 233–34; "French Bibles," 264–65).

42. The classroom alibi for the creation of a new, standard paratextual apparatus is affirmed by Laura Light ("Versions et révisions," 78–79, 85). See also Loewe, "Medieval History," 147.

43. See d'Esneval, "Division de la Vulgate," 560.

44. On the *pecia* system and the (often legal) requirement, common to thirteenth- and fourteenth-century universities, that students possess copies of set texts, see Graham Pollard's "The *Pecia* System in the Medieval Universities," p. 150.

45. See Light, "Versions et révisions," 90–92; Loewe, "Medieval History," 147.

46. Light, "French Bibles," 248; Poleg, *Approaching the Bible,* 110.

47. Light, "French Bibles," 248–49.

48. Poleg, *Approaching the Bible,* 138–40.

49. Beryl Smalley notes that Langton's commentaries often apply biblical lessons to local institutional questions, such as the right of masters to expect payment from pupils, and that he refers often to classroom situations; see Smalley, "Commentaries of Cardinal Stephen Langton."

50. This is the explanation given by Langton's most modern biographer, F. M. Powicke; see his *Stephen Langton,* p. 37. The attribution of the chapter system to Langton become commonplace after the work of Jean-Pierre Paulin Martin; see *Critique générale,* 461–74. Those who endorse the Langton attribution are led to date the chapter system's formation to roughly 1200 to 1206, although they acknowledge that the system changed slightly up until 1220 or 1230. See d'Esneval, "Division de la Vulgate," 561; Light, "Bible and the Individual," 233–34. Smalley notes that it was already being used in copying one of Langton's glosses in 1203; see *Study of the Bible,* 223–24.

51. See Powicke, *Stephen Langton,* 35; Saenger, "Anglo-Hebraic Origins," 179.

52. Trevet, *Annales sex regum Angliae,* 216. Translation from Powicke, *Stephen Langton,* 34.

53. Quoted in Smalley, *Study of the Bible,* 224; see also Carruthers, *Book of Memory,* 95–99.

54. Saenger, "Twelfth-Century Reception," 51–53.

55. Saenger, "Anglo-Hebraic Origins," 186–87.

56. Saenger, "Jewish Liturgical Divisions," 187. Others have noted the similarity: see van Banning, "Chapter Divisions of Stephan Langton," 144–45.

57. Saenger, "Anglo-Hebraic Origins," 201. Some caution is necessary; as Joseph Heinemann argues, there was no single cycle of *sedarim* that could be securely related to New Testament divisions. See Heinemann, "Triennial Lectionary Cycle."

58. See Saenger, "Twelfth-Century Reception," 38–40.

59. Quoted in Powicke, *Stephen Langton,* 36.

60. Van Banning, "Chapter Divisions of Stephan Langton," 157.

61. Paulin Martin, *Critique générale,* 472.

62. The Dominican reference tools based on the new chaptering system have also been understood as helping to popularize that system; see Rouse and Rouse, *Preachers, Florilegia, and Sermons,* 39. See also Poleg, *Approaching the Bible,* 128; Saenger, "Early Printed Page," 33.

63. de Bruyne, *Summaries, Divisions, and Rubrics,* 509.

64. I borrow "conciseness" from Bultmann, for whom it refers to the Gospel tendency to only narrate "short incidents, that would have occupied no more than a few minutes or hours"; see *Synoptic Tradition,* 307.

65. As Philipp Rosemann puts it, previous systems "treated the biblical text like a play, breaking it up into scenes according to the arrival or departure of a particular character or a change of location," whereas the modern chapters seem to ignore the usual modes of narrative segmentation (*Great Medieval Book*, 54–55).

66. A typical example of commentary on this moment: "It is an instructive example of the way in which the artificial division into chapters often mars the sense, that one verse of this section is found at the close of the last chapter, and the remainder in this" (Ellicott, *New Testament Commentary*, 444).

67. Interestingly, the divisional system to which De Bruyne gave the siglum I—a type found in the Book of Durrow and Book of Kells—places its division at 9:1 just like the Langton–Saint Albans version, along with several other Latin division systems, demonstrating some precedent for the choice here. See De Bruyne, *Summaries, Divisions, and Rubrics*, 510. Commentaries often simply reject the modern version; Ellicott's *New Testament Commentary* calls it "obviously wrong" (212).

68. See, e.g., Goswell, "Early Readers of the Gospels," 158–59.

69. See Barthélemy, " Traditions anciennes de division," 36–38; Moore, "Vulgate Chapters."

70. From the prologue to his *Postillae perpetuae in universam S. Scripturam*; see Minnis, Scott, and Wallace, *Medieval Literary Theory*, 269–70.

Chapter 4

1. I use here, for the purposes of clarity, Janet Cowan's edition of the Caxton text, which modernizes spelling and conventions of punctuation while retaining the original's syntax. See Malory, *Morte d'Arthur* (ed. Cowan), 1:212. Subsequent references refer to this edition and will be cited parenthetically in the text by volume and page number, using the abbreviation *MA*.

2. Saintsbury, *English Prose Rhythm*, 89.

3. In this sense Mathieu writes of two kinds of chapter gaps, the "bridge" (*pont*) and the "fall" (*chute*)—or, a linking function and a semiclosural function (*Changer de chapitre*, 41–45).

4. Read from the facsimile image of the Winchester MS, here folio 105v, available at *The Malory Project*, directed by Takako Kato and designed by Nick Heyward (http://www .maloryproject.com).

5. Malory, *Morte Darthur* (ed. Field), 1:207. Field's text is the latest to be based on the Winchester MS, and as such is an updating of the Eugene Vinaver editions that had first proclaimed the superiority of Winchester to Caxton's edition.

6. Or "en prose par chapitre": Philippe de Vigneulles, *Chanson de Garin le Loherain*, 2.

7. Colombo Timelli, *"Erec,"* 101; *"Cliges,"* 65.

8. Stephen of Bourbon, *Anecdotes historiques*, 9. Translation mine.

9. Quoted from Vincent of Beauvais, *Speculum quadruplex*, 3. Translation from Blair, *Too Much to Know*, 44. For more on the information design of the *Speculum maius*, see Armando Petrucci's *Writers and Readers in Medieval Italy*, pp. 137–38.

10. See, for instance, N. F. Blake's argument that in Caxton's edition of Malory, "each small episode tends to become the illustration of a moral and can be read independently. The work

has become something like a sermon on chivalry with innumerable, carefully indexed, exempla" (*Caxton and His World*, 110). Blake reasserts this claim in "Caxton at Work."

11. Philippe de Vigneulles, as Catherine Jones has pointed out, uses much the same vocabulary for his prosification as he does for his work with cloth, particularly the term "joindre," the stitching together of discrete elements. See Jones, *Philippe de Vigneulles*, 88.

12. Augustine, *Confessions*, ed. O'Donnell, 155; trans. Chadwick, 232.

13. I owe a debt here to the detailed and suggestive discussion of Augustine's schema in Eleanor Johnson's *Staging Contemplation* (pp. 27–30).

14. Ricoeur, *Time and Narrative*, 1:21.

15. Bede, *Reckoning of Time*, 13.

16. Bede, 15.

17. Bede, 16.

18. Atomism was, however, an increasingly attractive methodological guide in thirteenth- and fourteenth-century western Europe; see Pabst, *Atomtheorien des lateinischen Mittelalters*.

19. Ricoeur, *Time and Narrative*, 1:9.

20. Augustine, *Confessions*, trans. Chadwick, 243; ed. O'Donnell, 163.

21. Bede, *Reckoning of Time*, 15.

22. This might be even truer for prose than verse in Bede's thinking; see E. Johnson, *Staging Contemplation*, 207.

23. Hodgson, *Cloud of Unknowing*, 20. The Middle English orthography retained by Hodgson has been standardized in my quotations.

24. Hodgson, 17–18.

25. See E. Johnson, *Staging Contemplation*, 36–40.

26. Hodgson, *Cloud of Unknowing*, 20.

27. Hodgson, 3.

28. Hodgson, 3–4.

29. "Laboratory" is a term used by Tania Van Hemelryck, in "Le livre mis en prose à la cour de Bourgogne," p. 254.

30. Jakobson's term is cited by Jane Taylor, who usefully suggests "acculturation" as the governing concept behind these remediations ("Significance of the Insignificant," 183, 190). Georges Doutrepont called them "free translations" (*Mises en prose*, 335).

31. Van Hemelryck, "Livre mis en prose," 249–51.

32. Colombo Timelli, *"Erec,"* 19.

33. Lacy, "Adaptation as Reception," 201.

34. Doutrepont himself initiated this critique by referring to the *mises en prose* as a proto-modernism, one that eliminated ornament and preferred brevity and exactitude; Martha Wallen's reading of the prose *Erec* explains it as a deliberate ideological clarification and, by extension, simplification. See Doutrepont, *Mises en prose*, 394–96; Wallen, "Significant Variations," 187–96.

35. Matthieu Marchal argues that the function of the prosateurs' chapters was to clarify and "aerate" their sources ("Mise en chapitres," 187).

36. Colombo Timelli asserts that the headings and main text of the *Erec* manuscript are from the same hand (*"Erec,"* 11). Doutrepont believed that division into chapters was usually performed subsequent to the composition of the prose "translation"; Colombo Timelli agrees,

arguing that many headings seem to borrow their phrasing from sentences within chapters. See Doutrepont, *Mises en prose*, 472; Colombo Timelli, "Syntaxe et technique narrative," 214–15.

37. Chrétien de Troyes, *Burgundian "Erec" and "Cligès,"* 40. Subsequent references to the English text of both the prose *Erec* and *Cligès* refer to this edition and will be given parenthetically, using the abbreviation *BEC.*

38. Cited and translated by Jones, *Philippe de Vigneulles*, 93.

39. Marchal, "Mise en chapitres," 189.

40. Colombo Timelli, *"Cligès,"* 81, 89, 106.

41. See Colombo Timelli, *"Erec,"* 29.

42. Auerbach, *Mimesis*, 127–28.

43. The shortest chapter in the *Cligès* MS is 18 prose lines; the longest, 194 (Colombo Timelli, *"Cligès,"* 21).

44. See Lacy, "Adaptation as Reception," 199–202; Tasker Grimbert, "Refashioning Combat."

45. Chrétien de Troyes, *Cligès*, ed. Gregory and Luttrell, 119–20, lines 3344–57; trans. Harwood Cline, 98, lines 3323–37.

46. Chrétien de Troyes, *Cligès*, trans. Harwood Cline, 98, lines 3318–20.

47. As Colombo Timelli puts it, the brevity of the chapter form in the prose revisions isolates a particular event or act that could otherwise be lost in a continuous narrative; but that event is too particular to constitute an actual "episode" ("Syntaxe et technique narrative," 209).

48. A 1467 catalogue of Philip the Good's holdings mentions the primary MS of the prose *Erec*, giving us the latest possible date for its production. There have been persistent claims that the Burgundian *Erec* and *Cligès* come from the same prosateur or workshop, but this thesis has recently fallen out of favor; see Colombo Timelli, *"Erec et Cligès en prose."*

49. Chrétien de Troyes, *Erec et Enide*, ed. Roques, 55, lines 1793–96; trans. Gilbert, 95, lines 1795–98.

50. See Martha Wallen's argument that while Chrétien prefers "thinking beyond" the present crisis, the prosateur thinks within isolated episodes ("Significant Variations," 189–94).

51. Deacon, *Biography of William Caxton*, 35–36.

52. *Godeffrey of Boloyne*, 5.

53. *Caxton's Mirrour*, 6–7.

54. *Chronicles of England*, prologue.

55. Helen Cooper argues that the difference between the Winchester MS and Caxton's edition reveals how "multiple subdivisions of fictional texts are central to the conception of the printed book—they are indeed conventions that go back in English in large measure to Caxton himself" ("Opening Up," 259).

56. The lack of intertitles has one peculiar exception, at the start 17.7. The general absence of the headings in the text did not last: Wynkyn de Worde's 1498 edition of the *Morte* would use Caxton's headings as intertitles. See Holbrook, "On the Attractions," 336; Wade, "Chapter Headings of the *Morte*." Helen Cooper suggests that the lack of intertitles is a sign of Caxton mimicking the design of the Winchester MS ("Opening Up," 264).

57. See Kato, *Caxton's "Morte Darthur,"* 43.

58. See Holbrook, "On the Attractions," 341.

59. The presence of the Winchester MS in the Westminster workshop in the 1480s was first discovered by Lotte Hellinga and Hilton Kelliher; see their "Malory Manuscript." The role of the Winchester MS in the production process is still being debated, however; Holbrook argues that it would not have been used extensively for chaptering because ink stains are not often present on pages where Caxton's divisions occur, but Kato argues that Caxton would have consulted it while chaptering his setting copy. See Holbrook, "On the Attractions," 353; Kato, *Caxton's "Morte Darthur,"* 71–72.

60. Kato, *Caxton's "Morte Darthur,"* 49–50.

61. See Wade, "Chapter Headings of the *Morte*," 646–53. Holbrook, however, argues that the table of headings must have been largely completed before the main text was set by compositors ("On the Attractions," 337).

62. Figures from Takagi and Takamiya, "Caxton Edits," 170.

63. Takagi and Takamiya, 264.

64. Takagi and Takamiya, 170, 187.

65. Kato, *Caxton's "Morte Darthur,"* 29–31. Holbrook notes this aspect of Caxton's page design and calls it "salubrious"; Blake feels differently, describing how it "makes the texts more fragmentary" despite Caxton's attempts at unification of Malory's different tales. See Holbrook, "On the Attractions," 341; Blake, *Caxton and His World*, 110.

66. Blake, *Caxton and His World*, 109–10. Monica Fludernik has written on these formulae, arguing for two mutations by the onset of the realist novel: their replacement by clauses with temporal markers indicating simultaneity ("meanwhile"), and their location at the start of chapters rather than at the onset of episodes, which she calls "chapterification." Yet Caxton's text has already started to "chapterify" the Malorian formulae. See Fludernik, "Diachronization of Narratology."

67. As argued by William Matthews in "The Besieged Printer," pp. 49, 64.

68. On lexical echoing in the headings, see Wade ("Chapter Headings," 650–51).

69. "Obtrusive": see Kennedy, "Caxton," 228. "Solid and foursquare": Matthews, "Besieged Printer," 56. An excellent summary of the changes in textual fashion since Eugene Vinaver's edition of the Winchester MS, as well as the coinage of the term "Malorization," can be found in Meg Roland's "'Alas! Who May Truste Thys World.'"

70. McGann, *Modern Textual Criticism*, 84.

71. Word counts were calculated using the electronic edition compiled by the University of Michigan Humanities Text Initiative: *Morte Darthur*, ed. H. Oskar Sommer.

72. The high variability of book 5 may be because Caxton was borrowing chapter divisions from a different source here, his own *Chronicles of England*; see Takagi and Takamiya, "Caxton Edits," 171.

73. See Kato and Heyward, *Malory Project*, fol. 20r; Malory, *Morte Darthur*, ed. Field, 42.

74. On Caxton's chapters as designed to heighten rhetorical occasions, see Blake (*Caxton and His World*, 109).

75. See Malory, *Morte Darthur*, ed. Field, 168–69; Kato and Heyward, *Malory Project*, fol. 84r.

76. On pensiveness, plural meaning, and suspended endings, see Barthes's *S/Z: An Essay*, translated by Richard Miller (New York: Hill and Wang, 1974), pp. 216–17.

Chapter 5

1. L. Sterne, *Tristram Shandy*, 241.

2. Fielding, *Joseph Andrews*, 90.

3. *History of Charlotte Summers*, 1:30.

4. See Martin, *History and Power of Writing*, 329.

5. Lupton, *Knowing Books*, 41–45.

6. As Janine Barchas argues, the eighteenth-century novelistic table of contents—which could be just as easily pegged, as in Richardson, to letters as to chapters—may have aided rereading, but may have just as often worked, perhaps deliberately, to misdirect first readers (*Graphic Design*, 208–9).

7. Coventry, *New Species of Writing*, 24.

8. Coventry, *Pompey the Little*, 77.

9. For the former theory, see R. M. Flores's "Cervantes at Work"; for a full account of the byplay between manuscript and print that contributed to the chaptering errors, see Francisco Rico's *Texto del "Quijote,"* pp. 217–44.

10. *Life of Lazarillo de Tormes.*

11. That novel and Bible might be closest in their negotiations with discontinuous reading is the surmise of Jordan Stein, who suggests that the pressure toward continuous reading was reflected, if in uneven ways, across the book market of the late seventeenth century. See Stein, *When Novels Were Books*, 53–91.

12. See Pattie, "Great Codices," 70; Mandelbrote, "English Scholarship."

13. Fox, *John Mill and Richard Bentley*, 125.

14. There was a competing attribution popular throughout the period, however, which was that the system had been devised by Hugh of Saint Cher along with his subdivisions and concordance. One popular source for this theory was the ecclesiastical historian and controversialist Louis Ellies du Pin, whose 1699 *Dissertation préliminaire* offered one of the era's most detailed histories of textual division in Scripture. The *Dissertation*, translated into English the same year as its French publication, asserted that biblical chapters were an invention of the fifth century, and that Hugh's more capacious chapters were finally convenient enough to achieve widespread use. See du Pin, *Dissertation préliminaire* and *Compleat History*. This theory of the system's Dominican provenance was remarkably popular in the prefatory material of Victorian Bibles, in Britain and the United States; a good example is the SPCK (Society for Promoting Christian Knowledge) publication *The Holy Bible, According to the Authorized Version; with Notes, Explanatory and Practical*, edited by George D'Oyly and Richard Mant.

15. R. Boyle, *Style of the Holy Scriptures*, 60–61.

16. From the reprinting of Casaubon's notes in *Novi testamenti libri omnes*, 363.

17. Simon, *Histoire critique*, 416–17.

18. This is the constellation Frances Ferguson calls "dissenting textualism": see "Dissenting Textualism."

19. Locke, *Understanding of St. Paul's Epistles*, vii–viii.

20. In Ferguson's phrase, Locke "calls attention to the ways in which a text (in its parts) can be at odds with that same text (in its entirely)" ("Dissenting Textualism," 593).

21. Locke, *Reasonableness of Christianity*, 165.

22. On the debt that Locke owes here to Spinoza, both in the underlying epistemology and the setting in which it is best enacted—"the study of the leisured and secluded reader"—see John Drury's introductory essay to *Critics of the Bible*, p. 18.

23. So D. F. McKenzie reads this passage, as an argument for how print design can generate "religious and civil dissension": *Bibliography*, 55–57.

24. Locke, *Understanding of St. Paul's Epistles*, viii.

25. This section combines the Langton–Saint Albans chapters 3–7. By contrast, the last of Locke's sections of the text contains only four verses, 13:11–14. See Locke, *Paraphrase and Notes*, 14–33, 58.

26. It is an irony that haunted Locke; there is, for instance, his rueful admission that his *Essay concerning Human Understanding* was an attempt to make "incoherent parcels" cohere. Quoted in Jay, *Songs of Experience*, 48.

27. See Woolhouse, *Locke*, 433.

28. Higgins-Biddle's editorial preface to the Clarendon edition of *Reasonableness* covers the Houghton copy in detail, and explains how the dating of the copy's chaptering was established: the blotting of one marginal chapter number onto a letter dated August 1701 that was tucked into the pages of the copy. See Locke, *Reasonableness of Christianity*, cxxi–cxxii.

29. Jenkin, *Remarks*, 118–20.

30. Le Clerc, *Bibliothèque choisie*, 64–67.

31. See Jonathan Sheehan's account of the ways in which eighteenth-century English Bibles exhibited a self-conscious strangeness, in which "the gap between the Bible's divine content and its human form leaps into view" (*Enlightenment Bible*, 3).

32. Quoted in Mandelbrote, "English Bible," 56. See also Hitchin, "Politics."

33. On Simon's influence, see Mandelbrote's "English Bible," pp. 54–55.

34. Whiston, *Primitive New Testament*, 2v.

35. *Four Gospels*, 668.

36. *Four Gospels*, 669–72.

37. Doddridge, *Family Expositor*, 594.

38. *New Testament*, trans. Wynne, 1:v.

39. Gilpin, *Two Sermons*, 24.

40. From the preface to *Nouveau Testament*, trans. Le Clerc, 9r.

41. *Liberal Translation*, vi.

42. *Translation of the New Testament*, ix.

43. Blackwall, *Sacred Classics*, 124, 127, 129–30. To solve the dilemma of John 8, Blackwell recommended simply moving its beginning back to the present 7:53, one of several minor adjustments he advised.

44. *New Translation*, 2r. Wearing its influences proudly, the Doddridge Testament included a prefatory extract from Rousseau and an epigraph from Locke.

45. A curious detail in the relation between fiction and biblical chapter controversies is the case of Johann David Michaelis, German translator of Richardson's *Clarissa*, whose *Einleitung in das Neue Testament*, translated into English in 1793, took the standard Lockean line that the modern chapter system was an obstacle to comprehension, as chapters "often end abruptly in the middle of a connected discourse." See Michaelis, *Introduction to the New Testament*, 526.

46. Fielding, *Joseph Andrews*, 90.

47. Thomas Keymer, in his analysis of Fielding's metaphor and its aftereffects across mid-eighteenth-century fiction, emphasizes the aspect of collectivity, the fantasy that reading might unite a readership in "a single movement, sociable and progressive, towards shared understanding," as figured by the stagecoach's "carefully structured and phased course laid out for the reader's imagination . . . with a common terminus for all" (*Sterne*, 39). See also the discussion of the metaphor in J. Paul Hunter's *Occasional Form* (143–51).

48. For much of the period chapter breaks are not tied to pagination, and can occur at various places on a page with minimal white space. Later in the century the practice of beginning each chapter with a new page becomes more normative, a shift reflected in *Tristram Shandy*'s development: volumes 1–8 maintain the usual layout, but volume 9 shifts to the newer mode and its inevitably more lavish use of white space—possibly, as Peter de Voogd argues, to bump out Sterne's slightly more meagre text (De Voogd, "*Tristram Shandy*," 119).

49. L. Sterne, *Tristram Shandy*, 224. Subsequent citations in this chapter will be given parenthetically in the text with the abbreviation *TS*.

50. Fifteen to twenty minutes is the guess of Natalie Phillips for the eighteenth-century novelistic chapter: a figure that suggests the kinds of attention possible within that range. See Phillips, *Distraction*, 91.

51. Lupton, *Reading*, 30. On the nonequivalence between chapter and episode as an essential aspect of novelistic time: Mathieu, *Changer de chapitre*, 20–24.

52. From Müller, "Erzählzeit und erzählte Zeit."

53. Lesage, *Gil Blas*, 270.

54. Lennox, *Female Quixote*, 2:222.

55. Fielding, *Tom Jones*, 77.

56. See Eirian Yem's discussion of Ann Radcliffe's epigraphs as moral directions meant to counter readerly self-forgetfulness and immersion ("Forgetting Oneself").

57. On the Sternean moment and its "internal independent logic," see Amit Yahav's *Feeling Time*, p. 111.

58. The literature on *Tristram Shandy*'s rhythmic effects is vast and often contentious. Much of it revolves around the old question of duration versus punctuated time: which Sterne preferred, and which is truer to the experience of time in general. Where A. A. Mendilow argued for Sterne as an exponent of Bergsonian durée, more recently critics have recuperated the punctual: Amit Yahav situates the Sternean "beat" as a communal synchronization, and Joseph Drury explains *Shandy*'s interruptions as a moralized technique for rupturing the relentlessly goal-oriented drives of self-interest. See Mendilow, *Time and the Novel*, 169; Yahav, *Feeling Time*, 103–10; Joseph Drury, *Novel Machines*, 139.

59. See Dürrenmatt ("Problème de division") on Sterne's and Diderot's dismantling of any neoclassical clarity to the part-whole relationship.

60. Here I take my lead from J. Paul Hunter's contention, as against Shklovsky's defamiliarization, that *Tristram Shandy*'s play with the chapter form is interested in "articulating and ultimately in defending the convention, not in satire or dismissal or destruction." See Hunter, "From Typology to Type," 53.

61. Shklovsky, *Theory of Prose*, 152.

62. Equiano, *Interesting Narrative*, 161. Subsequent references will be given parenthetically in the text, with the abbreviation *IN*.

63. For a description of this chapter's form as "one long series of crises"—a shape defined by its shapelessness—see Laura Doyle's *Freedom's Empire*, p. 196.

64. Examples include Briton Hammon's *A Narrative of the Most Uncommon Sufferings and Surprizing Deliverance of Briton Hammon, a Negro Man*; James Albert Ukawsaw Gronniosaw's *Narrative of the Most Remarkable Particulars in the Life of James Albert Ukawsaw Gronniosaw, an African Prince, as Related by Himself*; and John Marrant's *Narrative of the Lord's Wonderful Dealings with John Marrant, a Black*—each of which is unchaptered. Ottobah Cugoano's *Thoughts and Sentiments on the Evil and Wicked Traffic of the Slavery and Commerce of the Human Species* is similarly unchaptered, although it possesses a "General Contents" abstract indexed to page numbers. Well-known captivity narratives vary their approach, from John Kingdon's unchaptered *Redeemed Slaves* to the untitled chapters of Penelope Aubin's *Noble Slaves*; the scheme of Mary Rowlandson's *Sovereignty and Goodness of God*, divided into twenty "removes," perhaps comes closest to Equiano's method but is far more openly systematic.

65. On Equiano's efforts to market *The Interesting Narrative*, see John Bugg's "The Other Interesting Narrative"; on the "novelization" of slave narrative, see Cathy Davidson's argument for Equiano as the "father of the American Novel" in "Olaudah Equiano, Written by Himself," p. 25; also see William Andrews's *To Tell a Free Story*.

66. Both frontispiece and subscriber list are analyzed in detail in Carretta (*Equiano the African*, 280–300); the frontispiece in particular is discussed by Srinivas Aravamudan in *Tropicopolitans*, pp. 244–45.

67. Quoted in Equiano, *Interesting Narrative*, xxvii.

68. As for example, the tripartite allegorical scheme described by Adam Potkay and Sandra Burr—patriarchal culture, followed by enslavement, followed by liberation—which aligns Equiano's story to biblical history. See Potkay and Burr's introduction to their *Black Atlantic Writers of the Eighteenth Century*, pp. 12–13.

69. Lowe, *Intimacies of Four Continents*, 46.

70. So Aravamudan writes, describing Equiano's life as "discontinuously rather than uniformly checkered, indeed cobbled together from disparate episodes, forming a patchwork quilt of different life experiences." See *Tropicopolitans*, 249–50. Laura Doyle notes how Equiano's narrative syntax resists singularity; events happen multiply, as "everyday, ongoing ontological crises" (*Freedom's Empire*, 193).

71. John Bugg, picking up on one of Equiano's other terms, calls these small-scale narrative units "trifles" and provides a narrative analysis of their scope; see "Equiano's Trifles."

72. The narrative's most consequential shift, Equiano's purchase of freedom from his owner Robert King, is in the first edition marked by a horizontal black line between paragraphs; but the second edition drops the line (perhaps because the paragraph break so marked in the first edition here occurs between pages), and no subsequent edition in Equiano's lifetime restores it. The effort to mark this pivotal moment as such—as a barrier breached—does not last, and whatever the reason may have been, it does not generally accord with Equiano's segmenting practices.

73. Indeed, in the eleventh chapter (and nine years later) Equiano returns to Monserrat, if briefly, on his voyage with Charles Irving to establish a Miskito Coast plantation: "On the fifth

of January [1776] we made Antigua and Montserrat" (*IN*, 204). Whether they landed there or merely skirted it, there is the sense here of the former "adieu" as provisional only—the gravitational pull of the trading networks Equiano plied meant that scenes of his enslavement were rarely permanently left behind.

74. Sharpe, *In the Wake*, 127.

75. I owe this language of folded time—associated with a time of endurance, in which certain repetitive labors are hidden—to Lisa Baraitser's description of "maintaining." See *Enduring Time*, 47–50.

76. This moment is read by Henry Louis Gates Jr. as reflecting the commodification of time in the form of the slave's labor—the master's ownership, that is, of time itself (*Signifying Monkey*, 154–55).

77. This is the aspect of Equiano's narrative that Cathy Davidson calls the "existential rug-pull" ("Olaudah Equiano," 20), although with attention to what Christina Sharpe discusses as the deep time of the "hold" in Black life, it seems more appropriate to remain with the not-wholly-figural resonance, not of having a rug pulled out from under you, but of falling into the space where personhood is erased. Sharpe: "The slave ship, the womb and the coffle, and the long dehumanizing project; we continue to feel and be the fall . . . out" (*In the Wake*, 74).

78. See N. Boyle, *Goethe*, 215, 240; Unseld, *Goethe and His Publishers*, 91–105.

79. Goethe, *Wilhelm Meister's Apprenticeship*, trans. Blackall, 158; *Wilhelm Meisters Lehrjahre*, 285. Subsequent parenthetical references in the text (with abbreviation *WM*) are to this Blackall translation. Thomas Carlyle's 1824 translation of the novel comes closer to the phrase's technical meaning merely by being more literal—in Carlyle it is rendered "tabulary scheme," retaining the specific contemporary connotations of "tabulation," including paratextual apparatuses for discontinuous reading; see *Wilhelm Meister's Apprenticeship*, trans. Carlyle, 106.

80. As cited in N. Boyle, *Goethe*, 406.

81. In 1922 the Czech composer Václav Tomášek complained to Goethe about the slack relationship of each chapter to the others, "die lockere Haltung der Capitel untereinander": see Gräf. *Goethe Über Seine Dichtungen*, 995. Oddly, Goethe's recorded response is that the fragmentation Tomášek notes is a result of the chapters being published in pieces first—a condition that only obtains for the *Wanderjahre*, not the *Lehrjahre*, which is specifically the subject of Tomášek's inquiry. Did Goethe misremember, or mishear the question? Was he deliberately misleading Tomášek? There is a similar oddity to Tomášek's query, because his primary example of the fragmentation of the novel's chapters is book 6, the unchaptered "Confessions of a Beautiful Soul"—neither Tomášek nor Goethe, it seems, bother to distinguish between books and chapters here. Suggestive as the anecdote is, it bears the marks of several overlapping confusions.

82. See Andrew Piper's description of Goethe's "crisis of the genitive" (*Dreaming in Books*, 15).

83. At an average of 1,178 words per chapter, the chapters of the *Theatralische Sendung* are just slightly smaller than those of the first five books of the *Lehrjahre*, which average roughly 1,300 words.

84. Such is the surmise of Helmut Müller-Sievers, the only scholar I am aware of to have noted this pattern of lengthening chapters. Müller-Sievers argues that the expansion is "surely a function of having to wrap up various strands of the story as well as countenancing the didactic and programmatic orientation of the Tower Society" ("Going On In," 248).

85. Curiously, Goethe prefaced "The Man of Fifty Years," in both the 1821 and substantially revised 1829 editions, with a disclaimer, insisting—as the latter edition had it—that the tale's "inner continuity . . . considered as to attitudes, emotions, and events, occasioned an uninterrupted presentation," as if the chapter breaks themselves did not count as interruptions. The irony in relation to narrative rhythm and its articulations is, here and elsewhere in the *Wanderjahre*, inscrutable. Goethe, *Wilhelm Meister's Journeyman Years*, 212.

86. "Das Leben erzählt sich ja gerade nicht, sondern es lebt sich" (Müller, *Morphologische Poetik*, 256).

87. See Bakhtin, "Bildungsroman," 17.

88. On the productive confusion between "point" and "period"—or transition and era—in the concept of epoch, see Hans Blumenberg's *Legitimacy of the Modern Age*, pp. 457–81; Reinhart Koselleck's "The Eighteenth Century as the Beginning of Modernity," p. 155; Peter Fritzsche's *Stranded in the Present*, pp. 6–18.

89. See, for instance, Goethe's 1817 "Geistesepochen," or "Stages of Man's Mind," in which the fourfold path of the self's epochs is rendered in tabular format at the essay's conclusion: "Geistesepochen," 298–300.

90. Whether Goethe actually said to defeated Prussian officers after Valmy "From this place and from this day a new epoch in world history [*eine neue Epoche der Weltgeschichte*] begins and you can say you were there to see it"—and Boyle, for one, doubts it—the terminology of "epochs" was dear to him since at least the writing of the *Italian Journey* of 1786–88. In 1787, thinking through the imminent publication of *Faust* part 1 and *Torquato Tasso*: "By that time I shall have lived through the most important period [*eine Hauptepoche*] in my life and rounded it off so neatly that I can pick up my duties again." A few weeks later, thinking back on his journey's beginning: "A year ago today I set out from Carlsbad. What a year it has been! And what a wonderful epoch began for me on the day which was both the birthday of our Duke and the birthday of my new life." And again, in January 1788, thinking ahead to his trip's conclusion, "when a definite period [*eine gewisse Epoche*] of my life will come to an end." As always, the word modulates—in fact collapses—historical and personal-historical registers; in 1786 he notes, on Roman history, how "one epoch follows upon another," and the periodizations of Italian history leave their mark on his own self-conception. See N. Boyle, *Goethe*, 128–29; Goethe, *Italian Journey*, 374, 383, 441, 133.

91. Narrative morcellation has throughout Goethe's career a bad odor—particularly in theatrical terms, with the *comédie à tiroir* or *Schubladenstück*, the play as an assemblage of scenes, as his frequent target—even as the chapter never comes in for such critique. In his translation of Diderot's *Rameau's Nephew*, a biographical note on the playwright Palissot contrasts the *Schubladenstück* with more dignified forms; and in *Elective Affinities*, Ottilie will lament that a life without love is only a *Schubladenstück*, a thing that "barely holds together" (*hängt nur kümmerlich zusammen*). See Goethe, *Rameaus Neffe*, 124; *Wahlverwandtschaften*, 195.

92. The binary I am sketching here owes something to Georges Gurvitch's description of "erratic time"—a time of present contingency, of "intervals and moments placed within duration" in which social norms collide with unexpected deviations—and "retarded time," a slower, future-oriented time appropriate to "closed groupings or those to which admission is difficult," such as the Tower Society. Both are, as Gurvitch stresses, times of historical

transition, but they operate at different scales and with different intensities. See Gurvitch, *Spectrum of Social Time*, 31–33.

93. Austen, *Persuasion*, 244. On the subject of timescales and periodization in Austen, see Michael Paulson's "Present, Period, Crisis" and Mary Favret's "Jane Austen's Periods" and *War at a Distance*, pp. 146–51, 161–72.

94. See Shields, "Zusammenhang (Nexus)."

Chapter 6

1. On the new recessiveness of the chapter heading, see my discussion in "Chapter Heads," pp. 161–64.

2. It is a comparison that has been made before, and more broadly; see Billington, *Faithful Realism*.

3. Tolstoy, *War and Peace*, 179. Subsequent references will be given parenthetically in the text, with the abbreviation *WP*.

4. The term is Galen Strawson's, from "Against Narrativity." See also Gary Saul Morson's account of Tolstoy's "polyphony of incident," which presents an argument for how "actions and events retain their radical autonomy" in *War and Peace*: Morson, *Hidden in Plain View*, 188. "Episode" as a term seems to mark not only a principle of detachability—what Fredric Jameson calls an "eternal affective present" and "the supersession of plot by scene"—but also the very dynamic between the detachable and the intrinsic that inevitably raises the question of how any given episode relates to those that surround it; as Matthew Garrett puts it, the episode is "an *integral* but also *extractable* unit of any narrative," a "relational" form negotiating between what is essential and what is excess. See Jameson, *Antinomies of Realism*, 83, 153; Garrett, *Episodic Poetics*, 3.

5. For a history-of-calculus contextualization of Tolstoy's argument, see Stephen Ahearn's "Tolstoy's Integration Metaphor from *War and Peace*." Zeno's paradox has been recently taken up in connection with Thomas Hardy by Daniel Wright: see "Thomas Hardy's Groundwork."

6. In the 1873 edition, for instance, the "parts" within the four books were eliminated and chapters were numbered continuously within each book. See Eikhenbaum, *Tolstoi in the Sixties*, 241. The Louise and Aylmer Maude translation erased the *toma* and termed the *chasti* "books," streamlining Tolstoy's schema into two levels: fifteen "books" (plus a "First" and "Second" epilogue) within which the chapters are distributed. The Maudes also replaced some chapter breaks with blank space, essentially incorporating chapters into units Tolstoy had not intended, while also providing chapter summaries in their table of contents, both reshaping and repurposing Tolstoy's chapter design into a model more familiar to an English-speaking audience. See Feuer, *Tolstoy*, 220.

7. Detecting those broader processes, unsurprisingly, has long been the goal of Tolstoyan criticism. Richard Gustafson's claim for "the paradigmatic action of the restoration of harmony" as one of these master processes, which "governs the novel not only as a whole but also in its parts," is itself a paradigm of this kind of reading; see *Leo Tolstoy*, 41. The "parts" to which Gustafson refers, however, are multichapter episodes—the book 2 passages of Natasha at the ball and the hunt—which Gustafson calls "delineated segments." The delineation is, of course, that

of the critic; the chapter form seems too partial to exemplify the larger process the critic identifies.

8. 1,285 words per chapter, to be exact—calculated with the Russian etext at https://ilibrary .ru/text/11/index.html (Tolstoy, *Voyna i mir*) The novel's shortest chapters are less than half that. What is more instructive yet is that its longest chapters, amounting to over 3,000 words, do not as a result depict whole scenes. They are either combinations of smaller scenes, as in the 3,600-word sixth chapter of book 1 part 1, which gathers the end of Anna Scherer's "at home," Andrei and Pierre's late supper, and Pierre's drunken carousing involving a bear; or swollen by subsidiary documents, as in the 3,200-word twenty-second chapter of the same part, largely devoted to an exchange of correspondence between Julie Karagin and Princess Marya Bolkonsky. Conversely, the memorable "scenes" or set pieces of the novel encompass several, often quite brief, chapters.

9. For the details of this chronological error, see Feuer (*Tolstoy*, 20, 224n30).

10. Morson is attentive to these temporal disjunctures, referring to them as "indiscernible steps" or "tiny changes," without, however, tying them to the form of the Tolstoyan chapter (*Hidden in Plain View*, 199, 221–22).

11. Bachelard, *Dialectic of Duration*, 47.

12. Doody, *True Story*, 309–12.

13. I take the term from Georges Mathieu's brief, evocative list of the "figures" of novelistic chapter openings (sunrise, waking, entering, arriving) and chapter closings (sleep, fainting, silence, exits, death). See Mathieu, "Pour une théorie," 218–19.

14. Klein, "How Time Is Encoded," 4.

15. Fludernik, "Diachronization of Narratology," 335–38.

16. See Morson's *Hidden in Plain View* (pp. 168–69) on Tolstoyan simultaneity and variability.

17. Genette, *Narrative Discourse*, 94–99, 109–12.

18. Breton, *Manifestes du surréalisme*, 19.

19. Klein, "How Time Is Encoded," 20.

20. Eikhenbaum, *Tolstoi in the Sixties*, 227–28.

21. Mathieu notes the point-of-view shift as a significant element of chapter division in Balzac and Hugo, among others ("Pour une théorie," 219).

22. Miller, *Jane Austen*, 65. Striking as the *Emma* example may be, it is not unique. Anthony Trollope, for one, repeats the feat in identical terms across the ninth and tenth chapters of *Framley Parsonage*, offering the same sentence ("And now, how was he to tell his wife?") in free indirect discourse at the end of one chapter and straight omniscience at the start of the next (pp. 112–13).

23. Grahame, *Wind in the Willows*, 61.

24. Gaskell, *Wives and Daughters*, 370. Subsequent references will be given parenthetically in the text, using the abbreviation *WD*.

25. This peculiarity of the manuscript, and of Gaskell's practice more generally, has been studied by Josie Billington; see "On Not Concluding" and *Faithful Realism*, 51–52.

26. In the case of *Wives and Daughters*, that norm—its average chapter length—is 4,489 words, with no chapters below 2,500 words and none above 7,500. Given the somewhat stricter parameters of the serial number, hovering around 15,000 words, this meant that three chapters

per installment was the norm, although other configurations were possible. But that norm must have operated as one of the several guidelines the *Cornhill*'s editors used in their segmenting of the text.

27. Yet Gaskell could and sometimes did confect her own chapter divisions, as the manuscripts of *The Life of Charlotte Bronte* and *Sylvia's Lovers* demonstrate, even if the latter also includes what look to be chapter breaks inserted after initial composition. See Billington, *Faithful Realism*, 198n17.

28. Dickens, *Letters*, 6:900. Taken from a letter dated February 27, 1850.

29. Dickens, 7:278–79. Taken from a letter dated February 18, 1854.

30. Dickens, 7:355. Dated June 17, 1854.

31. Dickens, 7:363. Dated July 2, 1854.

32. Dickens, 7:378. Dated July 26, 1854.

33. Dickens, 7:382. Dated July 31, 1854.

34. Billington calls this a "dislike of interruption," referring it to Gaskell's vision of the necessarily continuous "rhythm of life itself" (*Faithful Realism*, 51).

35. This is a critical consensus best expressed by Wendy Craik: "*Wives and Daughters* is her most agglomerate, least dissectible of novels. It does not fall into neat sections, or move to climaxes of undivided attention. Clear, coherent and perfectly connected as is all the action, structurally it is near-indivisible" (*Elizabeth Gaskell*, 227).

36. See, for instance, Linda Hughes and Michael Lund's discussion of how change comes to Molly "slowly, almost imperceptibly," and the relation of those changes to the novel's serial form (*Victorian Publishing*, 31), or Jenny Uglow's discussion of the carefully blurred calendrical scheme of the novel, which instructs us in "how one era blends into another" (*Elizabeth Gaskell*, 580).

37. Here I am giving a turn to John Plotz's argument that Victorian fictional "episodes," loosely agglomerated into a "plot," produce what he calls "semi-detachment," the moment at an episode's conclusion where its pertinence to the plot as a whole can seem only partial, in question, as yet unrevealed. In *Wives and Daughters* that "semi-detachment" arises instead out of the *refusal* of the episode and its replacement by the deliberately unplanned, thoroughly contingent, and almost aleatory quality of the chapter. See Plotz, *Semi-Detached*, 15.

Chapter 7

1. Translation mine. The text here, which would later license the neoclassical doctrine of the unity of time ("hypo mian periodon hēliou einai ē mikron exallattein"), can be taken to mean either the full twenty-four-hour period or simply the period of daylight; see Aristotle, *Poetics*, 9. The editor of this edition, Lucas, notes that twelve hours would suffice for "virtually all of Sophocles' and Euripides' plays" (94), and that several, such as Sophocles's *Electra*, begin at dawn.

2. Day's end, either in sleep or in rituals associated with the day's end, can be said to conclude *Iliad* 1, 7, 8, 9, 10, and 18, as well as *Odyssey* 1, 2, 3, 4, 5, 7, 14, 15, 16, 18, and 19. Notably, very few of these books encompass a single day only; they simply gesture to the end of a day at their conclusion. In this, they differ from the novelistic version this chapter studies, in which the relationship between chapter and day is more commonly 1:1. For more on methods of closure

in ancient internal divisions such as "books," see Don Fowler's *Roman Constructions* (pp. 251–59).

3. Apuleius, *Golden Ass or Metamorphoses*, 12–13.

4. See Junghanns, *Erzählungstechnik von Apuleius' Metamorphosen*, 126; Harrison, *Framing the Ass*, 183.

5. Auerbach, *Mimesis*, 12.

6. Bryony Randall asks, of the one-day novel such as *Mrs. Dalloway* or *Ulysses*, "what can be done in a day, and by whom?" This is, I will be arguing, exactly the question the day-chapter nexus poses in novels with a seemingly more capacious time span. See Randall, "Day's Time," 601.

7. It is particularly notable, as Ann Blair has suggested, in the sixteenth-century successors to Gellius, such as the 1522 *Dies geniales*, or "Festive days," of Alexander ab Alexandro, or Simone Maioli's 1597 *Dies caniculares*, or "Dog days." See Blair, *Too Much to Know*, 130–31.

8. Bakhtin, "Forms of Time," 248.

9. Dickens, *Pickwick*, 15.

10. Dickens, *David Copperfield*, 209–10. Subsequent references will be given parenthetically in the text with the abbreviation *DC*.

11. Krista Lysack has argued that devotional reading in the nineteenth century found itself caught between the "two chronotopes" of "liturgical time and industrial time," which nonetheless began to resemble each other in their concentration upon evening leisure time. In this way novel reading and religious reading share several structures; and as the evidence from diaries and letters gathered by Timothy Larsen shows, the chapter is still very much the unit of measurement for such Victorian Bible reading—as in the "chapter each night" model. See Lysack, "Productions of Time," 453; Larsen, *People of One Book*.

12. See S. Eliot, "Reading by Artificial Light." Eliot identifies some mid-century developments—paraffin or kerosene lamps, the safety match—that made such reading easier, without entirely eliminating the inconvenience, low visibility, and dangers attendant upon the manipulation of flammable material for light.

13. For the distinction between "empirical" time—that of the reader or listener—and the time of aesthetic forms, see Adorno (*Aesthetic Theory*, 137–38).

14. Pavel, *Lives of the Novel*, 227–28.

15. Sleep has been noted as a figure of chapter transition by Mathieu ("Pour une théorie," 219); see also Dionne, *Voix aux chapitres*, 312–13.

16. Shklovsky, *Theory of Prose*, 56.

17. Ong, *Art of Being*, 4, 16.

18. What David here performs—and Dickens's chapters invite—is a tradition of day review extending back to Cicero's recommendation in *De senectute* to "follow the practice of the Pythagoreans and run over in my mind every evening all that I have said, heard, or done during the day." Associated primarily with Seneca, the tradition of an end-of-day audit, oriented toward moral self-assessment and improvement, was taken up explicitly by early modern scholars and divines, particularly within a Calvinist strain. See Max Engammare, *On Time*, 98–99; Cicero, *De senectute*, 47.

19. As Plotz puts it, "to be caught up in a moment but also capable of pulling oneself away from that moment to reflect upon it" (*Semi-detached*, 122).

20. Koselleck, "'Space of Experience.'"

21. See particularly Philip Davis's account of Dickens's manuscript revisions to the novel, where minute adjustments are made, the addition of what Davis calls "holding words," often to disrupt temporal linearity. Davis, "Deep Reading," 73.

22. Available at https://github.com/JonathanReeve/chapterize. My thanks to Jessica Monaco for invaluable assistance in compiling and analyzing the data derived from Chapterize, and to Jonathan Reeve for training in its use.

23. Underwood, "Literary Time," 360.

24. For a good guide to the various quantifications involved in serialization, see Peter Shillingsburg's "Book Publishing and the Victorian Literary Marketplace" (p. 33).

25. See Reeve, "Fingerprinting the Chapter."

26. In this sense Victorian fiction seems to unlearn what Stuart Sherman calls the chronometry of eighteenth-century diaristic form and its close relationship to the novel of that period. Sherman concentrates on the advent of new and ever more abstract measurements (such as the clock's minute hand), which inflect the "everydayness" of the early British novel. Nor is the Victorian chapter necessarily attuned to the suddenness and particularity of the "moment" studied by Sue Zemka. See Sherman, *Telling Time*; Zemka, *Time and the Moment*.

27. "Supplementing human memory," Ted Underwood argues, "does not have to be a high-tech project" ("Literary Time," 350).

28. Le Bossu's calculation hides two important truths. The first is the interpretive scope involved in making even this seemingly simple count. Debate still exists over the number of the *Iliad*'s days, although the current consensus—from 51 to 55—seems to render his figure obsolete; at any rate, the idea of a definitive or "true" count is a chimera. The second is that Le Bossu is a late example of a tradition of narrative time reckoning in Homer stretching back to Greek scholia from the second and third centuries CE, which counted days as a way of describing the *Iliad*'s temporal design. See Nünlist, *Ancient Critic at Work*, 69–73.

29. G. Eliot, *Middlemarch*, 299. Subsequent references will be given parenthetically in the text, with the abbreviation *M*.

30. It is this particular, habitual combination in prose fiction—temporal-deictic adverbs such as "this evening" or "tomorrow" with a preterite—that Käte Hamburger adduced as proof that "the past tense of fictional narration is no statement of past-ness," that a present-like fictional reality supplants the retrospective function of the verb tense (*Logic of Literature*, 71–74, quote at 71).

31. Jonathan Crary's account of the sleepless time of globalized capital, or "24/7," describes a "cancellation of the periodicity that shaped the life of most cultures for several millennia," a gradual process Crary reads as starting in the first decades of the nineteenth century in Britain, but one that is as yet held at bay in *Middlemarch*'s world. Crary, 24/7, 29–30.

32. Bakhtin, "Forms of Time," 91–92.

33. Interestingly, to use the previous chapter's example, Gaskell's *Wives and Daughters*, while slightly less explicit in its calendrical scheme, covers approximately 1,200 days of elapsed time (from the late spring of 1827 to September 1830) and contains 163 represented days—or 14%, an oddly similar ratio. Without making any strong claims on the basis of these limited and somewhat fuzzy calculations, one might hazard that a strong disproportion between a wide temporal

frame and a small, select amount of narrated time within it is a trait of Victorian realism: not all time counts in the same way, and only a slice of it deserves attention.

34. Michon, "Compleat Time Experiencer."

35. Shklovsky, *Theory of Prose*, 154; Barthes, *Preparation of the Novel*, 40–41.

36. Deliberately so; my method here—both in terms of the small number of entities counted, and the simplicity of counting method (such as word counts)—adheres to the principle of "quantitative parsimony." As Dennis Tenen defines it: "For the purposes of literary analysis, quantitative parsimony implies a preference for modular, atomic models. . . . Complex intuitions about diegetic worlds—narrative structure—rely on a limited number of foundational building blocks, which, when articulated, can be used to construct more sophisticated analytical models with considerable explanatory potential" ("Toward a Computational Archeology," 123).

37. Blumenberg, *Legitimacy of the Modern Age*, 458–61.

38. In this sense, the day-chapter-epoch triad I outline here is different than some other significant triads in the sociology of time, such as Fernand Braudel's geographical *longue durée*, social *conjoncture*, and short-term *événements*; or Anthony Giddens's three durations of day-to-day repetition, the lifespan and its projects, and slow institutional time; or Thomas Luckmann's inner or bodily time, social or intersubjective time, and the "historical" time of biographical schemes. The primary difference is that the day-chapter-epoch triad is not any kind of constituent, nested relationship but instead a tug between imperfectly aligned, even antagonistic, structures that are nonetheless not all that dissimilar in scale. See Braudel, *Mediterranean*, 17–22; Giddens, "Time and Social Organization"; Luckmann, "Constitution of Human Life."

39. My claim here owes a debt to a specific aspect of Heideggerian thinking: that our temporality is unthinkable without a notion of "span" (*Spanne*) or unit, and that each unit we can imagine has a tension of its own, a quality that expresses not only its size or breadth but also the kind of concern it delimits. It is perhaps no unimportant coincidence that in section 80 of *Sein und Zeit*, immediately following his description of the temporal "span," Heidegger turns to what he argues is the fundamental or paradigmatic unit of our everyday concern: the day, the period of daylight, where we first learn to measure and to find in distinct time spans distinct kinds of existence. Heidegger, *Being and Time*, 458–80.

40. From an 1873 letter to Lewis Campbell: Maxwell, *Scientific Letters and Papers*, 840–41.

41. Ricoeur, *Time and Narrative*, 1:63.

42. It is a motif within Victorian fiction: the day as the fiercely limited timeframe within which certain exceptions to social norms could be experienced—as in the "perfect day" of Gissing's 1893 *The Odd Women*, the single cloudless day in the Lake District in which Everard Barfoot proposes a free, nonmarital union to Rhoda Nunn. Some flights from the conventional have only an ephemeral duration.

43. Time structures, Hartmut Rosa has argued, "perform the necessary 'translation' of systemic requirements into individual action orientations" (*Social Acceleration*, 224).

44. Taken from the transcription in Eliot's *Quarry for Middlemarch*, p. 46.

45. Eliot, 51. Brackets are present in the original.

46. See Allison, *Reductive Reading*, 61–88.

47. My sense of "preoccupation" here bears a resemblance to what Amanda Anderson has called "rumination," a nondeliberative and repetitive form of thought characterized better by its duration than its results; see Anderson, "Thinking with Character." With Anderson, I would

suggest that this directionless thinking is particularly common to the novel, even if I place its formal mechanisms somewhat differently than she does.

48. McGregor, *Reservoir 13*, 5. Subsequent references will be given parenthetically in the text, with the abbreviation *R*.

49. Eight of the novel's thirteen chapters include an extra or intercalary month-paragraph; McGregor's scheme is repetitive but not strictly regular, and the paragraphs, like the chapters, are of a moderately flexible length.

50. McGregor's first novel, *If Nobody Speaks of Remarkable Things* (2002), is a single-day story in the mode of *Ulysses* and *Mrs. Dalloway*, suggesting that he found his way to the subtler alignments of Victorian chapter design through an initial devotion to modernist time framings. On this earlier McGregor, see Randall ("Day's Time," 595–97) and Neal Alexander ("Profoundly Ordinary").

Chapter 8

1. Machado, *Quincas Borba*, 159–60. Subsequent references will be given parenthetically in the text, with the abbreviation *QB*.

2. Machado, *Posthumous Memoirs*, 28. Subsequent references will be given parenthetically in the text, with the abbreviation *PM*.

3. For a contrary account of this moment, see Earl Fitz's *Machado de Assis and Narrative Theory*, pp. 101–2. Fitz reads these chapters as articulating a conscious rejection of "traditional realistic novel form," while I am here emphasizing a mingled complicity and rejection, one that operates by affiliating itself—partially and ambivalently—with one strand of that form, a strand defined by an old-fashioned version of capitulation.

4. Candido, *On Literature and Society*, 105.

5. Schwarz, "Capitu," 72.

6. Machado, *Dom Casmurro*, 9. Subsequent references will be given parenthetically in the text with the abbreviation *Dom*.

7. As Schwarz argues, this "eccentric, even snobbish, display of bookish learning" may seem unworldly but is in fact related to "the harsh form of contemporary class society"—it has something peremptory about it (Schwarz, "Beyond Universalism," 49).

8. Machado's familiarity with the British fiction of his day was not inconsiderable; in 1870 his partial translation of *Oliver Twist* appeared as *Oliveira Twist* in *O Jornal da tarde*.

9. The phrase is Schwarz's, although the perception that with *Posthumous Memoirs* Machado had reinvented his work is a commonplace. See Schwarz, "Machadian Turning Point."

10. See the careful analysis of Ana Cláudia Suriani da Silva, who discusses the *mise en page* of Machado's chapter divisions in both serial and book forms: *"Philosopher or Dog?,"* 22–31. The page = chapter equation has been habitually ignored by Machado's translators, with the notable exception of Flora Thomson-DeVeaux's 2020 translation of the *Posthumous Memoirs*, which consciously respects it. Thomson-DeVeaux cites as inspiration the comparative study of bibliographic conventions of the *Posthumous Memoirs* by Castedo, Gruszynski, and Moraes, "Edition and Visual Culture."

11. The first edition of the novel included a third name here—Charles Lamb—that was cut in subsequent editions. See Rouanet, *Riso e melancholia*, 31–32.

12. An irony often noted: see Candido, *On Literature and Society*; Hansen, "*Dom Casmurro*"; Gledson, "*Dom Casmurro*."

13. Machado, *Esau and Jacob*, 89. Subsequent references will be given parenthetically in the text, with the abbreviation *EJ*.

14. Schwarz, *Master on the Periphery*, 156.

15. Schwarz identifies "dismissal" as a form of punctuation in Machado: "we will find the same concluding gesture in innumerable forms, ending a paragraph or chapter, dismissing some kind of aspiration or fancy," a "tic of irritation and impatience in the face of fancies and desires that have no right to exist" (Schwarz, 64).

16. On the ambiguities of Machado's racial identity and its entanglement with class status, see G. Reginald Daniel's *Machado de Assis*.

17. Over forty such uses in each of *Posthumous Memoirs*, *Dom Casmurro*, and *Esau and Jacob*, more than all but the most common nouns and proper names—the chapter is one of the most present "things" in Machado's world.

18. On Machado's chapters as sequential "traps"—"this one pulls the rug out from under that one, chapter Y belies that which was promised in chapter X, and so on"—see João Cezar de Castro Rocha's *Machado de Assis: Toward a Poetics of Emulation*, p. 197.

19. From a 1966 note to the 1953 paper "The Function and Field of Speech and Language in Psychoanalysis," the talk in which Lacan first directly confronts the practice of unpredictably terminated analytic sessions. As he notes, the *pierre de rebut* is for him also a *pierre d'angle*, a cornerstone—just as it is, in his way, for Machado. See Lacan, *Écrits*, 268.

20. One other such joke, if a much more prolonged one, is the long Sunday that begins *Quincas Borba*, occupying chapters 1–3 and 27–50 of the book edition and chapters 20–50 of the serial, which, as Silva notes, had to be spread between thirteen installments and six months of publication time. See Silva, *"Philosopher or Dog?,"* 144. As chapter 50 begins, conscious of the joke played on realist time, the narrator confesses to the reader: "No, my dear lady, that ever so long day isn't over yet" (*QB*, 68).

21. Studies of Machadian time inevitably have to find terms or images for this "nothing": for Rouanet it is "empty" or "zero time," while K. David Jackson employs the image from *Dom Casmurro* of a clock with no face but only a pendulum. See Rouanet, *Riso e melancolia*, 135–36; Jackson, *Machado de Assis*, 62–73.

22. Quoted in Coe, *Like a Fiery Elephant*, 169.

23. B. S. Johnson, *Albert Angelo*, 81. Subsequent references will be given parenthetically in the text, with the abbreviation *AA*.

24. A calculation based on the fact that Johnson labeled "first" and "last" sections, leaving twenty-five aleatory sections. Of course the reader is free to ignore even that minimal instruction, increasing the range of possibilities accordingly.

25. The text of the film and the introduction are highly similar; see B. S. Johnson, *Well Done God!*, 25; David Quantick, "The Unfortunates Part 2," YouTube, May 17, 2010, https://www .youtube.com/watch?v=UZGy3SQuPek. The film was originally broadcast as part of the BBC2 program *Release* on February 22, 1969.

26. See, e.g., Delpidge, "Bold Device."

27. As in: "For it was not until his body was appeased that he could come alive in his mind, as described in section six" (Beckett, *Murphy*, 6).

NOTES TO CHAPTER 8   333

28. See, for instance, Richard Holmes's review, "Leaves in the Wind."

29. Quoted in Coe, *Like a Fiery Elephant*, 231.

30. Hebert, "Man Inside the Box."

31. B. S. Johnson, *Well Done God!*, 25.

32. "Discontinuous" and "flowing": Barthes, *Preparation of the Novel*, 18.

33. Jameson, "Joyce or Proust?," 178.

34. For a description of that terminological problem in *Ulysses*—does it have "episodes" or "chapters"?—see Eric Bulson's *Ulysses by Numbers*, pp. 69–70.

35. Barthes, *S/Z*, 30.

36. B. S. Johnson, *Well Done God!*, 21.

37. Glyn White calls it *Trawl*'s "standardization," a feature "somewhat anomalous within Johnson's work" (*Reading the Graphic Surface*, 114).

38. B. S. Johnson, *Trawl*, 8. Subsequent references will be given parenthetically in the text, with the abbreviation *T*.

39. "I object to the word experimental being applied to my own work," Johnson wrote in 1970 at his most self-consciously artisanal; "certainly I make experiments, but the unsuccessful ones are quietly hidden away and what I choose to publish is in my sense successful—that is, it is the best way I can find of solving particular writing problems.... The relevant question is whether the device works or not" ("Disintegrating Novel (2)," 8).

40. Enough so that the novel's originally contracted publishers, Secker and Warburg, "completely nonplussed by the daunting practicalities of the idea," had to partner with the new imprint Panther Books to bring Johnson's idea into being. See Coe, *Like a Fiery Elephant*, 268–69.

41. On how for Johnson "the page remained a site to be liberated from the uniformity of standard block-print," see David James's "The (W)hole Affect," p. 36.

42. As quoted in Jonathan Coe's introduction to the novel's 2007 republication. See B. S. Johnson, *Unfortunates*, xii. Subsequent references will be given parenthetically in the text, with the abbreviation *U*, by page number and first words of the section.

43. See Ngai, *Theory of the Gimmick*, 60.

44. See Hebert, "Man Inside the Box"; Holmes, "Leaves in the Wind"; Wall, "Curious Box of Tricks."

45. Kermode, "Retripotent."

46. Wall, "Curious Box of Tricks."

47. Coe stresses Johnson's disdain for pop art and much of 1960s popular culture, and his preference for survivals of a vanishing class formation such as the music hall, as aspects of his "loyalty to a dying tradition" (*Like a Fiery Elephant*, 127–28). István Bart's comments to Coe are particularly telling:

> Bryan may look like an avant-garde writer, but what turns out, after so many years, to be his contribution is that in fact all the time he was writing a folklore, a folklore of a whole society, of this working-class past: attitudes that simply disappeared and will never come back and are gone. Even at the time he was making this world up: it was not real at the time. It was dead. There were just relics of it. He was making up a lore for himself, on which to fall back. It was quite obvious that this was the past, this was gone. Replaced by the sixties, seventies, non-partisan, non-political life where all the old working-class values were being broken down. (Coe, 409).

48. Two worthwhile explorations of Johnson's real and fantasmatic class identifications: Darlington, *British Terrorist Novels*, 103–13; Watts, "Mind Has Fuses."

49. Eco, *Open Work*.

50. It is a dynamic of remediation that plays out again in the form of the novel's 2010 BBC adaptation for radio: in its initial broadcast the sections had to be played in a fixed sequence, much like the bound Hungarian version, but once put online in digital form they could be again "randomized" (even if, hewing to the novel's design, the "first" and "last" sections were so designated). See Hand, *Listen in Terror*, 197–98.

51. The "randomness" effect has been called "superfluous" by Patrick Parrinder, "superficial" by Judith Mackrell, and "regressive" by Frank Kermode; even Johnson's close friend Zulfikhar Ghose remembered commenting to Johnson that the novel's "form is really no different than *David Copperfield*," to which Johnson responded, "Bollocks." Yet it has also had defenders, salient among them being Philip Tew, who insists that even the incomplete suppression of temporal ordering removes the "immediately apprehensible context" of sequencing and so successfully deflects aesthetic effects that require sequence, such as "suspense or tragic impulse." See Parrinder, "Pilgrim's Progress," 115; Mackrell, "B. S. Johnson," 55; Kermode, "Retripotent"; Ghose, "Bryan," 33; Tew, *B. S. Johnson*, 40.

52. For Glyn White, "the order of memories when not tied to locations in the first *fabula* is impossible to reconstruct"; but Markku Eskelinen's taxonomy of kinds of order in postmodern narrative classifies *The Unfortunates* as "fully ordered," meaning that while its *fabula* may be presented in a nonlinear fashion it is possible to completely reassemble. Occupying a middle ground, Kaye Mitchell argues that the act of reconstructing the novel's *fabula*, while a source of pleasure, is also only "contingent, subjective, and transient." See White, *Reading the Graphic Surface*, 115; Eskelinen, *Cybertext Poetics*; Mitchell, "*Unfortunates*," 63.

53. This idea, however, was not initially Johnson's; his editor David Farrer suggested the designation of a first and last section. See Coe, *Like a Fiery Elephant*, 238.

54. See Mitchell's "*The Unfortunates*," p. 63, for an analogous discussion of the novel's temporal-deictic language ("then," "at that time").

55. Coe notes in passing Johnson's love of tabular organization—such as filing cabinets of correspondence, or what one friend called his "clerk-ish" habits, nicely foregrounding the class tonality of his interest in kinds of order and preservation (*Like a Fiery Elephant*, 77).

56. White also identifies poignancy as the novel's primary affect, although he understands it differently—for him it seems to be the feeling of the sinister onrushing of time (and mortality), whereas I would emphasize it is the effect of the temporarily, even delusive, *cessation* of that onrushing that is "poignant." See White, *Reading the Graphic Surface*, 116.

57. Of *La pointe courte*, Varda said in a later interview: "The film was divided into chapters, so the two themes were never mixed together but I left open the possibility for the spectator to confront them or superpose them." See Kline, "Agnès Varda from 5 to 7," 3. The interview, by Pierre Uytterhoeven, appeared in *Positif* in 1962, shortly before the filming of *Cléo de 5 à 7*.

58. See Quart, "Agnès Varda," 6–7.

59. Kline, "Secular Grace," 24.

60. Very few have recognized the film as such; one exception is Jill Forbes, who reads it as "the exemplary Bildungsroman of May 1968 and beyond." See Forbes, "Gender and Space," 83.

61. "Ce film se déroule 'au temps présent' . . . les 'durées' sont vraies." From the preface to her screenplay: Varda, *Cléo de 5 à 7*, 8. Subsequent references will be given parenthetically in the text, with the abbreviation *C*.

62. As attested in Varda and Bastide, *Varda par Agnès*, 234. Varda insisted that the shooting schedule was for Marchand's sake—"I helped her by doing the film in the order of the screenplay, which is very rare"—although as Alison Smith points out, the interest in linear time had been part of Varda's aesthetic from the outset and marks her early work. See Varda's interview with Marie-Claire Barnet in the latter's *Agnès Varda Unlimited*, p. 203, and A. Smith, *Agnès Varda*, 142.

63. See Valerie Orpen's account of the shooting schedule in *Cléo de 5 à 7*, pp. 9–10, 23.

64. An "approximate rather than strict" equivalence between labeled and actual chapter times: see Ungar, *Cléo de 5 à 7*, 33.

65. On card cutting and filmic cutting: Hardy, "Agnès Varda's *Cléo*," 33. Hardy comments that Irma's instruction to "cut" might just as well be addressed to Varda herself, or at least Janine Verneau, the film's editor. The *card*, however, continued to have a significant presence in experimentally formatted narratives interested in aleatory sequence, as in Edward Gorey's *The Helpless Doorknob* (1989), Robert Coover's "Heart Suit" (2005), or Jedediah Berry's *The Family Arcana: A Story in Cards* (2015). A narrative made of separate cards can always be reshuffled. Madame Irma's cards, however, have an inexorable, unalterable sequence.

66. Orpen, *Cléo de 5 à 7*, 28.

67. Orpen notes that Varda is oversimplifying her own procedure here: "other subjectivities intrude in chapters that should in theory focus on just one" (34).

68. Not just little episodes, but other kinds of little timed experiences as well: the radio news report that plays in the taxi in chapter 4—the actual broadcast that played on Europe 1 on June 21, 1961—starts with the announcement that it is 17:20, then later 17:22, a short slice of contemporaneity that also confirms the accuracy, or honesty, of the film's time scheme. See Orpen, 17–18.

69. Sandy Flitterman-Lewis comments, on the latter claim, that chapter 12 actually comprises two long shots "joined by a cut that violates the 180-degree rule," significantly dividing this "long breath." See Flitterman-Lewis, *To Desire Differently*, 284.

70. From Kline's translation of a 1962 interview with Michel Capdenac: "Agnès Varda: The Hour of Truth," p. 19.

71. Bordwell, *Narration*, 158.

72. Meaning a middle ground, or productive confusion, between the sixth and seventh categories in Metz's famous eight-part syntagmatic chain. See Metz, *Film Language*, 130–33

73. Varda and Bastide, *Varda par Agnès*, 14.

74. As Roy Jay Nelson describes it, through their "semiotic separateness as 'symbolic' signs (in the Peircian sense) in what is essentially an iconic and indexical medium, these titles seem a direct message from the scenarist herself": see Nelson, "Reflections," 736.

75. Condensed into Varda's image dichotomy here is not just a subjective/objective relation but also the Bergsonian distinction between *durée* and *temps*—here not in a hierarchy but in a complicated simultaneity. See Bloch, "*Cléo de 5 à 7*."

76. A connection discussed by Forbes, who also notes that the street where Cléo lives, rue Huyghens, is named after the Dutch physicist who worked for a time at the observatory and is credited with inventing the pendulum clock. See Forbes, "Gender and Space," 88.

77. The bubble: it is how Corinne Marchand fondly remembered the film's shooting on its fiftieth anniversary. Asked if anything about the role had scared her, she answered: "Rester dans cette bulle merveilleuse que vous offre un tournage jusqu'à s'y noyer de bonheur! Pourquoi avoir peur!" (To stay inside that wonderful bubble that surrounds you while filming until you drown in happiness! Why be afraid?). Her response—there was no need to be afraid in the bubble, where time is suspended—was, perhaps unconsciously, reminiscent of Cléo's own trajectory. See Barnet, "Cléo's 50th Birthday," 199.

78. It is a fact about *Cléo* most elegantly formulated by Jean-Yves Bloch: the more respect is given to objective time, the more time becomes subjectivized. My argument here is that this dialectic is not fully palpable in the film until its final, elongated chapter. See Bloch, "*Cléo de 5 à 7*," 123–24.

79. Flitterman-Lewis's reading is the best representative of this consensus; for her, Cléo develops from "woman-as-spectacle" to "woman-as-social-being," a transformation from "narcissistic containment" to "empathy" centered on chapter 7, the singing of "Sans toi," the removal of her wig, change into her black dress, and abandonment of Angèle. See Flitterman-Lewis, *To Desire Differently*, 270–73.

Post Chapter

1. U. Johnson, *Anniversaries*, 2:1488–89.

2. U. Johnson, 2:1497.

3. "Chapter," or *Kapitel*, is in fact the term commonly applied to the novel's units. For a treatment of the analogues of these "chapters" as calendrical rather than diaristic, see D. G. Bond's *German History and German Identity*, pp. 87–128.

4. An instance: the print version of Chang-rae Lee's 2014 *On Such a Full Sea* is divided into twenty-six units, each introduced by an identical graphic device, without numeration or heading. Yet the electronic editions available on Google Books and the EBSCO platform produce a "Table of Contents" in which these units are listed as "Chapter 1" and following. The digital version, that is, needs indexical segmentation, and produces it by returning to the old form of the "chapter" that the print version had attempted to avoid. My thanks to Denise Cruz for pointing me to this specific example.

5. Vandendorpe, *From Papyrus to Hypertext*, 39.

6. See Bordwell, "Intensified Continuity"; Goble, "How the West Slows Down."

7. See Self, "Literary Influences."

8. It might look, that is, like the time that Jonathan Crary calls "24/7": "a generalized inscription of human life into duration without breaks, defined by a principle of continuous functioning" (24/7, 8).

9. Flusser, "Typewriters," 62.

10. Michael Dango has argued that although the novel-of-short-stories genealogy is one possible model for *Goon Squad*, its chapters, particularly their endings, rebel against that isolating framing ("Filtering").

11. Egan, "Rumpus Interview."

12. Egan, *Goon Squad*, 101. Subsequent references will be given parenthetically in the text, with the abbreviation *GS*.

13. Kreilkamp, *"Goon Squad" Reread*, 8.

14. See Egan, "This Is All Artificial."

15. The ways in which PowerPoint is both mobilized as a futuristic mode and also banalized in the process is charted by Zara Dinnen in *The Digital Banal*, pp. 149–51.

16. Kreilkamp, *"Goon Squad" Reread*, 107.

17. Krasznahorkai, *Chasing Homer*, 26.

BIBLIOGRAPHY

Adorno, Theodor. *Aesthetic Theory.* Translated by Robert Hullot-Kentor. Minneapolis: University of Minnesota Press, 1998.

Agamben, Giorgio. *Idea of Prose.* Translated by Michael Sullivan and Sam Whitsitt. Albany: State University of New York Press, 1995.

Ahearn, Stephen. "Tolstoy's Integration Metaphor from *War and Peace.*" *American Mathematical Monthly* 112 (2005): 631–38.

Aland, Kurt, and Barbara Aland. *The Text of the New Testament: An Introduction to the Critical Editions and to the Theory and Practice of Modern Textual Criticism.* Translated by Erroll Rhodes. Grand Rapids, MI: Eerdmans, 1995.

Alexander, Neal. "Profoundly Ordinary: Jon McGregor and Everyday Life." *Contemporary Literature* 54, no. 4 (2013): 720–51.

Allison, Sarah. *Reductive Reading: A Syntax of Victorian Moralizing.* Baltimore, MD: Johns Hopkins University Press, 2018.

Anderson, Amanda. "Thinking with Character." In *Character: Three Inquiries in Literary Studies,* edited by Amanda Anderson, Rita Felski, and Toril Moi. Chicago: University of Chicago Press. 127–40.

Andrews, William. *To Tell a Free Story: The First Century of Afro-American Autobiography, 1760–1865.* Urbana: University of Illinois Press, 1988.

Apuleius. *The Golden Ass or Metamorphoses.* Translated by E. J. Kenney. London: Penguin, 1998.

Aravamudan, Srinivas. *Tropicopolitans: Colonialism and Agency, 1688–1804.* Durham, NC: Duke University Press, 1999.

Aristotle. *Poetics.* Edited by D. W. Lucas. Oxford: Clarendon, 1968.

Arns, Paolo Evaristo. *La technique du livre d'après Saint Jérôme.* Paris: De Boccard, 1953.

Arsic, Branka. *On Leaving: A Reading in Emerson.* Cambridge, MA: Harvard University Press, 2010.

Aubin, Penelope. *The Noble Slaves: or, the Lives and Adventures of Two Lords and Two Ladies, Who were Shipwrecked; and cast upon a desolate Island, near the East Indies; in the Year 1710.* Dublin, 1722.

Auerbach, Erich. *Mimesis: The Representation of Reality in Western Literature.* Translated by Willard Trask. Princeton, NJ: Princeton University Press, 1953.

Augustine. *Confessions.* Translated by Henry Chadwick. Oxford: Oxford University Press, 1991.

———. *Confessions Volume I: Introduction and Text.* Edited by James O'Donnell. Oxford: Clarendon, 1992.

———. *Letters 1*–29**. Translated by Robert Eno. The Fathers of the Church vol. 81. Washington, DC: Catholic University of America, 1989.

Austen, Jane. *Persuasion*. Edited by Janet Todd and Antje Blank. Cambridge: Cambridge University Press, 2006.

Bachelard, Gaston. *The Dialectic of Duration*. Translated by Mary McAllester Jones. London: Bowman and Littlefield, 2000.

Bagnall, Roger. *Early Christian Books in Egypt*. Princeton, NJ: Princeton University Press, 2009.

Bakhtin, M. M. "The Bildungsroman and Its Significance in the History of Realism (Toward a Historical Typology of the Novel)." Translated by Vern McGee. In *Speech Genres and Other Late Essays*, edited by Caryl Emerson and Michael Holquist, 10–59. Austin: University of Texas Press, 1986.

———. "Forms of Time and Chronotope in the Novel." In *The Dialogic Imagination*, translated by Caryl Emerson and Michael Holquist, 84–258. Austin: University of Texas Press, 1981.

Baraitser, Lisa. *Enduring Time*. London: Bloomsbury, 2017.

Barchas, Janine. *Graphic Design, Print Culture, and the Eighteenth-Century Novel*. Cambridge: Cambridge University Press, 2003.

Barletta, Vincent. *Rhythm: Form and Dispossession*. Chicago: University of Chicago Press, 2020.

Barnes, Timothy. *Constantine and Eusebius*. Cambridge, MA: Harvard University Press, 1981.

Barnet, Marie-Claire. "Agnès Varda's Interview: Verbal Ping-Pong and Matching Points." In *Agnès Varda Unlimited: Image, Music, Media*, edited by Barnet, 203–9. Cambridge, UK: Legenda, 2016.

———. "Cléo's 50th Birthday: Questions-Answers." In *Agnès Varda Unlimited: Image, Music, Media*, edited by Barnet, 197–202. Cambridge, UK: Legenda, 2016.

Barthélemy, Dominique. "Les traditions anciennes de division du texte biblique de la Torah." In *Κατὰ τοὺς ὁ: "Selon les Septante": Trois études sur la Bible grecque des Septante, en hommage à Marguerite Harl*, edited by Gilles Dorival and Olivier Munnich, 27–51. Paris: Éditions du Cerf, 1995.

Barthes, Roland. "Introduction to the Structural Analysis of Narrative." In *Image, Music, Text*, translated by Stephen Heath, 79–124. New York: Hill and Wang, 1977.

———. *The Preparation of the Novel: Lecture Courses and Seminars at the Collège de France (1978–1979 and 1979–1980)*. Translated by Kate Briggs. New York: Columbia University Press, 2011.

———. *S/Z: An Essay*. Translated by Richard Miller. New York: Hill and Wang, 1974.

Beckett, Samuel. *Murphy*. London: Calder, 1998.

Bede. *The Reckoning of Time*. Translated by Faith Wallis. Liverpool: Liverpool University Press, 1999.

Berger, John. *G*. New York: Vintage, 1992.

Bible, in Two Volumes, with Prologues and Interpretation of Hebrew Names. British Library Add MS 18720.

Billington, Josie. *Faithful Realism: Elizabeth Gaskell and Leo Tolstoy; A Comparative Study*. Lewisburg, PA: Bucknell University Press, 2002.

———. "On Not Concluding: Realist Prose as Practical Reason in Gaskell's *Wives and Daughters*." *Gaskell Journal* 30 (2016): 23–40.

Birdsall, J. N. "The New Testament Text." In *The Cambridge History of the Bible: From the Beginnings to Jerome*, edited by P. H. Ackroyd and C. F. Evans, 308–77. Cambridge: Cambridge University Press, 2008.

Black, Stephanie. *Sentence Conjunctions in the Gospel of Matthew: Kai, De, Tote, Gar, Oun and Asyndeton in Narrative Discourse.* London: Sheffield Academic, 2002.

Blackwall, Anthony. *The Sacred Classics Defended and Illustrated.* Vol. 2. London, 1731.

Blair, Ann. *Too Much to Know: Managing Scholarly Information before the Modern Age.* New Haven, CT: Yale University Press, 2011.

Blake, N. F. *Caxton and His World.* London: Andre Deutsch, 1969.

———. "Caxton at Work: A Reconsideration." In *The Malory Debate: Essays on the Texts of "Le Morte Darthur,"* edited by Bonnie Wheeler, Robert Kendrick, and Michael Salda, 233–54. Cambridge, UK: D. S. Brewer, 2000.

Bloch, Jean-Yves. "*Cléo de 5 à 7*: Le violon et le métronome." *Études cinématographiques* 179–86 (1991): 119–39.

Blomkvist, Vemund. *Euthalian Traditions: Text, Translation and Commentary.* Berlin: de Gruyter, 2012.

Blumenberg, Hans. *The Legitimacy of the Modern Age.* Translated by Robert Wallace. Cambridge, MA: MIT Press, 1983.

Bond, D. G. *German History and German Identity: Uwe Johnson's "Jahrestage."* Amsterdam: Rodopi, 1993.

Bordwell, David. "Intensified Continuity: Visual Style in Contemporary American Film." *Film Quarterly* 55, no. 3 (2002): 16–28.

———. *Narration in the Fiction Film.* Madison: University of Wisconsin Press, 1985.

Bower, Gordon, John Black, and Terrence Turner. "Scripts in Memory for Text." *Cognitive Psychology* 11 (1979): 177–220.

Boyle, Nicholas. *Goethe: The Poet and the Age.* Vol. 2, *Revolution and Renunciation (1970–1803).* Oxford: Clarendon, 2000.

Boyle, Robert. *Some Considerations Touching the Style of the Holy Scriptures, Extracted from several parts of a Discourse (concerning divers Particulars belonging to the Bible) written divers Years since to a Friend.* London, 1661.

Boynton, Susan, and Diane Reilly, eds. *The Practice of the Bible in the Middle Ages.* New York: Columbia University Press, 2011.

Braudel, Fernand. *The Mediterranean and the Mediterranean World in the Age of Philip II.* Translated by Siân Reynolds. Vol. 1. New York: Harper and Row, 1972.

Braungart, Georg, Harald Fricke, Klaus Grubmüller, Jan-Dirk Müller, Friedrich Vollhardt, and Klaus Weimar, eds. *Reallexikon der deutschen Literaturwissenschaft.* Vol. 2. Berlin: de Gruyter, 2003.

Bray, John, Miriam Handley, and Anne C. Henry, eds. *Ma(r)king the Text: The Presentation of Meaning on the Literary Page.* Aldershot, UK: Ashgate, 2000.

Brennan, Teresa. *The Transmission of Affect.* Ithaca, NY: Cornell University Press, 2004.

Bretelle-Establet, Florence, and Stéphane Schmitt, eds. *Pieces and Parts in Scientific Texts.* Cham, Switzerland: Springer, 2018.

Breton, André. *Manifestes du surréalisme.* Paris: Jean-Jacques Pauvert, 1962.

Brontë, Charlotte. *Jane Eyre.* Edited by Stevie Davies. London: Penguin, 2006.

Brown, Marshall. "Plan vs Plot: Chapter Symmetries and the Mission of Form." *Stanford Literary Review* 4 (1987): 103–36.

Bugg, John. "Equiano's Trifles." *ELH* 80 (2013): 1045–66.

———. "The Other Interesting Narrative: Olaudah Equiano's Public Book Tour." *PMLA* 121 (2006): 1424–42.

Bulson, Eric. *Ulysses by Numbers*. New York: Columbia University Press, 2020.

Bultmann, Rudolf. *The History of the Synoptic Tradition*. Translated by John Marsh. Oxford: Blackwell, 1963.

Butler, Shane. "Cicero's *Capita*." In *The Roman Paratext: Frame, Texts, Readers*, edited by Laura Jansen, 73–111. Cambridge: Cambridge University Press, 2014.

Candido, Antonio. *On Literature and Society*. Translated by Howard Becker. Princeton, NJ: Princeton University Press, 1995.

Carretta, Vincent. *Equiano the African: Biography of a Self-Made Man*. Athens: University of Georgia Press, 2005.

Carrington, Philip. *According to Mark: A Running Commentary on the Oldest Gospel*. Cambridge: Cambridge University Press, 1960.

Carroll, Lewis. *Sylvie and Bruno*. London: Macmillan, 1889.

Carruthers, Mary. *The Book of Memory: A Study of Memory in Medieval Culture*. Cambridge: Cambridge University Press, 1990.

Cassiodorus Senator, Flavius Magnus Aurelius. *Cassiodorus: "Institutions of Divine and Secular Learning" and "On the Soul."* Translated by James Halpern. Liverpool: Liverpool University Press, 2004.

Castedo, Raquel da Silva, Ana Gruszynski, and André Moraes. "Edition and Visual Culture: *Brás Cubas* and Its Multiple Incarnations." *Comunicação, mídia e consumo* 10 (2013): 49–70.

Cavallo, Guglielmo. "On Rolls, Codices and Other Aspects of Ancient and Medieval Written Culture." In *The Shape of the Book: From Roll to Codex (3rd Century BC–19th Century AD)*, edited by Franca Arduini, 9–23. Florence: Mandragora, 2008.

Caxton's Mirror of the World. Translated by William Caxton. Edited by Oliver Prior. Early English Text Society Extra series 110. London: Kegan Paul, Trench, Trübner, 1913.

Chappell, Warren, and Robert Bringhurst. *A Short History of the Printed Word*. 2nd ed. Point Roberts, WA: Hartley and Marks, 1999.

Chartier, Roger. "Languages, Books, and Reading from the Printed Word to the Digital Text." *Critical Inquiry* 31 (2004): 133–52.

Chatman, Seymour. *Story and Discourse: Narrative Structure in Fiction and Film*. Ithaca, NY: Cornell University Press, 1978.

Chrétien de Troyes. *Cligés*. Edited by Stewart Gregory and Claude Luttrell. Cambridge, UK: D. S. Brewer, 1993.

———. *Cligès*. Translated by Ruth Harwood Cline. Athens: University of Georgia Press, 2000.

———. *Erec and Enide*. Translated by Dorothy Gilbert. Berkeley: University of California Press, 1992.

———. *Erec et Enide*. Edited by Mario Roques. Paris: Librairie Ancienne Honoré Champion, 1955.

Chrétien de Troyes in Prose: The Burgundian "Erec" and "Cligés." Translated by Joan Tasker Grimbert and Carol Chase. Cambridge, UK: D. S. Brewer, 2011.

Chronicles of England. London, 1480. STC 9991. Early English Books Online. https://www.eebo.chadwyck.com.

Cicero. *De inventione, De optimo genere oratorum, Topica*. Translated by H. M. Hubbell. LCL 386. Cambridge, MA: Harvard University Press, 1949.

———. *De senectute, De amicitia, De divinatione*. Translated by William Falconer. LCL 154. Cambridge, MA: Harvard University Press, 1923.

Clark, Gillian. "City of Books: Augustine and the World as Text." In *The Early Christian Book*, edited by William Klingshirn and Linda Safran, 117–38. Washington, DC: Catholic University of America Press, 2007.

Clune, Michael. *Writing against Time*. Stanford, CA: Stanford University Press, 2013.

Codex Alexandrinus (Gregory-Aland 02), Bible in Four Volumes: Volume 4 (New Testament). British Library Digitized Manuscripts. Royal MS 1 D VIII. http://www.bl.uk/manuscripts/FullDisplay.aspx?ref=Royal_MS_1_d_viii.

Codex Alexandrinus (Royal MS. 1 D V–VIII) in Reduced Photographic Facsimile: New Testament and Clementine Epistles. London: Trustees of the British Museum, 1909.

Codex Amiatinus: Novum Testamentum Latine interprete Hieronymo. Ex celeberrimo codice Amiatino omnium et antichissimo et praesstantissimo nunc primus edidit. Edited by Constantine Tischendorf. Leipzig: Avenarius and Mendelssohn, 1854.

Codex Vaticanus Graecae 1209. Biblioteca Apostolica Vaticana. MS Vat.gr.1209. https://digi.vatlib.it/view/MSS_Vat.gr.1209.

Coe, Jonathan. *Like a Fiery Elephant: The Story of B. S. Johnson*. New York: Continuum, 2005.

Colombo Timelli, Maria, ed. *"Cligès": Le livre de Alixandre Empereur de Constentinoble et de Cligés son filz; Roman en prose du XVe siècle*. Geneva: Droz, 2004.

———. *"Erec et Cligés en prose: Quelques repères pour une comparaison." Moyen français* 51, no. 3 (2002–3): 159–75.

———, ed. *"Erec": L'histoire d'Erec en prose; Roman du XVe siècle*. Geneva: Droz, 2000.

———. "Syntaxe et technique narrative: Titres et attaques de chapitre dans l'*Erec* Bourguignon." *Fifteenth-Century Studies* 24 (1998): 208–30.

Columella, Lucius Junius Moderatus. *Columella on Agriculture: "De re rustica."* Translated by E. S. Forster and Edward Heffner. 3 vols. Cambridge, MA: Loeb Classical Library, 1979.

Coogan, Jeremiah. "Transforming Textuality: Porphyry, Eusebius, and Late Ancient Tables of Contents." *Studies in Late Antiquity* 5 (2021): 6–27.

Cooper, Helen. "Opening Up the Malory Manuscript." In *The Malory Debate: Essays on the Texts of "Le Morte Darthur,"* edited by Bonnie Wheeler, Robert Kindrick, and Michael Salda, 255–84. Cambridge, UK: D. S. Brewer, 2000.

Coventry, Francis. *An Essay on the New Species of Writing Founded by Mr. Fielding: With a Word or Two upon the Modern State of Criticism*. London, 1751.

———. *The History of Pompey the Little: or, the Adventures of a Lap-Dog*. London, 1751.

Craik, Wendy. *Elizabeth Gaskell and the English Provincial Novel*. London: Methuen, 1975.

Crain, Andrew Downer. *The Ford Presidency: A History*. Jefferson, NC: Macfarland, 2009.

Crary, Jonathan. *24/7: Late Capitalism and the Ends of Sleep*. London: Verso, 2013.

Crawford, M. H. *Roman Statutes*. 2 vols. London: Institute for Classical Studies, 1996.

Croucher, Sheila. *Globalization and Belonging: The Politics of Identity in a Changing World*. Lanham, MD: Rowman and Littlefield, 2018.

Cugoano, Ottobah. *Thoughts and Sentiments on the Evil and Wicked Traffic of the Slavery and Commerce of the Human Species*. London, 1787.

Da, Nan. "Lao She, James, and Reading Time." *Henry James Review* 34 (2013): 285–95.

Dames, Nicholas. "Chapter Heads." In *Book Parts*, edited by Dennis Duncan and Adam Smyth, 151–64. Oxford: Oxford University Press, 2019.

———. "Trollope's Chapters." *Literature Compass* 7/9 (2010): 855–60.

Dango, Michael. "Filtering: A Theory and History of a Style." *New Literary History* 51 (2020): 177–207.

Daniel, G. Reginald. *Machado de Assis: Multiracial Identity and the Brazilian Novelist.* University Park: Penn State University Press, 2012.

Darlington, Joseph. *British Terrorist Novels of the 1970s.* Cham, Switzerland: Palgrave Macmillan, 2018.

Davidson, Cathy. "Olaudah Equiano, Written by Himself." *Novel: A Forum on Fiction* 40 (2006–7): 18–51.

Davies, Martin. "Making Sense of Pliny in the Quattrocento." *Renaissance Studies* 9 (1995): 240–57.

Davis, Philip. "Deep Reading in the Manuscripts: Dickens and the Manuscript of *David Copperfield.*" In *Reading and the Victorians*, edited by Matthew Bradley and Juliet John, 65–77. Farnham, UK: Ashgate, 2015.

Deacon, Richard. *A Biography of William Caxton: The First English Editor, Printer, Merchant and Translator.* London: Muller, 1976.

de Bruyne, Donatien. "Quelques documents nouveaux pour l'histoire du texte Africain." *Revue bénédictine* 27 (1910): 273–324.

———. *Summaries, Divisions, and Rubrics of the Latin Bible.* Edited by Pierre-Maurice Bogaert and Thomas O'Loughlin. Turnhout, Belgium: Brepols, 2014.

Delany, Samuel. *The American Shore: Meditations on a Tale of Science Fiction by Thomas M. Disch—"Angouleme."* Middletown, CT: Wesleyan University Press, 2014.

Delpidge, David. "Author with a Bold Device." *Books and Bookmen* 13 (1967): 12–13.

De Quincey, Thomas. *Autobiographical Sketches.* Boston, 1853.

d'Esneval, Amaury. "La division de la Vulgate latine en chapitres dans l'édition parisienne du XIIIe siècle." *Revue des sciences philosophiques et théologiques* 62 (1978): 559–68.

De Voogd, Peter. "*Tristram Shandy* as Aesthetic Object." In *Laurence Sterne's "Tristram Shandy": A Casebook*, edited by Thomas Keymer, 108–19. Oxford: Oxford University Press, 2006.

Dickens, Charles. *David Copperfield.* Edited by Jeremy Tambling. London: Penguin, 1996.

———. *The Letters of Charles Dickens.* Edited by Madeline House, Graham Story, and Kathleen Tillotson. Vols. 6 and 7. Oxford: Clarendon, 1988–1993.

———. *The Posthumous Papers of the Pickwick Club.* Edited by Mark Wormald. London: Penguin, 1999.

Dimock, Wai Chee. "Nonbiological Clock: Literary History against Newtonian Mechanics." *South Atlantic Quarterly* 102 (2003): 153–77.

———. *Through Other Continents: American Literature across Deep Time.* Princeton, NJ: Princeton University Press, 2008.

Dinnen, Zara. *The Digital Banal: New Media and American Literature and Culture.* New York: Columbia University Press, 2018.

Dionne, Ugo. *La voie aux chapitres: Poétique de la disposition romanesque.* Paris: Seuil, 2008.

Doddridge, Philip. *The Family Expositor: or, A Paraphrase and Version of the New Testament.* Vol. 2. London, 1740.

Doody, Aude. "Finding Facts in Pliny's Encyclopedia: The Summarium of the *Natural History.*" *Ramus* 30 (2001): 1–22.

———. *Pliny's Encyclopedia: The Reception of the "Natural History."* Cambridge: Cambridge University Press, 2010.

Doody, Margaret Anne. *The True Story of the Novel.* New Brunswick, NJ: Rutgers University Press, 1997.

Doutrepont, Georges. *Les mises en prose des épopées et des romans chevaleresques du XIVe au XVIe siècle.* Brussels: Palais des Académies, 1939.

Doyle, Laura. *Freedom's Empire: Race and the Rise of the Novel in Atlantic Modernity, 1640–1940.* Durham, NC: Duke University Press, 2008.

Drucker, Johanna. "Reading Interface." *PMLA* 128 (2013): 213–20.

———. *SpecLab: Digital Aesthetics and Projects in Speculative Computing.* Chicago: University of Chicago Press, 2009.

Drury, John, ed. *Critics of the Bible, 1724–1873.* Cambridge: Cambridge University Press, 1989.

Drury, Joseph. *Novel Machines: Technology and Narrative Form in Enlightenment Britain.* Oxford: Oxford University Press, 2017.

du Pin, Louis Ellies. *A Compleat History of the Canon and Writers of the Books of the Old and New Testament, By Way of Dissertation: With Useful Remarks on that Subject.* 2 vols. London, 1699.

———. *Dissertation préliminaire, ou prolégomènes sur la Bible.* 2 vols. Paris, 1699.

Duranti, Alessandro, and Charles Goodwin, eds. *Rethinking Context: Language as an Interactive Phenomenon.* Cambridge: Cambridge University Press, 1992.

Dürrenmatt, Jacques. "Un problème de division: Ou comment Sterne et Diderot chapitrèrent le roman." *Poétique* 96 (1993): 415–31.

Dyson, Henry. *Prolepsis and Ennoia in the Early Stoa.* Berlin: de Gruyter, 2009.

Eco, Umberto. *The Open Work.* Translated by Anna Cancogni. Cambridge, MA: Harvard University Press, 1989.

Edwards, James. "The Hermeneutical Significance of Chapter Divisions in Ancient Gospel Manuscripts." *New Testament Studies* 56 (2010): 413–26.

Edwards, Mark, trans. *Neoplatonic Saints: The Lives of Plotinus and Proclus by Their Students.* Liverpool: Liverpool University Press, 2000.

Egan, Jennifer. "The Rumpus Interview with Jennifer Egan." Interview by Alec Michod. *Rumpus*, June 23, 2010. https://therumpus.net/2010/06/the-rumpus-interview-with-jennifer-egan/.

———. "This Is All Artificial: An Interview with Jennifer Egan." Interview by Zara Dinnen. *Post45*, May 20, 2016. https://post45.org/2016/05/this-is-all-artificial-an-interview-with-jennifer-egan/.

———. *A Visit from the Goon Squad.* New York: Anchor, 2010.

Eikhenbaum, Boris. *Tolstoi in the Sixties.* Translated by Duffield White. Ann Arbor, MI: Ardis, 1982.

Eliot, George. *Middlemarch.* Edited by Rosemary Ashton. London: Penguin, 1994.

———. *Quarry for Middlemarch.* Edited by Anna Theresa Kitchel. Berkeley: University of California Press, 1950.

Eliot, Simon. "Reading by Artificial Light in the Victorian Age." In *Reading and the Victorians*, edited by Matthew Bradley and Juliet John, 15–30. Farnham, UK: Ashgate, 2015.

Ellicott, Charles John, ed. *A New Testament Commentary for Modern Readers, by Various Writers.* Vol. 1. London: Cassell, Petter and Gilpin, 1905.

Engammare, Max. *On Time, Punctuality, and Discipline in Early Modern Calvinism.* Cambridge: Cambridge University Press, 2010.

Epictetus. *Discourses: Book I.* Edited by Robert Dobbin. Oxford: Clarendon, 1998.

———. *Discourses, Fragments, Handbook.* Translated by Robin Head. Oxford: Oxford University Press, 2014.

———. *Entretiens.* Translated by Joseph Souilhé. Vol. 1. Paris: Les Belles Lettres, 1975.

Equiano, Olaudah. *The "Interesting Narrative" and Other Writings.* Edited by Vincent Carretta. Harmondsworth, UK: Penguin, 1995.

Eskelinen, Markku. *Cybertext Poetics: The Critical Landscape of New Media Literary Theory.* London: Continuum, 2012.

Eusebius of Caesarea. *Histoire ecclésiastique.* Edited by Gustave Bardy. 4 vols. Sources Chrétiennes vols. 31, 41, 55, 73. Paris: Éditions du Cerf, 1952–60.

Ezzyat, Youssef, and Lila Davachi. "What Constitutes an Episode in Episodic Memory?" *Psychological Science* 22, no. 2 (2011): 243–52.

Favret, Mary. "Jane Austen's Periods." *Novel: A Forum on Fiction* 42 (2009): 373–79.

———. *War at a Distance: Romanticism and the Making of Modern Wartime.* Princeton, NJ: Princeton University Press, 2010.

Felski, Rita, and Susan Fraiman. "Introduction." *New Literary History* 43, no. 3 (2012): v–xii.

Ferguson, Frances. "Dissenting Textualism: The Claims of Psychological Method in the Long Romantic Period." *Studies in Romanticism* 49 (2010): 577–99.

———. "Jane Austen, *Emma*, and the Impact of Form." *Modern Language Quarterly* 61, no. 1 (2000): 157–80.

Ferruolo, Stephen. "*Parisius-Paradisus*: The City, Its Schools. and the Origins of the University of Paris." In *The University and the City: From Medieval Origins to the Present*, edited by Thomas Bender, 22–46. Oxford: Oxford University Press, 1988.

Fessenbecker, Patrick. "In Defense of Paraphrase." *New Literary History* 44, no. 1 (2013): 117–39.

Feuer, Kathryn. *Tolstoy and the Genesis of "War and Peace."* Edited by Robin Feuer Miller and Donna Tussing Orwin. Ithaca, NY: Cornell University Press, 1996.

Fielding, Henry. *Amelia.* Edited by Martin Battestin. Middletown and Oxford: Wesleyan University Press and Clarendon, 1984.

———. *The History of the Adventures of Joseph Andrews.* Edited by Martin Battestin. Middletown and Oxford: Wesleyan University Press and Clarendon, 1967.

———. *The History of Tom Jones, a Foundling.* Edited by Martin Battestin and Fredson Bowers. Middletown and Oxford: Wesleyan University Press and Clarendon, 1974.

Fink, Peter. "The Evolution of Order in the Chapter Lengths of Trollope's Novels." *Literary and Linguistic Computing* 21, no. 3 (2006): 275–82.

Fitz, Earl. *Machado de Assis and Narrative Theory: Language, Imitation, Art, and Verisimilitude in the Last Six Novels.* Lewisburg, PA: Bucknell University Press, 2019.

Flatley, Jonathan. *Affective Mapping: Melancholia and the Politics of Modernism*. Cambridge, MA: Harvard University Press, 2008.

Flitterman-Lewis, Sandy. *To Desire Differently: Feminism and the French Cinema*. Urbana: University of Illinois Press, 1990.

Flores, R. M. "Cervantes at Work: The Writing of *Don Quixote*, Part I." *Journal of Hispanic Philology* 3 (1979): 133–60.

Fludernik, Monica. "The Diachronization of Narratology." *Narrative* 11 (2003): 331–48.

———. "Metanarrative and Metafictional Commentary: From Metadiscursivity to Metanarration and Metafiction." *Poetica* 35 (2003): 1–39.

Flusser, Vilém. "On the End of History." In *Writings*, translated by Erik Eisel, 143–49. Minneapolis: University of Minnesota Press, 2002.

———. "Why Do Typewriters Go 'Click'?" In *The Shape of Things: A Philosophy of Design*, translated by Anthony Matthews, 62–65. London: Reaktion, 1999.

Forbes, Jill. "Gender and Space in *Cléo de 5 à 7*." *Studies in French Cinema* 2 (2002): 83–89.

Forster, E. M. *Aspects of the Novel*. New York: Harcourt, Brace and World, 1956.

The Four Gospels, Translated from the Greek. Translated by George Campbell. Vol. 1. London, 1789.

Fowler, Don. *Roman Constructions: Readings in Postmodern Latin*. Oxford: Oxford University Press, 2000.

Fowler, Robert. *Let the Reader Understand: Reader-Response Criticism and the Gospel of Mark*. Harrisburg, PA: Trinity, 1996.

Fox, Adam. *John Mill and Richard Bentley: A Study of the Textual Criticism of the New Testament, 1675–1729*. Oxford: Blackwell, 1954.

Frampton, Stephanie Ann. *Empire of Letters: Writing in Roman Literature and Thought from Lucretius to Ovid*. Oxford: Oxford University Press, 2019.

Frede, Michael. "Stoic Epistemology." In *The Cambridge History of Hellenistic Philosophy*, edited by Keimpe Algra, Jonathan Barnes, Jaap Mansfield, and Malcolm Schofield, 295–322. Cambridge: Cambridge University Press, 1999.

Fredouille, Jean-Claude, Marie-Odile Goulet-Cazé, Philippe Hoffmann, and Pierre Petitmengin, eds. *Titres et articulations du texte dans les oeuvres antiques*. Paris: Institut d'Études Augustiniennes, 1997.

Freeman, Elizabeth. *Time Binds: Queer Temporalities, Queer Histories*. Durham, NC: Duke University Press, 2010.

Fritzsche, Peter. *Stranded in the Present: Modern Time and the Melancholy of History*. Cambridge, MA: Harvard University Press, 2004.

Frontinus, Sextus Julius. *Strategemata*. Edited by R. I. Ireland. Leipzig: Teubner, 1990.

Garfield, James. "Letter Accepting the Nomination for the Presidency." In *The Works of James Abram Garfield*, vol. 2, edited by Burke Hinsdale, 782–87. Boston, 1883.

Garrett, Matthew. *Episodic Poetics: Politics and Literary Form after the Constitution*. Oxford: Oxford University Press, 2014.

Gasché, Rodolphe. *The Idea of Form: Rethinking Kant's Aesthetics*. Stanford, CA: Stanford University Press, 2003.

Gaskell, Elizabeth. *North and South*. Edited by Dorothy Collin. London: Penguin, 1970.

———. *Wives and Daughters*. Edited by Pam Morris. London: Penguin, 2001.

Gates, Henry Louis, Jr. *The Signifying Monkey: A Theory of African-American Literary Criticism*. Oxford: Oxford University Press, 1988.

Gellius, Aulus. *The "Attic Nights" of Aulus Gellius*. Translated by J. C. Rolfe. 3 vols. Cambridge, MA: Loeb Classical Library, 1961.

Genette, Gérard. *Narrative Discourse: An Essay in Method*. Translated by Jane Lewin. Ithaca, NY: Cornell University Press, 1983.

———. *Paratexts: Thresholds of Interpretation*. Translated by Jane Lewin. Cambridge: Cambridge University Press, 1997.

The Geneva Bible: A Facsimile of the 1560 Edition. Madison: University of Wisconsin Press, 1969.

Gesner, Johann Matthias. *Scriptores Rei rusticae veteres Latini*. 2 vols. Leipzig: Caspar Fritsch, 1773–34.

Ghose, Zulfikhar. "Bryan." *Review of Contemporary Fiction* 5 (1985): 23–34.

Giddens, Anthony. "Time and Social Organization." In *Social Theory and Modern Sociology*, 140–65. Stanford: Stanford University Press, 1987.

Gilpin, William. *Two Sermons: The first, preached at the primary Visitation of the Bishop of Winchester, at Southampton, July 15th, 1788. The second, at the Visitation of the Chancellor of the Diocese, Sept. 13th, 1788*. London, 1788.

Gingrich, Brian. *The Pace of Fiction: Narrative Movement and the Novel*. Oxford: Oxford University Press, 2021.

Gissing, George. *New Grub Street*. London, 1891.

———. *The Odd Women*. London, 1893.

Gledson, John. "*Dom Casmurro*: Realism and Intentionalism Revisited." In *Machado de Assis: Reflections on a Brazilian Master Writer*, edited by Richard Graham, 1–22. Austin: University of Texas Press, 1999.

Goble, Mark. "How the West Slows Down." *ELH* 85 (2018): 305–39.

Godeffrey of Boloyne, or the Siege and Conqueste of Jerusalem by William, Archbishop of Tyre. Translated by William Caxton. Edited by Mary Noyes Colvin. Early English Text Society Extra Series 64. London: Kegan Paul, Trench, Trübner, 1893.

Goethe, Johann Wolfgang. "Geistesepochen, nach Hermanns neusten Mittelungen." In *Goethes Werke*, vol. 12, *Schriften zur Kunst, Schriften zur Literatur, Maximen und Reflexionen*, edited by Erich Trunz and Hans Joachim Schrimpf, 298–300. Munich: C. H. Beck, 1982.

———. *Italian Journey [1786–1788]*. Translated by W. H. Auden and Elizabeth Mayer. Harmondsworth, UK: Penguin, 1962.

———. *Rameaus Neffe*. Vol. 31 of *Goethes Werke*. Berlin: Gustav Hempel, 1868.

———. *Die Wahlverwandtschaften: Ein Roman*. Stuttgart: Reclam, 1956.

———. *Wilhelm Meister's Apprenticeship*. 3 vols. Translated by Thomas Carlyle. Edinburgh, 1824.

———. *Wilhelm Meister's Apprenticeship*. Translated by Eric Blackall. Princeton, NJ: Princeton University Press, 1995.

———. *Wilhelm Meister's Journeyman Years or The Renunciants*. Translated by Krishna Winston. New York: Suhrkamp, 1989.

———. *Wilhelm Meisters Lehrjahre*. Munich: Deutsches Taschenbuch Verlag, 1977.

Goffman, Erving. *Frame Analysis: An Essay on the Organization of Experience*. Boston, MA: Northeastern University Press, 1974.

Gorman, Michael. "Chapter Headings for Saint Augustine's *De Genesi ad litteram*." *Revue des études augustiniennes* 26 (1980): 88–104.

Goswell, Greg. "The Early Readers of the Gospels: The *Kephalaia* and *Titloi* of Codex Alexandrinus." *Journal of Greco-Roman Christianity and Judaism* 6 (2009): 134–74.

Gräf, Hans Gerhard, ed. *Goethe über seine Dichtungen: Versuch einer Sammlung aller Äusserungen des Dichters über seine poetischen Werke.* Vol. 2. Frankfurt, 1902.

Grafton, Anthony, and Megan Williams. *Christianity and the Transformation of the Book: Origen, Eusebius, and the Library of Caesarea.* Cambridge, MA: Harvard University Press, 2008.

Grahame, Kenneth. *The Annotated Wind in the Willows.* Edited by Annie Gauger. New York: Norton, 2009.

Gregory of Nyssa. *De hominis opificio.* Edited by J.-P. Migne. Patrologiae Cursus Completus, Series Graeca 44:124–256. Paris: Migne, 1863.

Grimmelshausen, Hans Jakob Christoffel von. *The Adventurous Simplicissimus: Being the Description of the Life of a Strange Vagabond Named Melchior Sternfels von Fuchshaim.* Translated by A.T.S. Goodrick. Lincoln: University of Nebraska Press, 1962.

Gronniosaw, James Albert Ukawsaw. *A Narrative of the Most Remarkable Particulars in the Life of James Albert Ukawsaw Gronniosaw, an African Prince, as Related by Himself.* Bath, UK, 1774.

Gurvitch, Georges. *The Spectrum of Social Time.* Translated by Myrtle Korenbaum. Dordrecht, Netherlands: Reidel, 1964.

Gustafson, Richard. *Leo Tolstoy: Resident and Stranger.* Princeton, NJ: Princeton University Press, 1986.

Haber, Tom. "The Chapter-Tags in the Waverley Novels." *PMLA* 45 (1930): 1140–49.

Hadot, Pierre. *Philosophy as a Way of Life: Spiritual Exercises from Socrates to Foucault.* Translated by Michael Chase. Oxford: Blackwell, 1995.

Hallo, William. "New Viewpoints in Cuneiform Literature." *Israel Exploration Journal* 12 (1962): 13–26.

Halporn, James. "Methods of Reference in Cassiodorus." *Journal of Library History* 16 (1981): 71–91.

Hamburger, Käte. *The Logic of Literature.* Translated by Marilynn Rose. Bloomington: Indiana University Press, 1973.

Hammon, Briton. *A Narrative of the Most Uncommon Sufferings and Surprizing Deliverance of Briton Hammon, a Negro Man.* Boston, MA, 1760.

Hand, Richard. *Listen in Terror: British Horror Radio from the Advent of Broadcasting to the Digital Age.* Manchester: Manchester University Press, 2014.

Hanks, William. "The Indexical Ground of Deictic Reference." In *Rethinking Context: Language as an Interactive Phenomenon,* edited by Alessandro Duranti and Charles Goodwin, 43–77. Cambridge: Cambridge University Press, 1992.

Hansen, João Adolfo. "*Dom Casmurro*: Simulacrum and Allegory." In *Machado de Assis: Reflections on a Brazilian Master Writer,* edited by Richard Graham, 23–50. Austin: University of Texas Press, 1999.

Hardy, Francesca Minnie. "Agnès Varda's *Cléo de 5 à 7*: A Triptych of the Textile." In *Agnès Varda Unlimited: Image, Music, Media,* edited by Marie-Claire Barnet, 27–43. Cambridge, UK: Legenda, 2016.

Harl, Marguerite. "Recherches sur le Περί ἀρχών d'Origène en vue d'une nouvelle édition: La division en chapitres." In *Studia Patristica* III, *Texte und Untersuchungen zur Geschichte der altchristlichen Literatur* 78, edited by F. L. Cross, 57–67. Berlin: Akademie-Verlag, 1961.

Harnett, Benjamin. "The Diffusion of the Codex." *Classical Antiquity* 36 (2017): 183–235.

Harrison, S. J. *Framing the Ass: Literary Texture in Apuleius' "Metamorphoses."* Oxford: Oxford University Press, 2013.

Hayot, Eric. "Against Periodization." *New Literary History* 42 (2011): 739–56.

Haywood, Eliza. *The History of Miss Betsy Thoughtless.* London: Pandora, 1986.

Hebert, Hugh. "The Man Inside the Box." *Guardian*, March 15, 1969.

Hegel, G.W.M. *Aesthetics: Lectures on Fine Art.* Translated by T. M. Knox. 2 vols. Oxford: Clarendon, 1974.

Heidegger, Martin. *Being and Time.* Translated by John Macquarrie and Edward Robinson. New York: Harper and Row, 1962.

Heiden, Bruce. "The Placement of 'Book Divisions' in the *Iliad*." *Journal of Hellenic Studies* 118 (1998): 68–81.

Heinemann, Joseph. "The Triennial Lectionary Cycle." *Journal of Jewish Studies* 19 (1968): 41–48.

Hellinga, Lotte, and Hilton Kelliher. "The Malory Manuscript." *British Library Journal* 3 (1977): 91–113.

Henderson, John. "Columella's Living Hedge: The Roman Gardening Book." *Journal of Roman Studies* 92 (2002): 110–33.

Henry, Paul. *Les états du texte de Plotin.* Paris: Desclée de Brouwer, 1938.

Hershbell, Jackson. "The Stoicism of Epictetus: Twentieth Century Perspectives." *Aufsteig und Neidergang der Römischen Welt* II 36 (1989): 2148–63.

Hesse, Carla. "Books in Time." In *The Future of the Book*, edited by Geoffrey Nunberg, 21–36. Berkeley: University of California Press, 1997.

Hiltzik, Michael. *The New Deal: A Modern History.* New York: Free Press, 2011.

The History of Charlotte Summers, the Fortunate Parish Girl. 2 vols. London, 1750.

Hitchin, Neil. "The Politics of English Bible Translation in Georgian Britain." *Transactions of the Royal Historical Society*, 6th ser., 9 (1999): 67–92.

Hodgson, Phyllis, ed. *"The Cloud of Unknowing" and the "Book of Privy Counselling."* Early English Text Society 218. Oxford: Oxford University Press, 1943.

Holbrook, Ellen. "On the Attractions of the Malory Incunable and the Malory Manuscript." In *The Malory Debate: Essays on the Texts of "Le Morte Darthur,"* edited by Bonnie Wheeler, Robert Kindrick, and Michael Salda, 323–65. Cambridge, UK: D. S. Brewer, 2000.

Holford-Strevens, Leofranc. *Aulus Gellius: An Antonine Scholar and His Achievement.* Oxford: Oxford University Press, 2003.

Holmes, Richard. "Leaves in the Wind." *The Times*, March 15, 1969.

Holtz, Louis. "Lets mots latin désignant le lire au temps d'Augustin." In *Les débuts du codex*, edited by Alain Blanchard, 105–13. Turnhout, Belgium: Brepols, 1989.

The Holy Bible, According to the Authorized Version; with Notes, Explanatory and Practical. Edited by George D'Oyly and Richard Mant. London, 1839.

Houghton, H.A.G. "Chapter Divisions, *Capitula* Lists, and the Old Latin Version of John." *Revue bénédictine* 121 (2011): 316–56.

Howley, Joseph. *Aulus Gellius and Roman Reading Culture: Text, Presence, and Imperial Knowledge in the "Noctes Atticae."* Cambridge: Cambridge University Press, 2018.

———. "Tables of Contents." In *Book Parts*, edited by Dennis Duncan and Adam Smyth, 65–79. Oxford: Oxford University Press, 2019.

Huber, Martin. "Kapitel." In *Reallexikon der deutschen Literaturwissenschaft*, vol. 2, edited by Georg Braungart, Harald Fricke, Klaus Grubmüller, Jan-Dirk Müller, Friedrich Vollhardt, and Klaus Weimar, 232–33. Berlin: de Gruyter, 2003.

Hughes, Linda, and Michael Lund. *Victorian Publishing and Mrs. Gaskell's Work.* Charlottesville: University Press of Virginia, 1999.

Hunter, J. Paul. "From Typology to Type: Agents of Change in Eighteenth-Century English Texts." In *Cultural Artifacts and the Production of Meaning: The Page, the Image, and the Body*, edited by Margaret Ezell and Katherine O'Brien O'Keeffe, 41–69. Ann Arbor: University of Michigan Press, 1994.

———. *Occasional Form: Henry Fielding and the Chains of Circumstance.* Baltimore, MD: Johns Hopkins University Press, 1975.

Irigoin, Jean. "Titres, sous-titres et sommaires dans les oeuvres des historiens grecs du 1er siècle avant J.-C. au Vè siècle après J.-C." In *Titres et articulations du texte dans les oeuvres antiques: Actes du colloque international de Chantilly 13–15 décembre 1994*, edited by Jean Claude Fredouille, Marie-Odile Goulet-Cazé, Philippe Hoffmann, and Pierre Petitmengin, 127–34. Paris: Institut d'Études Augustiniennes, 1997.

Isidore of Seville. *The "Etymologies" of Isidore of Seville.* Translated by Stephen Barney, W. J. Lewis, J. A. Beach, and Oliver Berghof. Cambridge: Cambridge University Press, 2006.

Jackson, K. David. *Machado de Assis: A Literary Life.* New Haven, CT: Yale University Press, 2015.

Jager, Eric. *The Book of the Heart.* Chicago: University of Chicago Press, 2000.

James, David. "The (W)hole Affect: Creative Reading and Typographic Immersion in *Albert Angelo*." In *Re-reading B. S. Johnson*, edited by Philip Tew and Glyn White, 27–37. Basingstoke, UK: Palgrave, 2007.

James, Henry. *The Ambassadors.* Edited by Adrian Poole. London: Penguin, 2008.

———. *The Complete Notebooks of Henry James.* Edited by Leon Edel and Lyall Powers. Oxford: Oxford University Press, 1987.

James, William. "A World of Pure Experience." In *Essays in Radical Empiricism*, 39–91. New York: Longmans, Green, 1912.

Jameson, Fredric. *The Antinomies of Realism.* London: Verso, 2013.

———. "Joyce or Proust?" In *The Modernist Papers*, 170–203. London: Verso, 2007.

Jay, Martin. *Songs of Experience: Modern American and European Variations on a Universal Theme.* Berkeley: University of California Press, 2005.

Jenkin, Robert. *Remarks on some books lately publish'd, viz. Mr. Basnage's History of the Jews, Mr. Whiston's Eight sermons, Mr. Lock's Paraphrase and Notes on St. Paul's Epistles, Le Clerc's Bibliotheque Choisie.* London, 1709.

Jerome. *Commentariorum in Isaiah prophetam libri duodeviginti.* Patrologia Latina 24. Edited by J. P. Migne. Paris, 1863.

Johnson, B. S. *Albert Angelo.* In *B. S. Johnson Omnibus.* London: Picador, 2004.

———. "The Disintegrating Novel (2)." *Books and Bookmen* 15 (September 1970): 8.

————. *Trawl*. In *B. S. Johnson Omnibus*. London: Picador, 2004.

————. *The Unfortunates*. With an introduction by Jonathan Coe. New York: New Directions, 2007.

————. *Well Done God!: Selected Prose and Drama of B. S. Johnson*. Edited by Jonathan Coe, Philip Tew, and Julia Jordan. London: Picador, 2013.

Johnson, Eleanor. *Staging Contemplation: Participatory Theology in Middle English Prose, Verse, and Drama*. Chicago: University of Chicago Press, 2018.

Johnson, Uwe. *Anniversaries: From a Year in the Life of Gesine Cresspahl*. Translated by Damion Searls. 2 vols. New York: NYRB Classics, 2018.

————. *Jahrestage: Aus dem Leben von Gesine Cresspahl*. Vol. 4. Frankfurt: Suhrkamp, 1983.

Johnson, William. *Readers and Reading Culture in the High Roman Empire: A Study of Elite Communities*. Oxford: Oxford University Press, 2010.

————. "Toward a Sociology of Reading in Classical Antiquity." *American Journal of Philology* 121 (2000): 593–627.

Jones, Catherine. *Philippe de Vigneulles and the Art of Prose Fiction*. Cambridge, UK: D. S. Brewer, 2008.

Junghanns, Paul. *Die Erzählungstechnik von Apuleius' "Metamorphosen" und ihrer Vorlage*. *Philologus* Suppl. 24.1. Leipzig: Dieterich, 1932.

Kafka, Franz. *The Trial*. Translated by Breon Mitchell. New York: Schocken, 1998.

Kato, Takako. *Caxton's "Morte Darthur": The Printing Process and the Authenticity of the Text*. Oxford: Society for the Study of Medieval Languages and Literature, 2002.

Kato, Takako, and Nick Heyward, eds. *The Malory Project*. http://www.maloryproject.com.

Kelber, Werner. *The Oral and the Written Gospel: The Hermeneutics of Speaking and Writing in the Synoptic Tradition, Mark, Paul, and Q*. Philadelphia, PA: Fortress, 1983.

Kennedy, Edward Donald. "Caxton, Malory, and the 'Noble Tale of King Arthur and the Emperor Lucius.'" In *The Malory Debate: Essays on the Texts of "Le Morte Darthur,"* edited by Bonnie Wheeler, Robert Kindrick, and Michael Salda, 217–32. Cambridge, UK: D. S. Brewer, 2000.

Kenyon, Frederick. "Book Divisions in Greek and Latin Literature." In *William Warner Bishop: A Tribute*, edited by Harry Miller Lydenberg and Andrew Keogh, 63–75. New Haven, CT: Yale University Press, 1941.

————. *Books and Readers in Ancient Greece and Rome*. Oxford: Clarendon, 1951.

Kermode, Frank. "Retripotent." *London Review of Books*, August 5, 2004.

Keymer, Thomas. *Sterne, the Moderns, and the Novel*. Oxford: Oxford University Press, 2002.

Kingdon, John. *Redeemed Slaves: Being a Short Narrative of Two Neopolitans Redeemed from Slavery on the Coast of Barbary, and carried Home to the Friends at Naples on the Christian Shore*. Bristol, 1780.

Kittay, Jeffrey, and Wlad Godzich. *The Emergence of Prose: An Essay in Prosaics*. Minneapolis: University of Minnesota Press, 1987.

Klein, Wolfgang. "How Time Is Encoded." In *The Expression of Time*, edited by Klein and Ping Li, 39–82. Berlin: de Gruyter, 2009.

Kline, Jefferson, trans. "Agnès Varda from 5 to 7," In *Agnès Varda: Interviews*, 3–16.

————, ed. and trans. *Agnès Varda: Interviews*. Oxford: University Press of Mississippi, 2013.

————, trans. "Agnès Varda: The Hour of Truth." 1962 interview by Michel Capdenac. In *Agnès Varda: Interviews*, 17–22.

————, trans. "A Secular Grace: Agnès Varda." 1965 interview in *Cahiers du cinéma*. In *Agnès Varda: Interviews*, 23–37.

Korpel, Marjo C. A. "Introduction to the Series Pericope." In *Delimitation Criticism*, edited by Korpel and Josef Oesch, 1–50. Assen: Van Gorcum, 2000.

Koselleck, Reinhart. "The Eighteenth Century as the Beginning of Modernity." In *The Practice of Conceptual History: Timing History, Spacing Concepts*, translated by Todd Samuel Presner, Adelheis Baker, Kerstin Behnke, and Jobst Welge, 154–69. Stanford, CA: Stanford University Press, 2002.

————. "'Space of Experience' and 'Horizon of Expectation': Two Historical Categories." In *Futures Past: On the Semantics of Historical Time*, translated by Keith Tribe, 255–75. New York: Columbia University Press, 2004.

Kramnick, Jonathan. "Against Literary Darwinism." *Critical Inquiry* 37 (2011): 315–47.

Kramnick, Jonathan, and Anahid Nersessian. "Form and Explanation." *Critical Inquiry* 43 (2017): 650–69.

Krasznahorkai, László. *Chasing Homer*. Translated by John Bakti. New York: New Directions, 2021.

Kreilkamp, Ivan. *"A Visit from the Goon Squad" Reread*. New York: Columbia University Press, 2021.

Kundera, Milan. *The Art of the Novel*. Translated by Linda Asher. London: Faber and Faber, 1999.

Lacan, Jacques. *Écrits*. Translated by Bruce Fink. New York: Norton, 2002.

Lacy, Norris. "Adaptation as Reception: The Burgundian *Cligès*." *Fifteenth-Century Studies* 24 (1998): 198–207.

Lake, Kirsopp. *The Text of the New Testament*. New York: Edwin Gorham, 1908.

Lambot, Cyril. "Lettre inedité de S. Augustin relative au 'De civitate Dei.'" *Revue bénédictine* 51 (1939): 109–21.

Landy, Joshua. *How to Do Things with Fictions*. Oxford: Oxford University Press, 2012.

Largus, Scribonius. *Scribonii Largi "Compositiones."* Edited by Sergio Sconocchia. Leipzig: Teubner, 1983.

Larsen, Timothy. *A People of One Book: The Bible and the Victorians*. Oxford: Oxford University Press, 2011.

Le Clerc, Jean. *Bibliothèque choisie, pour servir de suite à la Bibliothèque universelle*. Vol. 13. Amsterdam, 1707.

Lee, Chang-rae. *On Such a Full Sea*. New York: Riverhead, 2014. Retrieved from http://search.ebscohost.com.

Lehnert, Wendy. "Plot Units and Narrative Summarization." *Cognitive Science* 4 (1981): 293–331.

Lennard, John. "Mark, Space, Axis, Function: Towards a (New) Theory of Punctuation on Historical Principles." In *Ma(r)king the Text: The Presentation of Meaning on the Literary Page*, edited by John Bray, Miriam Handley, and Anne C. Henry, 1–11. Aldershot, UK: Ashgate, 2000.

Lennox, Charlotte. *The Female Quixote: or, The Adventures of Arabella*. 2 vols. London, 1752.

Lesage, Alain-René. *Histoire de Gil Blas de Santillane I*. Edited by René Etiemble. Paris: Gallimard, 1973.

Levin, Harry. *The Power of Blackness: Hawthorne, Poe, Melville*. New York: Knopf, 1958.

Levinson, Stephen. *Pragmatics*. Cambridge: Cambridge University Press, 1983.

A Liberal Translation of the New Testament. Translated by Edward Harwood. Vol. 1. London, 1768.

The Life of Lazarillo de Tormes, His Fortunes and Adversities. Translated by Ilan Stavans. New York: Norton, 2016.

Light, Laura. "The Bible and the Individual: The Thirteenth-Century Paris Bible." In *The Practice of the Bible in the Middle Ages*, edited by Susan Boynton and Diane Reilly, 228–46. New York: Columbia University Press, 2011.

———. "French Bibles c. 1200–30: A New Look at the Origin of the Paris Bible." In *The History of the Book in the West: 400 AD–1455*, edited by Jane Roberts and Pamela Robinson, 247–68. London: Ashgate, 2010.

———. "Versions et révisions du texte biblique." In *Le Moyen Age et la Bible*, edited by Pierre Riché and Guy Robrichon, 55–93. Paris: Beauchesne, 1984.

Lintott, Andrew. *Judicial Reform and Land Reform in the Roman Republic: A New Edition, with Translation and Commentary, of the Laws from Urbino*. Cambridge: Cambridge University Press, 1992.

Locke, John. *An Essay for the Understanding of St. Paul's Epistles, By Consulting St. Paul Himself*. London, 1707.

———. *A Paraphrase and Notes on the Second Epistle of St. Paul to the Corinthians*. London, 1706.

———. *The Reasonableness of Christianity, As Delivered in the Scriptures*. Edited by John Higgins-Biddle. Oxford: Clarendon, 1999.

Loewe, Raphael. "The Medieval History of the Latin Vulgate." In *The Cambridge History of the Bible: The West from the Fathers to the Reformation*, edited by G. W. H. Lampe, 102–54. Cambridge: Cambridge University Press, 1969.

Lombard, Peter. *Sententiae in IV libris distincti*. Edited by Ignatius Brady. 2 vols. Grottaferrata, Italy: Editiones Collegii S. Bonaventurae Ad Claras Acquas, 1971–81.

Long, A. A. "Stoic Psychology." In *The Cambridge History of Hellenistic Philosophy*, edited by Keimpe Algra, Jonathan Barnes, Jaap Mansfield, and Malcolm Schofield, 560–84. Cambridge: Cambridge University Press, 1999.

———. *Stoic Studies*. Cambridge: Cambridge University Press, 1996.

Long, A. A., and D. N. Sedley. *The Hellenistic Philosophers*. 2 vols. Cambridge: Cambridge University Press, 1987.

Lowe, Lisa. *The Intimacies of Four Continents*. Durham, NC: Duke University Press, 2015.

Lowry, Malcolm. *Selected Letters of Malcolm Lowry*. Edited by Harvey Breit and Margerie Bonner Lowry. Philadelphia, PA: Lippincott, 1965.

Luckmann, Thomas. "The Constitution of Human Life in Time." In *Chronotopes: The Construction of Time*, edited by John Bender and David Wellbery, 151–66. Stanford, CA: Stanford University Press, 1991.

Lupton, Christina. *Knowing Books: The Consciousness of Mediation in Eighteenth-Century Britain*. Philadelphia: University of Pennsylvania Press, 2011.

———. *Reading and the Making of Time in the Eighteenth Century*. Baltimore, MD: Johns Hopkins University Press, 2018.

Lysack, Krista. "The Productions of Time: Keble, Rossetti, and Victorian Devotional Reading." *Victorian Studies* 55, no. 3 (2013): 451–70.

Machado de Assis, Joaquim Maria. *Dom Casmurro*. Translated by Helen Caldwell. New York: Farrar, Straus, Giroux, 1991.

———. *Esau and Jacob*. Translated by Elizabeth Lowe. New York: Oxford University Press, 2000.

———. *The Posthumous Memoirs of Brás Cubas*. Translated by Flora Thomson-DeVeaux. London: Penguin, 2020.

———. *Quincas Borba*. Translated by Gregory Rabassa. New York: Oxford University Press, 1998.

Mackrell, Judith. "B. S. Johnson and the British Experimental Tradition: An Introduction." *Review of Contemporary Fiction* 5 (1985): 42–64.

Macpherson, Sandra. "A Little Formalism." *ELH* 82 (2015): 385–405.

Mak, Bonnie. *How the Page Matters*. Toronto: University of Toronto Press, 2011.

Malory, Sir Thomas. *Le morte d'Arthur*. Edited by Janet Cowen. 2 vols. London: Penguin 1969.

———. *Le morte Darthur*. Edited by P.J.C. Field. 2 vols. Cambridge, UK: D. S. Brewer, 2013.

———. *Le morte Darthur by Syr Thomas Malory; the original edition of William Caxton now reprinted and edited with an introduction and glossary by H. Oskar Sommer; with an essay on Malory's prose style by Andrew Lang*. Ann Arbor: University of Michigan Humanities Text Initiative, 1997. http://name.umdl.umich.edu/MaloryWks2.

Mandelbrote, Scott. "The English Bible and Its Readers in the Eighteenth Century." In *Books and Their Readers in the Eighteenth Century: New Essays*, edited by Isabel Rivers, 35–78. London: Continuum, 2001.

———. "English Scholarship and the Greek Text of the Old Testament, 1620–1720: The Impact of Codex Alexandrinus." In *Scripture and Scholarship in Early Modern England*, edited by Ariel Hessayon and Nicholas Keene, 72–93. Aldershot, UK: Ashgate, 2006.

Mann, Thomas. *Doctor Faustus: The Life of the German Composer Adrian Leverkuhn as Told by a Friend*. Translated by John Woods. New York: Vintage, 1999.

Marchal, Matthieu. "Mise en chapitres, rubriques et miniatures dans *Gérard de Nevers*." In *Mettre en prose aux XIVe–XVIe siècle*, edited by Maria Colombo Timelli, Barbara Ferrari, and Anne Schoysman, 187–95. Turnhout, Belgium: Brepols, 2010.

Marrant, John. *A Narrative of the Lord's Wonderful Dealings with John Marrant, a Black*. London, 1785.

Marrou, Henri-Irénée. "La division en chapitres des livres de *La cité de Dieu*." In *Mélanges Joseph de Ghellinck, S. J.*, 1:235–49. Gembloux: J. Duculot, 1951.

Martin, Henri-Jean. *The History and Power of Writing*. Translated by Lydia Cochrane. Chicago: University of Chicago Press, 1994.

Mathieu, Georges. *Changer de chapitre dans "Les Misérables."* Paris: Honoré Champion, 2007.

———. "Esquisse d'une poétique de la table des matières." In *La table des matières: Son histoire, ses règles, ses fonctions, son esthétique*, edited by Georges Mathieu and Jean-Claude Arnold, 449–76. Paris: Garnier, 2017.

———. "Pour une théorie du chapitre 2: Étudier la division d'un roman en chapitres; quelques réflexions méthodologiques." In *Deviser, diviser: Pratiques du découpage et poétiques du chapitre de l'Antiquité à nos jours*, edited by Sylvie Triaire and Patricia Victorin, 197–222. Montpellier, France: Presses universitaires de la Méditerranée, 2011.

Matthews, William. "The Besieged Printer." In *The Malory Debate: Essays on the Texts of "Le Morte Darthur*,*"* edited by Bonnie Wheeler, Robert Kindrick, and Michael Salda, 35–64. Cambridge, UK: D. S. Brewer, 2000.

Mattingly, Harold. "The Lex Repetundarum of the Tabula Bembina." *Philologus* 157 (2013): 87–93.

———. "The Two Republican Laws of the *Tabula Bembina*." *Journal of Roman Studies* 59 (1969): 129–43.

Maxwell, James Clerk. *The Scientific Letters and Papers of James Clerk Maxwell*. Edited by P. M. Harman. Vol. 2. Cambridge: Cambridge University Press, 1995.

McArthur, H. K. "The Earliest Divisions of the Gospels." In *Studia evangelica*, vols. 2–3, edited by Frank Leslie Cross, 266–72. Berlin: Akademie Verlag, 1964.

McCarthy, Tom. *Remainder*. New York: Vintage, 2005.

McCutcheon, R. W. "Silent Reading in Antiquity and the Future History of the Book." *Book History* 18 (2015): 1–32.

McGann, Jerome. *A Critique of Modern Textual Criticism*. Chicago: University of Chicago Press, 1983.

———. *The Textual Condition*. Princeton, NJ: Princeton University Press, 1991.

McGregor, Jon. *Reservoir 13*. New York: Catapult, 2017.

McGurl, Mark. *Everything and Less: The Novel in the Age of Amazon*. London: Verso, 2021.

McKendrick, Scot. "The Codex Alexandrinus, or The Dangers of Being a Named Manuscript." In *The Bible as Book: The Transmission of the Greek Text*, edited by Scot McKendrick and Orlaith O'Sullivan, 1–16. London: British Library, 2003.

McKenzie, D. F. *Bibliography and the Sociology of Texts*. Cambridge: Cambridge University Press, 1999.

Mendilow, A. A. *Time and the Novel*. London: Peter Nevill, 1952.

Metz, Christian. *Film Language: A Semiotics of the Cinema*. Translated by Michael Taylor. New York: Oxford University Press, 1974.

Metzger, Bruce. *Manuscripts of the Greek Bible: An Introduction to Palaeography*. Oxford: Oxford University Press, 1981.

———. *The Text of the New Testament: Its Transmission, Corruption, and Restoration*. Oxford: Oxford University Press, 1968.

Meyvaert, Paul. "Bede's *Capitula Lectionum* for the Old and New Testaments." *Revue bénédictine* 105 (1995): 348–80.

Michaelis, Johann David. *Introduction to the New Testament*. Translated by Herbert Marsh. Vol. 2. Cambridge, 1793.

Michon, John. "The Compleat Time Experiencer." In *Time, Mind, and Behavior*, edited by J. A. Michon and J. L. Jackson, 20–52. Berlin: Springer, 1985.

Mieszkowski, Jan. *Crises of the Sentence*. Chicago: University of Chicago Press, 2019.

Miller, D. A. *Jane Austen, or The Secret of Style*. Princeton, NJ: Princeton University Press, 2003.

Minnis, Alastair, A. B. Scott, and David Wallace, eds. *Medieval Literary Theory and Criticism, c. 1000–c. 1375: The Commentary Tradition*. Oxford: Oxford University Press, 1988.

Mitchell, Kaye. "*The Unfortunates*: Hypertext, Linearity, and the Act of Reading." In *Re-reading B. S. Johnson*, edited by Philip Tew and Glyn White, 51–64. Basingstoke, UK: Palgrave, 2007.

Moore, G. F. "The Vulgate Chapters and Numbered Verses in the Hebrew Bible." *Journal of Biblical Literature* 12 (1893): 73–78.

Morson, Gary Saul. *Hidden in Plain View: Narrative and Creative Potentials in "War and Peace."* Stanford, CA: Stanford University Press, 1987.

Mroczek, Eva. "Thinking Digitally about the Dead Sea Scrolls: Book History Before and Beyond the Book." *Book History* 14 (2011): 241–69.

Müller, Gunther. "Erzählzeit und erzählte Zeit" (1948). Reprinted in *Morphologische Poetik*, 269–86.

——. *Morphologische Poetik: Gesammelte Aufsätze*. Tübingen: Max Niemeyer Verlag, 1968.

Müller-Sievers, Helmut. "Going On In: Philosophy of Continuity and the Writing of Coherence in Goethe's *Wilhelm Meister's Apprenticeship*." In *Goethe's "Wilhelm Meister's Apprenticeship" and Philosophy*, edited by Sarah Vandegrift Eldridge and C. Allen Speight, 237–68. Oxford: Oxford University Press, 2020.

Muñoz, José Esteban. *Cruising Utopia: The Then and There of Queer Futurity*. New York: New York University Press, 2009.

Nancy, Jean-Luc. *Listening*. Translated by Charlotte Mandell. New York: Fordham University Press, 2007.

Nelson, Roy Jay. "Reflections in a Broken Mirror: Varda's *Cléo de 5 à 7*." *French Review* 56 (1983): 735–43.

The New Testament: Carefully collated with the Greek, and corrected; Dividing and Pointed According to the Various Subjects treated of by the Inspired Writers, With the common Division into Chapters and Verses in the Margin; and illustrated With Notes Critical and Explanatory. 2 vols. Translated by Richard Wynne. London, 1764.

A New Translation of the New Testament of our Lord and Saviour Jesus Christ, Extracted from the Paraphrase of the late Philip Doddridge, D. D. Vol. 1. London, 1765.

Newtson, Darren, and Gretchen Engquist. "The Perceptual Organization of Ongoing Behavior." *Journal of Experimental Social Psychology* 12 (1976): 436–50.

Ngai, Sianne. *Theory of the Gimmick: Aesthetic Judgment and Capitalist Form*. Cambridge, MA: Harvard University Press, 2020.

Le Nouveau Testament de Nôtre Seigneur Jesus-Christ, traduit sur l'original Grec; Avec des Remarques, où l'on explique le Texte, & où l'on rend raison de la Version. Translated by Jean le Clerc. Vol. 1. Amsterdam, 1703.

Novi testamenti libri omnes recens nunc editi cum notis Isaaci Casauboni. Geneva, 1615.

Novum Testamentum Graece. 27th ed. Edited by Eberhard and Erwin Nestle, Barbara and Kurt Aland, Johannes Karavidopoulos, Carlo Martini, and Bruce Metzger. Stuttgart: Deutsche Bibelgesellschaft, 1993.

Nünlist, René. *The Ancient Critic at Work: Terms and Concepts of Literary Criticism in Greek Scholia*. Cambridge: Cambridge University Press, 2009.

Obama, Barack. "Weekly Address: A New Chapter with Cuba." Obama White House Archives. Accessed October 12, 2018. https://obamawhitehouse.archives.gov/the-press-office/2016/02/20/weekly-address-new-chapter-cuba.

Der Oberrheinische Revolutionär. *Der Oberrheinische Revolutionär: "Das Buchli der hundert Capiteln mit XXXX Statuten."* Edited by Klaus Lauterbach. Hanover: Hahnsche Buchhandlung, 2009.

O'Donnell, James. *Avatars of the Word: From Papyrus to Cyberspace.* Cambridge, MA: Harvard University Press, 2000.

Ong, Yi-Ping. *The Art of Being: Poetics of the Novel and Existentialist Philosophy.* Cambridge, MA: Harvard University Press, 2018.

Orpen, Valerie. *"Cléo de 5 à 7" (Agnès Varda, 1961).* Champaign: University of Illinois Press, 2007.

Pabst, Bernhardt. *Atomtheorien des lateinischen Mittelalters.* Darmstadt, Germany: Wissenschaftliche Buchgesellschaft, 1994.

Palmer, Nigel. "Kapitel und Buch: Zu den Gliederungsprinzipien mittelalterlicher Bücher." *Frühmittelalterlicher Studien* 23 (1989): 43–88.

Parkes, Malcolm. *Pause and Effect: An Introduction to the History of Punctuation in the West.* Farnham, UK: Ashgate: 1992.

Parrinder, Patrick. "Pilgrim's Progress: The Novels of B. S. Johnson (1933–73)." *Critical Quarterly* 19 (1977): 45–59.

Pattie, Thomas. "The Creation of the Great Codices." In *The Bible as Book: The Manuscript Tradition,* edited by John Sharpe III and Kimberly Van Kampen, 61–72. London: British Library, 1998.

Paulin Martin, Jean-Pierre. *Introduction à la critique générale de l'Ancien Testament: De l'origine du Pentateuque.* Vol. 2. Paris: Maisonneuve, 1888.

Paulson, Michael. "Present, Period, Crisis: Desynchronization and Social Cohesion in Jane Austen." *Modern Philology* 116 (2018): 164–85.

Pavel, Thomas. *The Lives of the Novel: A History.* Princeton, NJ: Princeton University Press, 2013.

Petitmengin, Pierre. *"Capitula* païens et chrétiens." In *Titres et articulations du texte dans les oeuvres antiques,* edited by Jean-Claude Fredouille, Marie-Odile Goulet-Cazé, Philippe Hoffmann, and Pierre Petitmengin, 491–507. Paris: Institut d'Études Augustiniennes, 1997.

Petrucci, Armando. *Writers and Readers in Medieval Italy: Studies in the History of Written Culture.* Translated by Charles Radding. New Haven, CT: Yale University Press, 1995.

Philippe de Vigneulles. *La "Chanson de Garin le Loherain" mise en prose par Philippe de Vigneuelles de Metz: Table des chapitres aves les reproductions des miniatures d'après le manuscrit appartenant à M. le comte d'Hunolstein.* Paris: Leclerc, 1901.

Phillips, Natalie. *Distraction: Problems of Attention in Eighteenth-Century Literature.* Baltimore, MD: Johns Hopkins University Press, 2016.

Philo of Byzantium. *Philons "Belopoiika": Viertes Buch der "Mechanik."* Edited by H. Diels and E. Schramm. Berlin: Verlag der Akademie der Wissenschaften, 1919.

Piper, Andrew. *Dreaming in Books: The Making of the Bibliographic Imagination in the Romantic Age.* Chicago: University of Chicago Press, 2009.

Pisano, Stephen. "The Text of the New Testament." In *Prolegomena to Bibliorum sacrorum Graecorum Codex Vaticanus B,* 27–41. Rome: Istituto poligrafico a Zecca della Stato, 1999.

Plaks, Andrew. "Leaving the Garden: Reflections on China's Literary Masterwork." *New Left Review* 47 (2007): 109–29.

———. "Shui-hu Chuan and the Sixteenth-Century Novel Form: An Interpretive Reappraisal." *Chinese Literature: Essays, Articles, Reviews* 2, no. 1 (1980): 3–53.

Pliny the Elder. *Natural History*. Translated by Harris Rackham. Vol. 1. Cambridge, MA: Loeb Classical Library, 1938.

Plotz, John. *Semi-Detached: The Aesthetics of Virtual Experience since Dickens*. Princeton, NJ: Princeton University Press, 2017.

Poleg, Eyal. *Approaching the Bible in Medieval England*. Manchester: Manchester University Press, 2013.

Pollard, Graham. "The *Pecia* System in the Medieval Universities." In *Medieval Scribes, Manuscripts, and Libraries: Essays Presented to N. R. Ker*, edited by M. B. Parkes and Andrew Wilson, 145–61. London: Scolar, 1978.

Pompeius. "Commentum *Artis* Donati." In *Grammatici Latini*, edited by Heinrich Keil, vol 5. Hildesheim, Germany: Georg Olms, 1961.

Potkay, Adam, and Sandra Burr, eds. *Black Atlantic Writers of the Eighteenth Century: Living the New Exodus in England and the Americas*. New York: St. Martin's, 1995.

Pound, Ezra. *Pound/Joyce: The Letters of Ezra Pound to James Joyce, with Pound's Essays on Joyce*. Edited by Forrest Read. New York: New Directions, 1967.

Powicke, F. M. *Stephen Langton*. Oxford: Clarendon, 1928.

Price, Leah. *How to Do Things with Books in Victorian Britain*. Princeton, NJ: Princeton University Press, 2012.

Priscian. *Institutiones grammaticae*. Edited by Martin Hertz. Leipzig: Teubner, 1855.

Proust, Marcel. "À propos du 'style' de Flaubert." *Nouvelle revue française* 76 (1920): 72–90.

Public Papers of the Presidents of the United States: Gerald Ford, Containing the Public Messages, Speeches, and Statements of the President, 1975. Vol 1. Washington, DC: United States Government Printing Office, 1977.

Pym, Barbara. *Excellent Women*. Harmondsworth, UK: Penguin, 1978.

———. *Jane and Prudence*. New York: Harper and Row, 1981.

———. *Less than Angels*. New York: Dutton, 1980.

Quart, Barbara. "Agnès Varda: A Conversation." *Film Quarterly* 40 (1986–87): 3–10.

Quintilian. *Institutio oratoria*. Translated by H. E. Butler. 4 vols. Cambridge, MA: Loeb Classical Library, 1922.

Randall, Bryony. "A Day's Time: The One-Day Novel and the Temporality of the Everyday." *New Literary History* 47, no. 4 (2016): 591–610.

Raskin, Ellen. "Newbery Award Acceptance Material." *Horn Book* 55 (1979): 385–89.

Reeve, Jonathan. "Fingerprinting the Chapter." Jonathan Reeve: Computational Literary Analysis, March 7, 2018. https://jonreeve.com/2018/03/fingerprinting-the-chapter/.

Rico, Francisco. *El texto del "Quijote": Preliminares a una ecdótica del Siglo de Oro*. Barcelona: Ediciones Destino; Valladolid, Spain: Centro para la Edición de los Clásicos Españoles y Universidad de Valladolid, 2005.

Ricoeur, Paul. *Time and Narrative*. Translated by Kathleen McLaughlin and David Pellauer. 3 vols. Chicago: University of Chicago Press, 1984.

Riggsby, Andrew. "Guides to the Wor(l)d." In *Ordering Knowledge in the Roman Empire*, edited by Jason Kong and Tim Whitmarsh, 88–107. Cambridge: Cambridge University Press, 2007.

Roberts, C. H., and T. C. Skeat. *The Birth of the Codex*. London: British Academy, 1983.

Rocha, João Cezar de Castro. *Machado de Assis: Toward a Poetics of Emulation*. Translated by Flora Thomson-DeVeaux. East Lansing: Michigan State University Press, 2015.

Roland, Meg. "'Alas! Who may truste thys world': The Malory Documents and a Parallel-Text Edition." In *The Book Unbound: Editing and Reading Medieval Manuscripts and Texts*, edited by Siân Echard and Stephen Partridge, 37–57. Toronto: University of Toronto Press, 2004.

Rosa, Hartmut. *Social Acceleration: A New Theory of Modernity*. Translated by Jonathan Trejo-Mathys. New York: Columbia University Press, 2013.

Rosemann, Philipp. *The Story of a Great Medieval Book: Peter Lombard's "Sentences."* Peterborough, ON: Broadview, 2007.

Rouanet, Sérgio Paulo. *Riso e melancolia: A forma shandiana em Sterne, Diderot, Xavier de Maistre, Almeida Garret e Machado de Assis*. São Paolo: Companhia das Letras, 2007.

Rouse, Richard, and Mary Rouse. *Preachers, Florilegia, and Sermons: Studies on the "Manipulus florum" of Thomas of Ireland*. Toronto: Pontifical Institute of Medieval Studies, 1979.

Rowlandson, Mary. *The Sovereignty and Goodness of God, Together with the Faithfulness of His Promises Displayed; Being a Narrative of the Captivity and Restoration of Mrs. Mary Rowlandson*. Cambridge, MA, 1682.

Saenger, Paul. "The Impact of the Early Printed Page on the Reading of the Bible." In *The Bible as Book: The First Printed Editions*, edited by Paul Saenger and Kimberly Van Kampen, 31–51. London: British Library, 1999.

———. "Jewish Liturgical Divisions of the Torah and the English Chapter Division of the Vulgate Attributed to Stephen Langton." In *Pesher Nahum: Texts and Studies in Jewish History and Literature from Antiquity through the Middle Ages, Presented to Norman (Nahum) Golb*, edited by Joel Kraemer and Michael Wechsler, 187–202. Chicago: Oriental Institute, 2012.

———. "The Twelfth-Century Reception of Oriental Languages and the Graphic *Mise en page* of Latin Vulgate Bibles Copied in England. " In *Form and Function in the Late Medieval Bible*, edited by Eyal Poleg and Laura Light, 31–66. Leiden: Brill, 2013.

Saenger, Paul, and Laura Bruck. "The Anglo-Hebraic Origins of the Modern Chapter Division of the Latin Bible." In *La fractura historiográfica: Las investigaciones de Edad Media y Renacimiento desde el tercer milenio*, edited by Javier San José Lera, 177–202. Salamanca, Spain: Sociedad de Estudios Medievales y Renacentistas, 2008.

Saintsbury, George. *A History of English Prose Rhythm*. London: Macmillan, 1912.

Sandbach, F. H. "Ennoia and Prolepsis." In *Problems in Stoicism*, edited by A. A. Long, 22–37. London: Athlone, 1971.

Schlesinger, Robert. *White House Ghosts: Presidents and Their Speechwriters, from FDR to George W. Bush*. New York: Simon and Schuster, 2008.

Schröder, Bianca-Jeanette. *Titel und Text: zur Entwicklung lateinischer Gedichtüberschriften, mit Untersuchungen zu Lateinischen Buchtiteln, Inhaltsverzeichnissen und anderen Gliederungsmitteln*. Berlin: de Gruyter, 1999.

Schultze, Sidney. "The Chapter in *Anna Karenina*." *Russian Literature Triquarterly* 10 (1974): 351–59.

Schwarz, Roberto. "Beyond Universalism and Localism: Machado's Breakthrough." In *Two Girls*, 33–53.

———. "Capitu, the Bride of Dom Casmurro." In *Two Girls*, 57–91.

———. "The Machadian Turning Point." Translated by Julia Maria Dias Negreiros. *Novos estudos CEBRAP* 1 (2005): 15–38.

———. *A Master on the Periphery of Capitalism*. Translated by John Gledson. Durham, NC: Duke University Press, 2001.

———. *Two Girls and Other Essays*. Edited by Francis Mulhern. Translated by Nicholas Brown, Emilio Gauri, and John Gledson. London: Verso, 2012.

Scrivener, F.H.A. *A Plain Introduction to the Criticism of the New Testament, for the Use of Biblical Students*. London: George Bell, 1894.

Self, Will. "Will Self on Literary Influences." Interview by Five Books, July 31, 2012. https://fivebooks.com/best-books/will-self-influences/.

Sharpe, Christina. *In the Wake: On Blackness and Being*. Durham, NC: Duke University Press, 2016.

Sheehan, Jonathan. *The Enlightenment Bible: Translation, Scholarship, Culture*. Princeton, NJ: Princeton University Press, 2005.

Sherman, Stuart. *Telling Time: Clocks, Diaries, and English Diurnal Form, 1660–1785*. Chicago: University of Chicago Press, 1996.

Shields, Ross. "Zusammenhang (Nexus)." *Goethe-Lexicon of Philosophical Concepts* 1 (2021): 121–40.

Shillingsburg, Peter. "Book Publishing and the Victorian Literary Marketplace." In *A Companion to the Victorian Novel*, edited by William Baker and Kenneth Womack, 29–38. Westport, CT: Greenwood, 2002.

Shklovsky, Viktor. *Theory of Prose*. Translated by Benjamin Sher. London: Dalkey Archive, 1990.

Silva, Ana Cláudia Suriani da. *Machado de Assis's "Philosopher or Dog?": From Serial to Book Form*. Abingdon, UK: Legenda, 2010.

Simon, Richard. *Histoire critique du texte du Nouveau Testament*. Rotterdam, 1689.

Skeat, T. C. "The Codex Sinaiticus, the Codex Vaticanus, and Constantine." *Journal of Theological Studies* 50 (1999): 583–625.

———. "The Origin of the Christian Codex." *Zeitschrift für Papyrologie und Epigraphik* 102 (1994): 263–68.

———. "The Provenance of the Codex Alexandrinus." *Journal of Theological Studies* 6 (1955): 233–35.

Smalley, Beryl. "Studies on the Commentaries of Cardinal Stephen Langton (Part II)." *Archives d'histoire doctrinale et littéraire du moyen age* 5 (1930): 152–82.

———. *The Study of the Bible in the Middle Ages*. Notre Dame, IN: University of Notre Dame Press, 1964.

Smith, Alison. *Agnès Varda*. Manchester: Manchester University Press, 1998.

Smith, W. Andrew. *A Study of the Gospels in Codex Alexandrinus: Codicology, Palaeography, and Scribal Hands*. Leiden: Brill, 2014.

Smollett, Tobias. *The Adventures of Roderick Random*. Edited by Paul-Gabriel Boucé. Oxford: Oxford University Press, 1979.

Speer, Nicole, and Jeffrey Zacks. "Temporal Changes as Event Boundaries: Processing and Memory Consequences of Narrative Time Shifts." *Journal of Memory and Language* 53 (2005): 125–40.

Stallybrass, Peter. "Books and Scrolls: Navigating the Bible." In *Books and Readers in Early Modern England*, edited by Jennifer Andersen and Elizabeth Sauer, 42–79. Philadelphia: University of Pennsylvania Press, 2002.

Stein, Jordan. *When Novels Were Books*. Cambridge, MA: Harvard University Press, 2020.

Stephen of Bourbon. *Anecdotes historiques, légendes et apologues, tirés du recueil inédit d'Étienne de Bourbon, Dominicain du XIIIe siècle*. Edited by A. Lecoy de la Marche. Paris, 1877.

Sterne, Jonathan. *MP3: The Meaning of a Format*. Durham, NC: Duke University Press, 2012.

Sterne, Laurence. *The Life and Opinions of Tristram Shandy, Gentleman*. Edited by Ian Campbell Ross. New York: Oxford University Press, 1983.

Stevick, Philip. *The Chapter in Fiction: Theories of Narrative Division*. Syracuse, NY: Syracuse University Press, 1970.

Stock, Brian. *Augustine the Reader: Meditation, Self-Knowledge, and the Ethics of Interpretation*. Cambridge, MA: Harvard University Press, 1998.

Strawson, Galen. "Against Narrativity." *Ratio* 17 (2004): 428–52.

Sultana, Niloufar. "The Principle of Chapter- and Volume-Division in *Tristram Shandy*." *Language and Style* 20, no. 2 (1987): 185–202.

Takagi, Masako, and Toshiyuki Takamiya. "Caxton Edits the Roman War Episode: The Chronicles of England and Caxton's Book V." In *The Malory Debate: Essays on the Texts of "Le Morte Darthur,"* edited by Bonnie Wheeler, Robert Kindrick, and Michael Salda, 169–90. Cambridge, UK: D. S. Brewer, 2000.

Tasker Grimbert, Joan. "Refashioning Combat in Chrétien's *Cligès* for the Burgundian Court." *Cahiers de recherches médiévales et humanistes* 30 (2015): 353–72.

Taylor, Elizabeth. *A View of the Harbour*. London: Virago, 1987.

Taylor, Jane. "The Significance of the Insignificant: Reading Reception in the Burgundian *Erec* and *Cligès*." *Fifteenth-Century Studies* 24 (1998): 183–97.

Teeuwen, Mariken. *The Vocabulary of Intellectual Life in the Middle Ages*. Turnhout, Belgium: Brepols, 2003.

Tenen, Dennis. *Plain Text: The Poetics of Computation*. Stanford, CA: Stanford University Press, 2017.

———. "Toward a Computational Archeology of Fictional Space." *New Literary History* 49, no. 1 (2018): 119–47.

Tew, Philip. *B. S. Johnson: A Critical Reading*. Manchester: Manchester University Press, 2001.

Thibaudet, Albert. "Réflexions sur la littérature: Sur le style de Flaubert." *Nouvelle revue française* 74 (1919): 942–53.

Tolstoy, Leo. *Voyna i mir*. The Komarov Library. https://ilibrary.ru/text/11/index.html.

———. *War and Peace*. Translated by Richard Pevear and Larissa Volokhonsky. New York: Vintage, 2007.

A Translation of the New Testament from the original Greek, Humbly Attempted by Nathaniel Scarlett, assisted by men of piety and literature, with notes. London, 1798.

Trevet, Nicholas. *Annales sex regum Angliae*. Edited by Thomas Hog. London: English Historical Society, 1845.

Trollope, Anthony. *Framley Parsonage*. Edited by P. D. Edwards. Oxford: Oxford University Press, 1980.

Trump, Donald. "Remarks by President Trump in Joint Address to Congress." Trump White House Archives, February 28, 2017. https://www.whitehouse.gov/briefings-statements/remarks-president-trump-joint-address-congress/.

Trumpener, Katie. "In the Grid: Period and Experience." *PMLA* 127 (2012): 349–56.

Turner, Eric. *The Typology of the Early Codex*. Philadelphia: University of Pennsylvania Press, 1977.

Uglow, Jenny. *Elizabeth Gaskell: A Habit of Stories*. London: Faber and Faber, 1993.

Underwood, Ted. "Why Literary Time Is Measured in Minutes." *ELH* 85 (2018): 341–65.

Ungar, Stephen. *Cléo de 5 à 7*. London: Bloomsbury, 2020.

Unseld, Siegfried. *Goethe and His Publishers*. Translated by Kenneth Northcott. Chicago: University of Chicago Press, 1996.

van Banning, Joop H. A. "Reflections upon the Chapter Divisions of Stephan Langton." In *Method in Unit Delimitation*, edited by Marjo Korpel, Josef Oesch, and Stanley Porter, 141–61. Leiden: Brill, 2007.

Vandendorpe, Christian. *From Papyrus to Hypertext: Toward the Universal Digital Library*. Translated by Phyllis Aronoff and Howard Scott. Urbana: University of Illinois Press, 2009.

Van Hemelryck, Tania. "Le livre mis en prose à la cour de Bourgogne: Réflexions pour une approche codicologique d'un phénomène littéraire." In *Mettre en prose aux XIVe–XVIe siècle*, edited by Maria Colombo Timelli, Barbara Ferrari, and Anne Schoysman, 245–54. Turnhout, Belgium: Brepols, 2010.

van Oort, Johannes. *Jerusalem and Babylon: A Study Into Augustine's "City of God" and the Sources of His Doctrine of the Two Cities*. Leiden: Brill, 1991.

Varda, Agnès. *Cléo de 5 à 7: Scénario*. Paris: Gallimard, 1962.

Varda, Agnès, and Bernard Bastide. *Varda par Agnès*. Paris: Éditions Cahiers du cinéma, 1994.

Verey, Christopher. "A Northumbrian Text Family." In *The Bible as Book: The Manuscript Tradition*, edited by John Sharpe III and Kimberly Van Kampen, 105–22. London: British Library, 1998.

Vezin, Jean. "La division en paragraphes dans les manuscrits de la basse antiquité et du haut Moyen Age." In *La notion de paragraphe*, edited by Roger Laufer, 41–51. Paris: Éditions du CNRS, 1985.

Vincent of Beauvais. *Speculum quadruplex sive speculum maius*. Facsimile reprint of 1624 Douai ed. Graz, Austria: Akademische Druck, 1964.

von Soden, Hermann Freiherr. *Die Schriften des Neuen Testaments in ihrer ältesten erreichbaren Textgestalt hergestellt auf Grund ihrer Textgeschichte*. Vol. 1. Göttingen, Germany: Vandenhoeck and Ruprecht, 1911.

Wade, James. "The Chapter Headings of the *Morte Darthur*: Caxton and de Worde." *Modern Philology* 111 (2014): 645–67.

Wall, Stephen. "Curious Box of Tricks." *Observer*, February 23, 1969.

Wallen, Martha. "Significant Variations in the Burgundian Prose Version of *Erec et Enide*." *Medium Aevum* 51 (1982): 187–96.

Watts, Carol. "'The Mind Has Fuses': Detonating B. S. Johnson." In *Re-reading B. S. Johnson*, edited by Philip Tew and Glyn White, 80–91. Basingstoke, UK: Palgrave, 2007.

Weber, Robert. "La lettre grecque K employée comme signe de correction dans les manuscrits bibliques latins écrits 'per cola et commata.'" *Scriptorium* 9 (1955): 57–63.

Whiston, William. *Mr. Whiston's Primitive New Testament.* Vol. 1. London, 1745.

White, Glyn. *Reading the Graphic Surface: The Presence of the Book in Prose Fiction.* Manchester: Manchester University Press, 2005.

Wibier, Matthijs. "The Topography of the Law Book: Common Structures and Modes of Reading." In *The Roman Paratext: Frame, Texts, Readers,* edited by Laura Jansen, 56–72. Cambridge: Cambridge University Press, 2014.

Wierusz Kowalski, George. "Le découpage du texte évangélique selon les intérets des groups lecteurs." In *La notion de paragraphe,* edited by Roger Laufer, 11–21. Paris: Éditions du CNRS, 1985.

Williams, Megan. *The Monk and the Book: Jerome and the Making of Christian Scholarship.* Chicago: University of Chicago Press, 2006.

Wilson, Woodrow. "Closing a Chapter." In *President Wilson's Addresses,* edited by George McLean Harper, 77–79. New York: Henry Holt, 1918.

Winnicott, Donald. "The Theory of the Parent-Infant Relationship." In *The Maturational Processes and the Facilitating Environment,* 37–55. Madison, CT: International Universities Press, 1965.

Wiseman, D. J. "Books in the Ancient Near East and in the Old Testament." In *The Cambridge History of the Bible: From the Beginnings to Jerome,* edited by P. R. Ackroyd and C. F. Evans, 30–48. Cambridge: Cambridge University Press, 1970.

Witty, Frances. "Book Terms in the Vivarium Translations." *Classical Folia* 28 (1974): 62–82.

Woolf, Greg. "Literacy or Literacies in Rome?" In *Ancient Literacies: The Culture of Reading in Greece and Rome,* edited by William Johnson and Holt Parker, 333–82. Oxford: Oxford University Press, 2009.

Woolhouse, Roger. *Locke: A Biography.* Cambridge: Cambridge University Press, 2007.

Wright, Daniel. "Thomas Hardy's Groundwork." *PMLA* 134 (2019): 1028–41.

Yahav, Amit. *Feeling Time: Duration, the Novel, and Eighteenth-Century Sensibility.* Philadelphia: University of Pennsylvania Press, 2018.

Yem, Eirian. "Forgetting Oneself: Epigraphs and Escapism in Ann Radcliffe's Novels." *Journal for Eighteenth-Century Studies* 45 (2022): 305–21.

———. "'An Inordinate Number of Words': Epigraphs in *Daniel Deronda.*" *19: Interdisciplinary Studies in the Long Nineteenth Century* 29 (2020). https://doi.org/10.16995/ntn.1926.

Zacks, Jeffrey, Nicole Speer, and Jeremy Reynolds. "Segmentation in Reading and Film Comprehension." *Journal of Experimental Psychology: General* 138, no. 2 (2009): 307–27.

Zacks, Jeffrey, Nicole Speer, Khena Swallow, Todd Brewer, and Jeremy Reynolds. "Event Perception: A Mind-Brain Perspective." *Psychological Bulletin* 133, no. 2 (2007): 273–93.

Zemka, Sue. *Time and the Moment in Victorian Literature and Society.* Cambridge: Cambridge University Press, 2011.

INDEX

Page numbers in *italics* refer to figures.